CATO SUPREME COURT REVIEW

2006–2007

CATO SUPREME COURT REVIEW

2006–2007

CENTER FOR CONSTITUTIONAL STUDIES

CATO
INSTITUTE
Washington, D.C.

THE CATO SUPREME COURT REVIEW
(ISBN 978-1-933995-08-3) is published annually at the close of each Supreme Court term by the Cato Institute, 1000 Massachusetts Ave., N.W., Washington, D.C. 20001-5403.

CORRESPONDENCE. Correspondence regarding subscriptions, changes of address, procurement of back issues, advertising and marketing matters, and so forth, should be addressed to:

Publications Department
The Cato Institute
1000 Massachusetts Ave., N.W.
Washington, D.C. 20001

All other correspondence, including requests to quote or reproduce material, should be addressed to the editor.

CITATIONS. Citation to this volume of the *Review* should conform to the following style: 2005-2006 Cato Sup. Ct. Rev. (2006).

INTERNET ADDRESS. Articles from past editions are available to the general public, free of charge, at www.cato.org/pubs/scr.

ISBN 978-1-933995-08-3

Printed in the United States of America.

Cato Institute
1000 Massachusetts Ave., N.W.
Washington, D.C. 20001
www.cato.org

Contents

FOREWORD

The Roberts Court Emerges: Restrained or Active?

Roger Pilon

The Cato Institute's Center for Constitutional Studies is pleased to publish this sixth volume of the *Cato Supreme Court Review*, an annual critique of the Court's most important decisions from the term just ended, plus a look at the cases ahead—all from a classical Madisonian perspective, grounded in the nation's first principles, liberty and limited government. We release this volume each year at Cato's annual Constitution Day conference. And each year in this space I discuss briefly a theme that seemed to emerge from the Court's term or from the larger setting in which the term unfolded.

This was the first full term of the Roberts Court, of course, and many were the commentaries at term's end about how things may have changed from the long years of the Rehnquist Court. A useful context for those commentaries appeared early this year with the publication of ABC News correspondent Jan Crawford Greenburg's important new book, *Supreme Conflict*, which chronicled the largely failed struggle over the past quarter century of the politically ascendant conservative movement to reshape the Court in its own image. Ms. Greenburg concluded, however, that with the confirmation of John Roberts and Samuel Alito—more savvy and focused than the justices they replaced—the movement may have succeeded at last in putting its stamp on the Court. But what is that stamp? And do we see signs of it in this first full term?

During his confirmation hearings and after, Chief Justice Roberts made it clear that his was an evolutionary approach to legal change, if change there must be—that is one sense of "conservative." Cognizant of the need to bring the Court's independent minds together to some degree if the Court is to speak at all, he thought it better that the Court speak less ambitiously than it has in recent years, but with one voice, if possible—the two are not unconnected. There is much to be said for that view. Bitterly divided 5-4 decisions—to say nothing of fractured multi-opinion decisions—suggest fundamentally opposing visions of the Constitution and the law enacted under it. Yet the Constitution was written for all of us: it is the set of rules, we believe, on which we all agreed at the beginning. A deeply divided Court undercuts that conception of our basic law, undercuts the Court's own authority, and, more important still, nourishes the idea that all is politics, little is law.

Much as the chief justice may have wished to see the Court travel down that ecumenical path, it did not happen this term. By term's end, only one-quarter of the Court's cases were decided unanimously, the lowest percentage in a decade, whereas fully one-third ended in 5-4 splits, the highest percentage in a decade, with several dissents read from the bench. Of the 24 5-4 decisions, 19 were "ideological" insofar as all of the Court's conservatives or liberals were on one side or the other. In 13 of the 5-4 decisions, all of the Court's conservatives were in the majority; 6 decisions had all of the Court's liberals in the majority. But since 4 of those 6 were Texas death penalty cases, liberals fared even worse this term than the numbers alone would indicate. And as many have noted, Justice Anthony Kennedy was in the majority in all 24 5-4 decisions: in fact, he was in the majority in all but two of the Court's decisions; thus, it is no stretch to call this the Kennedy Court.

Not surprisingly, the Court's clear ideological outcome drew sharp commentary, especially from liberals. But conservatives responded that when looked at more closely the actual doctrinal shifts were slight: abortion is still legal, for example, and campaign finance regulations are still very much in place. From a deeper perspective, however, that result-oriented, ideological approach to analyzing the Court's term, so prominent today, plays directly into the contention that all indeed *is* politics, little is law. Were that true, it would mark the death of the rule of law, of course, along with the principle of equality that underpins it, as Chief Judge Danny Boggs brings out in his B. Kenneth Simon Lecture below.

Doubtless, there are many conservatives, like all too many liberals, who look at the Court and its decisions in just that result-oriented way, as if it were simply one more political branch of government, not the non-political branch charged with applying the law. But the more thoughtful conservatives who constituted the movement about which Jan Greenburg wrote were not of that sort. In fact, quite the opposite: they were rebelling against the Warren and Burger Courts that had, they believed, politicized the Constitution and the law by deciding cases as if they were *making* and not simply *applying* the law. Thus, the image they sought to stamp on the Court through the confirmation of new justices was one of judicial "restraint"—as opposed to the judicial "activism" they saw the Court's liberals practicing.

But all too often the kind of restraint those conservatives would have the Court exercise has taken the form, essentially, of deference to the political branches. We see that, in fact, in Judge Robert Bork's 1990 best-seller, *The Tempting of America*, which set forth what for some time had been the dominant strain of conservative constitutional thought on such matters. America's first principle as a nation, Judge Bork wrote, is self-government, which means "that in *wide areas* of life majorities are entitled to rule, if they wish, simply because they are majorities." Our second principle, he continued, is "that there are nonetheless *some* things majorities must not do to minorities, *some* areas of life in which the individual must be free of majority rule" (emphasis added).

That vision of America's moral, political, and legal foundations plays directly, of course, into the conception of judicial restraint as deference to the political branches. But it also affords an expansive role for politics—and, therefore, government—in our lives—for majorities to rule "in wide areas of life," leaving individuals free only "in some areas of life." Moreover, because it is largely indifferent substantively, it is a vision available not only to conservatives but to liberals as well. It came as no surprise, therefore, that when the Rehnquist Court began eventually to rediscover constitutional limits to Congress's enumerated powers and the constitutional rights of individuals to use their property free from government interference, liberals objected to the Court's "activism" and began urging judicial "minimalism." (Some conservatives did as well, it should be noted.) If "restraint," understood as deference, is to be the order of the day, those liberals said, let's practice it evenhandedly, not selectively.

And so we come to the question of whether terms like judicial "restraint" and "activism," whether invoked early on by conservatives or more recently by liberals, are useful for reflecting on the work or direction of the Court, because behind them there is always a substantive theory, where the focus inevitably ends. With "restraint" understood as deference to the political branches, that substantive theory is one of constitutional majoritarianism. And that implies, as a normative matter, that legitimacy is a function simply of political will.

But as articles in this *Review* have argued from its inception, that is not America's theory of legitimacy. If it were, the Constitution would never have been ratified. Anti-federalists, after all, were wary of the proposed Constitution from the start, for fear that it authorized too much government. Federalists sought to assure them by pointing to the document's many substantive limits on expansive government. Both sides understood the problem of majoritarian tyranny, of course. And far from grounding legitimacy in mere political will, both sides invoked reason and the theory of natural rights.

Thus, our first principle as a nation was not that in *wide areas of life* majorities were entitled to rule simply because they were majorities but rather that in wide areas individuals were entitled to be *free* simply because they were born free. Nevertheless, majorities were entitled to rule in *some* areas of life—our second principle—not because they were majorities but because we had *authorized* them to rule in those areas, pursuant to our natural right to govern ourselves as individuals. That is the theory of legitimacy that is implicit in the Declaration of Independence; in the Constitution, especially in its Preamble and its doctrine of enumerated powers; in the Bill of Rights, especially in the Ninth and Tenth Amendments; and later in the Civil War Amendments, which brought the states more fully, at last, under those principles.

That, of course, is a rich, *substantive* theory of the Constitution, grounded not simply in political will but in the substantive theory of natural rights, the foundation for our system of government. It has judges, who are authorized to say what the law is, deferring to the political branches only insofar as the actors in those branches are acting within the scope of their authority and consistent with the rights retained by the people, enumerated and unenumerated alike. Thus, judicial "restraint" under this view implies anything but a supine Court sanctioning vast government powers—as both liberal and conservative jurists do today—powers restrained only by rights expressly in the Constitution or rights gleaned from "evolving social values," common touchstones for conservative and liberal jurists, respectively. Rather, restraint on this view means applying the law fully and *actively*—not to be confused with judicial "activism." It means assiduously policing the Constitution, recognizing power when it is authorized, limiting it as it is limited.

Far from being free-standing descriptions of judicial behavior, then, the terms "activism" and "restraint," if at all helpful and not simply confusing, take their force from the underlying substantive law. And arguments invoking them, when employed other than for praise or obloquy, reduce inevitably to arguments over what the underlying law really is. That understanding is coming increasingly to be appreciated in conservative jurisprudential circles. So too, and more important still, is the richer, more substantive conception of the Constitution—as opposed to Judge Bork's majoritarian conception, its roots in the Progressive Era. The question for us, however, is whether the nominally "conservative" Roberts Court reflects this evolving conservative thought. As the articles below indicate, the answer is mixed. To illustrate that I will touch very briefly on just three of the decisions that are discussed more fully in those articles.

The issue of judicial restraint came up pointedly in what may turn out to be the most important decision of the term, *Federal Election Commission v. Wisconsin Right to Life, Inc.* (*WRTL II*), when Justice Antonin Scalia, joined in his concurrence by Justice Kennedy, and Justice Clarence Thomas, charged Chief Justice Roberts, writing for the Court, with "faux judicial restraint." Unfortunately, *WRTL II* is the kind of decision that is all but impossible to explain to the educated layman, an audience this *Review* tries to reach, because it is simply the latest in a series of campaign finance cases that got off on the wrong foot from the start. By now this law is so complex—and confused—that one would sooner read the Internal Revenue Code than plow through it. Nevertheless, Professor Lillian BeVier does an excellent job below of placing this decision in its doctrinal context, particularly as she shows how it reinserts the First Amendment in the campaign finance debate.

To abbreviate the decision for present purposes, the Court's five conservatives joined to find that because broadcast ads that were aired before the 2004 federal elections by Wisconsin Right to Life, Inc., a nonprofit ideological advocacy corporation, did not expressly advocate the election or defeat of a particular candidate, nor were they the functional equivalent of such express advocacy, the prohibition of corporate expenditures on such ads by §203 of the Bipartisan Campaign Reform Act of 2002 (BCRA) does not apply. Because §203 burdens political speech, the Court ruled, the Federal Election Commission (FEC) must show that applying it to restrict a particular ad secures a compelling governmental interest by narrowly tailored means. The FEC failed in that because the "intent-and-effect" test it proposed to judge whether such ads were the functional equivalent of express advocacy was no part of the law. For in *McConnell v. FEC*, which upheld a facial challenge to BCRA in 2003, the Court established no such test, nor did it address the intent-and-effect test the Court rejected in 1976 in *Buckley v. Valeo*, the Court's seminal campaign finance case. Thus, the Court found the WRTL ads outside the §203 prohibitions, as applied.

Justice Scalia's concurrence went further. In 1990 in *Austin v. Michigan Chamber of Commerce* the Court had upheld a Michigan statute prohibiting corporations from using treasury money for independent expenditures to support or oppose candidates in elections for state offices. Scalia dissented, but at least the decision was limited to express advocacy; issue ads remained protected under the First Amendment. In *McConnell*, however, the Court expanded "express advocacy" to include ads that are the "functional equivalent" of express advocacy. The problem there, Scalia said, as well as with Chief Justice Roberts's "susceptible-of-no-other-reasonable-interpretation" standard for discerning "express advocacy," in which he was joined only by Justice Alito, is that all such tests are impermissibly vague and thus ineffective in vindicating fundamental First Amendment rights. Any test that would protect all genuine issue ads, Scalia concluded, would cover so many ads nominally prohibited by §203 as to make §203 overbroad and hence unconstitutional. Indeed, he noted that the chief justice's claim that "§203 on its face does not reach a substantial amount of speech protected under the principal opinion's test . . . seems . . . indefensible," adding that seven justices on the Court, including the four dissenters, "agree that the opinion effectively overrules McConnell['s §203 holding] without saying so. This faux judicial restraint is judicial obfuscation."

Returning to the question of how judicial restraint or activism may have been at play in this case, it should be clear initially how difficult it is to apply those terms in so complex a case in so heavily and mistakenly litigated an area. The Court went astray at the outset when in *Buckley* it upheld many of the 1974 amendments to the Federal Election Campaign Act of 1971, thus deferring to Congress when it should instead have deferred more fully to the First Amendment. The Court's many campaign finance decisions since then have constituted a checkered history that has, if anything, only muddied the waters further. But little compares with *McConnell* in 2003, upholding BCRA's sweeping restrictions on political speech. There the Court stated plainly that it was concerned to show "proper deference to Congress' ability to weigh competing constitutional interests in an area in which it enjoys particular expertise." To its credit, therefore, the Roberts Court took it upon *itself* to weigh those "competing constitutional interests"—the duty ultimately of the Court, after all, not the Congress. (And as Professor BeVier points out, Congress was hardly a disinterested party in this matter.)

The question, then, is whether the Roberts Court got it right, whether it applied the law and not something else, and that is a much closer call. Again, as a matter of first principle, this whole body of law is wrong, as Justice Thomas noted in 2000 in his powerful dissent in *Nixon v. Shrink Missouri Pac*: "The analytic foundation of *Buckley* . . . was tenuous from the very beginning and has only continued to erode in the intervening years." But judicial restraint limits courts to issues properly before them, and that fundamental question was not before this Court.

In fact, in his concurrence joining the principal opinion of Chief Justice Roberts, Justice Alito adverts to just that point:

> because §203 is unconstitutional as applied to the advertisements before us, it is unnecessary to go further and decide whether §203 is unconstitutional on its face. If it turns out that the implementation of the as-applied standard set out in the principal opinion impermissibly chills political speech, we will presumably be asked in a future case to reconsider the holding in *McConnell* that §203 is facially constitutional.

That is proper judicial restraint, because the Court decides only questions properly before it—questions that, presumably, have been properly briefed and argued. Since this was an as-applied challenge, that restraint leaves open the possibility that an as-applied challenge might fail.

But the issue is narrower still, and it comes out in a Roberts footnote. The Court in *Buckley*, to avoid constitutionally fatal vagueness, had narrowed the statute so that it restricted only expenditures on express advocacy—ads employing such "magic words" as "vote for" or "vote against." The *Buckley* Court then struck down the narrowed statute on the ground that it still impermissibly restricted speech. "From this," Roberts writes,

> Justice Scalia concludes that "[i]f a permissible test short of the magic-words test existed, *Buckley* would surely have adopted it." We are not so sure. *The question in* Buckley *was how a particular statutory provision could be construed to avoid vagueness concerns, not what the constitutional standard for clarity was in the abstract, divorced from specific statutory language.* Buckley*'s intermediate step of statutory construction on the way to its constitutional holding does not dictate a constitutional test.* The *Buckley* Court's "express advocacy restriction was an endpoint of statutory interpretation, not a first principle of constitutional law." *McConnell*, 540 U.S., at 190. And despite Justice Scalia's claim to the contrary, our citation of *Buckley* along with other decisions in rejecting an intent-and-effect test does not force us to adopt (or reject) *Buckley*'s statutory construction as a constitutional test (emphasis added).

One can appreciate Justice Scalia's concern to cut to the quick, and in a proper case that is likely what Chief Justice Roberts will do. But the restraint we see exercised here, far from being deference to the political branches, appears simply to be preparing the ground for a future constitutional test. The Court got it right here.

The pair of public school integration cases that Professor Samuel Estreicher discusses below, *Parents Involved in Community Schools v. Seattle School District No. 1*, are far less complicated than *WRTL II*, notwithstanding the complex "racial tiebreaker" schemes the school districts before the Court had devised to try to structure their admissions policies so that the racial demographics of their particular schools reflected, roughly, the demographics of the larger community rather than those of the vicinities of the particular schools. Faced, that is, with de facto residential segregation, school district officials instituted "voluntary" integration plans to address what they saw as the problem of de facto school segregation when students were assigned to neighborhood schools. But when those plans failed to achieve the desired racial balances in particular schools, the districts assigned students, by race, to schools not of their choosing, often necessitating long bus rides for the affected students. Not surprisingly, the parents of those students sued the school districts, asking that the schemes be found unconstitutional as racially discriminatory.

The Court agreed with the parents, Chief Justice Roberts writing for the five conservatives who constituted the majority. Justice Kennedy concurred in part and concurred in the judgment. The Court's four liberals dissented. Applying strict scrutiny, Roberts found the racial tiebreaker schemes unconstitutional under the Fourteenth Amendment's Equal Protection Clause. Unlike in *Gratz* and *Grutter*, the 2003 University of Michigan college and law school decisions in which the Court found "diversity" to be a compelling state interest, here the goal was simply preventing racial imbalance, and "racial balancing is not transformed from 'patently unconstitutional' to a compelling state interest simply by relabeling it 'racial diversity,'" Roberts wrote. Moreover, narrow tailoring requires "serious, good faith consideration of workable race-neutral alternatives," yet here the districts failed to show that their objectives could not have been met with non-race-conscious means. "The way to stop discrimination on the basis of race," Roberts concluded, "is to stop discriminating on the basis of race."

For his part, Justice Kennedy agreed that the plans before the Court did not survive strict scrutiny, but he thought that parts of the plurality opinion implied that race-conscious plans could never be used, and he wanted to leave the door open on that question. Public schools have a legitimate interest in ensuring equal opportunity for all, he said, regardless of race. To achieve that, however, officials may need to devise race-conscious measures in a general way that do not treat students by race individually.

Some critics complained that the *Parents Involved* decisions constituted a clear example of conservative judicial activism, following as closely as they did on the heels of the University of Michigan decisions. Yet the Court carefully distinguished those sets of decisions. Moreover, that complaint presumes that the Michigan cases were rightly decided. They were not. Equal protection means what it says: from a consideration of first principles, government may classify and discriminate on the basis of race only for the most compelling of reasons. "Good" reasons are not good enough. It is unclear, as a practical matter, how much light there is between the plurality opinion and Justice Kennedy's. But here too the Court applied the law of the Constitution correctly, even if it left to another day the questions in this area of the law that were not before it.

In the final case I want to touch upon, *Wilkie v. Robbins*, the Court got it very wrong, as thoroughly detailed in the article below by Professor Laurence Tribe, who argued Mr. Robbins's case before the Court. Both the facts and the law in this case are complex. In a nutshell, the title Robbins took when he purchased a Wyoming ranch was unencumbered by a public easement the federal Bureau of Land Management (BLM) had obtained from the prior owner because BLM officials had failed to record it. Upon realizing their mistake, they "demanded" the easement from Robbins. Willing to negotiate a fair price for the easement, Robbins was unwilling to capitulate to the BLM's demands that he give the government the easement free of charge. With that, the officials began a campaign of egregious misconduct, a far-reaching plan of harassment designed to "bury" Robbins, to get his BLM permits, and to "get him out of business." The record is appalling.

After suffering years of illegal actions as well as abuses of authority otherwise lawful, followed by futile administrative appeals, Robbins brought suit against the BLM officials in federal court under *Bivens v. Six Unnamed Agents* for violation of his Fifth Amendment rights under the Takings Clause and for repeated attempts at extortion under the Racketeer Influenced and Corrupt Organizations Act (RICO). Following rulings on preliminary motions in the trail court and the Tenth Circuit, discovery was conducted, after which the defendants moved for summary judgment on qualified immunity grounds. The district court denied the motion as did the court of appeals, which held that Robbins had "a clearly established right to be free from retaliation for exercising his Fifth Amendment right to exclude the Government from his private property."

With that, the U.S. solicitor general, representing the BLM agents, petitioned the Supreme Court for certiorari on the RICO question, the *Bivens* question, and the qualified immunity question. But in its eventual decision on the merits, as Professor Tribe shows in exquisite detail,

> the Court did not answer the one question (qualified immunity) without which the case could not have reached it at all in

> this pre-trial, interlocutory posture. Bypassing that question, and remaining silent on the existence of any anti-retaliation right for property owners, the Court held that, even if such a right had been clearly established, and even if the defendants had knowingly violated it and thus were entitled to no immunity from trial or from liability for damages, they were nonetheless entitled to escape trial altogether inasmuch as the *Bivens* doctrine gave Robbins no cause of action against the officers who had made good on their threat to "bury" him for standing firm on his Fifth Amendment rights.

The procedural issue highlighted here goes directly, of course, to questions about the Court's "activism" or "restraint." I will return to it in a moment, but first a look at the arguments on the merits.

At bottom, Roberts's claim was really quite simple. As Tribe put it succinctly, the BLM agents were putting a proposition to Robbins, "Your easement or your life"—a variation on the mugger's proposition. More fully,

> the BLM agents engaged both in unlawful exercises of their otherwise legitimate regulatory powers and in entirely illegitimate acts—independently illegal acts performed under color of their office but outside their delegated authority—in order to coerce [Robbins] into relinquishing his property without the Government being forced actually to "take" it and thereby incur an obligation to pay just compensation.

In a word, Robbins was put to a choice between two of his entitlements: his right to exclude the government from his property—except, under the Fifth Amendment, after receiving just compensation; and his right to be free from gratuitous governmental harassment. He could have one or the other of his rights, but not both. That is the classic definition of "coercion." And as Tribe shows, the point is perfectly generalizable: not only property but any right of choice protected by the Constitution is susceptible to being relinquished if such practices are immune from sanction. Thus the Court's longstanding and widely applied hostility toward government retaliation against the exercise of constitutional rights—in First Amendment cases, compelled self-incrimination cases, access to federal court cases, and more, including property rights cases like *Dolan v. City of Tigard* and *Nollan v. California Coastal Commission.*

Justice David Souter wrote for the Court, with only Justices Ruth Bader Ginsburg and John Paul Stevens dissenting. In finding that *Bivens* gave Robbins no cause of action, however, Justice Souter was hard-pressed to distinguish this case from others in which he *would* allow a *Bivens* sanction: "[U]nlike punishing someone for speaking out against the Government, trying to induce someone to grant an easement for public use is a perfectly legitimate purpose: as a landowner, the Government may have, and in this instance does have, a valid interest in getting access to neighboring lands."

The problem with that argument is patent, of course. True, the government's interest is valid, but it cannot pursue that interest by any means. Fortunately, the Framers thought about that issue: they wrote the Fifth Amendment, which provides a means through which the government may *legitimately* pursue its interest. It can induce an owner to grant an easement simply by paying for it. But that oversight in Souter's argument is only compounded by his mischaracterization of Robbins's challenge, which he says "is not that the means the Government used were necessarily illegitimate; rather, [Robbins] says that defendants simply demanded too much and went too far." To the contrary, it was precisely those illegitimate means that drove Robbins to court. Yet Souter reduces the government's illegal acts to mere "hard bargaining."

Those comments barely begin the critique of the Court's argument, a much fuller version of which will be found in Professor Tribe's article. Readers of this *Review* will be especially disappointed, however, by the one-paragraph concurrence of Justice Thomas, joined by Justice Scalia—the same Justice Scalia who described the California Coastal Commission's action in *Nollan*, where the commission withheld a building permit in order to induce owners to grant it an easement, as "an out-and-out plan of extortion." Far more than in *Nollan*, *Robbins* involved a prolonged and systematic pattern of illegal actions by government officials; yet Thomas and Scalia would grant no remedy for those constitutional wrongs because, as Thomas writes, citing Scalia in *Correctional Services Corp.* v. *Malesko*, "*Bivens* is a relic of the heady days in which this Court assumed common-law powers to create causes of action." That is judicial "restraint" amounting to judicial abdication. When Thomas adds: "*Bivens* and its progeny should be limited 'to the precise circumstances that they involved,'" one can only ask, "Why?" If wrongly crafted here (to remedy egregious BLM behavior), why not also in *Bivens* (to remedy egregious behavior by federal narcotics agents)?

The Court's argument on the merits aside, it is, if anything, the procedural issues in this case that are most disturbing. Recall that *Robbins* was before the Supreme Court on an interlocutory appeal of the denial of a motion for summary judgment on qualified immunity grounds. As Professor Tribe notes, with narrow exceptions, "the general rule in the federal courts, as enacted by Congress, is of course that litigants may appeal only from *final judgments*, not interlocutory rulings such as a denial of a summary judgment motion." Rather than trying to summarize the complex arguments at issue here, let me simply move to Tribe's conclusion that if the rationale for interlocutory appellate review of the qualified immunity issue, where it can be authoritatively determined in advance that no violation of law has occurred, is to preclude needlessly subjecting officials to trial, that rationale has no application here unless the evidence is insufficient at the outset that the officials acted illegally. But "where the only issue the Court ends up addressing is a question of judicial policy as to what the appropriate remedy would have been on the *assumption* that the officials had in the end been found guilty of clearly unconstitutional conduct, the rationale for forgoing a trial and resolving that question on appeal *prior to trial* is altogether lacking." Indeed, "a Court that had previously taken care at least to respect the boundaries Congress had set on the appellate jurisdiction of the Supreme Court (and of the federal circuit courts) to review non-final judgments of the federal district courts left no doubt that its eagerness to cut back on *Bivens* exceeded even its fidelity to those jurisdictional boundaries."

We are left, then, with the question of whether the Roberts Court in this case was applying the law or making it. Professor Tribe makes a compelling case that the settled law on these issues was not applied. Mr. Robbins's constitutional rights were egregiously violated, yet he was left with no remedy—and hence, effectively, with no right. No "new" remedy had to be crafted, as the Court contended; it was necessary simply to apply an existing remedy to a new, but hardly novel, set of facts. Thus, the Court ignored the substantive law pertaining to the facts—engaging in "restraint" amounting to abdication—but that is tantamount to "activism" insofar as the Court is making the new law that emerges from ignoring the existing law.

And Congress's procedural instructions to the Court, pursuant to its constitutional authority to establish such rules, were ignored as well. Here, proper deference to Congress's authority *was* in order, but rather than stay within its authority, the "activist" Court reached out to issues it had no authority to decide. Yet the larger rationale for what the Court did had the cast of the "judicial restraint" that so many conservatives urge—deference to government and its officials. A court so unable or unwilling to discern and apply the law is a court engaged in *faux* restraint.

* * *

Each year we at the *Review* struggle mightily to produce this volume in the brief period between the end of the Court's term in late June and the time we release it to the public at Cato's annual Constitution Day conference on September 17. This year that task has been especially difficult because our editor in chief, Mark Moller, left for Chicago in mid-July to begin a teaching career at the DePaul University College of Law. And in mid-August our administrative and research assistant, Anne-Marie Dao, joined the Justice Department to gain experience for a year before law school beckons her. I want to thank Anne-Marie for the work she has continued to do, even after leaving, to bring this *Review* together. And I am especially grateful to Mark, who likewise continued to work on the *Review* even as he was preparing his classes. During his four years as the *Review*'s editor in chief, he has done a marvelous job. We wish Mark and Anne-Marie the very best.

Introduction

*Mark K. Moller**

The sixth volume of the *Cato Supreme Court Review* considers the first full term with a new conservative majority—led by Chief Justice John Roberts and joined by Justice Samuel Alito. Last term, I noted the "cacophony of conflicting predictions about where the Court, under its new chief justice, is headed." The take on the Court's term that has proved most influential is Supreme Court reporter Jan Crawford Greenburg's: She argues that the term has revealed "a Supreme Court engaged in a fierce battle of ideas, a big-picture struggle over the role of the Court and the direction it's going to take. . . . It's the Roberts Court v. the Stevens Court."[1] The "Roberts Court," according to Greenburg, embraces judicial modesty. The Stevens Court, in this view, is fighting to preserve a less "modest" judicial role.

Greenburg's description, however much it has caught on in the blogosphere, doesn't really tell us much: It's true there are two camps, a conservative one lead by the chief justice and a liberal one led by the dean of the Court's liberals, Justice Stevens. But it is far from clear what they are fighting over and it's not clear that "modesty" precisely captures what that is. Is the Roberts wing simply trying to restrain the extension of old precedent to new areas of the law—stopping, for example, the expansion of affirmative action precedent in higher education, like *Grutter v. Bollinger*, to public high schools? Is the Roberts Court trying to "roll back" precedents dating from the Warren and Brennan Courts—chipping away at certain judicially recognized rights that were once thought to be fixed points in the law, like the *Bivens* doctrine or the taxpayer

*Editor in Chief, *Cato Supreme Court Review*; assistant professor of law, DePaul University College of Law.

[1]Greenburg, Jan Crawford, "The Roberts Court," Legalities at [http://blogs.abcnews.com/legalities/2007/05/the_roberts_cou.html] (August 27, 2007).

standing doctrine in Establishment Clause cases—while the Stevens Court is trying to preserve them? Or is the Roberts Court staking out new, more aggressive judicial roles for the Court in certain areas: by beefing up, albeit incrementally, First Amendment scrutiny of campaign finance law, for example.

It turns out, it's a bit of all three. Whether you view each of these moves as "modest" depends, ultimately, on your view of what the law commands of the Court in each area. "Modesty," it turns out, is just a slogan for results that observers think aligns the rule of constitutional law and a proper theory of constitutional legitimacy. It's judicial "spin." And, from the standpoint of a liberty-oriented defense of constitutional legitimacy, the record of the Roberts and Stevens wings of the Court are, so far, decidedly mixed.

Judge Danny J. Boggs leads off this edition of the *Cato Supreme Court Review* by examining the Court's existing record from the vantage point of "rule of law" values. He examines three areas: free speech, racial preferences, and election law. In each area, he asks "whether the courts are applying one rule for the cows and refusing to apply that rule when the godly or the goodly are involved." The results, he argues, are mixed: In the area of speech rights, the Court has done reasonably well in acting in an evenhanded way. In the second area, racial preferences, Judge Boggs argues that courts have done quite poorly. And in the third area, election law, he argues the verdict is out, but reports on "dangers and prospects."

Professor Laurence H. Tribe leads off the *Review*'s analysis of this term's cases, focusing on the Court's treatment of constitutional remedies in *Wilkie v. Robbins*. Professor Tribe, who argued for the respondent before the Supreme Court, argues that *Robbins* is an important, and overlooked, bellwether for the viability of constitutional tort suits against federal officials under the *Bivens* line of cases. In *Robbins*, he argues, the Court dealt a "severe and unjustifiable blow both to individual rights—including, but not limited to, rights of private property—and to the role of *Bivens* remedies in implementing those rights, thus making them real." After this term, he says, "the best that can be said of the *Bivens* doctrine is that it is on life support with little prospect of recovery."

Next, Professor Lillian BeVier examines this term's foray into election law: *FEC v. Wisconsin Right to Life, Inc.* (*WRTL II*). In *WRTL II*, the Court revisits *McConnell* v. *FEC*, which, as Professor BeVier notes, was "an unambiguous rejection of the view that at the First Amendment's core is the principle of free political speech." While *McConnell* didn't overrule *Buckley v. Valeo,* she writes, it was dismissive of *Buckley*'s First Amendment foundations. In *WRTL II,* Professor BeVier argues, a new majority of the Court has "revived *Buckley* and thus breathed renewed life into the First Amendment."

Erik S. Jaffe examines the Supreme Court's unanimous decision in *Davenport v. Washington Education Association* and *Washington v. Washington Education Association,* and concludes that for what should have been an easy First Amendment case, the Court came to the right conclusion but for reasons that might do more harm than good. While the Court correctly reversed a Washington State Supreme Court decision that turned the First Amendment on its head and declared that unions had a First Amendment right to spend excess agency fees improperly appropriated from nonmember employees on political speech having nothing to do with collective bargaining, the Court emphasized broad discretion by the State in restricting speech rather than the countervailing First Amendment rights of the nonunion employees. The latter approach, argues Jaffe, would have been the correct rationale for the same result, and would not have required weakening various First Amendment Doctrines in order to reject the false rights claimed by the union

Hans Bader dissects the Court's First Amendment follies in *Morse v. Frederick,* popularly known as the "Bong Hits for Jesus" case. In *Morse,* the Court considered whether the First Amendment barred a school in Alaska from disciplining a student who displayed a banner with those cryptically offending words in view of students and administration officials. Bader argues that the Court, "in its zeal to give the government a win in the 'War on Drugs,' . . . upheld censorship of speech that posed little risk of causing drug use." Even so, he argues, *Morse* "has two bright spots for free speech advocates": First, the justices recognized that political speech advocating the legalization of drugs could not be banned under their ruling. Second, the Court implicitly rejected some lower court rulings that students' speech must be on matter of "public concern" to enjoy any protection.

Professor Brannon Denning examines the dog that didn't bark this term: federalism. He does so by a considering a decision in which the federalism "bark" was most glaringly silent: *Gonzales v.*

Carhart, in which the Court considered the constitutionality of the federal partial birth abortion ban. Neither the parties nor the Court's majority opinion addressed federalism concerns with the Congress's assertions of power to regulate abortion procedures; instead, the parties argued, and the Court decided, *Carhart* under the *Roe, Casey,* and *Stenberg* line of cases. However, Justice Clarence Thomas, in a short concurrence, hinted he'd be willing to consider Commerce Clause arguments against the ban if they were properly raised in subsequent cases. Professor Denning writes the "majority opinion that might have been," had those Commerce Clause arguments been raised by the parties in this case.

From abortion and federalism, we move to Article III standing and separation of powers. In *Massachusetts v. EPA*, the Court considered whether states have standing under the Clean Air Act to complain about the EPA's reticence to regulate global warming. The state won, but, argues Andrew P. Morriss, standing doctrine lost. As he says, "the Supreme Court took yet another significant step away from the Framers' vision of the judiciary and toward a politicized Supreme Court sitting as a super-legislature and super-regulator." Morriss argues that *Massachusetts v. EPA* is "but one piece of a broader trend toward regulation through litigation," in which "[a] wide range of interest groups, including state politicians, private interest groups, and federal regulators, are increasingly using the courts as a vehicle to impose regulatory measures the interest groups cannot obtain from legislatures and agencies."

In the Court's other major standing decision, *Hein v. Freedom from Religion Foundation*, the majority cut back on the once-settled principle, derived from *Flast v. Cohen*, that Establishment Clause challenges are an exception to the general rule against taxpayer standing. First Amendment litigator Robert Corn-Revere argues that the Court's decision in *Hein* has left *Flast* intact in form only. In reality, the Court has created a road map "by which the executive may circumnavigate judicial standing in Establishment Clause cases altogether, simply by supporting religious institutions on its own initiative."

Professor Samuel Estreicher considers the Court's latest foray into equal protection and affirmative action, *Parents Involved in Community Schools v. Seattle School District No. 1.* Estreicher argues that "as long as analysis of racial classification cases turns on the familiar two-prong inquiry into whether government has asserted a 'compelling interest' and, if so, whether the challenged program reflects 'narrow tailoring,' the Supreme Court jurisprudence in this area will prove deeply unsatisfying and difficult to predict." The Court, he says, needs "a clear, compelling principle" in this area, but hasn't yet identified it. Estreicher considers whether the Court's cases might be read to supply such a principle, and argues that they do, although the Court hasn't recognized it. He argues that this principle—which he calls the "non-preferment principle"—helps explain and unify the results in *Bakke, Grutter*, and *Parents Involved*.

Turning to regulatory law, Professor G. Marcus Cole dissects *Watters v. Wachovia Bank*, a preemption case involving a conflict between state and federal banking regulatory regimes. The issue raised in the case is whether federalism principles limit the statutory power of federal regulators to forbid a state from imposing certain regulations on a state mortgage lender. Cole argues that the federalism dilemma perceived by many conservatives and libertarians in this case is a false one. Federalism is an instrumental value, designed to promote individual liberty. In this case, he argues, "the interests of freedom . . . [are] advanced by federal control of banking regulation, and its concomitant limitations on state consumer protection laws."

Professor Thomas Lambert argues while the Court's decision in *Leegin Creative Leather Products, Inc. v. PSKS, Inc.*, which overruled the "much-maligned" 1911 *Dr. Miles* decision, is probably the most notable antitrust decision of October Term 2006, the Court's decision in *Weyerhaeuser Co. v. Ross-Simmons Hardwood Lumber Co.* may prove to be the most important in the long run. In *Weyerhaeuser*, the Court addressed the legal standard applicable to predatory bidding claims (*i.e.*, claims that bidders have driven prices up higher than necessary in an attempt to drive rival bidders from the market). "On first glance," says Lambert, "the matter addressed by the *Weyerhaeuser* Court looks quite narrow: Must a plaintiff complaining of predatory bidding make the same two-part showing as a predatory pricing plaintiff? In answering that narrow question in the affirmative, however, the Supreme Court may have unwittingly weighed in on one of the most hotly disputed matters in antitrust—how to define 'exclusionary conduct' under Section 2 of the Sherman Act." Lambert argues that the Court's resolution of that question is a salutary development, with important consequences for antitrust law.

In *Philip Morris v. Williams*, the Supreme Court considered anew due process restraints on excessive punitive damages, this time in the context of a very large punitive damage judgment against Philip Morris. The Court didn't validate the widespread anxiety among corporate defendants that a wholesale pull-back from due process review of punitive damages would follow in the wake of Justice Sandra Day O'Connor's departure from the Court. But the Court's decision was, even so, no model of clarity. Professor Michael Krauss performs a backward-looking, post-*Williams* survey of the Court's punitive damage case law, and suggests *Williams* is the culmination of a Court that has "no coherent view of punitive damages."

Finally, Glenn Harlan Reynolds surveys the Supreme Court term to come. He examines trends in the Court's caseload and ventures some predications about the hotly watched cases that are either on the Court's docket or expected to be added to its docket—including cases dealing with the right to bear arms, presidential powers, the right to *habeas*, and free speech on the Internet.

Challenges to the Rule of Law: Or, *Quod Licet Jovi Non Licet Bovi*

*Danny J. Boggs**

I chose for the title of my talk the somewhat mysterious: *Quod Licet Jovi Non Licet Bovi*. I did this for several reasons. The first was sheer publicity value. I thought it might sound more exotic than the usual sort of speech title, as for example, "Democracy and Tradition: Compare and Contrast," or "Class Actions: Disaster or Catastrophe."

The more serious reason, however, is that the phrase, which translates as "what is permitted to Jove (or Jupiter, the king of the gods) is not permitted to cows," has always seemed to me to symbolize the opposite of what I consider to be the rule of law. And the rule of law is what I perceive and consider judging to be about—at least it is why I went into judging rather than into some of the previous endeavors that Roger's introduction of me laid out at some length. The rule of law means that, to the extent that fallible judges are capable of adhering to it, the expectation is that when you go before a court, the outcome depends on the merits of your case, not your political status, relation to the court, or other personal characteristics. It does not mean that the law is a mechanical enterprise—it cannot be. But it should mean that the judge will apply the same standards to the merits of your case, as to those of any other case, whatever the color of your skin or the content of your character.

I'm going to examine three areas in which I think the courts have confronted or are confronting issues that call into question whether that concept of the rule of law is being applied and ask whether the courts are applying one rule for the cows and refusing to apply that rule when the godly or the goodly are involved. And for balance, the three areas will include one in which I believe that courts have generally done well despite occasional lapses and challenges. That is the area of speech rights. For the second area, racial preferences,

*Chief Judge, the United States Court of Appeals for the Sixth Circuit.

I believe that courts have done quite poorly. And in the third area, election law cases where the issues are coming increasingly into play, I don't know what the ultimate result will be, but I will examine both dangers and prospects.

At the outset, however, I need to make the obligatory, but I believe important, disclaimer that I am not opining on the outcome of any pending or impending issues that may come before me. I am primarily trying to discuss cases that have been decided and what I see as the consistencies or inconsistencies of some of the doctrine laid out in those cases.

I.

Beginning then with the issue of speech rights, courts have generally been willing to bite the bullet and give even the most unpopular speech the same protection as the popular. From the 1930s to the 1960s it was primarily the rights of communists, leftists, and protesters that were protected in cases like *Cohen v. California*,[1] the famous "Fuck-the-Draft" jacket case, *New York Times v. Sullivan*,[2] and *Stromberg v. California*,[3] involving communist campers. Yet even in the old cases, fascists, white supremacists, and Klan members were sometimes protected, as in the *Terminiello*[4] case involving anti-Semites in Chicago and *Brandenburg v. Ohio*[5] involving Klan members. Those cases gradually, but generally, established a tradition of broad and evenhanded protection of speech. The recent cases of *R.A.V. v. City of St. Paul*[6] and *Virginia v. Black*,[7] involving various efforts to suppress cross-burning, have mostly continued that tradition.

In recent years, most of the celebrated cases have involved two areas, both relating to education. One is clothing or symbols in elementary and secondary schools growing out of the *Tinker*[8] decision. The other is efforts in schools, especially colleges, to enforce

[1] 403 U.S. 15 (1971).

[2] 376 U.S. 254 (1964).

[3] 283 U.S. 359 (1931).

[4] Terminiello v. City of Chicago, 337 U.S. 1 (1949).

[5] 395 U.S. 444 (1969).

[6] 505 U.S. 377 (1992).

[7] 538 U.S. 343 (2004).

[8] Tinker v. Des Moines Indep. Cmty. Sch. Dist., 393 U.S. 503 (1969).

strictures against what is labeled "hate speech". Both of these areas began with doctrines or rubrics that threatened, nay, even invited, discriminatory application, but I believe that for the most part, courts have resisted that temptation.

Tinker involved a girl who, at the instigation of her parents, it turned out, wore a black armband to school as a protest against the Vietnam War. The Supreme Court upheld her right to do so as long as it was not "colliding with the rights of others"[9] or "materially and substantially interfer[ing] with the requirements of appropriate discipline."[10] In the past few years there have been numerous cases, all at lower levels, in which student rights have generally been upheld, regardless of whether the message could be considered as of the right or the left. Thus, even the Confederate flag usually has not been treated worse than leftist symbols, at least since the time that racial tensions were especially evident in particular schools. The standard, however, is quite problematic.

It is tempting for judges to let their own attitudes color their view of what a particular symbol or slogan means. The Supreme Court in *Tinker* clearly felt that protesting the Vietnam War with an armband was a benign, even laudable, act. Those seeking to uphold discipline against Confederate flag tee-shirts clearly thought that the message was much less benign, representing hate not heritage, to revert to the slogan of the flag defenders. But courts seem not to have grappled in a general way with how they should interpret symbols. Is there an objective standard for what they mean? Should it be the intent ascribed by the speaker or the meaning taken by the listener or observer? Clearly, during the Vietnam War the *Tinker* armband could have been taken as a personal affront to those in the armed forces and their children, since the wearer in many cases implied their complicity in war crimes and other evils. Or it could have been taken as simple support for pacifism, or anything in between.

In this ambiguity of symbols I experienced a very poignant example concerning the great Broadway hit *Les Miserables*. The heroic crowds in that musical are waving red flags, and those flags are potent symbols. A friend, a refugee from a communist country, said she

[9] *Id.* at 513.

[10] *Id.* (quoting Burnside v. Byars, 363 F.2d 744, 749 (1966)).

had a very hard time watching or enjoying the play because for her the red flag was a symbol of oppression that gave her offense. But that offense, even if expressed in a school rather than a theater, should not and generally has not led to judicial suppression. Courts have not resolved the philosophical tension, of course, but they have mostly upheld speech rights evenhandedly, at least in the absence of compelling evidence of physical confrontation or tension at the school.

But that limitation is also problematic as it invokes the specter of the "Heckler's Veto," conceptualized by my great old professor, Harry Kalven, and now taken as part of First Amendment law.[11] The heckler's veto stands for the idea that officials may suppress speech if those hearing it may be sufficiently incensed to try themselves to suppress it. It has been rejected in numerous cases from *Brown v. Louisiana*[12] to *Forsyth County*,[13] involving a license for a Klan march. But the standard of whether a symbol creates disruption leads to some rather strange results. If the audience includes very touchy and angry people, a speech or symbol might be restricted more readily than if the school is inhabited by Quakers or Zen masters, which seems a very odd doctrine. The "fighting words" doctrine, which at least by citation has enjoyed a revival since *R.A.V.*,[14] has the same problem. As a limit on freedom of speech when such speech tends to incite an immediate breach of the peace, the doctrine is anything but clear or easy to apply. Psychological testing asking people what it would take by way of insult or language to make them fight has found, not surprisingly, that there are substantial differences among groups. Women, for example, are less inclined to fight, which might mean that under the doctrine they could be subject to more offensive speech than the more testosterone-poisoned, which makes for an odd doctrine. Yet though these doctrinal dangers remain, courts usually have applied the doctrine evenhandedly.

But my benign view was tested recently in a case from the Ninth Circuit. After pro-gay rights activities in the Poway School District

[11] See Harry Kalven, Jr., The Negro and the First Amendment, 140–60 (1965).

[12] 383 U.S. 131 (1966).

[13] Forsyth County v. The Nat'l Movement, 505 U.S. 123 (1992).

[14] R.A.V. v. City of St. Paul, 505 U.S. 377 (1992).

in California, a student named Harper wore a tee-shirt that could be read at the least as expressing philosophical opposition to homosexuality. In a Ninth Circuit opinion,[15] Judge Reinhardt permitted the school to punish the wearer, drawing a sharp dissent from the panel and from a denial of rehearing *en banc*.[16] That led Judge Reinhardt to some rather remarkable rejoinders that in their starkness express what I would call the Jovi vs. Bovi view. Reinhardt said, "The dissenters still don't get the message [that you can't] strike[ ] at the very core of . . . [someone else's] dignity and self-worth."[17] And Judge Gould, in concurring with the denial of rehearing en banc, said, "Hate speech . . . in the form of a tee shirt misusing biblical text [can be punished to] protect [others] from psychological harm,"[18] which I also found quite striking because based on the judge's view about the proper use or misuse of a biblical text.

The tee-shirt that the student wore, after school-approved activities opposing his views, said on the front, "BE ASHAMED OUR SCHOOL EMBRACED WHAT GOD HAS CONDEMNED." And on the back it said "homosexuality is shameful."[19] The Ninth Circuit panel interpreted those words as being a direct attack on "the dignity and self-worth of individual students," though without any indication that it would have taken a similarly latitudinarian view of the message in *Tinker* with respect to, for example, the children of members of the armed forces or persons in junior ROTC. That case brings starkly to the fore the question of whether a court can make its own personal interpretation of the meaning of symbols, and it leads to a very strong possibility of the Jovi-Bovi distinction.

In contrast, the Second Circuit, shortly thereafter, forbade school officials from punishing a student who wore a tee-shirt described in its opinion as follows: "The front of the shirt, at the top, has large print that reads 'George W. Bush,' below it is the text, 'Chicken-Hawk-In-Chief,' [followed by] a large picture of the President's face, wearing a helmet, superimposed on the body of a chicken" surrounded by oil rigs, dollars signs, three lines of cocaine and a razor

[15] Harper v. Poway Unified Sch. Dist., 445 F.3d 1166 (9th Cir. 2006).

[16] *Id.* at 1052.

[17] *Id.* at 1053.

[18] *Id.* at 1053–54.

[19] *Id.* at 1171.

blade, and a martini glass with an olive. And under it is the line "World Domination tour." That was found insufficiently offensive.[20]

The plaintiff in the California case petitioned the U.S. Supreme Court for certiorari, which might have led one to think that a resolution was forthcoming. The Supreme Court found the case to be moot, however, which kept the Court from opining on the merits.[21] The Court did grant certiorari, however, and in doing so vacated the Ninth Circuit's opinion.[22] It could instead have simply denied certiorari, leaving the Ninth Circuit's decision in force. That the Court chose to grant cert and vacate the underlying judgment is at least some indication that they frowned on it.[23]

Another interesting, potentially problematic, case is in front of the Sixth Circuit. It involves a high school rule prohibiting students from wearing clothing that bears the Confederate flag.[24] The district court denied a motion from a student for a preliminary injunction enjoining the school from implementing this rule.[25] A Sixth Circuit panel (I was not on the case) affirmed the district court's decision, finding that the district court was not clearly wrong in determining that in a school with a recent history of racial tensions a Confederate flag might cause disruption—even absent any indication that Confederate flags had ever caused past disruptions at the school. A petition for rehearing *en banc* is currently pending.

Similarly, college hate speech cases have almost uniformly gone against the schools attempting to enforce speech codes. They are still on the books at many schools and can have a chilling effect on students who do not wish to risk the controversy, expense, and obloquy of challenging them, but they rarely survive despite reams of academic writing attempting to support them.[26] Two quick examples: in our

[20] Guiles v. Marineau, 461 F.3d 320, 330–31 (2d Cir. 2006).

[21] Harper v. Poway Unified Sch. Dist., 127 S. Ct. 1484 (2007).

[22] *Id.*

[23] See Tony Mauro, Court Vacates 9th Circuit Ruling Against Anti-Gay T-Shirt, First Amendment Center, March 5, 2007, at http://www.firstamendmentcenter.org/analysis.aspx?id=18251.

[24] D.B. v. Lafon, 217 F. App'x 518 (6th Cir. 2007).

[25] D.B. v. Lafon, 452 F. Supp. 2d 813 (E.D. Tenn. 2006).

[26] See, e.g., Mari J. Matsuda, Legal Storytelling: Public Response to Racist Speech: Considering the Victim's Story, 87 Mich. L. Rev. 2320 (1989); Thomas C. Grey, How to Write a Speech Code Without Really Trying: Reflections on the Stanford Experience, 29 U.C. Davis L. Rev. 891 (1996); Charles R. Lawrence III, "If He Hollers Let Him Go: Regulating Racist Speech on Campus," in Words That Wound: Critical Race

own circuit, district judge Avern Cohn struck down a university speech code in an opinion[27] that was apparently sufficiently resounding that the University of Michigan did not even attempt to appeal it to our circuit. Interestingly, Judge Cohn began his opinion, perhaps with sly intent, by quoting Lee Bollinger,[28] the same Lee Bollinger who as law dean and then president of the University of Michigan endorsed and implemented the code and would later be the defendant in *Grutter v. Bollinger*, the Supreme Court decision that upheld law school diversity admissions.[29] He quoted from Bollinger's own writings: "[J]udges, being human, will not only make mistakes but will sometimes succumb to the pressures exerted by the government to allow restraints [on speech] that ought not to be allowed. To guard against these possibilities we must give judges as little room to maneuver as possible and, again, extend the boundary of the realm of protected speech into the hinterlands of speech to minimize the potential harm from judicial miscalculation and misdeeds."[30] There, at least, Professor Bollinger wrote more truly than did Dean and President Bollinger.

More recently, in a similar speech code case, Georgia Tech agreed to a settlement in which the offending portions of the code, which were being used to support discipline against students only of a particular stripe, were excised and only provisions that dealt with direct physical threat were left in.[31] That has been the general trend. Thus, I would summarize this area of the law by saying that, despite a clear and strong effort on the part of many academics and groups to apply legal doctrine in a way that would sanctify the opinions of one side but not those of the other, the evenhanded application of speech rights seems mostly secure. But we will need to see the ultimate outcome of the doctrines raised in that *Harper v. Poway* case in the Ninth Circuit.

Theory, Assaultive Speech, and the First Amendment 53–58 (Mari Matsuda et al. eds., 1993).

[27] Doe v. Univ. of Mich., 721 F. Supp. 852 (E.D. Mich. 1989).

[28] *Id.* at 853.

[29] Grutter v. Bollinger, 539 U.S. 306 (2003). See Roger Pilon, Principle and Policy in Public University Admissions: *Grutter v. Bollinger* and *Gratz v. Bollinger*, 2002–2003 Cato Sup. Ct. Rev. 43 (2003).

[30] Lee Bollinger, The Tolerant Society 78 (1986).

[31] See Sklar v. Clough, 2007 U.S. Dist. LEXIS 49248 (N.D. Ga., July 6, 2007).

II.

The second area, the one where courts have not done so well in my view, is the area of racial preferences. It is true, of course, that governments often prefer some individuals, groups, or interests to others. To a great extent that is what modern governments do, even if it is not what the Founders primarily said was the proper role of government. At the same time, the Founders were quite aware of the practical dangers of such tendencies and sought to protect against them by structural features. *Federalist 51*, after all, was about how to control the general drive to get government to act in support of one's narrow interests. One aspect of this drive is called patronage. When your side wins political or legislative power, you get the spoils. While perhaps regrettable as a matter of political philosophy, if the role and reach of patronage are defined and enforced by law I don't think that it is necessarily antithetical to the rule of law. Over most of our history, it was thought that government employment was a legitimate area for patronage. Certainly since the presidency of Andrew Jackson it was accepted, and although later it might be limited by civil service legislation, it was not unconstitutional. Then came the *Branti*[32] case in 1980 that said that a person could not be fired for political affiliation or to open up a slot for the politically favored group. At first this ruling seemed limited—after all, being fired is a lot worse than simply not being hired.[33] But ultimately, in the case of *Rutan v. Republican Party of Illinois*,[34] the Court said that all government employment, except for narrowly defined areas, was off limits to patronage. At the time, in a case essentially overruled by *Rutan*, I wrote that minorities might well come to rue this decision as it might limit the opportunities for patronage that had been reaped by groups before them.[35] That prediction came to pass in a later case, *Middleton v. City of Flint*,[36] when we struck down racial preferences in some city employment, which were instituted after a new mayor

[32]Branti v. Finkel, 445 U.S. 507 (1980).

[33]See Messer v. Curci, 881 F.2d 219, 222–23 (6th Cir. 1989) (en banc); Messer v. Curci, 806 F.2d 667, 1986 U.S. App. Lexis 34146, at *10–11 (6th Cir. 1988) (Boggs, J., dissenting).

[34]497 U.S. 62 (1990).

[35]See *supra*, note 33.

[36]92 F.3d 396 (6th Cir. 1996).

was elected. Such preferences may easily have been upheld prior to *Rutan* if the mayor was simply preferring his political supporters who were, fortuitously, largely of one racial group.

I start with this backdrop because prime educational opportunities and the drive to give favored groups preferential access to those opportunities can very well be regarded as a species of patronage. Indeed, one of the arguments made for racial preference (mislabeled by some as "affirmative action")[37] is that it is important for certain perks offered by society to be spread around in some rough proportion to different groups. Courts seem today to eschew a clear definition of diversity, but a recent article in the *Harvard Law Review* by Professor Heather Gerken[38] stated plainly, I think, the principle involved: "when scholars usually use the term they mean that something . . . should roughly mirror the composition of the relevant population from which it draws its members; it should 'look like America,' . . . particularly in the wake of *Grutter v. Bollinger.*"[39] Of course, since there is only 100 percent of anything, such a principle absolutely, inevitably, and mathematically leads to the limitation of all other groups to their rough proportions, whether those groups are actually defined or are simply the residual of the preferred group.

I want then to examine the tie between proportionality and patronage. In *Grutter* it was noted that one of the most allegedly persuasive amicus briefs was submitted by military people arguing the need for a racially diverse officer corps.[40] Yet that argument seemed to

[37] See Grutter v. Bollinger, 288 F.3d 732, 774 (6th Cir. 2002) (en banc) (Boggs, J., dissenting) ("Standing alone, the term 'affirmative action' might mean anything from affirmative action to study harder to affirmative action to exclude minorities. However, as used in the context of our society's struggle against racial discrimination, the term first enters the public print and the national vocabulary in Executive Order 10925, issued by President John F. Kennedy on March 6, 1961, and subsequently incorporated into a wide variety of statutes and regulations. It ordered government contractors to 'take affirmative action to ensure that applicants are employed, and that employees are treated during employment, without regard to their race, creed, color, or national origin.' It is thus clear that whatever else Michigan's policy may be, it is not 'affirmative action.'").

[38] Heather Gerken, Second-Order Diversity, 118 Harv. L. Rev. 1099 (2005).

[39] *Id.* at 1102.

[40] See, e.g., Charles Lane, Stevens Gives Rare Glimpse of High Court's 'Conference'; Justice Details His Thoughts on Affirmative Action Case in Michigan, Wash. Post, Oct. 19, 2003, at A3.

me almost wholly implausible. As was noted, officers come largely from either ROTC or the military academies.[41] But it is hardly plausible that if more minorities go to the Harvards and Michigans of the world, they are *more* likely to go into ROTC than if they go to lesser-ranked state colleges, which almost invariably have much more active ROTC programs—indeed, even assuming the higher ranked schools permit ROTC programs.[42] And admission to the military academies is the one area where political patronage is *explicitly* enshrined in statute. Admission for the vast majority of spots requires sponsorship by a member of Congress, as enshrined in 10 U.S.C. § 4342 for West Point, and other statutes for the other academies.[43] And congressional membership is perhaps the most racially balanced high-ranking position in our society. Thus, that very patronage can ensure the desired balance.

Although they could have done so, the courts have not articulated or permitted a patronage system. Instead, in *Grutter* and similar decisions the Supreme Court has said that Jove can indeed be treated differently, so long as we blind ourselves as to the exact degree of preference that is being given to Jove and withheld from the cows. For that was the crucial distinction between *Grutter* and *Gratz*. If the numbers are explicit, as in *Gratz*,[44] preference will be struck down; if they are concealed, as in *Grutter*,[45] preferences will be permitted. It's rather interesting that in *Bakke* and *Grutter*, we had sixteen Supreme Court justices and they voted effectively 14-2 that there is no intellectually supportable difference between mere preferences, explicit preferences, and quotas.[46] Unfortunately for intellectual rigor, those two were the swing votes in each case. The two controlling votes thought that you could split the baby and impose burdens on people because of their race or ethnicity, as long as you weren't too explicit about it.

[41] See Grutter, 539 U.S. at 331 (citing Brief of Julius W. Becton, Jr. as Amici Curiae at 27 (Military amicus brief)).

[42] See, e.g., Harvard College, Other Programs, ROTC, at http://www.college.harvard.edu/academics/other_programs/rotc/ (specifying that Harvard undergraduates can only participate in ROTC by cross-registering for ROTC courses at MIT).

[43] See 10 U.S.C. §§ 6954, 9342.

[44] Gratz v. Bollinger, 539 U.S. 244 (2003).

[45] Grutter v. Bollinger, 539 U.S. 306 (2003).

[46] See *id.* and Regents of Univ. of Cal. v. Bakke, 438 U.S. 265 (1978).

The faults of that position are generally clear, in my view, and well argued in the dissents.[47] But I want to focus only on the Jovi-Bovi aspect of it. Of course, if you are going to treat Jovi different than Bovi, you have to be able to define which is which. Although the public controversy seems to rest on a reasonably clear idea, at the level of actual definition the question of who should or should not be favored is much less clear, indicating the lack of rule-of-law type standards. As late as 1980, for example, Ohio had a statutory preference for "Orientals," a "group" now often disfavored.[48] A series of Ohio decisions ultimately had eight judges on one side and seven judges on the other as to whether people of Lebanese background were entitled to be called "Orientals."[49] With that much trouble at the nomenclature level, deciding individual cases can be even more problematic.

As a personal aside, I observed this issue when one of my children was spontaneously offered a graduate school scholarship from a consortium that asked, after awarding it, for documentation that my son had "at least one Hispanic grandparent." As he was out of the country at the time, I assembled the necessary information with birth and marriage certificates going back a century. But the whole exercise of proving that he was, in analogy to the Nuremberg laws, a "Mischling, second-class," was a bit off-putting, to say the least.

There is a third consideration, which is the potential subdividing of what are currently considered to be favored and disfavored classes. In rough terms, most governmental and educational institutions today give racial preference to groups called "Hispanic" or "Latino" and those called "black" or "African-American," while imposing burdens on groups defined as "white" or "Asian." But I have noted, at least in private conversations with admissions officers, an increasing tendency to distinguish internally among Hispanics so that those who might be considered as coming from "more favored" areas, such as Cuba or Chile, receive less or no preference, in contradistinction to those from, say, Guatemala or Mexico. Similarly, a

[47] See, e.g., Grutter, 539 U.S. at 364 (Rehnquist, C.J., dissenting).

[48] See O.R.C. § 122.71(E) (1980).

[49] See Ritchey Produce Co. v. State of Ohio Dep't of Admin. Servs., 1997 Ohio App. LEXIS 4590 (Ohio App. 10 Dist., Oct. 7, 1007), rev'd, 707 N.E.2d 871 (1999).

series of articles has indicated displeasure among some black scholars and leaders with the distribution of those who are arriving on campus with the label "black," whether or not preference was accorded in their admission, because too many of them have parents from Africa or the Caribbean or are students whose racial mixture was created in recent years by having a non-black parent as opposed to having non-black ancestors in whatever quantity further up the family tree.[50] Finally, as shown by litigation over Lowell High School in San Francisco, which is Justice Stephen Breyer's alma mater, there have been efforts to distinguish among Asians so that one subgroup, such as Samoans or Filipinos, could obtain preference, or at least not be disadvantaged, whereas other subgroups, such as Vietnamese or Chinese, would continue to bear the racial burden.[51]

Very briefly, Lowell had a scheme whereby, in order to be admitted, you needed sixty-six out of a possible sixty-nine academic points if you were Chinese, fifty-nine if you were white or other Asian, and so on down the line for a variety of groups.[52] As a result of a consent decree the scheme was ultimately abandoned, but that decree has just expired[53] and it is unclear what the school is going to do. It is still very controversial. Under *Gratz* I don't think they could go back to so explicit a system. But under *Grutter* they could perhaps have exactly the same result by simply putting a bit of gauze over it. It is interesting to note, however, that in each of these efforts to create subdivisions, the change in generally accepted categories moves toward favoring groups that on average, sociologically, appear to lean more in the direction of liberal or statist views and against those of the opposite persuasion. That leads back to the question of whether what is really at work in this area is a version of patronage. Do the following thought experiment: If it suddenly happened that the students receiving racial preference in admission were to arrive on campus with ninety percent of them

[50] See Sara Rimer and Karen W. Arenson, Top Colleges Take More Blacks, but Which Ones?, N.Y. Times, June 24, 2004, at A1.

[51] See San Francisco NAACP v. San Francisco Unified Sch. Dist., 413 F. Supp. 2d 1051 (N.D. Cal. 2005).

[52] Group Preferences and the Law: Hearing Before the Subcomm. On the Constitution of the H. Comm. On the Judiciary, 104th Cong. (June 1, 1995) (written statement by Lee Cheng, Secretary of the Asian American Legal Foundation).

[53] *Id.*

clamoring to attend Cato conferences and registering Republican, how long do you think the educational institutions would continue to accord such preferences? I doubt very much that it would continue for very long.

Justice O'Conner suggested in *Grutter* that preferences might last only another twenty-five more years.[54] That would make the span from the first preference programs that were upheld to the end of that period to be almost exactly the same fifty-eight years as the time from the *Plessy* decision, which upheld separate-but-equal, to the *Brown* decision, which ended legally sanctioned school segregation. Maybe preferences will end that way, maybe they will persist longer, despite their inconsistency with equal protection, or they may end sooner. Thus far, however, I think courts have done a very bad job in this area. They permit the government to label some as cows and some as gods and assign benefits based on those labels, the very antithesis of the rule of law.

III.

The third area, and the one in which I say that the jury is still very much out, is that of election law. Many commentators have remarked on the expanding legalization and constitutionalization of elections.[55] This is not a wholly new phenomenon, nor a wholly unwarranted one. Elections are conducted according to laws and those laws, just as with any others, may ultimately lead to court cases and judicial resolution. There is in fact a very rich body of law concerning ballot counting in close elections, albeit usually for small local offices. Most of it came from the paper ballot days. What is a proper mark? What is a spoiled ballot?[56] Before Florida 2000, this seemed mostly the province of antiquarians and election junkies, but it was there. If the election is close enough, legitimate issues inevitably arrive. Perhaps the most notable example was the 1962 Minnesota governor's race, which was ultimately settled by ninety-one votes after a three-month recount supervised by the supreme

[54] Grutter, 539 U.S. at 343.

[55] See, e.g., Richard H. Pildes, Constitutionalizing Democratic Politics, in A Badly Flawed Election 155 (R. Dowrkin ed., 2002).

[56] See In re Application of Anderson, 264 Minn. 257 (Minn. 1962); 26 Am. Jur. 2d Elections § 336 (2006).

court of the state.[57] Florida 2000, of course, brought this area into blazing prominence. I'm not going to refight that litigation, but only use it to illustrate and make a few points. First, it doesn't mean that every election is going to be litigated. Florida was not just any close election; in percentage terms it was the closest state presidential election in our history, out of more than 2,000 state results. At that level of closeness, controversy was inevitable. But it does mean that suspicion about the role of the courts will arise: the Republicans suspected the Florida Supreme Court, the Democrats suspected the U.S. Supreme Court. Yet at the end of the day, it should be possible to discern some underlying principles in the election area that should be followed.

When the controversy started I was very aware of a recent on point and compelling case that had been decided in the Eleventh Circuit, which included Florida. It was called *Roe v. Alabama*,[58] and unlike *Roe v. Wade*, there really was a Mr. Roe who was the plaintiff. In the race for chief justice of Alabama the initial count favored the Republican candidate by 262 votes. Controversy arose over a large number of absentee ballots from one county. State law required a witness signature on the ballots, which these ballots lacked. But the county wanted to count those ballots and not enforce the requirement. Should those votes count? If they counted, the incumbent chief justice, a Democrat, would remain in office. If not, he would be replaced by the Republican opponent. The federal courts sent the case back to the Alabama courts for a state law decision.[59] The state supreme court, with the chief judge recused, but with his colleagues and campaign contributors sitting, said that state law did allow the counting.[60] The Eleventh Circuit, including a Democratic appointee, Rosemary Barkett, universally considered quite liberal, reversed unanimously, saying that you have to apply the law uniformly, even when the state doesn't want to.[61] To me, that was an appropriate court intervention, and not wildly controversial at the time. I was

[57] See Minnesota gubernatorial election, 1962, at http://en.wikipedia.org/wiki/Minnesota_gubernatorial_election%2C_1962.

[58] 68 F.3d 404 (11th Cir. 1995).

[59] See Roe v. Alabama, 43 F.3d 574 (11th Cir. 1995).

[60] See Roe v. Mobile County Appointment Board, 676 So. 2d 1206 (Ala. 1995).

[61] See Roe, 68 F.3d at 409.

surprised that the case was not widely adverted to and used during the Florida litigation.

On the other hand, a 2004 Ohio election challenger case illustrates the potential for unequal application of the law.[62] There, lower courts had forbidden Republican challengers, named as defendants, from exercising their rights under a state law providing for challenges to persons said to be unqualified to vote. Democrats were not party to the case and, at least by the anecdotal evidence, were not sitting on pins and needles waiting to see how the appeal would be resolved. As it turned out, a panel of our court, on which I did not sit, ultimately overturned the ruling,[63] permitted both parties equally to have observers and challengers. Justice Stevens refused to stay that decision.[64]

Finally, let me simply mention a few cases that raise claims of election fraud. In the Sixth Circuit we upheld the ability of state election commissions to have what I call a truth-declaring function. We allowed a commission to give an opinion on the factual claims of candidates, but we struck down their ability to impose punishment based on that view or to disqualify the candidate.[65] Obviously, I thought that was the proper decision because I wrote it. At a subsequent symposium, counsel from both sides said that we had split the baby correctly, and they both agreed with the decision. But cases allowing courts to adjudicate whether arguments used in elections are fraudulent are especially problematic. Such decisions would not be made behind the veil of ignorance. And they would come at the time when the temptation to bend the principles in favor of one party or another are the greatest. At the same time I think that court intervention cannot be ruled out or even always discouraged. We cannot allow partisans, for their own purposes, to bend or ignore the laws that have been enacted. And that is the lesson of the Eleventh Circuit case that I mentioned.

It is a tough area. We have yet to see fully what the courts will do, and there are many cases bubbling up. I'll mention three cases the

[62] See Spencer v. Blackwell, 347 F. Supp. 2d 528 (S.D. Ohio 2004).

[63] See Summit County Democratic Cent. & Exec. Comm. v. Blackwell, 388 F.3d 547 (6th Cir. 2004).

[64] See Spencer v. Pugh, 543 U.S. 1301 (2004).

[65] Pestrak v. Ohio Elections Comm., 926 F.2d 573 (6th Cir. 1991).

Sixth Circuit has seen recently. One involved voting technologies.[66] A second involved an effort to strike a Michigan referendum from the ballot where the district court and a panel of our court on which I did not sit denied an injunction.[67] And a third arose when a candidate went into federal court to seek the polling data of an opponent and to censor the questions being asked on the opponent's polls.[68] These are just examples that are emblematic of the challenges that will face courts in this area in the years ahead.

In summary, then, in all three of these areas, and others too, where the temptation is to favor Jovi and burden Bovi, courts must avoid the temptation of such jurisprudence in order to merit and retain the trust of the people. They must try to adhere to principles and rules laid down as far ahead as possible and must explain themselves in ways that show that they are sensitive to the ever-present dangers of stepping outside the rule of law.

[66] See Stewart v. Blackwell, 444 F.3d 843 (6th Cir. 2006). En banc rehearing never occurred as the appeal became moot. The panel opinion was vacated. See Stewart v. Blackwell, 473 F.3d 692 (6th Cir. 2007), cert. denied, 127 S. Ct. 646 (2007).

[67] See Coalition to Defend Affirmative Action v. Granholm, 473 F.3d 237 (6th Cir. 2006).

[68] See Carl Chancellor, State Auditor Candidates Reach Deal, Akron Beacon Journal, Oct. 6, 2006, at B4; Complaint, Sykes v. Taylor et. al., No. 5:06-cv-02145-JG (N.D. Ohio).

Death by a Thousand Cuts: Constitutional Wrongs Without Remedies After *Wilkie v. Robbins*

*Laurence H. Tribe**

I. Introduction

Many constitutional violations are discrete events: FBI agents conduct a warrantless wiretap; a judge enjoins the publication of an article criticizing a political leader; a public school principal fires a teacher for expressing his doubts about the Darwinian theory of evolution; a public school teacher leads her class in a group prayer; a government agency takes private property and refuses to pay just compensation. For these kinds of well-defined and bounded violations, some legal remedy is almost always available to the victim—whether in federal court, in state court, or before an administrative agency subject to judicial review. Other constitutional violations consist of an episodic series of small events—events that in isolation may verge on the trivial. But—as the metaphor "death by a thousand cuts" suggests—a series of small harms, in unison or in sequence, can add up to one very large harm indeed. This article explores the problems raised by those constitutional wrongs that consist of such patterns of behavior. It does so through a close examination of the Supreme Court's recent decision in *Wilkie v. Robbins*,[1] a case that addressed precisely the sort of pattern that, viewed as a whole, can render unconstitutional the conduct involved, and the plan to engage in it.

I should disclose at the outset that I represented the respondent, a cattle rancher named Frank Robbins, pro bono before the Supreme

*Carl M. Loeb University Professor, Harvard University. For excellent research assistance with this article, I thank Emily Gumper, Harvard Law School J.D. 2007, and Daniel Gonen, Harvard Law School J.D. 2007. For any errors, I of course have myself to blame.

[1] 127 S. Ct. 2588 (2007).

Court, working with the Harvard Law School Supreme Court Litigation Clinic. His case involved a pattern of harassment, intimidation, and threats by federal employees who demanded that he grant an easement to the public. The pattern involved federal government officials who sought to wear down his resolve in insisting that the government either negotiate a purchase of the easement or take it through eminent domain and pay him just compensation. But this article is about more than just one Supreme Court case. It is about property rights in general because, after *Robbins*, government officials have a blueprint for obtaining private property without having to pay for it. All they need do is single out a property owner and gradually bring the government's vast regulatory and other powers to bear on the owner's shoulders, making it clear that the resulting burden will be lifted if—but only if—the owner will simply "give" some valuable property interest to the government.[2] More broadly, however, this article also addresses constitutional rights generally, exploring the future viability of constitutional tort suits against federal officials under the Supreme Court's *Bivens* line of cases.[3] I argue that the Supreme Court's decision in *Robbins* dealt a severe and unjustifiable blow both to individual rights—including, but not limited to, rights of private property—and to the role of *Bivens* remedies in implementing those rights, thus making them real.

The Court's *Bivens* analysis in *Robbins* acknowledged that both state and federal avenues of relief could well prove inadequate in the kind of situation Robbins faced—and did indeed prove inadequate to protect Robbins from the cumulative harm he was made

[2] All of us are potentially subject to an almost unthinkable degree of government intrusion into our lives and businesses, much of it lawful when engaged in for lawful purposes. One need only imagine having a police officer constantly hovering over one's shoulder ready to impose a fine any time one jaywalks, drives over the speed limit, fails to stop fully at a stop sign, or takes an improper deduction on one's tax return to understand the damage that government officials could do once they set their minds to it. It simply cannot be the case that, when the government sets out to invoke all of its powers against an individual for the demonstrable purpose of getting that individual to waive a clearly established federal constitutional right, and when that individual is able to prove that, but for this forbidden purpose, those powers would not have been invoked, no remedy is available from the federal courts unless Congress has expressly enacted one. Yet that appears to be the result after *Robbins*, at least when the right is one that attaches to private property.

[3] See Bivens v. Six Unknown Named Agents of Fed. Bureau of Narcotics, 403 U.S. 388 (1971).

to suffer for insisting on his rights as a property owner. But even while conceding that the combined effect of all the non-*Bivens* relief available to Robbins was predictably insufficient to address a *pattern* of conduct whose unconstitutionality lay in what the pattern was designed to accomplish and in the harm the pattern inflicted in the course of that effort, the *Robbins* Court declined to fill the resulting remedial gap with the usual form of *Bivens* relief. Instead, the Court departed from the core premise of *Bivens*—that the importance of constitutional rights justified implying a cause of action directly from the Constitution; and for the first time since *Bivens* it held, without any indication from Congress that it disfavored the application of a *Bivens* remedy in such circumstances, that a private citizen could not sue a government official for a constitutional violation, even in the absence of any alternative to such a suit that would operate to deter that kind of violation or at least redress it when deterrence failed.

The Court reached that conclusion by transforming the *Bivens* presumption in favor of a federal cause of action into a general, all-things-considered, balancing test. What makes the ruling in *Robbins* especially frustrating is not only the Court's unacknowledged and unexplained transformation of *Bivens* but also its mishandling, in *Robbins* itself, of the balancing test it purported to be applying. Thus, the Court held that a *Bivens* action was unavailable for Robbins's takings claim because of the supposedly inherent difficulty of defining a workable standard to determine when a pattern of conduct goes so far as to violate a constitutional right. Apart from everything else that may be said (and will be said below) to address that concern as a supposed justification for leaving rights without protection, one decisive irony is that the Court's holding will not serve even to avoid the problem ostensibly motivating it, because substantively identical claims will get to federal court anyway—either as claims for injunctive and/or damages relief against state officials under 42 U.S.C. § 1983,[4] or, in piecemeal form, as claims against federal officials via judicial review of final agency action under the Administrative Procedures Act (hereafter, the APA).[5]

[4] 42 U.S.C. § 1983 (2000).

[5] 5 U.S.C. §§ 551–559, 701–706 (2000 & Supp. IV 2004). The *Robbins* Court may have taken solace from the thought that it was saving the lower courts the burden of defining a workable standard for Robbins's Fifth Amendment claim. Any such thought would have been mistaken, however, not only because of the availability of

After Justice David Souter's opinion for the Court in *Robbins*, an opinion at once evasive in its logic and immodest in its reach, the best that can be said of the *Bivens* doctrine is that it is on life support with little prospect of recovery. In *Robbins*, the Court denied a cattle rancher whose business was deliberately ruined a *Bivens* remedy against the federal agents who retaliated against him over a nearly decade-long period—by means both of independently illegal acts and of abuses of their regulatory authority—for his refusal to surrender his Fifth Amendment Takings Clause rights by granting the government an easement across his property without just compensation. That rejection of a remedy under *Bivens* should have come as no surprise to anyone watching the recent trajectory of the *Bivens* doctrine. It certainly did not come as a surprise to me, as the brief writer and oral advocate for Robbins and as the attorney who had argued and lost *Schweiker v.Chilicky*,[6] the decision that had dealt the most recent major blow to *Bivens* as a precedent. But it was a bitter disappointment nonetheless. Hope springs eternal, and when it is born of a source as deeply embedded in our culture as the Bill of Rights and the principle of government accountability for constitutional wrongs, its trashing is never an easy experience.

Although the Court's failure to afford a *Bivens* remedy was no surprise, the same cannot be said about the lengths to which the Court went to reach the *Bivens* question and to answer that question as it did. The Court sacrificed on a false altar of judicial modesty—false because the Court's holding was based on its unexplained shirking of a prototypically judicial function—both the limited appellate jurisdiction of the federal courts and the bedrock principle that the government's objectives "cannot be pursued by means that needlessly chill the exercise of basic constitutional rights."[7] Private

§ 1983 suits against state officials but also because of the Court's endorsement, however lukewarm, of Robbins's administrative remedies. See *infra* note 88.

[6] 487 U.S. 412 (1988) (denying a *Bivens* remedy for consequential injury suffered by Social Security claimants whose claims were wrongfully denied as part of an allegedly unconstitutional scheme, where Congress had provided a comprehensive mechanism for reinstating wrongfully withheld benefits but no mechanism for remedying the kind of injury alleged by respondents).

[7] United States v. Jackson, 390 U.S. 570, 582 (1968).

property rights are thus once again relegated to "the status of a poor relation" of many other constitutional guarantees.[8]

The remainder of this article proceeds as follows. Part II discusses the factual background of *Robbins* and the legal arguments on both sides. Part III then explores the *Robbins* opinion with regard to its implications for property and other individual rights. Part IV focuses on the *Robbins* Court's *Bivens* analysis and discusses the Court's willingness to allow wrongs without remedy. Part V focuses on how the Court exceeded thoroughly settled limits on its exercise of interlocutory appellate jurisdiction by reaching the *Bivens* issue in this case rather than deciding simply whether the conduct by Bureau of Land Management (BLM) officials that Robbins had alleged and sought to establish at trial violated a clearly established constitutional right against retaliation for the exercise of one's Fifth Amendment property rights. Part VI then briefly concludes the article.

II. The Background of the Litigation: Oh, Give Me a Home Where the Bureaucrats Roam . . . "Your Easement Or Your Life!"

A. The Factual Background of the Case

In the early 1990s, a Wyoming office of the federal Bureau of Land Management (the BLM) was on a mission to obtain an easement over a portion of the South Fork Owl Creek Road cutting across the High Island Ranch, a privately owned cattle and guest ranch in Hot Springs County, Wyoming. Driven by a wholly legitimate desire to increase already existing access to the national forest abutting the ranch, the BLM was able to convince the ranch's then-owner, George Nelson, to grant the U.S. government a public easement over the Owl Creek Road in exchange for a right of way over a portion of a nearby road on federal land.

In a bungle that initiated the chain of events ultimately leading to this lawsuit, the BLM failed to record the easement Nelson had granted. Shortly afterward, Nelson sold his ranch to Frank Robbins,

[8]See James W. Ely Jr., "Poor Relation" Once More: The Supreme Court and the Vanishing Rights of Property Owners, 2004–05 Cato Sup. Ct. Rev. 39 (2005) (arguing that the Supreme Court's recent Takings Clause jurisprudence threatens the promise of Justice Rehnquist's declaration in *Dolan v. City of Tigard*, 512 U.S. 374, 392 (1994), that the Takings Clause should not be "relegated to the status of a poor relation"). But see *infra* text accompanying notes 114–25.

who was completely unaware of the government's easement. Under the applicable Wyoming law, the BLM's failure to record meant that Robbins took title free of the government's Nelson easement. Upon realizing their embarrassing mistake, BLM officials called Robbins and "demanded an easement to replace Nelson's."[9] When Robbins proved willing to negotiate a fair price but "unwilling to capitulate" to the BLM's "unilateral demands"[10] that he provide the easement free of charge, the BLM officials, apparently just as unwilling to accept the consequences of their own mistake and pursue one of the legally available means for obtaining the easement,[11] instigated a campaign of actions designed, as one former BLM employee reported, to "bury" Robbins.[12] It quickly became apparent that this was no idle threat. BLM officials embarked on a scheme to "get . . . [Robbins's] permits and get him out of business,"[13] engaging in a pattern of egregious misconduct consisting of both independently illegal actions and demonstrable abuses of lawful authority, substantiated by "ample evidence"[14] on the summary judgment record.[15]

[9] Wilkie v. Robbins, 127 S. Ct. 2588, 2593 (2007).

[10] *Id.* at 2609 (Ginsburg, J., concurring in part and dissenting in part). Robbins was informed by one of the BLM officials that "the Federal Government does not negotiate." *Id.* at 2593.

[11] The BLM's legal options for acquiring that kind of property interest in privately owned land amounted to just three: First, the agency could acquire the property through donation by, purchase from, or exchange with a willing seller or donor. Second, the agency could take the property through eminent domain, but only if certain statutory conditions were met and with the permission of the attorney general. See *infra* note 145. Third, BLM regulations permit the agency to require an "applicant for a right-of-way" across federal lands, "as a condition of receiving the right of way, to grant the United States an equivalent right of way that is adequate in duration and rights." It appears that the arrangement the BLM had orchestrated with Nelson relied on those BLM regulations but did not meet their "equivalence" condition, see Brief for the Respondent at 4, Wilkie v. Robbins, 127 S. Ct. 2588 (2007) (No. 06-219) (hereinafter Resp't Br.), but nothing in Robbins's claim depended on that failure. Another BLM regulation provides that an applicant for a permit for grazing on federal lands may be required to accord the BLM limited administrative access across private lands for the "orderly management and protection of the public land," but that proviso could not furnish a legal basis for obtaining the general access to the road demanded by the BLM. See Resp't Br. at 1-2 (citations omitted).

[12] Joint Appendix at 49, 52, Wilkie v. Robbins, 127 S. Ct. 2588 (2007) (No. 06-219) (plaintiff's third amended complaint, ¶ 42) (hereinafter Joint Appendix).

[13] Robbins, 127 S. Ct. at 2594.

[14] See Robbins v. Wilkie, No. 98-CV-201-B, 2004 WL 3659189, at *6 (D. Wyo. Jan. 20, 2004) (district court's order denying defendant's motion for summary judgment).

[15] It is settled that, on an interlocutory appeal from a decision refusing to grant officers summary judgment on the basis of qualified immunity, the district court's evaluation of the factual proof as to its denial of summary judgment is binding on each appellate court to consider the matter. Johnson v. Jones, 515 U.S. 304, 313–20 (1995).

The agents' independently unlawful actions included intentionally trespassing on Robbins's land,[16] inciting a neighbor to ram a truck into Robbins while he was on horseback,[17] breaking into his guest lodge,[18] filing trumped-up felony charges against him without probable cause,[19] and pressuring other government agents to impound Robbins's cattle without cause.[20] The officials' actions that might have been lawful in other circumstances but were unauthorized as means to the unconstitutional and thus illegal ends to which they were put here—the extraction, without any payment or exchange, of an easement to which the government had no colorable claim[21]—included canceling the right-of-way previously negotiated with Nelson that was to have run with the land;[22] filing doubtful administrative charges against Robbins and selectively enforcing others,[23] and then relying upon these charges to deny Robbins the recreational use and grazing permits essential to his cattle drive business;[24] refusing to

[16] Robbins, 127 S. Ct. at 2594.

[17] Joint Appendix, *supra* note 12, at 49, 67.

[18] Wilkie v. Robbins, 127 S. Ct. 2588, 2596 (2007).

[19] Joint Appendix, *supra* note 12, at 55–56, 68–71; Resp't Br., *supra* note 11, at 6–7.

[20] Robbins, 127 S. Ct. at 2596.

[21] It is necessary to note here the government's persistent (and persistently misleading) characterization of the defendants as engaged throughout the entirety of the case in "attempt[s] to secure a *reciprocal* right of way over private land intermingled with public lands." Cert. Pet. at 10–11, Robbins v. Wilkie (No. 98-CV-201-B) (emphasis added). In support of this strain of argument, the government relied on the authority it had invoked under the BLM regulations in its dealings with Nelson to require an "applicant for a right-of-way" across federal lands, "as a condition of receiving the right of way, to grant the United States an equivalent right of way that is adequate in duration and rights." *Id.* at 3. However, as Justice Ginsburg noted in dissent, in its reliance on those regulations, the BLM was at best "on shaky legal ground," Robbins, 127 S. Ct. at 2609 (Ginsburg, J., dissenting in part), given that Robbins was not himself an applicant for a right-of way, and no law required Robbins to make up for the BLM's neglectful loss of the first easement. *Id.* In any event, even assuming the stability of that legal ground, the ground surely caved in by the end of the first year of the BLM's eight-year campaign, when it cancelled the right-of-way it had negotiated with Nelson.

[22] *Id.* at 2594. BLM officials cancelled the right-of-way in 1995, at the same time canceling whatever dubious argument they may have had for claiming, as they nonetheless continued to do throughout this litigation, that they were merely engaged in attempts to "secure a reciprocal right of way."

[23] *Id.* at 2595. The Court noted that "[o]ne Bureau employee, Edward Parodi, was told by his superiors to 'look closer' and 'investigate harder' for possible trespasses and other permit violations." *Id.* at 2594.

[24] *Id.* at 2595–96.

keep the main access route to Robbins's property passable while fining Robbins for repairing the access road that the previous owner had been allowed to maintain;[25] and interfering with his business by "videotap[ing] ranch guests during [a cattle] drive, even while the guests sought privacy to relieve themselves."[26]

B. The Litigation

In attempting to respond to the rising mountain of dubious and selective charges against him, Robbins fought a predictably losing battle through the administrative appeals process to the Interior Board of Land Appeals (IBLA)—which, among other things, held itself to be without statutory authority to consider Robbins's essential claim that the actions taken against him were unconstitutionally motivated and formed part of a pattern of unconstitutional harassment.[27] Simultaneously, he was defending himself against the false criminal charges brought against him and attempting to run his business in the face of the BLM officials' attempts to make that as difficult as possible. Furthermore, the administrative appeals process afforded Robbins no opportunity to seek redress for the numerous individual actions of the BLM officials unrelated to "final agency action," or for the cumulative effect of the officials' independently unlawful actions, as the Court expressly recognized:

> But Robbins's argument for a remedy that looks at the course of dealing as a whole, not simply as so many individual incidents, has the force of the metaphor Robbins invokes, "death by a thousand cuts." Brief for Respondent 40. It is one thing to be threatened with the loss of grazing rights, or to be prosecuted, or to have one's lodge broken into, but something else to be subjected to this in combination over a period of six years, by a series of public officials bent on making life difficult. Agency appeals, lawsuits, and criminal defense take money, and endless battling depletes the spirit along with the purse. The whole here is greater than the sum of its parts.[28]

[25] *Id.* at 2595.

[26] *Id.* at 2596.

[27] See Frank Robbins v. B.L.M., 170 I.B.L.A. 219, 227–30 (2006), cited in Wilkie v. Robbins, 127 S. Ct. 2588, 2598 n.5 (2007).

[28] Wilkie v. Robbins, 127 S. Ct. 2588, 2600–01 (2007).

In 1998, having already endured four years of harassment, Robbins brought an action in federal court against the BLM officials, under *Bivens v. Six Unnamed Agents,*[29] for violation of his Fifth Amendment rights under the Takings Clause.[30] Robbins also brought RICO claims against the defendants for their repeated attempts to extort the easement from him.[31]

The district court granted the defendants' motion to dismiss both claims, but the Tenth Circuit reversed and held both that Robbins had pleaded damages with adequate specificity under RICO and that the APA and the Federal Tort Claims Act (FTCA) did not preclude relief under *Bivens,* except with regard to violations consisting of final agency action for which review under the APA was available.[32]

On remand to the district court, the defendants again moved to dismiss Robbins's claims, this time solely on qualified immunity

[29] 403 U.S. 388 (1971).

[30] Originally, Robbins also alleged claims under the Fourth Amendment for malicious prosecution as well as various due process claims under the Fifth Amendment; these were dismissed on qualified immunity grounds at a later stage of the litigation, and no appeal was taken from those dismissals. In addition, Robbins voluntarily dismissed claims against the U.S. government originally included in his complaint.

[31] The Racketeer Influenced and Corrupt Organization Act (RICO), 18 U.S.C. §§ 1961–1968 (2000 ed. and Supp. IV), is a criminal statute that also provides for a civil cause of action, and imposes liability for engaging in a "pattern of racketeering activity." *Id.* § 1962(c). The Act defines such racketeering activity to include acts of extortion, as defined under the Hobbs Act, 18 U.S.C. § 1951 (2000), or under state law. 18 U.S.C. §§ 1961(1)(A)–(B) (2000 ed., and Supp. IV). The gist of Robbins's RICO claim was that actions of the BLM officials constituted a series of attempts to extort the easement from him, which in turn constituted an indictable offense under the Hobbs Act definition of racketeering as an attempt to "obtain[] . . . property from another, with his consent . . . under color of official right." 18 U.S.C. § 1951(b)(2). Robbins also asserted that the conduct violated Wyoming's blackmail statute, Wyo. Stat. Ann. § 6-2-402, another RICO predicate. The Court held without dissent that the RICO claim was not actionable, on the ground that "the conduct alleged does not fit the traditional definition of extortion," Robbins, 127 S. Ct. at 2608, which "focused on . . . the sale of public favors for private gain," not "on behalf of the Government." *Id.* at 2606 (footnote omitted); *id.* at 2618 n.11 (Ginsburg, J., concurring in part and dissenting in part). Although I do not agree either with the Court's interlocutory assumption of ancillary appellate jurisdiction to reach the RICO question or with the substance of its answer, the Court's disposition of the matter was a unanimous windmill against which this article makes no effort to tilt.

[32] See Robbins v. Wilkie, 300 F.3d 1208, 1211–13 (10th Cir. 2002).

grounds, and the court denied the motion.[33] After discovery, the defendants moved for summary judgment on qualified immunity. The district court denied that motion and defendants appealed that decision. After properly determining that it had interlocutory appellate jurisdiction to decide the qualified immunity issue under *Mitchell v. Forsyth*'s extension of the collateral order appeal doctrine to orders denying qualified immunity on legal as opposed to factual grounds,[34] the court of appeals affirmed, holding that Robbins had "a clearly established right to be free from retaliation for exercising his Fifth Amendment right to exclude the Government from his private property,"[35] reasoning that "[b]ecause retaliation tends to chill citizens' exercise of their Fifth Amendment right to exclude the Government from private property, the Fifth Amendment prohibits such retaliation as a means of ensuring that the right is meaningful."[36] In addition, the court of appeals—without pausing to consider whether it was acting within its appellate jurisdiction over the defendants' interlocutory appeal of the district court's qualified immunity decision—entertained the defendants' argument that the *Bivens* claim was precluded by the APA and/or the FTCA, and reinstated its holding from the first round of appeals that neither the APA nor any other source of law precluded *Bivens* relief for violations unrelated to final agency action.

The solicitor general, representing the BLM agents, then petitioned for certiorari on the RICO question, the *Bivens* question, and the qualified immunity question (couched in terms of the existence of a clearly established anti-retaliation right in property rights cases), in that order. The Supreme Court granted certiorari on all three questions. In its eventual decision on the merits, however, the Court did not answer the one question (qualified immunity) without which the case could not have reached it at all in this pre-trial, interlocutory posture. Bypassing that question, and remaining silent on the existence of any anti-retaliation right for property owners, the Court held that, even if such a right had been clearly established, and even

[33] The district court dismissed other claims for violations of the Fourth and Fifth Amendments. Those claims are not addressed here.

[34] 472 U.S. 511, 528–30 (1985).

[35] Robbins v. Wilkie, 433 F.3d 755, 765–67 (10th Cir. 2006).

[36] *Id.* at 766.

if the defendants had knowingly violated it and thus were entitled to no immunity from trial or from liability for damages, they were nonetheless entitled to escape trial altogether inasmuch as the *Bivens* doctrine gave Robbins no cause of action against the officers who had made good on their threat to "bury" him for standing firm on his Fifth Amendment rights.[37]

C. *The Fifth Amendment Right Not to Have One's Property Taken by the Government Without Receiving Just Compensation*

The constitutional claim at the heart of *Robbins* is one that may at first seem novel to many students of the Takings Clause, but it is, in fact, central to the constitutional protection of private property—and, indeed, to the effective protection of every constitutional right that takes the form of recognizing in individuals an entitlement to choose, within defined constraints, among possible courses of conduct. Obvious examples are the right to choose what to say, whether and how to pray, whether and when to end a pregnancy, and what to do with one's private property—whether to donate it to the public gratis, or sell it to the public for a fair price.[38] In the protection of private property in particular, modern Takings Clause jurisprudence is generally divided into physical takings and regulatory takings. The claim in *Robbins* falls into neither camp. It is not a physical takings claim because the BLM never actually claimed to have acquired an easement across his land; and it is not a regulatory takings claim because Robbins never alleged that any legislative or administrative enactment had deprived him of all economically beneficial use of his land or of any distinct bundle of property rights in that land.

The thrust of Robbins's claim was that the BLM agents engaged both in unlawful exercises of their otherwise legitimate regulatory powers and in entirely illegitimate acts—independently illegal acts performed under color of their office but outside their delegated authority—in order to coerce him into relinquishing his property

[37] Wilkie v. Robbins, 127 S. Ct. 2588, 2604–05, 2608 (2007).

[38] The option of simply holding onto the property forever, or until the public offers whatever extortionate price one might choose to charge, is understood to be beyond the rights that the Takings and Just Compensation Clauses confer whenever exercise of the "takings" or "eminent domain" power is legislatively authorized.

without the government being forced actually to "take" it and thereby incur an obligation to pay just compensation. Had it succeeded, this strategy would have accomplished a literal transfer to the government (with no pretense of compensation) of what are unquestionably compensable property rights in a way that would have entirely circumvented the just compensation requirement by making a "taking" of any variety—either literal or regulatory—unnecessary. For the government would never need to exercise its eminent domain power to take property or its lawmaking power to enact regulations that so affect property uses as to constitute a de facto taking—either of which might force it to pay—if it were free instead to leverage the myriad ways in which its powers can be brought to bear on an individual or on any other rights-bearing entity, and use that leverage to force a property owner into surrendering the owner's property free of charge.

The point is one that could as easily be made with respect to essentially any right of choice protected by the federal Constitution. If a constitutional provision or principle prohibits abridgment of a right that takes the form of a *choice* someone is entitled to make—for instance, a right to freedom of speech or to the free exercise of religion, or a right to be free from compelled self-incrimination—then government may escape whatever preventive or remedial regime protects persons from deprivation of that right if it is free simply to induce the rights-holder "voluntarily" to relinquish the right, either by threatening to inflict injury by independently unlawful means unless the right is relinquished ("your right or your life!"), or by threatening to withhold some privilege or benefit that government is entitled to condition upon other forms of forbearance on the part of the privilege-seeker but not upon sacrifice of the right in question.[39]

[39] The Fifth Amendment's Takings Clause, like its Self-Incrimination Clause but unlike, say, the First Amendment's Free Speech Clause or the First Amendment's Free Exercise of Religion Clause, has long been understood to give the government a clear but costly path along which it may extract what it wants from someone: If you want someone's property for a legitimate public use such as increasing access to a national forest, use eminent domain and pay the owner just compensation; if you want the psychological "property" held in someone's mind for a legitimate public purpose such as law enforcement or legislative oversight, swear the person in as a witness and give that witness immunity from criminal prosecution based on his answers or their fruits. Rights to insist that the government pursue the constitutionally designated path if it wishes to obtain one's property or one's testimony are uniquely

Not all rights are of this character, of course. Some rights, like the Establishment Clause right to live in a non-theocratic state, or the Eighth Amendment right to be free of cruel and unusual punishments, or the Article I right to be free of ex post facto laws or of bills of attainder, do not have a choice-making structure that lends itself to the distinctive sort of circumvention illustrated by what was done to Robbins by agents of the BLM in order to induce him to give up his easement and to waive his right to just compensation. But the right not to be deprived of one's private property for public use without just compensation—like the Fifth Amendment right not to be compelled to incriminate oneself without the compensating assurance provided by an appropriate grant of immunity from criminal prosecution[40]—seems paradigmatic of those choice-based rights with respect to which the technique of circumvention employed against Robbins must be deemed unconstitutional if the right is not to be rendered essentially unenforceable.

The Fifth Amendment claim in *Robbins* viewed in this light fits comfortably within the Supreme Court's longstanding and widely applied hostility toward government retaliation against the exercise of constitutional rights.[41] The anti-retaliation principle as a free-standing claim is most often seen in First Amendment cases,[42] but it has also been recognized in the context of numerous other rights, including the Fifth Amendment privilege against compelled self-incrimination,[43] the right to demand a criminal trial by

vulnerable insofar as agents of the government are given an incentive to traverse the less costly path of pressuring one to waive such rights.

[40] See *supra* note 39.

[41] See, e.g., Bordenkircher v. Hayes, 434 U.S. 357, 363 (1977) ("[F]or an agent of the State to pursue a course of action whose objective is to penalize a person's reliance on his legal rights is 'patently unconstitutional.'"); *id.* ("To punish a person because he has done what the law plainly allows him to do is a due process violation of the most basic sort . . ."); Perry v. Sindermann, 408 U.S. 593, 597 (1972) ("[Government] may not deny a benefit to a person on a basis that infringes his constitutionally protected interests . . ."); Griffin v. California, 380 U.S. 609, 614 (1965) (striking down "a penalty imposed by courts for exercising a constitutional privilege"). See *supra* note 39.

[42] See, e.g., Hartman v. Moore, 126 S. Ct. 1695, 1704 (2006); Crawford-El v. Britton, 523 U.S. 574 (1998); Mt. Healthy Sch. Dist. Bd. of Educ. v. Doyle, 429 U.S. 274, 282, 287 (1977).

[43] In *Griffin v. California*, 380 U.S. 609 (1965), the Court held that a prosecutor's comment on a defendant's failure to testify violated the Fifth Amendment because "it is a penalty imposed by courts for exercising a constitutional privilege." *Id.* at

jury,[44] the right of access to the federal courts,[45] and the right to travel interstate.[46] In *Dolan v. City of Tigard*,[47] the Court applied this anti-retaliation principle specifically to the Takings Clause.

614. In the context of government employment, the Court has repeatedly condemned government retaliation against employees or independent contractors who refused to waive their Fifth Amendment rights. See Lefkowitz v. Turley, 414 U.S. 70, 83–84 (1973) (holding that disqualification of independent contractors from receiving government work for refusing to waive their privilege against self-incrimination was unconstitutional); Uniformed Sanitation Men Ass'n v. Comm'r of Sanitation, 392 U.S. 280, 283–84 (1968) (holding that dismissal of state employees who refused to give testimony that could have been used against them in a criminal prosecution violated the Fifth Amendment); Gardner v. Broderick, 392 U.S. 273, 279 (1968) (''[T]he mandate of the great privilege against self-incrimination does not tolerate the attempt, regardless of its ultimate effectiveness, to coerce a waiver of the immunity it confers on penalty of the loss of employment.''); Garrity v. New Jersey, 385 U.S. 493, 500 (1967) (holding that ''the protection of the individual . . . against coerced statements prohibits use in subsequent criminal proceedings of statements obtained under threat of removal from office. . .'').

[44]See United States v. Goodwin, 457 U.S. 368, 384 (1982) (holding that a prosecutor may not vindictively bring greater charges against a defendant who demands a jury trial). In *United States v. Jackson*, 390 U.S. 570 (1968), the Court held that legislative retaliation for the exercise of the jury trial right was also unconstitutional and struck down a statute that authorized the imposition of the death penalty only after a jury trial. See *id.* at 582–83. The Court found that making the ''risk of death,'' *id.* at 571, the price for exercising the right to a jury trial ''needlessly penalizes the assertion of a constitutional right.'' *Id.* at 583.

[45]See Terral v. Burke Constr. Co., 257 U.S. 529, 532 (1922) (''[A] state may not, in imposing conditions upon the privilege of a foreign corporation's doing business in the state, exact from it a waiver of the exercise of its constitutional right to resort to the federal courts, or thereafter withdraw the privilege of doing business because of its exercise of such right, whether waived in advance or not.'').

[46]See Mem'l Hospital v. Maricopa County, 415 U.S. 250, 254–70 (1974) (holding unconstitutional a state statute requiring a year's residence in the county as a condition of an indigent's receiving medical care at the county's expense); Shapiro v. Thompson, 394 U.S. 618, 629–31 (1969) (holding that a state statute conditioning receipt of welfare benefits on one year of residence could not be justified by unconstitutional purpose of discouraging migration to the state).

[47]512 U.S. 374 (1994). See *id.* at 385 (''Under the well-settled doctrine of 'unconstitutional conditions,' the government may not require a person to give up a constitutional right—here the right to receive just compensation when property is taken for a public use—in exchange for a discretionary benefit conferred by the government where the benefit sought has little or no relationship to the property.''). Although the *Dolan* Court invoked the doctrine of unconstitutional conditions rather than retaliation, the two merge analytically when an individual is put to the choice of exercising a right, on the one hand, or receiving some government benefit or avoiding some government penalty, on the other hand. Cf. Crawford-El v. Britton, 523 U.S. 574, 588 n.10 (1998)

In *Robbins*, the retaliation issue was front and center in that the BLM was indisputably (on the record before the Court) retaliating against Robbins precisely for refusing to surrender his property without compensation and thus waive his Fifth Amendment right. Given that this property right would seem perfectly suited to, and inadequately protected without, an effective remedy against just this kind of circumvention, it is worse than ironic that the *Robbins* Court displayed no sensitivity whatever to the need for such a remedy. I say "worse than ironic" because, as is well known, the Supreme Court has spent much of the past few decades in a largely unsuccessful effort to delineate the situations in which government regulation of property uses amounts to a taking.[48] Yet in *Robbins* the Court turned its back on what amounts to a far more blatant form of government interference with private property rights—a form that cannot be tolerated at all if such rights are to be meaningfully protected. The BLM's strategy of acquisition through coercive acts that fall short of the direct application of physical force to wrest possession or ownership from a property holder could be used in any number of situations in which government officials want to avoid the procedural or substantive constraints of the eminent domain process. After *Robbins*, this kind of shadowy end run around the Takings Clause appears not to trigger any form of legal redress.[49]

("Retaliation is thus akin to an 'unconstitutional condition' demanded for the receipt of a government-provided benefit.").

[48] See, e.g., Richard A. Epstein, The Seven Deadly Sins of Takings Law: The Dissents in Lucas v. South Carolina Coastal Council, 26 Loy. L.A. L. Rev. 955, 966 (1993); Andrea L. Peterson, The Takings Clause: In Search of Underlying Principles Part I—A Critique of Current Takings Clause Doctrine, 77 Cal. L. Rev. 1299 (1989); Carol M. Rose, Mahon Reconstructed: Why the Takings Issue Is Still a Muddle, 57 S. Cal. L. Rev. 561, 566 (1984); Jed Rubenfeld, Usings, 102 Yale L.J. 1077, 1081 (1993). For developments in the Supreme Court's modern regulatory takings jurisprudence, see Keystone Bituminous Coal Ass'n v. Debenedictus, 480 U.S. 470 (1987); Hodel v. Irving, 481 U.S. 704 (1987); First English Evangelical Lutheran Church of Glendale v. County of Los Angeles, 482 U.S. 304 (1987); Nollan v. Cal. Coastal Comm'n, 483 U.S. 825 (1987); Lucas v. South Carolina Coastal Council, 505 U.S. 1003 (1992); Dolan v. City of Tigard, 512 U.S. 374 (1994); Palazzolo v. Rhode Island, 533 U.S. 606 (2001); Tahoe-Sierra Pres. Council, Inc. v. Tahoe Reg'l Planning Agency, 535 U.S. 302 (2002); and Lingle v. Chevron U.S.A., 544 U.S. 528 (2005).

[49] Unless the defendant is a state government official. Presumably, a property owner would have a cause of action against such an official under 42 U.SC. § 1983 (2000). See *infra* text accompanying notes 87–88.

D. An Analysis of the Government's Arguments in Robbins

The solicitor general, arguing for the BLM officials before the Supreme Court, offered several arguments for the surprising claim that no cognizable Fifth Amendment right was involved in *Robbins*. First, the solicitor general argued that the Fifth Amendment right to just compensation is "owed by (and can be violated only by) the government itself, not by federal officials in their individual capacity."[50] But the notion that the Fifth Amendment's property clauses are uniquely directed against the government does not withstand even the most elementary look at the constitutional text. The First Amendment, for example, commands that "*Congress* shall make no law ... abridging the freedom of speech,"[51] yet an individual public official can clearly be liable for violating an individual's free speech rights. In contrast, the Fifth Amendment uses the passive voice in declaring "nor shall private property *be taken*. . . ."[52] If one of these amendments had been uniquely directed at the government, surely it would be the First and not the Fifth. More fundamentally, it is a staple of our jurisprudence that the Constitution's rights-securing strictures are directed not only at government in the abstract, but also at the human agencies and entities through which government brings power to bear upon individuals.[53] For the government to question that foundational principle at this late date ought to have been an embarrassment. Unsurprisingly, the Court did not take up (or even respond to) the invitation to do so.

Second, the solicitor general argued that the Constitution's text ensures that the only remedy for a Takings Clause violation is an award of just compensation—that is, payment to the owner of the fair market value of the taken property—and that the injunctive and declaratory relief and consequential damages Robbins sought were thus constitutionally unavailable for a Takings Clause violation.[54]

[50] Brief for the Petitioners at 29, Wilkie v. Robbins, 127 S. Ct. 2588 (2007) (No. 06-219) (hereinafter Pet'r Br.).

[51] U.S. Const. amend. I (emphasis added).

[52] *Id.* amend. V (emphasis added).

[53] See, e.g., Ex Parte Young, 209 U.S. 123 (1908); Home Telephone & Telegraph Co. v. City of Los Angeles, 227 U.S. 278 (1913).

[54] See Pet'r Br., *supra* note 50, at 43 ("[A] plaintiff may not sue individual government employees for a taking; his sole remedy under the Fifth Amendment is to seek just compensation under the Tucker Act once a taking has occurred.").

According to this argument, Robbins could have had no Fifth Amendment claim unless and until the government actually acquired an easement across his property—something it never succeeded in acquiring—and, even then, he could have sued only for the fair value of the easement, not for the considerably larger amount of damages he suffered as a result of the BLM officials' campaign of harassment. But a plurality of the justices, including two who were in the majority in *Robbins*,[55] had previously rejected the counterintuitive notion that a property owner can assert no Takings claim unless and until property has been taken and just compensation has been denied. In *City of Monterey v. Del Monte Dunes at Monterey*,[56] the plurality observed that, when government repudiates its duty to provide just compensation, "either by denying just compensation in fact or by refusing to provide procedures through which compensation may be sought, it violates the Constitution. In those circumstances the government's actions are not only unconstitutional but unlawful and tortious as well."[57] The normal rule that a plaintiff in tort can recover any damages that naturally flow from the injury would then apply. And constitutional torts should be no different in this regard.[58] The plurality in *Del Monte Dunes* observed that the fact that, in most Takings Clause claims, the proper measure of damages will turn out to equal the amount of just compensation "is neither surprising nor significant."[59] This is so because in most takings claims—where the government simply takes some property without paying for it—the only injury is the loss of the property taken. In contrast, if government officials showed up at some unsuspecting person's home, forcibly removed its inhabitants, smashed

[55] The plurality consisted of Justices Kennedy and Thomas, both of whom were in the majority in *Robbins*, as well as the late Chief Justice Rehnquist and Justice Stevens, the latter joining Justice Ginsburg's dissent in *Robbins*.

[56] 526 U.S. 687 (1999).

[57] *Id.* at 717.

[58] See Memphis Cmty. Sch. Dist. v. Stachura, 477 U.S. 299, 306 (1986) ("[W]hen § 1983 plaintiffs seek damages for violations of constitutional rights, the level of damages is ordinarily determined according to principles derived from the common law of torts."); Smith v. Wade, 461 U.S. 30, 48–49 (1983) (same); Carey v. Piphus, 435 U.S. 247, 257–58 (1978) (same).

[59] City of Monterey v. Del Monte Dunes at Monterey, Ltd., 526 U.S. 687, 718 (1999).

up valuable personal possessions, and then informed the homeowner that the house now belonged to them, the homeowner would presumably be able to recover damages for personal injury and property destruction in addition to the value of the home—whether under the Takings Clause alone or under that clause augmented by the Fourth Amendment's ban on "unreasonable seizures," a ban the Court has applied to the forcible removal of a mobile home even where nothing akin to a "privacy" interest was disturbed.[60]

In addition, the Court has repeatedly barred government acts, whether involving unilateral executive conduct or the issuance of judicial injunctions or decrees, that would have amounted to an uncompensated taking without ever suggesting that the aggrieved property owners ought to have waited for the taking to occur and only then sued for just compensation.[61] Under the solicitor general's theory that the only remedy for a taking is just compensation, all of these cases would have been dismissed. And, under the solicitor general's theory, in a case such as *Kaiser Aetna v. United States*,[62] the Army Corps of Engineers might have forgone its suit seeking an injunction against a private marina owner that would have opened the marina to the public, and instead threatened the owner with frivolous criminal prosecutions or incited speedboat owners to ram the recalcitrant marina owner's sailboats unless the owner caved to that pressure and simply granted the desired easement to the neighboring public.

The solicitor general's arguments in this regard—which the Court neither accepted nor rejected but appears to have simply ignored—rested in significant part on a basic misconception of the historical origins and development of the Takings Clause. The Framers were less concerned with the risk of uncompensated interference with

[60] See Soldal v. Cook County, 506 U.S. 56, 65–66, 72 (1992).

[61] See, e.g., Dolan v. City of Tigard, 512 U.S. 374, 396 (1994) (striking permit condition that would have effected a taking); Nollan v. Cal. Coastal Comm'n, 483 U.S. 825, 841–42 (1987) (same); Hodel v. Irving, 481 U.S. 704, 713–18 (1987) (striking down federal statute under Takings Clause); Kaiser Aetna v. United States, 444 U.S. 164, 169, 178–80 (1979) (denying an injunction in suit brought by the federal government that would have required owners of a private marina to allow public access to their facilities); Pa. Coal Co. v. Mahon, 260 U.S. 393, 416 (1922); see also E. Enters. v. Apfel, 524 U.S. 498, 519–22, 538 (1998) (plurality opinion) (concluding that federal statute should be struck down under the Takings Clause).

[62] 444 U.S. 164 (1979).

private property by legislative acts than with takings of property by executive officials acting without legislative authority. The Takings Clause can be traced back to Article 39 of the Magna Carta, which itself was prompted by "the barons' complaints against King John" for expropriating supplies.[63] Article 39 declared that "[n]o freeman shall be taken or imprisoned or disseised or exiled or in any way destroyed, nor will we go upon him nor send upon him, except by the lawful judgment of his peers or by the law of the land."[64] The result was a limit on the king's power to take private property—he could do so only with the consent either of the owner or of Parliament.[65] In practice, compensation was usually paid to the owner, but this was not an "inviolable rule."[66] The fear was not of uncompensated takings per se, but rather of the unconstrained abuse of power by the king.

The English custom of not requiring compensation for a legislatively authorized taking was brought over to the colonies and persisted until the Vermont Constitution of 1777 first introduced a compensation requirement.[67] The only other pre-Fifth Amendment compensation provisions, in the Massachusetts Constitution of 1780 and the Northwest Ordinance of 1787, were both motivated by a

[63]Matthew P. Harrington, "Public Use" and the Original Understanding of the So-Called "Takings" Clause, 53 Hastings L.J. 1245, 1290 (2002).

[64]Magna Carta art. 39, reprinted in William Sharp McKechnie, Magna Carta: A Commentary On The Great Charter Of King John 375 (1958).

[65]William Michael Treanor, Note, The Origins and Original Significance of the Just Compensation Clause of the Fifth Amendment, 94 Yale L.J. 694, 698 (1985).

[66]William Michael Treanor, The Original Understanding of the Takings Clause and the Political Process, 95 Colum. L. Rev. 782, 788 n.28 (1995); see also James W. Ely, Jr., "That due satisfaction may be made:" The Fifth Amendment and the Origins of the Compensation Principle, 36 Am. J. Legal Hist. 1, 15 (1992).

[67]See Treanor, *supra* note 66, at 827. The Vermont compensation provision came about due to a widely perceived injustice Vermonters felt they had suffered at the hands of the New York legislature. When England transferred the Vermont territory from New Hampshire to New York, the colonial government of New York "refused to make regrants of [Vermonters'] lands to the original proprietors and occupants, unless at the exorbitant rate of 2300 dollars fees for each township; and did enhance the quit-rent, three fold, and demanded an immediate delivery of the title derived before, from New-Hampshire." *Id.* at 828 (quoting Vt. Declaration of Rights pmbl. (1777), reprinted in 1 Bernard Schwartz, The Bill of Rights: A Documentary History 319, 320 (1971)).

"specific source of concern during the revolutionary era"—"[u]ncompensated seizures by the military."[68]

The same concern with military impressments during the Revolutionary War was probably the main motivating factor behind the Fifth Amendment's Property Clauses.[69] Professor William Treanor, who has written the most extensive scholarly account of the historical background of the Property Clauses, cites two pieces of historical evidence for this proposition. First, in a 1778 essay, John Jay denounced "the Practice of impressing Horses, Teems, and Carriages by the military, without the Intervention of a civil Magistrate, and without any Authority from the Law of the Land."[70] Second, St. George Tucker, the "author of the most prominent constitutional law treatise in the early republic," who provided the "only more or less contemporaneous statement of why the [Takings] clause was passed,"[71] wrote that the clause "was probably intended to restrain the arbitrary and oppressive mode of obtaining supplies for the army, and other public uses, by impressment, as was too frequently practised during the revolutionary war."[72] Other scholars have endorsed the view that the Property Clauses were chiefly aimed at preventing the unauthorized seizure of property by executive branch officials.[73]

[68] Treanor, *supra* note 66, at 831.

[69] *Id.* at 835.

[70] John Jay, A Hint to the Legislature of the State of New York (1778), in 1 John Jay: The Making of a Revolutionary, Unpublished Papers 1745–1780, at 461 (Richard B. Morris ed., 1975); *id.* at 462 ("[It is] the undoubted Right and unalienable Priviledge of a Freeman not to be divested . . . [of] Property, but by Laws to which he has assented. . . . Violations of this inestimable Right by the King of Great Britain, or by an American Quarter Master; are of the same Nature. . .").

[71] Treanor, *supra* note 66, at 836.

[72] *Id.* at 831–32 (quoting 1 William Blackstone, Commentaries with Notes of Reference to the Constitution and Laws, of the Federal Government of the United States; and of the Commonwealth of Virginia 305–06 (St. George Tucker ed., 1803)).

[73] See, e.g., Robert Brauneis, The First Constitutional Tort: The Remedial Revolution in Nineteenth-Century State Just Compensation Law, 52 Vand. L. Rev. 57, 103 (1999); Andrew S. Gold, Regulatory Takings and Original Intent: The Direct, Physical Takings Thesis "Goes Too Far," 49 Am. U. L. Rev. 181, 214 (1999); Matthew P. Harrington, Regulatory Takings and the Original Understanding of the Takings Clause, 45 Wm. & Mary L. Rev. 2053, 2067 (2004) ("[A]n examination of the history leading up to the inclusion of the Compensation Clause in the constitutional text reveals the clause was less about concerns with land use regulation or confiscation than it was about military impressments.").

This history suggests that the Framers, while primarily concerned with military seizures accompanied by the use or threat of physical violence, would have been just as disturbed by the unauthorized acts of executive officials who used subtler forms of coercion and intimidation in an effort to obtain private property gratis. It also seems likely that the Framers would have considered those property owners who resisted military impressments and endured injury as a result to have suffered a clear constitutional violation.

The solicitor general also argued that there was no anti-retaliation principle implicit in the Fifth Amendment, unlike the First, because the Just Compensation Clause itself provides an incentive to assert Fifth Amendment rights, leaving no reason to worry about a "chilling effect" against assertion of the underlying right.[74] According to the solicitor general, it is the concern with such a chilling effect alone that justifies the existence of a freestanding retaliation claim in the First Amendment context.[75] But it has long been settled that an unwarranted burden on the exercise of a federal constitutional right need only *penalize* exercise of that right—it need have no *deterrent effect at all*—in order to be deemed unconstitutional per se.[76] And as far as chilling effect is concerned, the fact that Robbins had been invoking his Fifth Amendment rights for a dozen years in numerous forums and managed to hold out to the bitter end as he faced continued retaliation hardly means that the great majority of property owners would be similarly willing—or able—to stand on their rights while their lives were made to collapse around them. If others in Robbins's shoes—others who have either shallower pockets or softer spines—are not to be chilled into caving to their governmental tormenters, those who would torment them until they succumb must surely be confronted with the counter-threat that nothing short of a *Bivens* remedy, limited by the appropriately crafted rules of qualified immunity, can provide.

[74]See Pet'r Br., *supra* note 50, at 14.

[75]See *id.*

[76]See Memorial Hospital v. Maricopa County, 415 U.S. 250, 257–58 (1974) (holding that the fact that there was no evidence that a durational residency requirement for free non-emergency health care did not actually deter anyone from exercising his or her right to travel did not save the restriction from strict scrutiny).

The solicitor general argued, finally, that allowing Robbins's Fifth Amendment claim to go forward would unleash a flood of litigation that would cripple federal land management,[77] an argument on which the Court seized and expanded.[78] There are several responses to this floodgates concern. The first is the basic point made by Justice Harlan in his *Bivens* concurrence: That the violation at issue attacks the Constitution itself surely implies that concerns about spawning too many lawsuits should never suffice to stay the Court's hand in framing an otherwise necessary and appropriate federal damages remedy.[79]

Second, it is unreasonable to imagine that adding Fifth Amendment actions to the long list of claims the solicitor general trumpeted as already being available to (albeit insufficient for) an individual such as Robbins—state tort suits, APA actions, and First Amendment suits where the retaliation is against those petitioning the government for just compensation or other redress[80]—would make a qualitative difference in overall litigation burdens.

Third, the Court has already developed an elaborate jurisprudence of causation, burden shifting, criteria of seriousness, and the like in First Amendment retaliation cases,[81] in right to travel claims,[82] in Title VII claims,[83] in *Batson* challenges,[84] and under 42 U.S.C. § 1983,[85] all of which would be available here.

Fourth, and finally, if upholding a *Bivens* cause of action for violations of the identical Property Clauses of the Fifth and Fourteenth

[77] See Reply Brief for the Petitioners at 11, Wilkie v. Robbins, 127 S. Ct. 2588 (2007) (No. 06-219).

[78] See Robbins, 127 S. Ct. at 2604.

[79] See Bivens v. Six Unknown Named Agents, 403 U.S. 388, 410–11 (1971) (Harlan, J., concurring).

[80] See Pet'r Brief, *supra* note 50, at 27, 40.

[81] See, e.g., Hartman v. Moore, 126 S. Ct. 1695, 1704 (2006); Mt. Healthy City Sch. Dist. Bd. of Educ. v. Doyle, 429 U.S. 274, 287 (1977).

[82] See Starns v. Malkerson, 401 U.S. 985 (1971), summarily aff'g 326 F. Supp. 234 (D. Minn. 1970) (upholding one-year residency requirement for reduced, instate tuition rate); cf. Sosna v. Iowa, 419 U.S. 393 (1975) (upholding one-year residency requirement for divorce).

[83] See McDonnell Douglas Corp. v. Green, 411 U.S. 792 (1973).

[84] See Batson v. Kentucky, 476 U.S. 79 (1986).

[85] See St. Mary's Honor Center v. Hicks, 509 U.S. 502, 506 n.1 (1983).

Amendments would unleash a flood of such claims, then we should have already seen such a flood in claims brought against state officials under § 1983. As Justice Ginsburg tellingly emphasized in her *Robbins* dissent, the existence of § 1983 offers a "controlled experiment" as to whether a flood of Property Clause claims is likely to occur.[86] Needless to say, no such flood has materialized.

Two further observations should be made about § 1983. First, the existence of a presumed Fifth Amendment claim against state officials under § 1983 embarrassingly undercuts what turns out to be the Court's principal justification for not recognizing a *Bivens* cause of action in *Robbins*—the supposed "difficulty in defining a workable cause of action."[87] For, flood or no flood, courts will be unable to avoid defining the contours of the underlying Fifth Amendment claim in whatever § 1983 cases are filed against state officers who are as lawless in their pursuit of property as the BLM agents here were. Thus, the Court's holding in *Robbins* will have done nothing to avoid the inevitable judicial costs.[88] Instead—and

[86] Wilkie v. Robbins, 127 S. Ct. 2588, 2616 (2007) (Ginsburg, J., concurring in part and dissenting in part).

[87] *Id.* at 2601.

[88] This is so for yet another reason: Suppose that the next time the BLM charges someone like Robbins with trespass—or takes any final agency action that adversely affects his property interests to pressure him into giving up an easement or other property right without just compensation—the victim of the agency's persecution does what the Court seems to expect him to do and challenges the action through administrative avenues, asserting his Fifth Amendment claim as a defense to the adverse administrative action. Although the IBLA has explicitly disclaimed jurisdiction to consider such a claim, see Robbins v. Bureau of Land Mgmt., 170 I.B.L.A. 219, 226 (2006), cited in Robbins, 127 S. Ct. at 2598 n.5, one must suppose that the defendant would follow the Court's advice, *id.* ("[Robbins] could have advanced the [constitutional] claims in federal court whether or not the IBLA was willing to listen to them."), and advance his claim in a federal court exercising judicial review under the APA. Although such review would ordinarily be limited to the factual record the agency had compiled, the end result would be exactly the situation the Court purportedly wanted to avoid by denying the *Bivens* claim: a federal court will be confronted with a claim of accumulating retaliation for having refused to waive the right to just compensation.

This time, there would be no way for the federal court to avoid the issue, given that the APA clearly gives a litigant the right to challenge each final agency action. That federal court will thus need to engage in the very same process of line-drawing aggravated by the fact that it would see only one at a time of the thousand cuts to which tomorrow's Robbins will have been subjected—that the Supreme Court thought was too difficult. And, regrettably, the court would need to undertake this line-drawing process within the confines of the APA, which drastically limits the eviden-

this is the second point—*Robbins* will simply have created an anomaly in which identical conduct by state and federal officials will result in drastically different sets of liabilities. Given the gradual eclipse of *Bivens*, this ironic asymmetry is likely to grow as the Bill of Rights, which applies of its own force only to the federal government, will as a practical matter pose less of an obstacle to federal lawlessness than to state lawlessness. State officials will be held personally accountable for violations of clearly established constitutional rights while their federal counterparts will confront no such reckoning, even when they could not qualify for immunity on the theory that the rights they violated had not yet been clearly established. While there may have been a time when there was greater reason to fear constitutional violations by state officials than by their federal counterparts, ours is not such a time.

III. The *Robbins* Opinion—Conceiving the Inconceivable

A. Manipulating Rights Out of Existence

The Supreme Court had for decades treated as "inconceivable"[89] the notion that any of the Constitution's guarantees of individual rights could be "manipulated out of existence"[90] through the crude device of having government officials demand the surrender of those rights on pain of suffering deprivations of benefits or privileges that would not have been imposed but for this unlawful purpose and

tiary possibilities, for judicial review under the APA is generally limited to the administrative record. See 5 U.S.C. § 706 (2000). Since the IBLA would not allow Robbins to introduce evidence supporting his constitutional claims, see Robbins, 170 I.B.L.A. at 228–30, a federal court would not have had an adequate administrative record before it on judicial review.

A federal court exercising judicial review under the APA is also limited in its remedial choices. The APA permits a court only to order, or set aside, agency action, see 5 U.S.C. § 706—equitable relief that "is useless to a person who has already been injured," Butz v. Economou, 438 U.S. 478, 504 (1978), and who cannot demonstrate that the illegal conduct is ongoing or likely to be repeated, see Lujan v. Defenders of Wildlife, 504 U.S. 555 (1992); City of Los Angeles v. Lyons, 461 U.S. 95, 101–02 (1983). Moreover, given the unending variety of means employed by petitioners, it is difficult to imagine that respondent could have secured, or a court could have crafted, an effective injunction against the conspiracy. See, e.g., O'Shea v. Littleton, 414 U.S. 488, 495–97 (1974); Int'l Longshoremen's Ass'n, Local 1291 v. Phila. Marine Trade Ass'n., 389 U.S. 64, 76 (1967); see also Fed. R. Civ. P. 65(d).

[89] Frost v. R.R. Comm'n of Cal., 271 U.S. 583, 594 (1926).

[90] *Id.*

that, in extreme instances such as many of those involved in *Robbins,* could not otherwise lawfully have been imposed for *any* reason. In *Robbins,* the Court did the "inconceivable" in effectively holding that federal officials may, without incurring any risk of liability, burden individuals without limit until they surrender their Fifth Amendment right not to have their property taken without just compensation. That holding unquestionably leaves private property rights in worse shape than the Court found them, although it is difficult to be precise about the extent of the damage. On the one hand, the Court did not purport to decide whether the official actions taken in this case were so clearly unconstitutional as to make qualified immunity unavailable; indeed, it did not decide whether those actions were unconstitutional at all. Rather, the Court considered only "whether to devise a new *Bivens* damages action for retaliating against the exercise of ownership rights,"[91] an undertaking that proceeds on "the *assumption* that a constitutionally recognized interest is adversely affected by the actions of federal employees."[92] But, on the other hand, the path that the Court chose came perilously close to contradicting that assumption—in part by its seeming indifference to the fact that its approach left the "constitutionally recognized interest" it assumed had been "adversely affected" worth very little.[93]

At its root, the Court's reasoning in refusing to recognize Robbins's cause of action for damages rested on the view that recognizing claims of the kind he advanced would entail unworkable line-drawing along a spectrum of government behavior, at one end of which lies good-faith negotiation within the terms of government's regulatory authority and at the other end of which lies unconstitutional coercion. Delineating the bounds of unconstitutional conduct, the Court claimed, would involve an inquiry into whether the official action merely "went too far" and was thus simply "too much." The Court contrasted the typical retaliation claim it had recognized in the past as instead "turn[ing] on an allegation of impermissible

[91] Robbins, 127 S. Ct. at 2597.

[92] *Id.* at 2598 (emphasis added).

[93] *Id.*

purpose and motivation" and thus as being susceptible of "definite answers" to a more simple "what for" question:[94]

> A judicial standard to identify illegitimate pressure going beyond legitimately hard bargaining would be endlessly knotty to work out, and a general provision for tortlike liability when Government employees are unduly zealous in pressing a governmental interest affecting property would invite an onslaught of *Bivens* actions.[95]

But, however close cases are to be resolved, the Court was wrong not to see the conduct of the BLM agents in this case as falling so manifestly on the wrong side of the line as to pose no close question at all. The source of the Court's myopia on this point appears to have been its evident determination to follow the government's lead in characterizing the BLM's ongoing campaign of coercion as nothing more than a "continuing process in which each side has a legitimate purpose in taking action contrary to the other's interest."[96] But this version of the facts, as Justice Ginsburg's dissent shows convincingly,[97] simply cannot be squared with the district court's findings—by which the Court was bound—that the coercive and punitive steps the BLM agents took would not have occurred but for Robbins's insistence on his rights under the Takings Clause and would have

[94] *Id.* at 2601. To the degree that the Court's concern was with delineating the difference between permissible persuasion and forbidden coercion, see *id.* at 2601–04, it was treating as distinctive to this property context a problem that is in fact ubiquitous, and one that comes down to defining the baseline of threats and offers that are to be allowed in the Government's dealings with individuals, whether on a one-off basis or continuously. See also *infra* text accompanying notes 114-25, discussing the Court's ineffective attempt to distinguish property-based relationships between the government and its private neighbors—relationships implicating the rights of private landowners to just compensation—from relationships between the government and its employees or between the government and private citizens generally—relationships implicating the rights of private individuals to such liberties as freedom of expression.

[95] *Id.* at 2604.

[96] *Id.* at 2603 n.10.

[97] See Wilkie v. Robbins, 127 S. Ct. 2588, 2609–11 (2007) (Ginsburg, J., concurring in part and dissenting in part) (noting that the "full force of Robbins' complaint" is "not quite captured in the Court's restrained account of his allegations" and providing a more "complete rendition"); see also *id.* at 2614–15 (taking exception to the Court's "dubious characterization" of the government action in Robbins's case as involving a "perfectly legitimate" objective).

ceased the moment Robbins agreed to waive those rights and to drop his demand for just compensation.[98]

Just as problematic, and ultimately even more puzzling, is the concession in Justice Souter's opinion for the Court that "Robbins does make a few allegations, like the unauthorized survey and the unlawful entry into the lodge, that charge defendants with illegal action plainly going beyond hard bargaining."[99] Those actions standing alone, the Court's opinion suggests, *would* give rise to a *Bivens* cause of action for unconstitutional retaliation—because, "[i]f those were the only coercive acts charged, Robbins could avoid the 'too much' problem by fairly describing the Government behavior alleged as illegality in attempting to obtain a property interest for nothing."[100] Really? Why in the world, if a pattern of independently unlawful actions solves the "too much" problem, is the problem not solved just as well where, as in Robbins's case, officials *not only* act in independently unlawful ways but *also* abuse their lawful authority? How could it possibly be the case that the *addition* of actions taken in abuse of regulatory authority can render independently unlawful conduct *less* rather than *more* subject to redress by an action for damages?

The only explanation the Court offers is to assert that "defendants' improper exercise of the Government's 'regulatory powers' is essential to [Robbins's] claim."[101] Even if that were so, and even if "the bulk of Robbins's charges [went] to actions that, on their own, fall within the Government's enforcement power,"[102] it would be flatly false to say, as the Court inexplicably does, that "Robbins's challenge, therefore, is not to the object the Government seeks to achieve. . . ."[103] For, without any doubt, Robbins's challenge is *precisely* to "the object

[98]See Robbins v. Wilkie, No. 98-CV-201-B, 2004 WL 3659189, at *6 (D. Wyo. Jan. 20, 2004) (holding that evidence that "[d]efendants did intend and agreed to extort and punish [Robbins]"—including evidence of "[d]efendants' alleged motive and intent, threats, lies, trespass, disparate treatment and harassment"—compelled denial of defendants' summary judgment motion).

[99]Robbins, 127 S. Ct. at 2603.

[100]*Id.*

[101]*Id.*

[102]*Id.* at 2604.

[103]*Id.* at 2601.

the Government seeks to achieve"—namely, the acquisition of his property without the compensation guaranteed by the Fifth Amendment. To the degree that Robbins could establish, at the trial that the Court has denied him, that he was seriously injured by a campaign of conduct orchestrated by the BLM—including both flatly illegal acts and acts lawful in the abstract but unlawful when engaged in to punish the assertion of constitutional rights—that *would not have occurred but for his insistence on his Fifth Amendment rights* as an owner of private property, his case is analytically indistinguishable from one in which a property owner who continuously petitions the government for redress of grievances under the First Amendment is subjected to a relentless campaign of retaliatory acts—some illegal in themselves and others unlawful only because they would not have been taken but for the owner's insistence on exercising his First Amendment rights—that ends up driving him out of business.

Beyond this basic point, it must be added that the Court's peculiar suggestion that the mere "improper exercise" of the BLM officials' delegated "regulatory powers" is "essential" to Robbins's claim, besides being irrelevant, has the disadvantage of coming from thin air. To be sure, the many actions by BLM officials taken in abuse of powers formally entrusted to them aggravated the *magnitude* of the consequential harm Robbins suffered and thus the appropriate measure of his *Bivens* damages. But what made the Court imagine, for whatever it was worth, that this subset of the officials' actions was a *sine qua non* of the *Bivens* claim that Robbins advanced? The only authority the Court's opinion adduces for that supposition was a cryptic reference to "Brief for Respondent 21."[104]

Having written that brief, I know it well, but I reread page 21 (and the surrounding pages) to discover what the Court could possibly have been referencing. I can report that I remain mystified. Quite to the contrary of the Court's assertion, a reader of the brief could not avoid noting that, in responding to the solicitor general's argument that the BLM agents were simply exercising vigorously the powers delegated to them "for the orderly management and protection of the public lands,"[105] the brief stressed the finding of the district court—a finding "not subject to review on interlocutory

[104] *Id.*

[105] Resp't Br., *supra* note 11, at 20 (quoting 43 C.F.R. §4130.3-2(h)).

appeal''[106]—that ''the summary judgment evidence substantiated respondent's claim in his complaint that the incursions on his land were undertaken for an entirely different, and unlawful, purpose: to coerce and retaliate.''[107] The brief concluded, on the page cited by the Court, that ''this case has nothing to do with 'the sort of give and take that both Congress and this Court' have approved in the public lands context, . . . and everything to do with the kinds of abuse of power the Fifth Amendment [was] enacted to redress.''[108]

The most one can say in the Court's defense on this crucial point is that the brief did from time to time lump together *all* of the unlawful behavior on the part of the BLM officials—both the behavior that would have been unlawful regardless of motive and the behavior that was rendered unlawful solely by its unconstitutional aim—describing the officials as ''using their regulatory powers to harass, punish, and coerce a private citizen into giving the Government his property without payment.''[109] But that is precisely what the *Robbins* Court itself described as the kind of '''what for' question [that] has a ready answer in terms of lawful conduct,''[110] so that the claim Robbins brought plainly *did* ''fit the prior retaliation cases,'' which, the Court stressed, ''turn on an allegation of impermissible purpose and motivation.''[111] For Robbins to have treated together both the impermissibly motivated exercises of otherwise lawful regulatory authority and the conduct that was independently unlawful even without regard to its motive could by no stretch be confused with a concession that his complaint was simply that the BLM agents had been guilty only of overzealous bargaining and of doing ''too much'' of a good thing. Justice Souter's opinion thus seems uncharacteristically confused insofar as it argues that Robbins's claim called on the Court to confront an intractable ''problem of degree''[112] rather than to ''answer[] a 'what for' question or two.''[113]

[106] Resp't Br., *supra* note 11, at 21.

[107] *Id.*

[108] *Id.* (quoting Pet'r Br. at 46).

[109] Resp't Br., *supra* note 11, at 21.

[110] Wilkie v. Robbins, 127 S. Ct. 2588, 2601 (2007).

[111] *Id.*

[112] *Id.* at 2604.

[113] *Id.* at 2601.

Even accepting the Court's strained version of the facts of the case and of the character of the claim Robbins had made, its refusal to recognize a cause of action for a pattern of retaliation through the manifest abuse of official regulatory authority in a manner intentionally calculated to circumvent the Constitution's protections for private property is deeply problematic. Especially noteworthy is the Court's frankly lame attempt to contain the reach of its holding to the property context. In particular, it would be impossible to say with any confidence how the Court will apply *Robbins* in dealing, for example, with a pattern of official retaliation for someone's exercise of the First Amendment right to criticize government action. Justice Souter's opinion for the Court describes "the standard retaliation case recognized in our precedent" as one in which "the plaintiff has performed some discrete act in the past, typically saying something that irritates the defendant official," so that the question in the ensuing *Bivens* action against that official becomes "whether the official's later action against the plaintiff was taken for a legitimate purpose" such as "firing to rid the workplace of a substandard performer," or instead "for the purpose of punishing for the exercise of a constitutional right."[114] As the Court's opinion envisions the matter, in such a "standard case" the "plaintiff's action is over and done with, and the only question is the defendant's purpose."[115] The Court then contrasts *Robbins* by noting that, in this case, "the past act or acts (refusing the right-of-way without compensation) are simply particular steps in an ongoing refusal to grant requests for a right-of-way."[116] Because "[t]he purpose of the continuing requests is lawful (the Government still could use the right-of-way),"[117] "we are confronting a continuing process in which each side has a legitimate purpose in taking action contrary to the other's interest."[118]

But exactly the same thing could arise in a First Amendment context, with a government agency or agent engaging in an ongoing series of retaliatory steps to punish an individual for his ongoing protests and to bring such constitutionally protected protests to an

[114] *Id.* at 2602–03 n.10.

[115] *Id.* at 2603 n.10.

[116] *Id.*

[117] *Id.*

[118] *Id.*

end. It is only the Court's transparent manipulation of the level of generality at which it describes the "purpose of the continuing requests" by the BLM agents in *Robbins*—that purpose obviously ceases to be lawful once one recognizes it not simply as the acquisition of a useful right-of-way but as the circumvention of the Just Compensation Clause with respect to that right-of-way—that enables the Court to distinguish between retaliation claims pressed by property owners under the Fifth Amendment and retaliation claims pressed by government employees or private citizens under the First Amendment.[119]

Although the Court accuses Robbins of "chang[ing] conceptual gears [to] consider the more abstract concept of liability for retaliatory or undue pressure on a property owner for standing firm on property rights,"[120] it is in fact the Court that changes conceptual gears by describing the purpose of such retaliation as the legitimate one of acquiring an easement but *not* describing the purpose of retaliation against an employee or citizen for standing firm on his free speech rights as the legitimate one of reducing hostility and strife.

The Court also changes conceptual gears when it transforms a claim of retaliation for the exercise of a constitutional right into a claim of "retaliation, probably motivated by spite,"[121] leading it to the odd conclusion that Robbins was arguing "that the presence of malice or spite in an official's heart renders any action constitutionally retaliatory, even if it would otherwise have been done in the name of legitimate hard bargaining,"[122] something the Court rightly noted "is not the law of our retaliation precedent."[123] But that was never Robbins's argument. On the contrary, he asked only for the right to "be placed in no worse a position than if he had not engaged in the [constitutionally protected] conduct"[124] of refusing to give up

[119] *Id.*

[120] *Id.* at 2604.

[121] *Id.* at 2603 n.10.

[122] *Id.*

[123] *Id.*

[124] Mt. Healthy City School Dist. v. Doyle, 429 U.S. 274, 287 (1977) (enunciating retaliation standard for First Amendment cases).

an easement without just compensation—invoking the very principle that the Court in *Robbins* reiterated as controlling retaliation claims.[125]

B. The Background Principle of Unconstitutional Conditions in Robbins

The Court's decision was also particularly unsettling when considered in light of the Court's application of the doctrine of unconstitutional conditions—long invoked with regard to a broad range of constitutional rights[126]—to the specific context of the Takings Clause. In both *Dolan v. City of Tigard*[127] and *Nollan v. California Coastal Commission*,[128] the Court invalidated the state's conditioning of a discretionary grant of a development permit upon the property owner's provision of a property interest to the state.[129] Thus, under the unconstitutional conditions doctrine as developed in the context of the Takings Clause, the government "may not require a person to give up a constitutional right—here, the right to receive just compensation when property is taken for public use—in exchange for a discretionary benefit conferred by the government where the benefit has little or no relationship to the property."[130] Whatever the limits of the doctrine, it clearly affords the government no defense where, as in Robbins's case, the government demanded not only that Robbins give up his right to just compensation in exchange for a "discretionary benefit," like a grazing or special use permit, but also as a condition of his incontestable entitlement to conduct his business free from the scourge of false criminal charges, illegal trespass on his land, and continued harassment of his business and

[125] Wilkie v. Robbins, 127 S. Ct. 2588, 2603 n.10 (2007).

[126] See, e.g., Mem'l Hospital v. Maricopa County, 415 U.S. 250, 256 (1974) (right to interstate travel); cf. Harman v. Forssenius, 380 U.S. 528, 542 (1965) (Twenty-Fourth Amendment); Zablocki v. Redhail, 434 U.S. 374, 387 & n.12 (1978) (right to marry).

[127] 512 U.S. 374 (1994).

[128] 483 U.S. 825 (1987).

[129] In *Nollan*, a state agency included the granting of a public easement as a condition in granting homeowners the right to build an addition to their home. Nollan, 482 U.S. at 827–28. In *Dolan*, a city required a business owner who wanted a land-use variance in order to expand her store and pave the parking lot to dedicate a portion of her land to the public. Dolan, 512 U.S. at 379–80.

[130] Dolan, 512 U.S. at 392; see also Nollan, 483 U.S. at 836–37.

customers.[131] But because, as discussed above, the Court was particularly fixated on those elements of the allegations involving abuses of regulatory authority rather than independently illegal acts, I consider next the Court's failure to see that even those "mere" abuses of authority likewise fell afoul of the unconstitutional conditions doctrine.

This incongruity may have been apparent to the Court, explaining its seemingly willful refusal to address those cases directly while both speaking in their language and reaching a result (albeit, as I shall argue, a patently incorrect result) within their framework. Those cases lurk in the background of a statement that lies at the heart of the Court's reasoning:

> [T]he Government was not offering to buy the easement, but it did have valuable things to offer in exchange, like continued permission for Robbins to use Government land on favorable terms (at least to the degree that the terms of a permit were subject to discretion).[132]

Here, the Court clearly envisions the government permissibly conditioning various favorable outcomes within its discretionary authority—granting as opposed to denying grazing and recreational use permits, choosing not to disproportionately seek out infractions and selectively enforce administrative regulations against Robbins—upon his uncompensated surrender of the easement. But the fact that the agents' actions were "subject to discretion" is the beginning, not the end, of the inquiry under *Dolan* and *Nollan*. In those cases, in holding that imposing the condition constituted a taking for which compensation must be made available, the Court made clear that the problem was the lack of a sufficiently close "fit" or "nexus"

[131] See Mitchell N. Berman, Coercion Without Baselines: Unconstitutional Conditions in Three Dimensions, 90 Geo. L.J. 1, 15–18 (2001).

[132] Wilkie v. Robbins, 127 S. Ct. 2588, 2602 (2007). The Court's careful formulation of the government's stance as that of one "offer[ing] something in exchange," *id.*, for the easement is a gross mischaracterization of the long course of hostile government action taking place *after* the cancellation of the right of way—a course of action that surely lacked the flavor of good-faith bargaining the Court attributes to it. See *supra* notes 21–23.

between the government's permissible reasons for granting or withholding the discretionary benefit and the Government's reasons for imposing the particular condition on granting that benefit.[133]

The relevant question, then, is the relationship between the reasons for which the BLM officials could, as a general matter of discretion, withhold "permission . . . to use Government land on favorable terms" and their reasons for conditioning this permission on Robbins's surrender of the easement. Here, as Justice Ginsburg irrefutably demonstrates in her dissent,[134] the objectives of the agents' conditioning of the right—to regain the "carelessly lost" easement gratis so as simultaneously to benefit the agency and cover the agents' tracks, and to punish Robbins for his stubborn failure to gratify that desire—are far from, and in fact bear no real relation to, any of the legitimate reasons for the government's exercise of its discretionary authority.[135]

[133] See Nollan, 483 U.S. at 837 ("T]he lack of nexus between the condition and the original purpose of the building restriction converts it to something other than it was. The purpose then becomes, quite simply, the obtaining of an easement to serve some valid governmental purpose, but without payment of compensation. Whatever may be the outer limits of 'legitimate state interests' in the takings and land-use context, this is not one of them. In short, unless the permit condition serves the same governmental purpose as the development ban, the building restriction is not a valid regulation of land use but 'an out-and-out plan of extortion.'").

[134] Robbins, 127 S. Ct. at 2614–15 (Ginsburg, J., concurring in part and dissenting in part).

[135] The Court's elision of permissible ends with allowable means in *Robbins* is inconsistent with its previous recognition of the importance of precisely this means-ends distinction in the context of the Takings Clause. In *Nollan v. Cal. Coastal Comm'n*, 483 U.S. 825 (1987), the Court rejected any notion that the California Coastal Commission's legitimate end of obtaining an easement for public access across the waterfront cured the means it chose—requiring that property owners who wanted to build an addition to their house grant the easement in exchange for a building permit—of a constitutional infirmity. *Id.* at 841–42. In *Nollan*, the Court held that the different purposes behind the permit requirement, which preserved visual access to the shore, and the easement, which would have promoted physical access to the shore, lacked an essential nexus that made the conditional permit amount to a taking. *Id.* at 837–39.

Whether or not one agrees with the *Nollan* analysis, surely the lack of nexus between the BLM's desire for an easement across Robbins's land and the purposes behind the BLM's power to charge individuals with trespassing on federal lands is all the greater. The Court's motivating concern in *Nollan*—that, without a nexus requirement, the government might tend to overregulate land use and might "leverage" its power to grant exemptions as currency to buy any property interest it desired, *id.* at 837 n.5—is fully applicable to the situation in *Robbins*.

C. Caught Between a Rock and a Hard Place: Distinguishing Between a "Taking" and a "Giving"

Robbins served as an ideal case in which to condemn the government's strategy of circumventing the Takings Clause precisely because it was a case in which the strategy *failed.* Had the government been successful, it would have had a powerful argument that no "taking" had occurred because Robbins had merely been "persuaded" to give up his property—in other words, that there had been a "giving" for which just compensation is not required. That is what made the solicitor general's argument that, because no taking occurred, no property right was violated and no remedy was constitutionally required, so disingenuous. But, although the Court did not advert to, much less embrace, the solicitor general's inverted form of argument, it also unfortunately said nothing to reject it.

Notably, the explicit rejection of just this upside-down argument was central to the Supreme Court's analysis in the analogous situation of guilty pleas induced by the death penalty provision of the Lindbergh Anti-Kidnapping Act.[136] In *United States v. Jackson*[137] the Court struck down the portion of the Act that authorized the death penalty because the Act made that penalty available only in cases tried by a jury—i.e., only in cases in which the accused refused to plead guilty and refused to waive his Sixth Amendment right to a jury trial. The Court reasoned that this scheme put in place an unjustified and therefore impermissible penalty on the exercise of the constitutional right to trial by jury.[138] Subsequently, the Court made plain that entering guilty pleas under the influence of this problematic statutory scheme would not in itself enable those who had done so to assert that their pleas were coerced by their fear that they risked being sentenced to death if they went to trial and insisted on a jury.[139] Far from representing a retreat from *Jackson,* the Court's decision to uphold those guilty pleas and the life sentences to which they led underscored the linchpin of *Jackson*'s analysis: It was the very fact that the structural defect in the Lindbergh Act's capital

[136] P.L. No. 73-232, 48 Stat. 781 (1934) (codified as amended at 18 U.S.C. § 1201 (2000)).

[137] 390 U.S. 570 (1968).

[138] *Id.* at 583.

[139] See Brady v. United States, 397 U.S. 742, 746, 758 (1970) (holding a *Jackson*-induced waiver "voluntarily and intelligently made").

punishment scheme could not be cured *post hoc*—by rejecting as coerced those waivers of the right not to plead guilty and of the right to demand a jury that the scheme induced—that required the Court to strike the scheme down *on its face* rather than upholding it and waiting to invalidate particular *applications* of its punitive structure as products of forbidden coercion.[140] In other words, it was the fact that the statutory scheme was structured to penalize, without adequate justification, the assertion of Sixth Amendment rights, coupled with the inability to cure the problem case-by-case, that rendered the Act unconstitutional *on its face*. Consistent with that theory, those who had surrendered their rights when the statutory scheme was applied to them (before having been facially invalidated) were presumed to have done so voluntarily. Just so, if Robbins had succumbed to the threats made against him rather than standing his ground while his business was essentially destroyed, the government could have argued that, whatever pressure the BLM had applied to Robbins, he had relinquished the easement voluntarily and could not claim it had been "taken."

D. The Problem of Unauthorized Takings

Even if Robbins could somehow have established that his relinquishment of the easement under the government's unrelenting pressure amounted to an involuntary taking rather than a voluntary "giving," neither the Just Compensation Clause nor the Tucker Act[141] would have allowed Robbins to recover for what would nonetheless have amounted to an *unauthorized* taking of his property by executive branch officials. For the Supreme Court has long held that the taking of property by executive officials without congressional authorization cannot subject the United States to liability for just compensation.[142] Because Congress and Congress alone possesses the power of the purse, the executive branch must not be permitted to accomplish

[140] See Jackson, 390 U.S. at 583 ("The power to reject coerced guilty pleas and involuntary jury waivers might alleviate, but it cannot totally eliminate, the constitutional infirmity in the capital punishment provision of the Federal Kidnaping Act.").

[141] 28 U.S.C. § 1491 (2000). This Act waives the federal government's sovereign immunity for certain types of claims, including takings claims.

[142] See, e.g., Reg'l Rail Reorganization Act Cases, 419 U.S. 102, 127 (1974); United States v. N. Am. Transp. & Trading Co., 253 U.S. 330, 333 (1920) (per Brandeis, J.); Hooe v. United States, 218 U.S. 322, 335–36 (1910).

what would in effect be a congressionally unapproved appropriation of public money by the expedient of seizing private property and leaving the aggrieved owner to bring a claim for just compensation against the United States.[143]

This point has special relevance here because the BLM officials had no source of legislatively granted authority for the pattern of conduct they employed in their pursuit of the easement from Robbins—the same easement that they had originally acquired from the prior owner of Robbins's ranch but had negligently lost through their failure to timely record it. Congress entrusted the BLM with limited authority to acquire property interests through statutorily provided means beyond outright purchase from or exchange with a willing seller—specifically, via eminent domain if it makes a showing of necessity to "secure access to public lands,"[144] or as a condition imposed on an applicant for a right-of-way across federal land.[145] And even if the requisite showing of necessity could have been made, Congress conferred no statutory authority on BLM officials to harass and threaten a property owner in order to acquire a property interest from him gratis, outside the eminent domain process. Because the actions of the BLM officials thus clearly amounted to an unauthorized attempt to obtain private property from its rightful owner, Robbins could not have sought compensation from the United States itself, under the Tucker Act or otherwise, had the BLM officials succeeded in their scheme of constitutional circumvention—a feature of the case about which the Court in *Robbins* was oddly silent but one that plainly gave it its particular poignancy.

E. *The Implications of* Robbins *for the Future of Property (and Other Fifth Amendment) Rights: The Shortest Cut*

The unavailability of a claim for just compensation against the United States means that in a case like *Robbins*, the remedy "is *Bivens*

[143]See Youngstown Sheet & Tube Co. v. Sawyer, 343 U.S. 579, 588 (1952); *id.* at 631–32 & n.2 (Douglas, J., concurring).

[144]43 U.S.C. § 1715(a)(2000). It is doubtful that such a showing would have been possible on the facts in *Robbins*, especially given the stringent way in which the necessity requirement has been defined and policed. See United States v. 82.46 Acres of Land, 691 F.2d 474, 477 (10th Cir. 1982). In general, takings by the federal government must be effectuated through condemnation proceedings initiated by the attorney general that afford property owners significant substantive and procedural protections, as well as an important measure of political oversight and accountability. See 40 U.S.C. §§ 3111–3118; Fed. R. Civ. P. 71A.

[145]See *supra* note 11.

or nothing."[146] Without the threat of personal liability under *Bivens*, officials working for a federal agency that seeks to acquire a private property interest but either lacks statutory authority to obtain it by eminent domain or has insufficient funds in its budget to purchase it for its fair market value have nothing to lose and much to gain by using the kinds of harassing behavior that the BLM employees used against Robbins.[147] If the officials are successful in getting the property owner to give in, then they have gained a property interest for free.[148] If they are unsuccessful, they face no personal liability after *Robbins*, and the unavailability of any claim against the United States means that their superiors would be unlikely to discipline or constrain them. While this kind of behavior seems not to have occurred with much frequency in the past—or at least seems not to have generated any noticeable waves of litigation—the *Robbins* decision could encourage it to happen with greater frequency in the future.

Beyond the likely behavioral effects of *Robbins* in prompting outright circumvention of the just compensation requirement, the decision is likely to cast a long shadow over the recent revival of the Court's concern to seek out regulations it determines to be tantamount to a taking and therefore invalid in the absence of (often unavailable) just compensation. In cases striking down legislative

[146] This is a paraphrase of Justice Harlan's oft-quoted observation that a cause of action against a federal official for a constitutional violation is especially appropriate when "it is damages or nothing." Bivens v. Six Unknown Named Agents of Fed. Bureau of Narcotics, 403 U.S. 388, 410 (1971) (Harlan, J., concurring). A claim against the United States under the FTCA was not enough to preclude a *Bivens* cause of action against prison officials in *Carlson v. Green*, 446 U.S. 14 (1980). See *id.* at 23 ("[W]e cannot hold that Congress relegated respondent exclusively to the FTCA remedy. . . ."). The fact that Robbins would not have had a claim against the United States only strengthens the argument that he should be able to assert a claim against the officials involved.

[147] One might wonder why federal officials would go to such lengths to secure property for the benefit of the government. One answer is that what is good for the employer often tends to be good for the employee. In the *Robbins* case, the BLM employees obviously had an incentive to avoid looking sloppy and wasteful due to their own negligence in losing the original easement, and may also have harbored an inchoate hope that they would be rewarded financially, through monetary bonuses or raises, for their efforts against Robbins, especially if those efforts proved successful.

[148] There might be whatever costs their efforts entailed, but in the case of truly malicious officials who are "out to get someone," the costs of their efforts, as internalized by the officials themselves, would be negative.

development bans[149] and conditional development permit terms,[150] the Court has effectively reiterated its earlier declaration that "[a] strong public desire to improve the public condition [will not] warrant achieving the desire by a shorter cut than the constitutional way of paying for the change."[151] With *Robbins*, however, the Court effectively turns its back on government action that amounts to a still shorter cut, accomplishing a complete transfer of indisputably compensable property rights in ways that circumvent the just compensation requirement by making a "taking" of any variety—either literal or regulatory—unnecessary.

The danger the Court's decision poses for the Fifth Amendment right not to have one's property taken for public use without just compensation is acute. If anything, the case for remedying this kind of cumulative retaliatory injury to private property (including both physical property and the intellectual "property" embodied in one's potentially self-incriminating testimony under oath) through circumvention of the just compensation requirement (or of the requirement of witness immunity) is stronger than the case for remedying similarly inflicted injuries to other constitutionally protected interests. For *Robbins* all but invites government officials eager to obtain someone's physical or intellectual property but either lacking the requisite statutory authority[152] or unwilling to sacrifice the resources that a taking would necessitate (or the successful criminal prosecution that "use immunity" might frustrate) to squeeze the prospective source of the desired property or information by making his life as difficult as they can, both by withholding whatever discretionary benefits they would otherwise have granted and by initiating a torrent of independently unlawful actions that their target will be unable to fend off or be compensated for.

To be sure, the Court does not directly condone such tactics in *Robbins*. Indeed, it even concedes that the tactics here may have

[149] See Lucas v. S.C. Coastal Council, 505 U.S. 1003 (1992).

[150] See Dolan v. City of Tigard, 512 U.S. 374 (1994); Nollan v. Cal. Coastal Comm'n, 483 U.S. 825 (1987).

[151] Pa. Coal Co v. Mahon, 260 U.S. 393, 416 (1922).

[152] That such authority is needed both for a taking and for a grant of use or transactional immunity follows from elementary considerations of the separation of powers, as well as from the guarantee that neither liberty nor property may be taken "without due process of law."

violated the Constitution.[153] And the Court avoids embracing the government's remarkable suggestion that the conduct at issue in *Robbins* could not have violated the Fifth Amendment because no actual taking occurred. At the same time, the Court equally carefully avoids *rejecting* that astonishing suggestion, steering clear of the Fifth Amendment issue altogether and confining its ruling to the further demolition of what little remains of *Bivens.*

Whatever the Court's reasons for reaching out to dispose of the case on that basis, the result can only encourage others to engage in violations similar to those committed by the BLM agents in this case. *Robbins* obviously gives federal officials a green light in this respect unless and until Congress enacts a specifically applicable cause of action for damages against such officials. And even at the state level, where the availability of damages relief under 42 U.S.C. § 1983 might theoretically discourage some state actors from doing essentially what the BLM agents did here, that deterrence is certainly weakened by the Court's apparent reluctance to condemn the conduct involved here as flatly unconstitutional. For state actors bent on circumventing the just compensation requirement can hardly avoid noticing the Supreme Court's studious avoidance of a holding condemning what the BLM agents did to Frank Robbins as a clear violation of the Constitution. And at least some such state actors might well conclude that, if any of them were to get hammered in a § 1983 action for acting just as the BLM officials did, the Court would come to the rescue by finding the retaliatory tactics at issue not *clearly* enough unconstitutional to overcome qualified immunity.

IV. *Robbins* and the Jurisprudence of Wrongs Without Remedies

Looking back after reading the Court's opinion, one must conclude that the introduction to the Court's decision on the merits said it all. "The first question" before it, the Court says at the outset, "is *whether to devise a new Bivens damages action* for retaliating against the exercise of ownership rights. . . ."[154] By describing the anti-retaliatory

[153] Wilkie v. Robbins, 127 S. Ct. 2588, 2604 (2007) ("The point here is not to deny that Government employees sometimes overreach, for of course they do, and they may have done so here if all the allegations are true.").

[154] *Id.* at 2597 (emphasis added).

Bivens damages action invoked in these circumstances by Robbins as "new," a Court that had for years displayed a dwindling inclination to respect the spirit of *Bivens,* much less to extend its letter, made clear what its answer would be. And—as we shall shortly see—by describing the *Bivens* question as properly before it *at all* on this purely interlocutory appeal from a qualified immunity dismissal, a Court that had previously taken care at least to respect the boundaries Congress had set on the appellate jurisdiction of the Supreme Court (and of the federal circuit courts) to review non-final judgments of the federal district courts left no doubt that its eagerness to cut back on *Bivens* exceeded even its fidelity to those jurisdictional boundaries.

The *Robbins* Court described its decision to reject a damages remedy for retaliatory violations of the Fifth Amendment by federal agents as based on "the reasonable fear that a general *Bivens* cure would be worse than the disease."[155] Justice Souter's opinion, however, suggests so strong an antipathy to the *Bivens* cause of action as to call into question any meaningful distinction between the Court's purported application of *Bivens*, on the one hand, and Justice Thomas's avowal, on the other, that he "would not extend *Bivens* even if its reasoning logically applied to this case."[156] If, as I develop below, the *Bivens* line of cases exhibits a basic schizophrenia with regard to the Court's view of the federal judiciary's authority and responsibility to fashion remedies for violations of the federal Constitution, its ruling in *Robbins* suggests a stubborn refusal to accept treatment.

To appreciate the degree to which the Court's decision represents a nearly pathological insistence on retaining the appearance of the judicial responsibility that *Bivens* recognized while simultaneously seeking any excuse not to exercise that responsibility, it is necessary to provide a brief overview of what one commentator has aptly dubbed "*Bivens*'s non-doctrine."[157]

A. The Bivens *Framework*

In *Bivens v. Six Unknown Named Agents,*[158] the Court held that the victim of a Fourth Amendment violation by federal officials could

[155] *Id.* at 2604.

[156] *Id.* at 2608 (Thomas, J., joined by Scalia, J., concurring).

[157] Gene R. Nichol, Bivens, Chilicky, and Constitutional Damages Claims, 75 Va. L. Rev. 1117, 1128 (1989).

[158] 403 U.S. 388 (1971).

recover damages against the officials in federal court even though Congress had not provided a statutory vehicle for such redress. In *Davis v. Passman*,[159] and *Carlson v. Green*,[160] the Court held that *Bivens*'s reasoning required recognition of damages remedies for Fifth Amendment and Eighth Amendment violations by federal officials, respectively, and reiterated that under *Bivens* the victims of constitutional violations by federal officials are presumptively entitled to recover damages in federal court unless either (1) "defendants demonstrate 'special factors counselling hesitation in the absence of affirmative action by Congress'" or (2) "defendants show that Congress has provided an alternative remedy which it explicitly declared to be a substitute for recovery directly under the Constitution and viewed as equally effective."[161]

Both *Davis* and *Carlson* stressed that alternative remedies developed by Congress would not preclude relief under *Bivens* unless those remedies were "equally effective" and Congress expressly declared that they were meant to supplant the *Bivens* remedy of an action for damages. Both of these glosses on the "adequate alternative" exception to the presumptive availability of *Bivens* relief were rejected by the Court in *Bush v. Lucas*.[162] In *Bush*, the Court denied a *Bivens* remedy to a federal civil service employee who alleged that he had been discharged for protected speech in violation of the First Amendment. Noting that Congress could indicate its intent to preclude the *Bivens* remedy "by statutory language, by clear legislative history, *or perhaps even by the statutory remedy itself*,"[163] the Court reasoned that a *Bivens* remedy was implicitly precluded by Congress's design, in the civil employment context, of an "elaborate remedial system that has been constructed step by step, with careful

[159] 442 U.S. 228 (1979). In *Davis*, the Court held that the plaintiff, an assistant to the defendant Congressman, could recover damages for violation of her right to equal protection under the Fifth Amendment when she was terminated on the basis of her gender.

[160] 446 U.S. 14 (1980). In *Carlson*, the Court held that a prisoner could recover damages against individual prison officials for neglect of his medical needs despite the availability of relief against the government under the FTCA, reasoning that Congress had not expressly declared the FTCA remedy to supplant the *Bivens* remedy and that the *Bivens* remedy was a more effective deterrent.

[161] Carlson, 446 U.S. at 19 (citing *Bivens*, 403 U.S. at 397, and *Davis*, 442 U.S. at 245–47).

[162] 462 U.S. 367 (1983); see *id.* at 380–90.

[163] *Id.* at 378 (emphasis added).

consideration to policy considerations. . . ."[164] Furthermore, the Court held the congressionally created remedial scheme precluded *Bivens* recovery even where it assumed those alternative remedies would not "compensate him fully for the harm he suffered."[165]

Although the *Bush* Court purported to find in the design of the civil service remedial system a "special factor[] counseling hesitation,"[166] the real thrust of *Bush* was to expand the class of cases in which congressionally created remedies would be held to preclude *Bivens* recovery far beyond the small, if not null, set in which Congress has explicitly declared a *Bivens* remedy to be supplanted and the somewhat larger set in which Congress might plausibly be said to have implied such preclusion.[167] Congress rarely makes (and does not often imply) a decision to preclude the possibility of relief of the sort contemplated in *Bivens*, and where it does, a *Bivens* claim is unlikely to be brought in the first place. *Bush* thus can be viewed as the Court's arrival at something of an equilibrium with regard to the limits upon its remedial authority imposed by congressional action in a field. Indeed, the *Bivens* inquiry as originally conceived arguably placed too little stock in Congress's legislative authority to devise remedies for constitutional violations.[168] This judicial disdain for Congress's exercise of its remedial powers parallels the disdain the Court has famously shown in reviewing the constitutionality of congressional legislation enacted under Section 5 of the Fourteenth Amendment, in a long series of closely divided decisions.[169]

In addition to the development, described above, of the circumstances in which Congress's legislative *activity* in a field may be

[164] *Id.* at 388.

[165] *Id.* at 372.

[166] *Id.* at 380.

[167] Nonetheless, *Bush*'s use of the "special factors" exception to reach its result contributed to the expansion of that exception into the unprincipled inquiry the Court conduced in *Robbins*. See Nichol, *supra* note 157, at 1147.

[168] See Nichol, *supra* note 157, at 1143–45 (arguing that Congress's authority to legislate remedies for constitutional violations means that it may in some instances supplant a *Bivens* remedy).

[169] See, e.g., Bd. of Trustees v. Garrett, 531 U.S. 356 (2001); United States v. Morrison, 529 U.S. 598 (2000); Florida Prepaid Educ. Expense Bd. v. College Savings Bank, 527 U.S. 627 (1999); City of Boerne v. Flores, 521 U.S. 507 (1997). See generally Laurence H. Tribe, American Constitutional Law 258–67 (3d. ed. 2000); *id.* at 604 n.35.

taken to preclude recognition of a *Bivens* remedy, the Court also developed the theory that Congress's special sphere of constitutional *authority*—even if unexercised—with regard to a particular domain itself constitutes a "special factor counselling hesitation." Thus, in both *Chappell v. Wallace*[170] and *United States v. Stanley*,[171] the Court held that Congress's special authority over military matters precluded judicial creation of a *Bivens* remedy for injuries arising incident to military service.[172] Under this understanding of the "special factors" exception, the judicial branch is to refrain from intruding into substantive fields whose regulation the Constitution is thought to entrust exclusively to Congress.[173]

To summarize, the early line of *Bivens* cases essentially recognized the judiciary's authority to fashion remedies, including money damages, as part of its core responsibility to hear cases and controversies properly within its grant of subject matter jurisdiction under Article III as implemented by 28 U.S.C. § 1331. And this judicial authority was to be presumptively exercised unless either (1) a congressionally

[170] 462 U.S. 296 (1983).

[171] 483 U.S. 669 (1987).

[172] See Chappell, 462 U.S. at 304 ("[C]ongress, the constitutionally authorized source of authority over the military system of justice, has not provided a damages remedy for claims by military personnel that constitutional rights have been violated by superior officers. Any action to provide a judicial response by way of such a remedy would be plainly inconsistent with Congress' authority in this field."). While the *Stanley* Court also noted that a judicially created remedy would be damaging in its disruption of military life, that construal of the "special factors" inquiry is unjustified, given that *Bivens* contemplated the inquiry as one into the proper *source* of remedies for constitutional violations, not into the *merits* of a particular remedy. See Bush v. Lucas, 462 U.S. 367, 380 ("The special factors counseling hesitation in the creation of a new remedy in *Standard Oil* and *Gilman* did not concern the merits of the particular remedy that was sought. Rather, they related to the question of who should decide whether such a remedy should be provided.").

[173] In his opinion for the majority in *Stanley*, Justice Scalia denied the dissent's claim that under his reasoning "all matters within congressional power are exempt from *Bivens*," noting that "[w]hat is distinctive here is the specificity of [U.S. Const. Art. I, 8, cl. 14's authorization for Congress "[t]o make Rules for the Government and Regulation of the land and naval Forces] and the insistence (evident from the number of Clauses devoted to the subject) with which the Constitution confers authority over the Army, Navy, and militia upon the political branches." Stanley, 483 U.S. at 682. Dean Nichol has argued that, in finding this sort of "special factor," the Court essentially applies the political question doctrine under a different name. See Nichol, *supra* note 157, at 1152.

crafted remedial scheme provided adequate alternative relief or (2) the Constitution's grant to Congress of special policy-making authority over a particular field precluded judicial intervention without specific congressional invitation.

B. The Beginning of the End for Bivens

With its decision in *Schweiker v. Chilicky*,[174] the Court began to dismantle this scheme, substituting in its place an essentially unprincipled search for any factor that would allow it to shirk the judicial responsibility recognized in the earlier cases. In *Chilicky* the Court held that the denial of Social Security disability benefits pursuant to a policy inconsistent with the Fifth Amendment Due Process Clause does not give rise to a cause of action for money damages because of the elaborate remedial scheme Congress had constructed to redress erroneous benefits termination. The Court's reliance on its earlier holding in *Bush* was unpersuasive, for in *Chilicky* there was no evidence that the congressional scheme, which aimed only to remedy erroneous benefits determinations caused by mistake or oversight, was intended to address the distinct problem posed by cases, like *Chilicky*, in which the deliberately adopted *procedure* for termination was itself alleged to be unconstitutional. Indeed, the decision in *Chilicky* left the victims with no remedy other than the reinstatement of their missed benefits even where the unconstitutional cutoff of their disability payments had resulted in death or grave illness.[175] The Court's decision in *Chilicky* drew considerable scholarly criticism, with at least one commentator observing that *Chilicky* inaugurated "an open-ended balancing approach whereby judges attempt to decide whether a damages claim serves the public good."[176] Fulfilling that prognosis, the Court in *Robbins* openly adopted just such an approach.

C. The Bivens *Issue in* Robbins

The *Robbins* Court did not hold—nor could it plausibly have said—that a *Bivens* remedy was precluded in light of other adequate remedies available in that case. Indeed, the remedies available to Robbins plainly constituted no targeted "elaborate remedial scheme

[174] 487 U.S. 412 (1988).

[175] For a fuller discussion of *Chilicky*, see Tribe, *supra* note 169, at 485 n.134.

[176] Nichol, *supra* note 157, at 1150.

constructed step by step,"[177] but were merely a hodge-podge of the generically available forms of administrative relief provided under the broad terms of the Administrative Procedure Act, state tort law remedies,[178] and defenses to criminal charges.[179] If it was a stretch for the *Chilicky* Court to find that the existing Social Security benefits remedial scheme precluded a *Bivens* remedy, it would have been an even more extreme deformation in Robbins's case. In truth, if the "remedies" available to Robbins sufficed to render *Bivens* unavailable, then most of the ink spilled in the long line of *Bivens* cases could have been saved, for remedies of the sort available to Robbins were ubiquitous in those cases.

To leave no doubt about how far it was going in cutting into *Bivens*, the Court in *Robbins* expressly conceded—as we have already seen—that, while individual remedies may have been available for many of the numerous harms Robbins suffered, these did not amount to a remedy for the *cumulative effect* of the BLM's long campaign of harassment. The Court thus seemed fully cognizant of what it was leaving unremedied when it acknowledged that "[i]t is one thing to be threatened with the loss of grazing rights, or to be prosecuted, or to have one's lodge broken into, but something else to be subjected to this in combination over a period of six years, by a series of public officials bent on making life difficult."[180] And the Court was nothing but realistic when it conceded Robbins's point that "[a]gency appeals, lawsuits, and criminal defense take money, and endless battling

[177] Bush v. Lucas, 462 U.S. 367, 388 (1983).

[178] State tort law remedies were potentially available in *Bivens* and were specifically held not to preclude recognition of a damages action. See Bivens v. Six Unknown Named Agents of Fed. Bureau of Narcotics, 403 U.S. 388, 394–95 (1971). For an argument that the Court's decision in *Correctional Services Corp. v. Malesko*, 534 U.S. 61 (2001), portended reconsideration of even that basic principle, see Daniel Meltzer, The Supreme Court's Judicial Passivity, 2002 Sup. Ct. Rev. 343, 361 (noting that "[i]f the *Bivens* decision once seemed, as a general matter, to extend constitutional tort remedies against federal officials as broadly as 42 U.S.C. § 1983 does against state and local officials, and to confirm the authority of federal courts to fashion appropriate remedies for violation of federal constitutional rights, *Malesko* suggests that the future may look different").

[179] See Wilkie v. Robbins, 127 S. Ct 2588, 2600 (2007) (describing the "forums of defense and redress open to Robbins" as "a patchwork, an assemblage of state and federal, administrative and judicial benches applying regulations, statutes and common law rules").

[180] *Id.* at 2600–01.

depletes the spirit along with the purse," leading the Court, in the end, to accept as apt Robbins's characterization of the agents' action as "death by a thousand cuts,"[181] and to offer its own description that this was a situation in which, without doubt, "[t]he whole here is greater than the sum of its parts."[182] The point would have been difficult to deny. For a person in Robbins's situation, paying a fine of a few hundred dollars on an administrative trespass charge, while not an insubstantial sum, is trivial when compared with the thousands of dollars it would cost to contest each charge all the way up through the administrative process and the federal courts via the APA. For Robbins, winning was as good (bad) as losing. Every charge meant additional time and money spent regardless of the outcome. And for the officials bent on bleeding Robbins dry, these administrative challenges fed right into their plans.

Just as the *Robbins* Court could not have claimed that an adequate alternative remedial scheme was available to Robbins, so it could not claim to be deferring to Congress's special authority under the Constitution with regard to the federal government's property ownership rights.[183] In essence, the *Robbins* Court has written the "specialness" out of the "special factors" inquiry altogether by grossly mischaracterizing "*Bivens* step two"[184]—its new term for the special

[181] *Id.* at 2600 (citing Resp't Br., *supra* note 11, at 40).

[182] *Id.* at 2601.

[183] Indeed, the Court's (mis)characteriziation of the government's status throughout this case as Regular Joe Landowner itself undermines any such claim. See, e.g., Robbins, 127 S. Ct. at 2602 (noting that "in many ways, the Government deals with its neighbors as one owner among the rest (albeit a powerful one)"). The Court sought to analogize the facts in *Robbins* to a situation in which "a private landowner, when frustrated at a neighbor's stubbornness in refusing an easement, may press charges of trespass every time a cow wanders across the property line or call the authorities to report every land-use violation." *Id.* The analogy shockingly ignores the Constitution's central premise that the government, being uniquely powerful, is uniquely in need of restraints that would be wholly out of place in our fundamental law's treatment of private parties. On the approach suggested by Justice Souter's opinion, one might as well say that, just as a private landowner, when frustrated at a neighbor's political views or voting behavior, may opt to press charges of trespass every time a cow wanders across the property line even though that landowner would not otherwise be so insistently punitive, so may the government. But the law is, of course, otherwise: The Government is not free, in the way a private party would be, to withhold lenity in a manner deliberately calculated to prevent or punish constitutionally protected speech.

[184] *Id.* at 2600.

factors inquiry—as the "weighing [of] reasons for and against the creation of a new cause of action, the way common law judges have always done."[185] This way of framing the inquiry suggests that the Court is engaged in the policy-driven creation of any old common law cause of action, as opposed to a federal cause of action specifically crafted as necessary to remedy and deter a violation of the United States Constitution. But powerful principles underlying the Constitution itself give rise to a strong presumption that violations of federal constitutional rights are redressable by appropriate relief in the federal courts.[186] While an absolute and simplistic understanding of that principle must be—and has been—rejected,[187] surely it should furnish a baseline to guide the Court in its performance of the quintessentially judicial task of determining which remedies are available for any given constitutional violation.

D. The Future of Bivens

While the Court's prior *Bivens* cases had set the stage for *Robbins*, *Robbins* appears to represent the first time the Court has found a *Bivens* remedy unavailable to redress a run-of-the-mill constitutional claim against a federal official in the absence of an alternative remedial scheme that is even arguably designed to be comprehensive.[188] *Robbins* thus marks the Court's first genuine departure from *Bivens*'s "core holding."[189] The Court's foray into the unhinged and uncabined balancing inquiry foreshadowed in *Chilicky* adopts a newly "open-ended special factors methodology" that seems both "unmanageable" and "inconsistent with a reasonable concept of separation

[185] *Id.*

[186] See Tribe, *supra* note 169, at 599–605 (discussing constitutional presumption that "for every right there should be a remedy").

[187] *Id.*; see also Richard H. Fallon, Jr. & Daniel J. Meltzer, New Law, Non-Retroactivity, and Constitutional Remedies, 104 Harv. L. Rev. 1731, 1784–86 (1991).

[188] The Court had previously rejected *Bivens* claims against organizations as opposed to individuals, finding the purpose of deterring agents of government to be inapplicable, see Corr. Serv. Corp. v. Malesko, 534 U.S. 61 (2001) (suit against private corporation); FDIC v. Meyer, 510 U.S. 471 (1994) (suit against federal agency), and in the special situation of lawsuits involving harm to military personnel arising from active service, see United States v. Stanley, 483 U.S. 669, 679 (1987); Chappell v. Wallace, 462 U.S. 296, 304 (1983), finding congressional primacy in those spheres to be dispositive, but none of those decisions is comparable to *Robbins*.

[189] Wilkie v. Robbins, 127 S. Ct. 2588, 2613 (2007) (Ginsburg, J., concurring in part and dissenting in part).

of powers."[190] It is one thing for a cause of action to redress constitutional violations to be deemed presumptively available in the absence of a narrow set of judicially defined exceptions, but quite another for the Supreme Court to assume virtually unchecked power to decide *which* constitutional rights, and which kinds of constitutional violations, yield an implied cause of action for damages (against non-immune government actors) and which ones do not. That this newly assumed power has been exercised to the detriment of Fifth Amendment rights peculiarly in need of the protection that only a *Bivens* remedy could have ensured merely underscores how lawless and arbitrary is the enterprise on which the Court has now embarked. If the Court's exercise of essentially unbridled discretion to decide which constitutional violations to remedy is troubling in itself,[191] its unconvincing reasons for withholding a remedy here are more troubling still.

The Court's assertion that "any damages remedy for actions by Government employees who push too hard for the Government's benefit may come better, if at all, through legislation,"[192] rings particularly hollow; for the Court, tellingly, provides no explanation of *why* Congress is in a better position to perform the prototypically judicial line-drawing functions with which the Court appears to have decided not to dirty its hands in this context. And, indeed, were Congress to step into the remedial void the Court leaves with its decision, enacting a statute providing a cause of action for damages for retaliation in violation of a property owner's Fifth Amendment rights by federal officers—or perhaps crafting an even broader statute similar to 42 U.S.C. § 1983—it would fall to the Court to perform exactly the sort of line-drawing it shrinks from here, a task the Court is already obligated to undertake in cases reaching it under § 1983. But, unfortunately, the Court's decision not to overrule *Bivens* altogether, despite the hostility to that precedent demonstrated by

[190] Nichol, *supra* note 157, at 1151.

[191] See *id.* at 1150; Meltzer, *supra* note 179, at 356–62; see also Dickerson v. United States, 530 U.S. 428, 460–61 (2000) (Scalia, J., dissenting) (contrasting the open-ended judicial power to craft prophylactic rules like the requirement of *Miranda* warnings with the congruence and proportionality the Court demands of Congress in crafting prophylactic remedies under Section 5 of the Fourteenth Amendment).

[192] Robbins, 127 S. Ct. at 2604–05.

the lengths to which the Court went to find a "special factor" pointing to the result reached in *Robbins*, makes congressional action in the field less, not more, likely.

V. Stretching Jurisdictional Limits to the Breaking Point

Not only has the Court's hesitation about fashioning monetary remedies for the victims of constitutional violations produced incoherence in the *Bivens* framework; beyond that, this hesitation evidently motivated the Court to compromise its fidelity to jurisdictional limits. To see that this is so and that the Court's avoidance of the constitutional merits simply cannot be understood as an instance of judicial modesty, one must remember that the posture of the *Robbins* case before the Court was an *interlocutory appeal* of the denial of a motion for summary judgment on qualified immunity grounds. The general rule in the federal courts, as enacted by Congress, is of course that litigants may appeal only from *final judgments*, not interlocutory rulings such as a denial of a summary judgment motion.[193] To be sure, there is a set of narrow exceptions to the final judgment rule, one of which allows immediate appeals of denials of qualified immunity.[194] The allowance of interlocutory appeals of pretrial denials of qualified immunity extends not only to the qualified immunity standard of whether the defendants violated clearly established law,[195] but also to the "inextricably intertwined"[196] issues of whether any right was violated[197] (i.e., whether any constitutional tort was committed), and "the definition of an element of th[at] tort."[198]

But the question of *remedy*—whether a federal suit for damages under *Bivens* would be an available form of relief *if* the conduct

[193] See 28 U.S.C. § 1291 (2000); see also Will v. Hallock, 126 S. Ct. 345, 347–49 (2006).

[194] See Mitchell v. Forsyth, 472 U.S. 511, 530 (1985).

[195] See Harlow v. Fitzgerald, 457 U.S. 800, 818 (1982).

[196] Swint v. Chambers County Comm'n, 514 U.S. 35, 51 (1995).

[197] The Supreme Court has held that the proper procedure in a qualified immunity determination is to first assess "whether the plaintiff has alleged the deprivation of an actual constitutional right at all, and if so, proceed to determine whether that right was clearly established at the time of the alleged violation." Conn v. Gabbert, 526 U.S. 286, 290 (1999). Thus, the issue of whether a right exists at all is properly before an appellate court on interlocutory appeal of the qualified immunity issue.

[198] Hartman v. Moore, 126 S. Ct. 1695, 1702 n.5 (2006).

alleged were proven and *if* that conduct constituted a violation of a clearly established federal constitutional rule—had never before been deemed "inextricably intertwined" with the logically and functionally distinct question *whether* the conduct alleged constituted such a violation as a matter of law and therefore was not entitled to qualified immunity. And, of course, it is *only* the supposedly inextricable entwinement of that remedy issue with the qualified immunity issue that could *bring* the remedy issue—i.e., the availability of *Bivens* relief for the sort of violation alleged—within the limited interlocutory appellate jurisdiction that permitted the court of appeals, and the Supreme Court, to hear *Robbins* at all in the interlocutory posture presented. Thus, even assuming—as the *Robbins* Court ultimately held—that the district court was *wrong* in holding that a *Bivens* action was available to Robbins, if no question of qualified immunity had ever been raised, the defendants would presumably have had to stand trial and only then, if they lost at trial and were aggrieved by the *Bivens* relief granted against them, would they have been able to appeal the *Bivens* issue to the court of appeals and then on to the Supreme Court, where they would in the end presumably have been vindicated.[199]

To be sure, they would in that instance have undergone a trial that could have been avoided altogether had the district court decided at the outset—rightly, on the hypothesis that the Supreme Court's take on the *Bivens* issue would have been unaffected by the intervening proceedings—that no *Bivens* remedy was available. But in that respect, their situation would have been identical to that of many other defendants who lose a dispositive summary judgment motion or motion to dismiss that they should in principle have won and who, if they prevail after trial—e.g., because they are found to have acted for legitimate reasons, or are found not to have done what the complaint alleged they did—are just out of luck with respect to their claim that, had the motion been correctly ruled upon in the first instance, they would have been spared the burdens of trial and not just been handed a favorable post-trial verdict.

[199] Only "presumably," however, because one cannot say with confidence that the Court's *Bivens* calculus would remain unaffected by the district court's trial and the circuit court's analysis on appeal.

While there is a surface allure to the notion that a litigant should be able immediately to appeal *any* order denying a claim of right to prevail without trial, Congress has expressly decided that it is wiser to save all appeals for the end of a case rather than having a case bounce around repeatedly from trial court to appellate court.[200] Thus, had the BLM officials not challenged the district court's pretrial denial of their qualified immunity claim, or had that challenge been regarded as frivolous, they would not have been entitled, on any view of the settled law that survives the *Robbins* Court's holding,[201] to appeal in an interlocutory posture the holding that a *Bivens* remedy was available against them. The jurisdictional issue the *Robbins* Court therefore had to resolve as a threshold matter was whether the insertion of a qualified immunity issue into this case should have been permitted to transmute the situation into one where not only the existence of qualified immunity but also the existence of a *Bivens* remedy could get resolved on appeal in advance of trial. In other words, should the *Bivens* issue be able to take a ride on the "jurisdictional coattails"[202] of the qualified immunity issue, for purposes of pre-trial, interlocutory appellate review?

Considering the purposes of allowing interlocutory appeals of qualified immunity denials, the answer clearly ought to have been "no." The sole reason for permitting interlocutory review of the qualified immunity question is that the Court has defined qualified immunity from liability for a constitutional tort—when the prerequisites of such immunity are met—as conferring upon the officials involved not just freedom from the ultimate imposition of monetary liability, but also freedom from the burdens of being put on trial.[203] The theory is that forcing government officials to suffer through a trial where, even on the plaintiff's allegations and evidence, it can be authoritatively determined in advance that there was no violation of clearly established law needlessly distracts officials from their duties, chills their legitimate exercise of discretionary authority, and

[200]See Will v. Hallock, 126 S. Ct. 952, 958 (2006). In *Will*, the Supreme Court held that federal agents who had appealed the denial of their defense of judgment bar in a *Bivens* action had to stand trial and await a final judgment before appealing the issue. See *id.* at 957.

[201]See Wilkie v. Robbins, 127 S. Ct. 2588, 2597 n.4 (2007).

[202]See Swint v. Chambers County Comm'n, 514 U.S. 35, 44 n.2 (1995).

[203]See Mitchell v. Forsyth, 472 U.S. 511, 525–26 (1985).

wrongly deters public service.[204] That theory justifies interlocutory appellate review of the qualified immunity issue. But the theory has no application to a case such as *Robbins*—unless there is insufficient evidence at the outset that the government officials acted for legally impermissible reasons, and that they were indeed guilty of conduct whose unconstitutionality was unmistakable and should clearly have been understood as such by those officials. Where the only issue the Court ends up addressing is a question of judicial policy as to what the appropriate remedy would have been on the *assumption* that the officials had in the end been found guilty of clearly unconstitutional conduct, the rationale for forgoing a trial and resolving that question on appeal *prior to trial* is altogether lacking. For, absent a convincing or at least an arguable claim of qualified immunity—i.e., a truly plausible argument that the sort of retaliation that this case involved did not violate any clearly established constitutional rule—this case could not be regarded as one in which there was a social interest in insulating the government officials from suit. Permitting the BLM officials to escape any trial at all solely because of the Court's concerns about defining a workable standard for *Bivens* relief gave them a complete windfall.

The Court's sole argument to the contrary, relegated to a footnote, was that the same reasoning it had used in *Hartman v. Moore*[205] to conclude that the definition of an *element* of the alleged constitutional tort was properly before it on interlocutory appeal of a qualified immunity defense applies "to the recognition of the entire cause of action."[206] It becomes plain that this is little more than a play on words once one sees that, in this case, the phrase "recognition of the entire cause of action" means not the existence of a clear constitutional right and its violation but only the availability of damages relief against the violator. So, while the Court's comparison of the case to *Hartman v. Moore* may have some superficial plausibility, it has no basis in law or logic in light of Congress's legislative decision to rule out interlocutory appeals on questions whose resolution is distinct from the question of whether, even on the allegations

[204] See *id.*; Harlow v. Fitzgerald, 457 U.S. 800, 816 (1982).

[205] 126 S. Ct. 1695 (2006).

[206] Robbins, 127 S. Ct. at 2957 n.4.

made and evidence adduced, the defendant can be said, as a matter of law, to have violated no clearly established constitutional right.[207]

VI. Conclusion

In *Robbins*, the Supreme Court acknowledged that a pattern of conduct may infringe a constitutional right, but failed to provide a remedy for this manifestly important category of wrongs. To rule out a *Bivens* remedy in such cases, the Court had to stretch its jurisdictional limits and depart from the presumption of *Bivens* relief, moving instead into the realm of judicial balancing. Only time will tell what effects *Robbins* will have on property rights, or constitutional rights more generally. We may see government officials increasingly making end runs around the Just Compensation Clause by the means of coercive waiver. We may see a flood of *Robbins*-style claims under § 1983 or the APA, in which case courts will be forced to develop a workable standard, a challenge for which they are well-equipped—notwithstanding the doubts expressed on that score by the Court in *Robbins*. Or we may see relatively few lawsuits, in which case the Court's fear of a flood of claims without any way to separate the wheat from the chaff was unwarranted. Whichever of these outcomes comes to pass, *Robbins* portends a bleak future for the core premise of *Bivens* that every constitutional wrong should have some kind of remedy—and for the meaningful enforcement of the Bill of Rights against renegade government officials.

[207]In *Hartman*, the Court concluded that a plaintiff alleging retaliatory prosecution had to prove that there was no probable cause for the prosecution. See Hartman, 126 S. Ct. at 1706. If a prosecutor has probable cause, then there has been no constitutional violation, and the reasons for immunity from suit are fully applicable. In contrast, where the sole issue is not the elements of the right, but only the existence of a damages remedy and thus of a "cause of action" for damages, those reasons are entirely absent.

First Amendment Basics *Redux:* *Buckley v. Valeo* to *FEC v. Wisconsin Right to Life*

*Lillian R. BeVier**

In 2002, hard on the heels of the Enron debacle, Congress passed and President Bush signed the Bipartisan Campaign Finance Reform Act (BCRA, or McCain-Feingold).[1] The Act imposed extensive new regulations on and restrictions of campaign finance practices. Its two most notorious titles were Title I, which prohibited so-called soft-money contributions to national political parties,[2] and Title II, which prohibited corporations and unions from making independent expenditures from their general treasury funds to broadcast ''electioneering communications''—communications that mention candidates for federal office by name within thirty days of a primary or sixty days of a general election.[3] Profound differences of opinion existed about the wisdom and the likely effects of BCRA, and its

*David and Mary Harrison Distinguished Professor, University of Virginia Law School. Rob Painter, University of Virginia Law School Class of 2009, provided superb research help.

[1] Bipartisan Campaign Finance Reform Act of 2002, Pub. L. No. 107-155, 116 Stat. 81.

[2] *Id.* at 82. In brief, the soft money provisions bar national political parties from ''solicit[ing], receiv[ing], or direct[ing] to another person a contribution, donation, or transfer of funds or any other thing of value, or spend any funds, that are not subject to the limitations, prohibitions, and reporting requirements of this Act.'' *Id.* The prohibition of soft money contributions was intended to prevent unregulated (and thus unlimited) contributions being made to political parties in order indirectly to benefit candidate campaigns and thus circumvent restrictions on direct, or hard money, contributions to candidates. For a summary of ''soft money'' rules and practices before the enactment of BCRA, see Note, Soft Money: The Current Rules and the Case for Reform, 111 Harv. L. Rev. 1323, 1323–28 (1998).

[3] Bipartisan Campaign Finance Reform Act, 116 Stat. at 88.

constitutionality was always in doubt.[4] Indeed, conventional wisdom has it that President Bush signed the legislation only because he was convinced that the courts would invalidate it.[5] The electioneering communications prohibition was thought to be particularly vulnerable to First Amendment challenge. In a 329-page set of opinions, however, rendered after taking volumes of testimony, a divided three-judge district court sustained the Act almost in its entirety.[6] A majority of the Supreme Court affirmed in an opinion with respect to Titles I and II that was co-authored by Justices John Paul Stevens and Sandra Day O'Connor and joined by Justices David Souter, Ruth Bader Ginsburg, and Stephen Breyer.[7]

Champions of campaign finance regulation understandably regarded *McConnell* as a "stunning triumph,"[8] and not merely because of the result. Although its reasoning has been called "unusually sloppy and incoherent" even by stalwart supporters of regulation,[9] the majority opinion in *McConnell* was clear about one vitally important fact: it was an unambiguous rejection of the view that at the First Amendment's core is the principle of free political speech. Indeed, the majority in *McConnell* was quite plainly disheartened by

[4]See, e.g., Constitutional Issues Raised by Recent Campaign Finance Legislation Restricting Freedom of Speech: Hearing Before the Subcomm. On the Constitution of the H. Comm. on the Judiciary, 107th Cong. 5 (2001) (statement of Rep. Chabot, Chairman, Subcomm. on the Constitution) (noting that "the tension between certain campaign finance proposals and the first amendment is clear, even to those supporting such regulations").

[5]See, e.g., Akhil Reed Amar & Vikram David Amar, Breaking Constitutional Faith: President Bush and Campaign Finance Reform, FindLaw, Apr. 5, 2002, http://writ.news.findlaw.com/amar/20020405.html (suggesting that President Bush justified signing an unconstitutional bill "by punting to the judiciary"); Capital Gang (CNN television broadcast Mar. 23, 2002), transcript available at http://transcripts.cnn.com/TRANSCRIPTS/0203/23/cg.00.html (last visited July 27, 2007) ("[President Bush] figures, as do many other people who voted for this bill, that the Supreme Court will strike down some of its more obnoxious, unconstitutional provisions.").

[6]McConnell v. FEC, 251 F.Supp.2d 176 (D.D.C. 2003).

[7]McConnell v. FEC, 540 U.S. 93 (2003).

[8]Richard Briffault, McConnell v. FEC and the Transformation of Campaign Finance Law, 3 Election L.J. 147 (2004).

[9]Richard L. Hasen, Symposium: The Law of Democracy: Campaign Finance after McCain-Feingold: Buckley is Dead, Long Live Buckley: The New Campaign Finance Incoherence of McConnell v Federal Election Commission, 153 U. Pa. L. Rev. 31, 33 (2004).

what became of politics when free political speech was the universal baseline. Thus, it paid "only cursory attention to the First Amendment interests" at stake.[10] At the same time, the majority exhibited no skepticism about the possibility either that the legislators who passed BCRA might have had malign self-protective motives or that BCRA might produce anything other than benign results.[11] *McConnell* did not purport to overrule *Buckley v. Valeo*,[12] the Court's seminal campaign finance regulation case, but it did turn a very cold shoulder indeed to the First Amendment premises that had provided the touchstone of *Buckley*'s analysis (if not, perhaps, all of its holdings).[13] In *Federal Election Commission v. Wisconsin Right to Life, Inc.* (*WRTL II*),[14] the case that is the subject of this essay, a new majority of the Court revived *Buckley* and thus breathed renewed life into the First Amendment.

Before sorting out the strands of *WRTL II*, though, it is necessary to make a brief return—one of several this essay will make—to *Buckley*. Returning to *Buckley* may seem unnecessary to aficionados of the "rich tapestry"[15]—or is it the "patternless mosaic?"[16]—of the First Amendment law of campaign finance regulation, who are already familiar with the doctrinal structure that that law is heir to. It is *Buckley*'s First Amendment foundations that are of interest here, not the rickety doctrinal house the Court built upon them. *WRTL II* returned to and rebuilt those foundations, and that is what matters most about it.

[10] *Id.* at 34.

[11] Justice Stevens recognized, however, that this legislation would not be the final line of sandbags dropped in the way of the flood: "We are under no illusion that BCRA will be the last congressional statement on the matter. Money, like water, will always find an outlet." McConnell, 540 U.S. at 224.

[12] 424 U.S. 1 (1976) (per curiam).

[13] See generally Lillian R. BeVier, McConnell v. FEC: Not Senator Buckley's First Amendment, 3 Election L.J. 127 (2004) (summarizing specific respects in which McConnell rejected Buckley's underlying First Amendment premises).

[14] Federal Election Comm'n v. Wisconsin Right to Life, Inc., 127 S. Ct. 2652 (2007) (WRTL II).

[15] Allison Hayward, The Per Curiam Opinion of Steel: Buckley v. Valeo as Superprecedent? Clues from Wisconsin and Vermont, 2005–06 Cato Sup. Ct. Rev. 195, 196 (2006).

[16] Daniel Hays Lowenstein, A Patternless Mosaic: Campaign Finance and the First Amendment after Austin, 21 Capital U. L. Rev. 381 (1992).

In *Buckley*, the Court addressed the constitutionality of the Federal Election Campaign Act of 1971, as amended in 1974 (FECA),[17] which was at the time "by far the most comprehensive reform legislation" that Congress had ever passed.[18] Among other provisions, FECA limited both contributions to and independent expenditures in behalf of candidates for federal office. The D.C. Circuit sustained most of those restrictions. It thought they served "a clear and compelling interest" in preserving the integrity of the electoral process.[19] The Supreme Court reversed. In a *per curiam* opinion, which decisively announced the fundamental premises from which it reasoned, the Court insisted that

> contribution and expenditure limitations operate in an area of the most fundamental First Amendment activities. Discussion of public issues and debate on the qualifications of candidates are integral to the operation of the system of government established by our Constitution. . . . "[I]t can hardly be doubted that the constitutional guarantee has its fullest and most urgent application precisely to the conduct of campaigns for political office."[20]

Given this affirmation, it was surprising that the Court sustained the contribution limitations. This aspect of *Buckley* has been consistently both challenged by First Amendment partisans[21] and exploited by advocates of reform.[22] And a majority of the Court has never wavered

[17] Federal Election Campaign Act of 1971, Pub. L. No. 92-225, 86 Stat. 3, amended by the Federal Election Campaign Act Amendments of 1974, Pub. L. No. 93-443, 88 Stat. 1263.

[18] Buckley v. Valeo, 519 F.2d 821, 831 (D.C. Cir. 1975), rev'd, 424 U.S. 1 (1976).

[19] *Id.* at 841. The D.C. Circuit held one provision of the FECA, § 437a, unconstitutionally vague and overbroad. *Id.* at 832.

[20] Buckley v. Valeo, 424 U.S. 1, 14 (1976).

[21] Cf., e.g., Colorado Republican Fed. Campaign Comm. v. Federal Election Comm'n, 518 U.S. 604, 631 (1996) (Thomas, J., concurring) (arguing that the Court should "reach the facial challenge in this case" and advocating the "reject[ion of] the framework established by *Buckley v. Valeo*").

[22] Cf., e.g., Nixon v. Shrink Missouri Gov't PAC, 528 U.S. 377 (2000) (deeming a state statute limiting campaign contributions constitutionally sufficient even without empirical evidence demonstrating the presence or perception of the corruption the regulation was enacted to combat); Federal Election Comm'n v. Beaumont, 539 U.S. 146 (2003) (holding that nonprofit advocacy organizations may also be constitutionally barred from making direct contributions and expenditures in particular electoral contexts); McConnell v. Federal Election Comm'n, 540 U.S. 93 (2003) (sustaining a

from its conclusion that the contribution limitations "entailed only a marginal restriction on the contributor's ability to engage in free communication";[23] there was "no indication" that the limitations "would have any dramatic adverse effect on the funding of campaigns and political associations";[24] and they served the compelling governmental interest in preventing *quid pro quo* corruption of "current or potential office holders" or the appearance of such corruption.[25]

More directly relevant to *WRTL II*, however, is the Court's conclusion in *Buckley* that the expenditure limitations imposed by FECA § 608(e)(1) constituted "substantial rather than merely theoretical restraints on the quantity and diversity of political speech."[26] The Court very narrowly construed § 608(e)(1), reading it to restrict only expenditures on words of express advocacy. Still the Court found that the restrictions served no compelling government interest. They did not serve to prevent corruption. And the reformers' claim that government could use them in pursuit of an interest in "equality" was emphatically rejected. The equality goal embodied the "concept that government may restrict the speech of some elements of our society in order to enhance the relative voice of others,"[27] but the Court was emphatic that pursuit of such a goal was "wholly foreign to the First Amendment."[28]

BCRA is a far more ambitious attempt to remake the federal campaign finance process than FECA was. Advocates of BCRA had always chafed mightily against the First Amendment constraints that *Buckley* imposed on their reform efforts.[29] The rationale and results in a number of the campaign finance cases decided after 1976

ban on the use of soft money by political parties and upholding the prohibition of "electioneering communications").

[23] Buckley, 424 U.S. at 20–21.

[24] *Id.* at 21.

[25] *Id.* at 26–27.

[26] *Id.* at 19.

[27] *Id.* at 48–49.

[28] *Id.*

[29] See BeVier, *supra* note 13, at 140–41 (noting arguments of campaign finance reformers that demonstrated their disdain for Buckley).

had significantly weakened *Buckley*'s First Amendment foundations.[30] Eventually, the advocates of reform were able to devise a strategy to exploit those weaknesses. BCRA embodied that strategy, the majority of the Court embraced it in *McConnell*, and *Buckley*'s First Amendment foundations yielded to the sustained pressure.

In sustaining the soft money ban, *McConnell* relied principally on several post-*Buckley* cases that had interpreted *Buckley*'s "lesser scrutiny" for contribution limitations to dictate virtually no judicial scrutiny of them at all. If *Buckley* could be thought to have rested on an implicit premise of distrust of legislative judgment regarding restrictions that "operated in an area of the most fundamental First Amendment freedoms," *McConnell* replaced it with an explicit premise of deference to legislatures. In addition, again relying on post-*Buckley* cases, the *McConnell* majority thoroughly repudiated *Buckley*'s narrow definition of corruption as *quid pro quos* between contributors and candidates. Such an expansive "interpretation of the First Amendment would render Congress powerless to address the more subtle but equally dispiriting"[31] kind of corruption represented by the granting of access to office-holders in exchange for soft money contributions. Indeed, the Court went so far as to announce that soft-money contributions could be regulated "[e]ven if . . . access did not secure actual influence, [because] it certainly gave the appearance of such influence."[32]

The way the *McConnell* Court dealt with the electioneering communications ban is of more central concern here because what the Court actually held when it sustained the ban turns out to have been the source of the disagreement that drove the major doctrinal wedge between the majority and the dissent in *WRTL II*. A distinction between "express advocacy" and "issue advocacy" had emerged from the *Buckley* Court's reading of § 608(e)(1): that reading had left corporations and unions free to spend treasury funds on broadcast political ads about issues—ads that also mentioned federal candidates by name during election season—but only so long as the ads avoided the "magic words" of express advocacy—words like "vote for" or "vote against." *McConnell* held that the distinction was

[30] *Id.* at 129–35 (summarizing cases).

[31] McConnell v. FEC, 540 U.S. 93, 153 (2003).

[32] *Id.* at 150.

merely "an endpoint of statutory interpretation, not a first principle of constitutional law."[33] Nowhere in *Buckley*, the *McConnell* Court said, had the Court "suggested that a statute that was neither vague nor overbroad would be required to toe the same express advocacy line."[34] Therefore, since § 203's electioneering communications restrictions raised "none of the vagueness concerns that drove our analysis in *Buckley*,"[35] the Court sustained them, reading its "prior decisions regarding campaign finance regulation" to dictate that it must "respect . . . the legislative judgment that the special characteristics of the corporate structure require particularly careful regulation."[36]

Instead of being concerned to fulfill what *Buckley* had understood as *the Court's* distinctive role as guardian of "fundamental First Amendment freedoms," *McConnell* invoked "*Congress'* ability to weigh competing constitutional interests in an area in which it enjoys particular expertise."[37] For this, among other reasons, the First Amendment law of campaign finance regulation that emerged from *McConnell* departed almost completely *in principle* from the law that had emerged from *Buckley*. Instead of paying tribute to freedom of political speech, the *McConnell* Court embraced restriction with an enthusiasm wholly unencumbered by skepticism about the possibility that malign legislative motives might have prompted BCRA's passage or that perverse consequences might ensue from its enforcement. The upshot was that the *McConnell* majority effectively renounced free political speech in favor of a vision of the more perfect democracy that they believed BCRA's regulatory regime embodied.[38]

[33] *Id.* at 190.

[34] *Id.* at 192.

[35] *Id.* at 194.

[36] *Id.* at 205 (internal quotation marks omitted). The precise basis for the "respect for the legislative judgment" that the Court's prior decisions supposedly embodied is not easy to discern in those cases. See BeVier, *supra* note 13.

[37] McConnell v. FEC, 540 U.S. 93, 95 (2003) (emphasis added).

[38] "'[W]hat we have is two important values in direct conflict: free speech and our desire for healthy campaigns in a healthy democracy' and '[y]ou can't have both.'" FEC v. Wisconsin Right to Life, Inc., 127 S. Ct. 2652, 2686 (2007) (Scalia, J., concurring) (quoting former House Minority Leader Richard Gephardt).

The *McConnell* majority lost its fifth vote when Justice O'Connor retired, and the new majority coalesced to resurrect *Buckley*'s First Amendment premises in *WRTL II*.[39] Chief Justice John Roberts and Justice Samuel Alito, along with *McConnell* dissenters Justices Anthony Kennedy, Antonin Scalia, and Clarence Thomas, agreed to do this, although they disagreed about how to go about it. The chief justice and Justice Alito thought *Buckley* could be revived without overruling *McConnell*. Justices Kennedy, Scalia, and Thomas thought not. The important fact, though, is that for the moment, at least, freedom is once again triumphant. In what follows, I will describe this development and offer an assessment of its import.

I. From *McConnell* to *WRTL II*

A. Randall v. Sorrell

The new majority that decided *WRTL II* had its first encounter with the utopian dreams of reform advocates in *Randall v. Sorrell*,[40] a case that the Court decided in 2006. In a 6-3 decision, the Court invalidated Vermont's Act 64, a set of stringent restrictions on campaign giving and spending enacted by the Vermont legislature in 1997. Specifically, the act instituted strict ceilings on the total campaign expenditures a candidate for state office could make during a given election cycle, with the permissible amount dependent on the position sought.[41] Contributions were also capped, limiting the sums that citizens could donate to both candidates and political parties during each electoral window.[42]

Randall was a surprising and interesting decision for several reasons that bear mentioning here. First, although only Chief Justice Roberts joined his opinion in its entirety, it was Justice Breyer who announced the Court's judgment invalidating Act 64. That Justice

[39] Federal Election Comm'n v. Wisconsin Right to Life, Inc., 127 S. Ct. 2652 (2007).

[40] 126 S. Ct. 2479 (2006).

[41] The expenditure limits correspond to the scope of the office's constituency and the importance of the job: "governor, $300,000; lieutenant governor, $100,000; other statewide offices, $45,000; state senator, $4,000 (plus an additional $2,500 for each additional seat in the district); state representative (two-member district), $3,000; and state representative (single member district), $2,000." *Id.* at 2486.

[42] The law permitted contributions of $400, $300, and $200 to candidates for governor, state senator, and state representative, respectively, and a contribution of $2,000 to a political party. *Id.*

Breyer wrote for the Court an opinion *invalidating* both contribution and expenditure limits is striking, since he had previously portrayed himself rather consistently as a champion of regulation—or at least as an advocate of the view that there are First Amendment interests on both sides of campaign finance regulation debates.[43]

Second, Act 64 was the first head-on legislative challenge to *Buckley*'s holding that limits on individual *expenditures* in candidate elections are unconstitutional. Justice Breyer's prior writings on[44] and off[45] the Court seemed to signal that he would be sympathetic to such a challenge. Indeed, he had quite explicitly stated his view that the *Buckley* holding with respect to expenditure limits ought to be read "to give the political branches sufficient leeway to enact comprehensive solutions to the problems posed by campaign finance" and that, were it not so read, it would have to be reconsidered.[46] But his *Randall* opinion decisively invoked the principle of stare decisis in support of the conclusion that *Buckley* dictated not only that Vermont's expenditure limitations could not stand but also that the state's asserted justification for them—namely, that they were necessary to prevent elected officials from spending too much time raising money—had been decisively if only implicitly rejected by *Buckley*.[47]

The third aspect of *Randall* that is worth noting here was that the Court had never before held that limits on contributions were too

[43]"[T]his is a case where constitutionally protected interests lie on both sides of the legal equation. . . . We [cannot] expect that mechanical application of the tests associated with 'strict scrutiny'—the tests of 'compelling interests' and 'least restrictive means'—will properly resolve the difficult constitutional problem that campaign finance statutes pose." Nixon v. Shrink Missouri Gov't. PAC, 528 U.S. 377, 400 (2000) (Breyer, J., concurring).

[44]"[T]he legislature understands the problem—the threat to electoral integrity, the need for democratization—better than do we. We should defer to its political judgment that unlimited spending threatens the integrity of the electoral process." *Id.* at 403–04.

[45]See Stephen Breyer, Active Liberty: Interpreting Our Democratic Constitution 39–55 (2005).

[46]Nixon, 528 U.S. at 405.

[47]"In our view, it is highly unlikely that fuller consideration of this time protection rationale would have changed *Buckley*'s result. The *Buckley* Court was aware of the connection between expenditure limits and a reduction in fundraising time." Randall, 126 S. Ct. at 2490.

low. Instead, in case after case—beginning with *Buckley* and continuing up to and including *McConnell*—the Court had assumed an increasingly hands-off posture of deference to legislative judgments about appropriate contribution limits.[48] That in *Randall* it would not merely scrutinize but overturn the legislature's determination was, to say the least, an unexpected development.

The fourth and final aspect of the *Randall* opinions that is noteworthy for my purposes in this essay is that, just as they did in *McConnell*, and just as they continued to do in *WRTL II*, the opinions reflected profound and fundamental disagreements. The approaches of the two new justices' to campaign finance regulation remained opaque after *Randall* because, on the crucial question of the validity of the restrictions at issue, each of them joined Justice Breyer's opinion, which straddled rather than confronted the core issues. By contrast, the other justices's differences with one another were not matters merely of analytical nuance, nor did they reflect simple disagreements about facts. Instead, their views were poles apart. Justice Stevens on one end of the continuum abandoned the First Amendment ship almost entirely. He was much more explicit about this in *Randall* than he had been in *McConnell*: whereas in *McConnell* he purported to leave *Buckley* intact, in *Randall* he asserted in no uncertain terms that he thought that *Buckley* had been "quite wrong to equate money and speech"[49] because, as he had noted in his *Shrink Missouri* concurrence, "money is property; it is not speech."[50] Thus, in Justice Stevens's view, the Court should grant the same generous and uncritical deference to legislative judgments about contribution and expenditure limitations that it presently accords to regulations of the time, place, and manner of speech. Tenaciously at the other end of the continuum, Justices Thomas and Scalia also asserted that *Buckley* had been wrongly decided—but they thought that, in permitting legislatures to limit contributions, *Buckley* "provide[d]

[48]See Buckley, 424 U.S. at 83 (asserting that the appropriate contribution threshold is "best left in the context of this complex legislation to congressional discretion"); McConnell, 540 U.S. at 95 (applying a "less rigorous review standard [that] shows proper deference to Congress' ability to weigh competing constitutional interests in an area in which it enjoys particular expertise").

[49]Randall v. Sowell, 126 S. Ct. 2479, 2508 (2006) (Stevens, J., dissenting).

[50]Nixon v. Shrink Missouri Gov't PAC, 528 U.S. 377, 398 (2000) (Stevens, J., concurring).

insufficient protection to political speech,"[51] not that it provided too much.

B. Back to Buckley—*Again*

McConnell upheld the facial validity of BCRA § 203's ban on corporate and union spending for "electioneering communications." In 2006, however, the Court unanimously concluded that *McConnell* did not preclude as-applied challenges,[52] and it was just such a challenge that *WRTL II* sustained. But the decision goes so far toward eviscerating § 203 that it effectively overrules *McConnell*'s holding that the section is valid on its face. Indeed, a majority of the justices are quite explicit that this is the decision's effect. Chief Justice Roberts's principal opinion claimed that the Court had "had no occasion to revisit"[53] *McConnell*, but Justice Scalia's concurring opinion for himself and Justices Kennedy and Thomas scorned the claim for its "faux judicial restraint."[54] And Justice Souter's dissent, joined by Justices Stevens, Ginsburg, and Breyer, similarly concluded that "*McConnell*'s holding that § 203 is facially constitutional is overruled."[55]

Understanding the claim about *WRTL II*'s overruling effect requires another short return to *Buckley* and then to *McConnell* and the facial attack against which *McConnell* sustained § 203. That facial attack was grounded in the claim that § 203 was overbroad. How eager the Court should be—or has been in the past—to sustain as-applied challenges to facially-valid laws is a matter of some dispute.[56]

[51] *Id.* at 2505 (Thomas, J., dissenting).

[52] Wisconsin Right to Life, Inc. v. Federal Election Comm'n., 546 U.S. 410 (2006) (WRTL I).

[53] Federal Election Comm'n v. Wisconsin Right to Life, Inc., 127 S. Ct. 2652, 2674 (2007).

[54] *Id.* at 2683 n.7 (Scalia, J., concurring).

[55] *Id.* at 2699 (Souter, J., dissenting).

[56] Compare Brief for Appellants John McCain et al. at 39, McCain v. Wisconsin Right to Life, Inc., 127 S. Ct. 2652 (2007) (No. 06-970) ("[A]n as-applied challenge should succeed only if the plaintiff can show that the ad itself and the circumstances of its creation and airing demonstrate that there is no reasonable prospect the ad is likely to influence the election."), with Brief for Appellee Federal Election Commission at 41–42, McCain v. Wisconsin Right to Life, Inc., 127 S.Ct. 2652 (2007) (Nos. 06-969, 06-970) (asserting that, although "the overbreadth of the prohibition is not sufficiently substantial for facial invalidation," this "does not shift the strict scrutiny burden from the government and force challengers to prove that the mentioned options are inadequate").

In principle, of course, a facially valid law regulating First Amendment activity is not necessarily constitutional in all its applications. The conclusion that a law is not facially overbroad does not entail either that it can never be unconstitutional as-applied or that the Court should tend to be systematically unsympathetic to as-applied challenges.[57] And, again in principle, there is no reason why a decision such as *WRTL II* that sustains an as-applied challenge to a law that the Court has previously explicitly held to be facially valid should be thought entirely to compromise the law's facial validity, as so many people think that *WRTL II* does. It is plausible to conclude, for example, that a law that prohibits civil service employees from actively engaging in partisan political activities or soliciting campaign contributions from their coworkers might be constitutional on its face but unconstitutional if applied to prohibit them from wearing political buttons or displaying bumper stickers.[58] Nevertheless, *WRTL II* is thought completely to eviscerate *McConnell* because of the way *McConnell* supposedly resolved the question about the source of the *Buckley* Court's narrow construction of FECA's expenditure limitations.

Thus, we must once again return to *Buckley* itself and FECA § 608(e)(1), because the language the Court used when evaluating that section was once again the source of controversy. The Court held that the language of § 608(e)(1) that limited individual and group expenditures "relative to a clearly identified candidate"[59] was unconstitutionally vague, and to eliminate the vagueness, it thought itself impelled to interpret the phrase "relative to" to mean "advocating the election or defeat of" a candidate.[60] Even this interpretation did not eliminate the vagueness problem, however, because of the stubborn fact that "the distinction between discussion of issues and candidates and advocacy of election or defeat of candidates may often dissolve in practical application."[61] Then, in the holding whose

[57] Cf. Broadrick v. Oklahoma, 413 U.S. 601, 615 (1973) (holding that overbreadth challenges may be sustained only when a statute's overbreadth is "not only . . . real, but substantial as well, judged in relation to the statute's plainly legitimate sweep").

[58] Cf. *id.*

[59] Federal Election Campaign Act Amendments of 1974, Pub. L. No. 93-443, § 101(e)(1), 88 Stat. 1265 (codified at 18 U.S.C. § 601(e)(1)) (repealed 1976).

[60] Buckley v. Valeo, 424 U.S. 1, 42 (1976).

[61] *Id.*

constitutional underpinnings became the subject of so much debate, the Court concluded that

> in order to preserve the provision against invalidation on vagueness grounds . . . [§ 608(e)(1)] must be construed to apply only to expenditures for communications that in express terms advocate the election or defeat of a clearly identified candidate for federal office.[62]

And in a footnote announcing what became known as the "magic words" test of express advocacy, the Court acknowledged that its construction

> would restrict the application of § 608(e)(1) to communications containing words of express advocacy of election or defeat, such as "vote for," "elect," "support," "cast your ballot for," "Smith for Congress," "vote against," "defeat," "reject."[63]

Nearly all the appellate courts that had considered this aspect of *Buckley* had concluded that the holding was not merely a product of statutory construction necessitated by the need to cure the vagueness inherent in the difficulty of distinguishing in practice between "discussion of issues and candidates" and "advocacy of election or defeat of candidates."[64] Rather, they thought the narrow construction had been dictated by the First Amendment need to protect discussion of issues.[65] They read *Buckley* to hold that any exception to the

[62] *Id.* at 44.

[63] *Id.* at 44 n.52

[64] *Id.* at 42.

[65] See, e.g., FEC v. Christian Action Network, 110 F.3d 1049, 1064 (4th Cir. 1997) (concluding that Buckley limited the FEC's regulatory authority over express advocacy to communications containing the "magic words"); Maine Right to Life Comm. v. FEC, 914 F. Supp. 8, 10–11 (D. Me. 1996) (concluding that Buckley and FEC v. Massachusetts Citizens for Life, 479 U.S. 238 (1986), taken together, require the "magic words" approach), aff'd, 98 F.3d 1 (1st Cir. 1996), cert. denied, 522 U.S. 810 (1997). Two frequently cited passages in the *Buckley* opinion seemed to support this conclusion. In one, the Court stated that "[s]o long as persons and groups eschew expenditures that in express terms advocate the election or defeat of a clearly identified candidate, they are free to spend as much as they want to promote the candidate and his views." Buckley, 424 U.S. at 45. In the other, it asserted that "[a]dvocacy of the election or defeat of candidates for federal office is no less entitled to protection under the First Amendment than the discussion of political policy generally or advocacy of the passage or defeat of legislation." *Id.* at 48.

First Amendment that would permit restrictions of expenditures on express advocacy would have to be confined within a very narrow regulatory space so as to keep "the discussion of political policy generally or advocacy of the passage or defeat of legislation"[66] as free as possible.

Although many champions of free political speech have criticized *Buckley* for not protecting enough speech,[67] the decision actually left a very considerable amount of speech unrestricted.[68] To the dismay of reform advocates, it turned out to be very easy for corporations and unions to engage in political advertising during election campaigns without using words of express advocacy. When political activists, primarily but not exclusively non-profit advocacy corporations, realized the full implications of what *Buckley* left them free to do, they began spending enthusiastically from their corporate treasuries on such advertising.[69] The amount of this spending, and the content of the ads on which it was spent, alarmed reform advocates. They mobilized their own constituencies and brought considerable intellectual and financial resources to bear on a First Amendment counter-attack.[70]

[66] Buckley v. Valeo, 424 U.S. 1, 42 (1976).

[67] See Brief of Amici Curiae the Center for Competitive Politics et al. in Support of Appellees at 6–7 Federal Election Comm'n v. Wisconsin Right to Life, Inc., 127 S. Ct. 2652 (2007) (Nos. 06-969, 06-970) (contending that "*Buckley* . . . denigrated the First Amendment value of candidate contributions as a form of expression and association by arguing that such contributions involved only symbolic and inarticulate expressions of support and ultimately produced only speech-by-proxy").

[68] Prior to BCRA, expenditures on issue ads by political parties, labor unions, trade and business associations, corporations, and ideological interest groups were not subject to either the contribution limits or the disclosure requirements that restricted the giving and spending of those who contributed to candidate campaigns or expressly advocated the election or defeat of particular candidates. For a summary of the statutory scheme that applied to issue ads, see David A. Pepper, Recasting the Issue Ad: The Failure of the Court's Issue Advocacy Standards, 100 W. Va. L. Rev. 141 (1997).

[69] See Deborah Beck et al., Annenberg Pub. Policy Ctr., Issue Advocacy Advertising During the 1996 Campaign 3 (1997) (dicussing the ascendancy of the "thorny new practice" of issue advocacy); Jeffrey D. Stanger & Douglas G. Rivlin, Annenberg Pub. Policy Ctr., Issue Advocacy Advertising During the 1997–1998 Election Cycle 1 (1998) (estimating that spending on issue ads during the 1997–1998 election cycle had grown to between $275 and $340 million); Glenn Moramarco, Regulating Electioneering: Distinguishing Between "Express Advocacy" & "Issue Advocacy" 9 (Brennan Ctr. for Justice Campaign Fin. Reform Series, 1998) (identifying "multi-million dollar electioneering campaigns [engaged in] under the guise of 'issue advocacy'").

[70] The Illinois Civil Justice League reports that more than "$140 million was spent" by the campaign finance reform lobby during the decade preceding 2005. Illinois

The strategy the reformers developed had three principal components. The first component consisted of crafting and developing the implications of an argument to the effect that a constitutionally significant difference exists between "election-related" spending, which the First Amendment permits to be regulated, and spending on general "political speech," which the First Amendment protects.[71] The argument implied, of course, that restrictions on "election-related" speech about candidates—speech that had the intent or the effect of influencing voters and thereby of affecting federal election outcomes—were more likely to survive First Amendment scrutiny than were restrictions on speech about general political issues.

Civil Justice League, Watching the Watchdogs: How George Soros & Other Special Interest Foundations Have Hijacked Campaign Finance Reform in Illinois 2 (April 12, 2005), http://www.icjl.org/WatchingWatchdogs.pdf. The Brennan Center for Justice, an organization heavily involved in the research underpinning the holding in *McConnell*, was the recipient of "contributions totaling $3.8 million from the Soros, Joyce, Ford and Carnegie foundations" during the same period. *Id.* at 4. An editorial printed in the *Washington Times* further details giving by "liberal foundations" to "campaign-finance 'reform' groups like . . . the Brennan Center for Justice," citing "a recent report by the nonpartisan Political Money Line [entitled] Campaign Finance Lobby: 1994–2004. Propaganda and the Money Trail, Wash. Times, Mar. 23, 2005, at A16. The report asserts that "Pew [Charitable Trusts] spent an average of $4 million a year over 10 years promoting reform" and that "[s]even other foundations—including the Carnegie Corp. ($14 million), the Joyce Foundation ($13.5 million), George Soros' Open Society Institute ($12.6 million)—cumulatively ponied up another $83 million." *Id.*

[71] See C. Edwin Baker, Campaign Expenditures and Free Speech, 33 Harv. C.R.-C.L. L. Rev. 1, 49–50 (1998) (drawing a line "between election-oriented expression and the broader realms of political expression" for the purposes of First Amendment analysis); Richard Briffault, Issue Advocacy: Redrawing the Elections/Politics Line, 77 Tex. L. Rev. 1751, 1763 (1999) (noting the existence of a "line that distinguishes electoral speech from other political speech"); Burt Neuborne, The Supreme Court and Free Speech: Love and a Question, 42 St. Louis U. L.J. 789, 808–10 (1998). Professor Neuborne's article provides convincing evidence that distinguishing between election-related speech and other political speech emerged from the shared agenda of campaign finance reformers. See Neuborne, 42 St. Louis U. L. J. at 800 n.47:

> I acknowledge a debt to Professor C. Edwin Baker who raised the possibility of viewing election campaigns as discrete institutions at a campaign finance symposium at Brooklyn Law School, and who subsequently circulated a thoughtful draft of an article urging his position. I also benefited from a Brennan Center working group on campaign finance reform chaired by Ronald Dworkin, that includes Frank Sorauff, Roy Schotland, Rick Pildes, Richard Briffault, Josh Rosenkranz, and myself.

(citation omitted).

The second component of the reformers' strategy was rhetorical. It consisted of relentlessly asserting that, because they mentioned candidates by name, many so-called issue advocacy advertisements were "intended to affect the outcome of federal elections" and were therefore "not really advertisements about issues but . . . a form of electioneering without the words of express advocacy" and hence amounted to "sham issue advocacy."[72] Characterizing independently funded ads that mentioned both candidates and issues during election campaigns as "sham issue ads" implied that ads that mentioned candidates were *by definition* not issue ads. In addition, the reformers implied that such ads were dishonorable, dishonest, and illegitimate by virtue of what the reformers asserted to be the fact that they were intended to influence candidate elections rather than solely to engage in discussion of issues.[73]

The third component of the reform advocates' intellectual strategy was to persist in claiming that *Buckley*'s "magic words" holding did not reflect a *constitutionally mandated* limitation on Congress's ability to restrict election-related speech. They did not regard such a limitation as necessary in order that discussion of issues during election campaigns would not be caught in the regulators' net. Instead, they argued, the magic words holding was merely an artifact of vagueness concerns. The vagueness problem could be cured by statutory specificity, which reform advocates were able to supply with their precise definition of "electioneering communications."[74] Then, assuming the Court could be persuaded of the merits of the constitutional argument that restrictions on corporate and union spending for election-related speech were different from and more tolerable than restrictions on political speech generally, Congress could close the "loophole" that permitted corporations and unions to engage in the "sham

[72] Richard L. Hasen, The Surprisingly Complex Case for Disclosure of Contributions and Expenditures Funding Sham Issue Advertising, 48 UCLA L. Rev. 265, 267–68 (2000).

[73] See, e.g., Hasen, *supra* note 72.

[74] "The term 'electioneering communication' means any broadcast, cable, or satellite communication which—(I) refers to a clearly identified candidate for Federal office; (II) is made within—(aa) 60 days before a general, special, or runoff election for the office sought by the candidate; or (bb) 30 days before the primary or preference election, or a convention or caucus of a political party that has authority to nominate a candidate, for the office sought by the candidate; and (cc) in the case of a communication which refers to a candidate for an office other than President or Vice President, is targeted to the relevant electorate." 2 U.S.C. § 434(f)(3)(A)(i).

issue advocacy" that mentioned candidates by name during election campaigns.

Two other developments helped regulatory advocates make their case that *Buckley* was no longer a firewall of protection for political speech but rather had become a platform of support for further restrictions. First, in cases decided since *Buckley*, the Court had made clear its willingness to embrace an increasingly broad view of what constituted the "corruption" whose reality or appearance legislatures could prevent. For example, in *Austin v. Michigan Chamber of Commerce*,[75] the Court relied on an anti-corruption rationale to sustain state legislation prohibiting corporations and unions from making independent expenditures on candidate elections. In doing so, the Court said that the concept of corruption included "the corrosive and distorting effects [on the integrity of the electoral process] of immense aggregations of wealth that are accumulated with the help of the corporate form."[76] Henceforward, it appeared, legislatures could restrict contributions and expenditures in order to prevent not merely the corruption of *officeholders* or potential officeholders but also to cure a much more amorphous kind of corruption, namely the corruption of *the political process*. And later, in *Nixon v. Shrink Missouri Government PAC*,[77] the Court expanded the conception of corruption of officeholders so that it "was not confined to bribery of public officials, but extended to the broader threat from politicians too compliant with the wishes of large contributors."[78]

The second post-*Buckley* development that helped reform advocates was the Court's ever-increasing willingness to defer to legislative judgments about the necessity for restrictions on political giving and spending. From the somewhat less skeptical attitude it adopted in *Buckley* to contribution limitations than to expenditure restrictions, the Court progressed in *Austin* to permissiveness about a complete ban on independent corporate expenditures in support of or opposition to candidates and thence, in *FEC v Beaumont*,[79] to a general posture of explicit and uncritical deference to legislative judgments

[75] 494 U.S. 652 (1990).

[76] *Id.* at 660.

[77] 528 U.S. 377 (2000).

[78] *Id.* at 389.

[79] Federal Election Comm'n v. Beaumont, 539 U.S. 146 (2003).

restricting the political spending of corporations. The Court read its own prior cases as having acknowledged that the "special characteristics of the corporate structure" required such deference.[80] It refused to "second-guess a legislative determination as to the need for prophylactic measures where corruption is the evil feared," because the "special benefits conferred by the corporate structure . . . [carry a genuine] potential for distorting"[81] the political process.

C. The First Amendment Resurrected

BCRA and the *McConnell* decision that sustained its provisions were the culmination of the intellectual and judicial developments just described. *WRTL II* goes far, in turn, to subvert them. *WRTL II* challenges *McConnell*'s fundamental First Amendment premises, thereby substantially undermining its authority. It is time now to turn to it.

Wisconsin Right to Life, Inc. (WRTL), is a non-profit ideological advocacy corporation. In August 2004 it wanted to fund with general treasury funds some broadcast ads objecting to the filibusters by Senate Democrats of several of President Bush's judicial nominees. The proposed ads, which WRTL labeled "grass roots lobbying," would have mentioned incumbent Senator Russ Feingold by name, though without using the "magic words" of express advocacy, within 30 days of the 2004 Wisconsin primary. WRTL knew the ads would violate § 203's prohibition on electioneering communications but it believed it had a First Amendment right to run them. Accordingly, WRTL sought declaratory and injunctive relief against § 203's enforcement by the Federal Election Commission (FEC). The district court denied the requested relief on the ground that, when the Court in *McConnell* sustained § 203 on its face, its reasoning had left "no room for the kind of 'as applied' challenge" that WRTL sought to bring.[82] The Supreme Court unanimously disagreed, held that

[80] *Id.* at 153 (quoting Federal Election Comm'n v. National Right to Work Comm., 459 U.S. 197, 209 (1982)) (citing National Right to Work, 459 U.S. at 207; Austin v. Michigan Chamber of Commerce, 494 U.S. 652, 658–59 (1990); Federal Election Comm'n v. Massachusetts Citizens for Life, Inc., 479 U.S. 238, 257–58 (1986); Federal Election Comm'n v. National Conservative Political Action Comm., 470 U.S. 480, 500–501 (1985)).

[81] *Id.* at 157–58 (citations and internal quotation marks omitted).

[82] Wisconsin Right to Life, Inc. v. Federal Election Comm'n, 2004 U.S. Dist. LEXIS 29036, at 6 (D.D.C. 2004).

McConnell did not foreclose as-applied challenges, and remanded the case.[83] In a complete about face, the district court then sustained WRTL's as-applied challenge.[84] It read *McConnell* to have held that BCRA was constitutional only insofar as it proscribed corporate and union expenditures on express advocacy and its "functional equivalent."[85] Whether WRTL's proposed ads constituted express advocacy's functional equivalent depended on whether the court should consult only the "language within the four corners"[86] of the ads or try to evaluate them in their context—*i.e.*, by looking to their purpose and intended effects. The FEC and the interveners (FEC hereafter), including Senator McCain, argued that the ads should be interpreted in their appropriate context and that when that were done it could be seen that they did constitute the functional equivalent of express advocacy. WRTL argued that only the words mattered, and the words were not the functional equivalent of express advocacy. The district court decided that its analysis should be confined to the ad's language. It agreed with WRTL that

> [d]etermining intent and the likely effect of an ad on the viewing public is . . . too conjectural and wholly impractical if future as-applied challenges are going to be evaluated on an emergency basis by three-judge panels prior to and during the BCRA blackout period leading up to federal primary and general elections.[87]

And, read literally, the court held, the ads did not constitute express advocacy or its functional equivalent.

Thus the key district court holdings that the Supreme Court affirmed in *WRTL II* were, first, that whether an ad constitutes the functional equivalent of express advocacy should be determined by its words alone and not by its purpose or effect and, second, that the words of WRTL's proposed ads were not express advocacy's functional equivalent. It is these holdings that are thought to eviscerate *McConnell*'s conclusion that § 203 is facially valid. I agree that

[83] Wisconsin Right to Life, Inc. v. Federal Election Comm'n, 546 U.S. 410 (2006) (per curiam) (WRTL I).

[84] Wisconsin Right to Life, Inc. v. Federal Election Comm'n, 466 F. Supp. 2d 195 (2006).

[85] *Id.* at 204.

[86] *Id.* at 207.

[87] *Id.* at 205.

WRTL II guts *McConnell*, but it does so not alone or even most significantly by virtue of its holding. More importantly, it guts *McConnell* because it resurrects the First Amendment.

The chief justice's principal opinion repeatedly signals a perspective that represents an entirely different view of the First Amendment than the one reflected in *McConnell*. The opinion affirmed in no uncertain terms that "[b]ecause BCRA § 203 burdens political speech, it is subject to strict scrutiny"[88]—surprisingly citing *McConnell* for the point. (On the very page of the opinion that the chief justice cited, however, *McConnell* had emphasized its "respect for the 'legislative judgment that the special characteristics of the corporate structure require particularly careful regulation.'"[89]) And the chief justice invoked, as *Buckley* did,[90] but *McConnell* most definitely did not,[91] the implications of *New York Times v Sullivan*'s "profound national commitment to the principle that debate on public issues should be uninhibited, robust and wide open."[92]

Chief Justice Roberts understood, as had the district court, that resolving the as-applied challenge to § 203 required the Court to distinguish between issue advocacy and the functional equivalent of express advocacy, a distinction he well understood often dissolved in practice. Accordingly, he emphasized the importance of crafting a test that would "provide a safe harbor for those who exercise First Amendment rights."[93] The FEC claimed that *McConnell* established that the constitutional test for functional equivalence was "whether

[88] Federal Election Comm'n v. Wisconsin Right to Life, Inc., 127 S. Ct. 2652, 2664 (2007).

[89] McConnell, 540 U.S. at 205 (internal citations omitted).

[90] Buckley v. Valeo, 424 U.S. 1, 14 (1976).

[91] In the portion of the *McConnell* opinion that sustained the ban on corporate and union spending for electioneering communications, the Court did not mention *New York Times*. McConnell, 540 U.S. at 203–09. And when it did mention the case in connection with the disclosure requirements, it disdained its relevance. *Id.* at 197 (quoting the district court opinion, 251 F. Supp. 2d at 237, that celebrated "informed choices in the political marketplace" and implied that *New York Times* was antithetical to "precious First Amendment values."). For discussion of the *McConnell* Court's treatment of *New York Times*, see BeVier, *supra* note 13, at 142–44.

[92] New York Times v. Sullivan, 376 U.S. 254, 270 (1964).

[93] WRTL II, 127 S. Ct. at 2665.

the ad is intended to influence elections and has that effect."[94] Rejecting that claim, the Chief Justice exhibited the kind of concern to protect free political debate that was at the heart of *Buckley*: the intent-based standard was unacceptable, he said, because it "would chill core political speech."[95] An objective standard was required, one that would entail minimal discovery, eliminate the threat of protracted litigation, and preclude both open-ended factual inquiries and complex legal arguments.[96] He announced a test and applied it as follows:

> [A]n ad is the functional equivalent of express advocacy only if the ad is susceptible of no reasonable interpretation other than as an appeal to vote for or against a specific candidate. Under this test, WRTL's three ads are plainly not the functional equivalent of express advocacy. First, their content is consistent with that of a genuine issue ad: The ads focus on a legislative issue, take a position on the issue, exhort the public to adopt that position, and urge the public to contact public officials with respect to the matter. Second, their content lacks indicia of express advocacy: The ads do not mention an election, candidacy, political party, or challenger; and they do not take a position on a candidate's character, qualifications, or fitness for office.[97]

Chief Justice Roberts characterized the FEC as having advocated the "perverse[]" view that "there can be no such thing as a genuine issue ad during the blackout period."[98] Emphasizing once again

[94] *Id.* at 2664.

[95] *Id.* at 2665.

[96] *Id.* at 2666.

[97] *Id.* at 2667. Justice Souter's dissenting opinion asserts that the backup provision of BCRA's electioneering communication definition is "essentially identical" to the chief justice's test. *Id.* at 2704 (Souter, J., dissenting). The backup provision defines electioneering communications as ads that are "*suggestive* of no *plausible meaning* other than an exhortation to vote for or against" a candidate. 2 U.S.C. § 434(f)(3)(A)(ii) (italics added). Note Justice Souter's implicit claim, which is that the italicized language carries the identical meaning as "*susceptible of no reasonable interpretation other than* as an appeal to vote for or against a specific candidate." It is a sure bet that Chief Justice Roberts would not be persuaded that the two phrases carry identical meanings.

[98] Federal Election Comm'n v. Wisconsin Right to Life, Inc., 127 S. Ct. 2652, 2668 (2007).

"what we have acknowledged at least since *Buckley*: that 'the distinction between discussion of issues and candidates [which is protected] and advocacy of election or defeat of candidates [which may be restricted] may often dissolve in practical application,'"[99] the chief justice proceeded neatly to hoist the appellants on the petard of the highly speech-protective rationale that the Court recently deployed to protect virtual child pornography: "'The Government may not suppress lawful speech [i.e., genuine issue ads] as the means to suppress unlawful speech [i.e., express advocacy]. Protected speech does not become unprotected merely because it resembles the latter. The Constitution requires the reverse.'"[100]

Since WRTL's proposed ads were not the functional equivalent of express advocacy, the next question was whether any compelling governmental interests justified restricting them. The FEC had attempted to bring the spectre of circumvention to bear on this analysis by arguing that regulating express advocacy was necessary to prevent speakers from subverting the compelling governmental interest in preventing candidate corruption. *McConnell* had conceded that the risk of circumvention of contribution limits might be posed by some large independent expenditures for express advocacy and on issue ads that were their functional equivalent. The FEC tried to bootstrap this concession into support for the proposition that only an intent-and-effect definition of "functional equivalent" could ensure that expenditures on issue ads did not circumvent the rule against independent expenditures on express ads—which might be regulated to avoid circumvention of the rule against corporate contributions.[101] But "[e]nough is enough," said the chief justice.[102] "[A] prophylaxis-upon-prophylaxis approach to regulating expression is not consistent with strict scrutiny."[103]

The First Amendment perspective reflected in *McConnell* was finally completely eradicated when Chief Justice Roberts rejected the argument that the ban on issue ads could be supported by the interest in preventing the kind of corruption to which the Court

[99] *Id.* at 2669 (citing Buckley, 424 U.S. at 42).

[100] *Id.* at 2670 (citing Ashcroft v. Free Speech Coalition, 535 U.S. 234, 255 (2002)).

[101] Cf. McConnell v. FEC, 540 U.S. 93, 205 (2003).

[102] WRTL II, 127 S. Ct. at 2672.

[103] *Id.*

referred in both *Austin* and *McConnell*, namely, the corruption represented by "the corrosive and distorting effects of immense aggregations of wealth that are accumulated with the help of the corporate form."[104] Accepting the argument, the chief justice said, "would call into question our holding in *Bellotti* that the corporate identity of a speaker does not strip corporations of all First Amendment rights."[105]

The unqualified reliance on *Bellotti* seems particularly significant. It suggests that *WRTL II*, despite the fact that it sustains only an as-applied challenge, will not readily succumb to interpretations that limit its First Amendment implications. WRTL originally couched its challenge to § 203 as a frontal attack, for example, insisting that all—and, by negative implication, only—"grass roots lobbying" should be exempt from its prohibitions. Chief Justice Roberts's opinion in *WRTL II* speaks of the necessity to protect *political speech*, not just grass roots lobbying. In addition, some of WRTL's *amici* had thought that WRTL's status as a non-profit advocacy corporation should be the factor that protected its speech, but the Chief Justice's reliance on *Bellotti* belies such a limitation. Thus, although it is true that Chief Justice Roberts did not explicitly overrule *McConnell*, his opinion seems to have sustained an as-applied challenge to BCRA in First Amendment terms even broader than either WRTL had originally sought or many of its amici had advocated.[106]

Justice Scalia wrote a vigorous opinion concurring in the judgment, and the fact and nature of his dispute with the Chief Justice occasioned considerable attention in the national media.[107] He refused to join Chief Justice Roberts's opinion not because he read the opinion as having gone too far to undermine § 203's facial validity but rather because he thought the First Amendment required the Court to go further. The chief justice's refusal to overrule *McConnell* outright, Justice Scalia argued, amounted to an ill-conceived and unwarranted attempt at judicial moderation—"faux judicial restraint" tantamount to "judicial obfuscation."[108] "[T]he principal

[104] Austin, 494 U.S. at 660.

[105] Federal Election Comm'n v. Wisconsin Right to Life, Inc., 127 S. Ct. 2652, 2673 (2007) (citing First National Bank v. Bellotti, 435 U.S. 765, 778 (1978)).

[106] *Id.* at 2673 n.10.

[107] See, e.g., Linda Greenhouse, Even in Agreement, Scalia Puts Roberts to Lash, N.Y. Times, June 28, 2007, at A1.

[108] WRTL II, 127 S. Ct. at 2684 n.7 (Scalia, J., concurring).

opinion's attempt at distinguishing *McConnell* is unpersuasive enough,"[109] wrote Justice Scalia, and "[t]he promise of an administrable as-applied rule that is both effective in the vindication of First Amendment rights and consistent with *McConnell*'s holding is [so] illusory"[110] that Chief Justice Roberts' refusal to overrule could not be justified. Justice Scalia regarded any test—including the test that the principal opinion adopted—that turned on the public's or a court's perception of an ad's import as inevitably failing to provide "the degree of clarity necessary."[111]

For Justice Scalia, as for the chief justice, the important thing was to "avoid the chilling of fundamental political discourse."[112] He, too, emphasized that "the line between electoral advocacy and issue advocacy dissolves in practice," but for him this fact represented "an indictment of the statute, not a justification of it."[113] He found each of the clear rules that advocates had offered "incompatible with *McConnell*'s holding that § 203 is facially constitutional."[114] Indeed, he said, "*any* clear rule that would protect all genuine issue ads would cover such a substantial number of ads prohibited by § 203 that § 203 would be rendered substantially overbroad"[115] and therefore facially invalid. Justice Scalia's conclusion was that *McConnell*'s contrary holding that § 203 is facially valid *should* and *could* be overruled, and he offered three reasons for this conclusion. First, it was wrongly decided in the first place. Second, it was impossible to devise an administrable as-applied rule to protect issue advocacy. And third, the case had not generated a settled body of law that relied upon it.

Justice Souter wrote for the dissenters. His opinion paid virtually no attention to the First Amendment premises on which the majority relied. His footnotes addressed some of the details of the chief justice's argument, but in the body of his opinion he did not make a sustained effort to refute either the chief justice's or Justice Scalia's

[109] *Id.*

[110] *Id.* at 2685.

[111] *Id.* at 2680.

[112] *Id.*

[113] *Id.* at 2681.

[114] *Id.* at 2683.

[115] *Id.*

fundamental premises.[116] Justice Souter began his dissent by describing neither the facts of the case before the Court nor the specifics of the doctrinal dispute that it presented. Rather, he offered a lengthy introduction that emphasized that huge sums of money are spent on political campaigns, recounted the empirical support he thought existed for the proposition that these sums—in particular insofar as they derive from the "concentrations of money in corporate and union treasuries"—represent a threat to democratic integrity, summarized the legislative efforts that had tried to control the money flow, and recapitulated the case law that had sustained it.[117] He read what *McConnell* had said about § 203 as having "exemplified a tradition of repeatedly sustain[ing] legislaton aimed at the corrosive and distorting effects of immense aggregations of wealth that are accumulated with the help of the corporate form."[118] Before undertaking to address the specific issue before the Court, he concluded his opening paragraphs with the following assertion, which captures the essence of his view that corporate participation in politics threatens democracy:

> From early in the 20th century through the decision in *McConnell,* we have acknowledged that the value of democratic integrity justifies a realistic response when corporations and labor organizations commit the concentrated moneys in their treasuries to electioneering.[119]

In view of this introduction and of the assumptions about corporate involvement in politics upon which it is based, it was hardly surprising that when Justice Souter finally addressed the merits of the controversy before the Court in *WRTL II* he disagreed with virtually every one of the chief justice's conclusions. To him it

[116] Chief Justice Roberts also responded specifically to Justice Souter's arguments (as he did to Justice Scalia's) in footnotes rather than in the text of his opinion. However, in the process of responding to the FEC's arguments and refuting their First Amendment premises, the chief justice implicitly responded to Justice Souter's very similar views.

[117] Federal Election Comm'n v. Wisconsin Right to Life, Inc., 127 S. Ct. 2652, 2687 (2007) (Souter, J., dissenting).

[118] *Id.* at 2696 (citing McConnell, 540 U.S. at 205) (omitting internal quotations and citations).

[119] *Id.* at 2697.

seemed blindingly obvious that WRTL's ads were the functional equivalent of express advocacy:

> [A]ny Wisconsin voter *who paid attention* would have known that Democratic Senator Feingold supported filibusters against Republican presidential judicial nominees, that the propriety of the filibusters was a major issue in the senatorial campaign, and that WRTL along with the Senator's Republican challengers opposed his reelection because of his position on filibusters.[120]

Justice Souter thought that the chief justice's "severely limited" test for "functional equivalence" was "flatly contrary to *McConnell*,[121] that his refusal to consider the context of an ad and its electioneering purpose amounted to an unwarranted blindness to the fact that any ad's "electioneering purpose" will easily be "objectively apparent from [its] content and context," and that the PAC alternative provides corporations '"with a constitutionally sufficient opportunity to engage in express advocacy."'[122]

II. What's Next: An Assessment

The disagreement between the majority and the dissenters in *WRTL II* has deep roots in the fundamentally different premises from which they reason about the First Amendment and campaign finance reform legislation. In *WRTL II*, that disagreement played itself out in doctrinal terms in a difference of opinion about how the First Amendment requires the Court to deal with the intractable fact that drove the Court in *Buckley* to hold FECA § 608(e)(1) unconstitutionally vague, which the majority in *WRTL II* repeatedly emphasized, namely, that

[120] *Id.* at 2698 (emphasis added). Chief Justice Roberts questioned whether Justice Souter's confidence in his implicit conclusion that Wisconsin voters routinely "paid attention" was justified. He cited a "prominent study" that found "that during the 2000 election cycle, 85 percent of respondents to a survey were not even able to name at least one candidate for the House of Representatives in their own district." *Id.* at 2667 n.6 (citation omitted).

[121] *Id.* at 2699.

[122] *Id.* at 2702 (citing McConnell, 540 U.S. at 203–04 (quoting Beaumont, 539 U.S. at 162)). Chief Justice Roberts responded to this argument of Justice Souter in a footnote, asserting that he had "overstate[d] his case" because "PAC's impose well-documented and onerous burdens, particularly on small nonprofits. See *MCFL*, 479 U.S. 238, 253–55 (1986) (plurality opinion)." *Id.* at 2671 n.9.

> the distinction between discussion of issues and candidates and advocacy of election or defeat of candidates may often dissolve in practical application. Candidates, especially incumbents, are intimately tied to public issues involving legislative proposals and governmental actions. Not only do candidates campaign on the basis of their positions on various public issues, but campaigns themselves generate issues of public interest.[123]

The basic issue is whether the Court is required to maintain the distinction between discussion of issues and candidates and advocacy of election or defeat of candidates when setting the limits of legislative power to regulate the political speech of corporations. Should the Court regard discussion of "issues and candidates" as *more* protected, *less* protected, or protected *to the same extent* as "advocacy of election or defeat of candidates"? The answer has become more divisive since the Court seems to have accepted the proposition that it is sometimes permissible to prohibit corporations and unions from making independent expenditures from their general treasury funds on express advocacy.[124] The practical difficulty of discerning the difference between express advocacy and discussion of issues has forced the Court to decide whether legislative power to restrict express advocacy should include the power also to restrict issue advocacy.

For the *WRTL II* majority, the answer to this question is a resounding no. Whatever difficulties might be presented in practice by the

[123] Buckley v. Valeo, 424 U.S. 1, 42 (1976).

[124] A majority of the Court has never directly questioned this conclusion, though members of the Court have challenged it from time to time. In United States v. UAW-CIO, 352 U.S. 567 (1957), the Court held that indirect contributions to union officials were covered by 18 U.S.C. § 610, which prohibited any corporation or labor organization from making a "contribution or expenditure in connection with" any election for federal office. The majority did not reach the issue of the statute's constitutionality, but Justice William O. Douglas did, in a dissent joined by Chief Justice Earl Warren and Justice Hugo Black. Justice Douglas described the constitutional issue, which he regarded as "fundamental to the electoral process and to the operation of our democratic society," as being "whether a union can express its views on the issues of an election and on the merits of the candidates, unrestrained and unfettered by the Congress." 352 U.S. at 593 (Douglas, J., dissenting). He objected to the majority's "innuendo" that "'active electioneering'" by union spokesmen is not covered by the First Amendment because he thought such a conclusion "ma[de] a sharp break with our political and constitutional heritage." *Id.* at 595 (Douglas, J., dissenting).

distinction between express and issue advocacy, the majority thinks that a clear First Amendment difference exists *in principle* between the two. They think that this difference requires the Court to exercise great care to define express advocacy narrowly. That is what *Buckley* tried to do when it described the "magic words" test, and it is plausible (though barely) to argue that *McConnell* preserved this narrow definition by concluding (if it did conclude) that § 203's prohibition of "electioneering communications" was constitutional only insofar as it applied to the functional equivalent of magic words. For the *WRTL II* majority, the conclusion that follows from that narrow definition of the speech that can be banned is that the *Court* must strictly police the boundary of express advocacy so as to leave discussion of issues *and candidates* as free as possible—since "candidates, especially incumbents, are intimately tied to public issues."

For the *WRTL II* dissenters, on the other hand, the distinction between express and issue advocacy was not merely difficult to draw but had become meaningless over the years—"a line in the sand drawn on a windy day."[125] They read *McConnell* as having held that all corporate and union "*electioneering speech*"—not just speech using words of express advocacy but all speech that has the purpose of affecting election outcomes—is "prohibitable."[126] What that implied for them was that, in order to *maximize* legislative power rather than to minimize it, the line had to be drawn between electioneering speech "clearly intended to influence the election" and "pure" issue ads. In other words, only "pure" issue ads were exempt from restriction. "[I]f an ad is reasonably understood as going beyond a discussion of issues (that is, if it can be understood as electoral advocacy), then by definition it is not 'genuine' or 'pure.'"[127] The dissent did not read *McConnell* as even having acknowledged a First Amendment freedom to spend corporate funds on genuine issue ads. In fact, they read it to have *rejected* the idea that "speakers possess an inviolable First Amendment right to engage in" issue

[125] Federal Election Comm'n v. Wisconsin Right to Life, Inc., 127 S. Ct. 2652, 2694 (2007) (Souter, J., dissenting) (citing McConnell, 540 U.S. at 126 n.16 (quoting "the former director of an advisory organization's PAC")).

[126] *Id.* at 2695.

[127] *Id.* at 2699.

advocacy.[128] To the dissenters, *McConnell* merely "left open the possibility of a 'genuine' or 'pure' issue ad that might not be open to regulation under § 203."[129]

Given that the majority and dissenting opinions approach and answer the basic issue posed in *WRTL II* so differently, perhaps Justice Scalia's criticism of the "faux judicial restraint" of the chief justice's opinion is well-taken. Perhaps judicial honor—and the rule of law—would have been fully satisfied only by a straightforward overruling of a precedent left standing with its theoretical heart cut out and its head severed. It is most definitely true that the fundamental premises of the chief justice's opinion were thoroughly inconsistent with those that animated the *McConnell* majority. And, despite its potential vagueness, the as-applied test he announced clearly did eviscerate § 203. Justice Souter, moreover, certainly understood that the chief justice's test would render § 203's limitations on "corporations corrosive spending when they enter the political arena . . . open to easy circumvention."[130] Chief Justice Roberts insisted that in future cases where doubts exist the tie must "go[] to the speaker, not the censor,"[131] and he tried to soothe Justice Scalia's doubts by carefully specifying that "no reasonable interpretation" means "*no reasonable interpretation*."[132] His admonitions may well prove insufficient to curb the enthusiasm of regulators, of course. Much will depend on how the FEC interprets *WRTL II*. Justice Alito's short concurrence suggests that, should regulators and courts misread the clear message of the principal opinion, the Court is likely to step in[133]—a promise of potential relief from abuse that Justice Scalia found wholly inadequate.[134] Nevertheless, what is worth emphasizing—and worth celebrating—is that it is *Buckley*'s theoretical heart, and not *McConnell*'s, that is now pumping with renewed vigor.

That reality is no doubt what most disturbed Justice Souter and the other dissenting justices. *WRTL II* is just the latest in the line of

[128] *Id.* at 2695 (citing McConnell, 540 U.S. at 190).

[129] *Id.* at 2699 (citing McConnell, 540 U.S. at 206–07).

[130] *Id.* at 2705.

[131] *Id.* at 2669.

[132] *Id.* at note 7.

[133] *Id.* at 2674 (Alito, J., concurring).

[134] *Id.* at 2682 n.5 (Scalia, J., concurring).

cases in which Justices Souter, Stevens, and Ginsburg have appeared to regard the right to free political speech that *Buckley* endorsed and *WRTL II* reaffirmed as a threat to, rather than the fundamental building block of, democracy.[135] (Justice Breyer has more often joined them than not.[136] Because of his *Randall* opinion, however, which purported to rely in part on *Buckley*, he must be credited with a tendency to value freedom somewhat more highly than his colleagues.)

In what follows, I will try to expose the nub of the controversy among the justices over the First Amendment and campaign finance regulation. I aim for transparency, and in doing so I will generalize about the roots of the controversy in a manner that I acknowledge runs the risk of oversimplifying what are in fact complex and subtle lines of argument. But the nub of the controversy lies in this: the majority and the dissents in *WRTL II* (or in any of the campaign finance cases that the Court has decided since *Austin*) occupy *no* common First Amendment ground. Though they disagree in good faith, both of their points of view cannot be right, and the differences that exist between them are at such a fundamental level that they leave scant room for compromise. Some commentators imply that "balancing" might help to untie the Gordian knot,[137] but without more clarity than they or the Court itself has provided about the nature and content of the interests to be assessed a balancing approach carries little prospect of success. Reading the differing opinions in search of an opening wedge for genuine engagement, one finds the justices talking past one another. They share neither empirical assumptions nor theoretical premises. For the majority in *WRTL II*, freedom to spend money on political speech—including

[135] Cf. Nixon v. Shrink Missouri Gov't PAC, 528 U.S. 377 (2000); Austin v. Michigan Chamber of Commerce, 494 U.S. 652 (1990); Colorado Republican Fed. Campaign Comm. v. Federal Election Comm'n, 518 U.S. 604 (1996); Federal Election Comm'n v. Beaumont, 539 U.S. 146 (2003); McConnell v. Federal Election Comm'n, 540 U.S. 93 (2003); Randall v. Sorrell, 126 S. Ct. 2479 (2006).

[136] See cases cited *supra* note 135.

[137] Richard L. Hasen, *supra* note 9, at 62 (urging the Court to engage in "careful balancing and policing for self-dealing under the participatory self-government rationale"); cf. Allison Hayward, *supra* note 15, at 216 (suggesting that, while there is "no coherent middle road," it is nevertheless impossible to "reason a path absent some ad hoc balancing based on the justices' individual experience, biases, and what may appear 'perfectly obvious' to them").

freedom of corporations to spend money on political speech about issues—is *the answer*. More speech coming from more points of view is always better than less speech coming from fewer. Restricting speech threatens democracy. Chief Justice Roberts, for example, thought that *WRTL II* was quintessentially a case "about political speech."[138] And in Justice Scalia's view, "perhaps [the Court's] most important constitutional task is to assure freedom of political speech."[139]

The dissenters take an utterly opposing view. From their perspective, corporate and union freedom to spend money on political speech is *the problem*. Justice Souter's dissent articulates their position in a nutshell:

> Devoting concentrations of money in self-interested hands to the support of political campaigning [as freedom permits corporations and unions to do] . . . threatens the capacity of this democracy to represent its constituents and the confidence of its citizens in their capacity to govern themselves. These are the elements summed up in the notion of political integrity, giving *it* [not freedom] a value second to none in a free society.[140]

The competing positions have manifested themselves in a multiplicity of ways as the debate on the Court has played out. The issues and the arguments have varied in detail, of course, and I have described the doctrinal point at which they came to a head in *WRTL II*. A few examples of the major differences in basic perspective will suffice to illustrate the irreconcilable tension these differences reflect. First, a caveat about what follows. I acknowledge that I am convinced by the First Amendment views expressed by Chief Justice Roberts and Justice Scalia. I will not undertake in these pages further to advocate the merits of their views—or of my own. In many forums, I have articulated and attempted to defend my normative position

[138] Federal Election Comm'n v. Wisconsin Right to Life, Inc., 127 S. Ct. 2652, 2673 (2007).

[139] *Id.* at 2686 (Scalia, J., concurring).

[140] *Id.* at 2689 (Souter, J., dissenting) (emphasis added).

that most campaign finance regulations are unconstitutional, ineffective, and likely to do more harm than good.[141] In addition I have in prior writings tried to make clear both the many deficiencies I observe in the empirical underpinnings of the case for regulation, as well as the difficulty I think exists in giving meaningful content to rhetorical invocations of such vague concepts as "electoral integrity" and the like.[142]

The current majority believes that political freedom is both unambiguously good and central to democratic government. They regard it, moreover, as having been very much at stake in *WRTL II*. They think that the First Amendment protects the right to spend money to speak about politics because freedom to speak about political issues is at the amendment's core, and speaking costs money. When corporations and unions spend money to engage in political speech, the majority does not worry that the ideas and issues that they discuss—or the fact that it is corporations and unions that discuss them—will corrode or distort or harm the political process. It has sometimes been thought that the First Amendment protects corporate and union speakers because corporations and unions *qua* corporations and unions, just like natural persons have First Amendment rights, but the majority in *WRTL II* implicitly rejected such a conclusion. Instead, the majority justices focused on protecting the *speech*:

[141] See, e.g., Lillian R. BeVier, Campaign Finance 'Reform' Proposals: A First Amendment Analysis (Cato Institute, 1997) (providing "a full accounting of regulation's cost to political freedoms"); Lillian R. BeVier, Money and Politics: The First Amendment and Campaign Finance Reform, 73 Cal. L. Rev. 1045 (1985) (arguing that the general application of fatal strict scrutiny analysis to laws regulating political giving and spending is "not merely plausible but probably correct"); Lillian R. BeVier, Campaign Finance Reform: Specious Arguments, Intractable Dilemmas, 94 Colum. L. Rev. 1258 (1994) (articulating "a number of reasons for skepticism about the soundness of contemporary arguments in support of campaign finance reform" as of the Court's ruling in Austin v. Michigan Chamber of Commerce); Lillian R. BeVier, The Issue of Issue Advocacy, 85 Va. L. Rev. 1761 (1999) (identifying "the explicitly normative, quasi-theoretical, nondoctrinally anchored case for regulating issue advocacy" and "outlining some reasons for rejecting it"); Lillian R. BeVier, What Ails Us? A Review of Ackerman and Ayres, Voting with Dollars: A New Paradigm for Campaign Finance, 112 Yale L.J. 1135 (2003) (asserting that "reforming [the campaign finance] system" will not remedy the problems of citizen disengagement and interest-group competition); BeVier, *supra* note 13 (noting that the McConnell majority "turned the First Amendment around").

[142] See sources cited in *supra* note 141.

"These cases are about political speech,"[143] affirmed the chief justice, who was echoed by Justice Scalia's insistence that it is the Court's "most important constitutional task to assure freedom of political speech."[144]

The majority has obviously concluded that having access to many voices and being able to evaluate the differing views they express enables citizens to hold their government accountable more effectively than they can when speech—whatever the identity of the speaker—is restricted. Perhaps as a corollary, they also appear to think that legislators are too likely to be self-interested and too eager to retain the power they have already acquired to be trusted to guard the "integrity of democracy."[145] As the majority sees the political world, a host of intractable realities renders legislators impotent to reduce the amount of money spent on attempting to acquire political power. They think efforts by legislators to rid politics of money—even if such efforts were benignly motivated—will always be plagued by unintended consequences and hence that such efforts have been and always will be futile.[146]

With FECA and BCRA, Congress has created a pervasive regulatory regime that has concentrated power in Washington-based interest groups, stifled grass roots political activity, embedded incumbent office-holders, and undermined the already fragile incentives that individuals have to participate in efforts to hold their government

[143] WRTL II, 127 S. Ct. at 2673. Except to dismiss the "notion that a ban on campaign speech could also embrace issue advocacy," because to do so would call into question the Court's holding in "*Bellotti* that the corporate identity of a speaker does not strip corporations of all free speech rights," the chief justice took almost no notice of the fact that Wisconsin Right to Life is a corporation. *Id.*

[144] *Id.* at 2686 (Scalia, J., concurring).

[145] See McConnell, 540 U.S. 93, 263 (Scalia, J., dissenting):

> Those in power, even giving them the benefit of the greatest good will, are inclined to believe that what is good for them is good for the country. . .The first instinct of power is the retention of power, and, under a Constitution that requires periodic elections, that is best achieved by the suppression of election-time speech.

[146] See Federal Election Comm'n v. Wisconsin Right to Life, Inc., 127 S. Ct. 2652, 2686-87 (2007) (Scalia, J., dissenting) (finding "wondrous irony" in the "fact that the effect of BCRA has been to concentrate more political power in the hands of the country's wealthiest individuals and their so-called 527 organizations, unregulated by § 203").

accountable. Thus, the majority's perception of how the First Amendment requires the Court to go about determining the constitutionality of campaign finance regulations marries its commitment to the political freedom that is at stake to its deep skepticism about whether government regulation of political activity can ever be benignly motivated or benevolent in its effects.

The current dissenters disagree both about what is at stake and about political reality. To them, campaign finance regulation is not about freedom. It is about money, and about the need to neutralize its political leverage. Justice Souter's dissent repeatedly invokes the threat to "political integrity,"[147] posed by "money in huge amounts,"[148] "huge sums"[149] of money, "money in self-interested hands,"[150] "vast sums" of money,[151] and "immense aggregations of wealth."[152] The dissenters think that the need to "restrict[] the electoral leverage of concentrations of money in large corporations"[153] trumps whatever interest in political freedom might be at stake. Indeed, Justice Souter's dissent suggests that freedom to spend money to speak about political issues is no more protected by the First Amendment than is freedom to spend money to grow wheat for one's own consumption[154] or to pay child laborers.[155] That at least seems to be an appropriate inference: the Court should accord legislators the same deference when regulating political expenditures as it accords them when regulating the economy. Perhaps the dissenters simply do not value political freedom as highly as they value "democratic integrity," but there is no doubt that they do not regard freedom as importantly at risk in the regulation of expenditures on political speech by corporations and unions.

When they turn to assessing political reality, and they review the history of campaign finance, the dissenters perceive that Congress

[147] *Id.* at 2689 (Souter, J., dissenting).

[148] *Id.* at 2687.

[149] *Id.* at 2688.

[150] *Id.* at 2689.

[151] *Id.* at 2694.

[152] *Id.* at 2696.

[153] *Id.* at 2687.

[154] Wickard v. Filburn, 317 U.S. 111 (1942).

[155] Hammer v. Dagenhart, 247 U.S. 251 (1918).

has achieved "steady improvement of the national election laws."[156] They regard BCRA as but the most recent step on the road to a well-functioning democracy.[157] From those facts, and from the perspective implicit in the lengthy introduction to Justice Souter's *WRTL II* opinion, one can infer that the dissenters regard the progression of laws regulating campaign finance practices since the Tilman Act in 1907 as having achieved their goal of "sustain[ing] the active, alert responsibility of the individual citizen in a democracy for the wise conduct of government."[158] For the dissenters, the fact that BCRA and its antecedent statutory reforms are necessary to counter the threat that "concentrated wealth" poses to "electoral integrity"—especially the concentrated wealth possessed by corporations—is both palpable and self-evident:

> This century-long tradition of legislation and judicial precedent rests on facing undeniable facts and testifies to an equally undeniable value. Campaign finance reform has been a series of reactions to documented threats to electoral integrity obvious to any voter, posed by large sums of money from corporate or union treasuries, with no redolence of 'grassroots' about them. . . . From early in the 20th century through the decision in *McConnell*, we have acknowledged that the value of democratic integrity justifies a realistic response when corporations and labor organizations commit the concentrated moneys in their treasuries to electioneering.[159]

Yet parsing Justice Souter's opinion for the "undeniable facts" upon which he claims the "century-long tradition" rests, one does not find much empirical evidence regarding anything other than evidence of the amounts of money that have recently been spent on state and federal elections,[160] of the statements of politicians who have railed against moneyed interests,[161] and of the increasingly

[156] McConnell v. FEC, 540 U.S. 93, 117 (2003).

[157] *Id.* at 224.

[158] Federal Election Comm'n v. Wisconsin Right to Life, Inc., 127 S. Ct. 2652, 2690 (2007) (Souter, J., dissenting).

[159] *Id.* at 2697.

[160] *Id.* at 2687–88.

[161] *Id.* at 2689–90.

stringent legislation that Congress has passed.[162] Opinion polls are cited, for example, to support the factual claim that "pervasive public cynicism" exists;[163] congressional debates and Senate reports are cited for the proposition that more reforms were needed when BCRA was being considered;[164] and rhetoric on the floor of the Senate is cited as though it reliably stated empirical fact.[165] In addition, the "value" to which Justice Souter says century-long tradition testifies is only "undeniable" if one ignores, as his opinion unfortunately does, the competing values that others—not merely, but certainly including, the current majority—have identified.[166] The value that Justice Souter treasures may indeed be the one that ought to trump, but its primacy is at the very least hardly "undeniable." Still, Justice Souter's words stand as vivid exemplars of the unbridgeable chasm between his and the other dissenters' fundamental premises and the deeply held convictions of those in the current majority on the Court who disagree.

There is little hope for reconciliation of the competing views of the current majority and the dissenters. Their disagreement is far more fundamental than a simple dispute about doctrine or about what *McConnell* held and whether *WRTL II* actually or only in effect overrules it. The problem—and it is a problem that has plagued the

[162] *Id.* at 2689–97. A few scholarly efforts have been made to challenge some of the empirical assumptions that support Justice Souter's opinion, but he does not join issue with their claims. See, e.g., David M. Primo and Jeffrey Milyo, Campaign Finance Laws and Political Efficacy: Evidence from the States, 5 Election L.J. 23, 36 (2006) (reporting results of a study of the link between campaign finance laws and citizen perceptions of democratic rule, which found that "the effect of campaign finance laws is sometimes perverse, rarely positive, and never more than modest"); Nathaniel Persily and Kelli Lammie, The Law of Democracy: Campaign Finance after McCain-Feingold: Perceptions of Corruption and Campaign Finance: When Public Opinion Determines Constitutional Law, 153 U. Pa. L. Rev. 119, 174 (2004) (reporting results of a study concluding that citizens of countries with radically different systems of campaign finance regulation share Americans' lack of '"confidence in the system of representative government,"' which suggests that campaign finance reformers might be surprised and "disappointed by the intractability and psychological roots of that lack of confidence").

[163] *Id.* at 2688.

[164] *Id.* at 2694.

[165] *Id.* at 2690 (recounting the lamentation of an early reformer).

[166] See, e.g., Richard A. Epstein, McConnell v. Federal Election Commission: A Deadly Dose of Double Deference, 3 Election L.J. 231 (2004).

Court since *Buckley*—is that the justices do not reason from the same premises, either as a matter of First Amendment principle or as a matter of the empirical assumptions that drive their respective analyses. They assess the worth of political freedom differently. They entertain wildly divergent assessments of the need for legislation to "promote democracy."[167] And they hold entirely disparate views about either the possibility that legislation can actually effectuate genuine improvement or the reliability of the elected officeholders who claim to have acted as guardians of the interests of those who seek to have them voted out of office.

I have not aimed in this brief essay to make once again the case for freedom and against regulation. My aim, rather, has been to demonstrate the nature of the chasm of theory, perception, and passionate conviction that separates those who advocate regulation of the political process from those who reject it in principle. Bridging the gap that exists between them will require more than cogent legal argument about matters of doctrinal detail. Rather, it will require one group or the other to relinquish fundamental beliefs about our constitutional democracy and about the role of the Court in preserving it. Compromise on such matters is not in the cards. Thus, the prospects for reconciliation cannot be thought bright.

[167] Briffault, *supra* note 8, at 149.

When Easy Cases Make Bad Law: *Davenport v. Washington Education Association* and *Washington v. Washington Education Association*

*Erik S. Jaffe**

It seems uncharitable to be critical of a case in which the side you supported prevailed, but that is the odd position in which I find myself regarding the Supreme Court's recent decision in *Davenport v. Washington Education Association* (decided together with *Washington v. Washington Education Association*).[1] Despite the laudable result, the Court in *Davenport* took a rather circuitous path to that result and ended up doing violence to the First Amendment along the way. Rather than simply stating that the lower court had gotten things exactly backwards—finding a First Amendment right in favor of the Union rather than the nonunion employees regarding coerced excess "agency" fees the Union had no valid justification for charging in the first place—the Court instead took a restrictive approach to the First Amendment and emphasized state discretion in order to turn back the Union's challenge. That emphasis on state discretion, rather than on nonunion-employee rights, likely will encourage further uncertainty and litigation in states such as Washington that improperly allow unions to intentionally collect agency fees in excess of their chargeable expenses. The Court's approach to the First Amendment, and its treatment of the supposed state interest in the "integrity" of the elections process said to support the limited opt-in requirement in this case, could also have untoward consequences in the campaign finance area.

*Solo appellate attorney, Erik S. Jaffe, P.C.

[1] 127 S. Ct. 2372 (2007). My support for the prevailing side took the form of filing a brief on behalf of the Cato Institute, the Reason Foundation, and the Center for Individual Freedom, as *amici curiae* in support of the petitioners in the combined cases (available at http://www.esjpc.com/WEA-Cato-Amicus-Final.pdf).

I. Background

The Supreme Court's decision in *Davenport* is the latest in a long line of cases addressing the First Amendment implications of so-called "union-shop" and "agency-shop" agreements. Under a union-shop agreement, an employer agrees to hire only union members; consequently, anyone who wants to work for the employer must join the union. An agency-shop agreement does not require employees to join the union, but instead requires employees who are not members of the union to pay an "agency" fee to the union. The union in such arrangements has the obligation to represent all employees in collective bargaining and related activities, and the agency fee is intended to eliminate "free-riding" by nonmembers.

As the Supreme Court observed in *Davenport,* a long line of cases has established that while agency-shop agreements are permissible and serve the supposedly important interest in avoiding free-riding by nonmembers on the collective bargaining efforts of members, such agreements, particularly with regard to public-sector employees, also impinge upon the First Amendment rights of nonmembers by forcing them to support the speech of the union.[2] Over the years the balance that had been struck is that nonmember employees can be forced to contribute only to union expenses that are "germane" to the collective bargaining and related activities on which the employees are supposedly free-riding. As for expenses attributable to union activities that are *not* germane to collective bargaining and the like, and especially expenses for ideological speech and activity by the union, such expenses are not properly chargeable to nonmembers. Ordinarily, the separation of chargeable and non-chargeable expenses results in an agency fee that is somewhat less than regular union dues given that unions spend a portion of the dues they receive from members on activities and speech that are not chargeable to nonmembers. The state of Washington, however, does things a bit differently.

Washington permits a union that negotiates an agency–shop agreement with an employer to collect agency fees from nonmember employees at a level *equal* to the amount that members of the union

[2]127 S. Ct. at 2376–77 (citing and discussing Machinists v. Street, 367 U.S. 740 (1961), Abood v. Detroit Bd. of Ed., 431 U.S. 209 (1977), Teachers v. Hudson, 475 U.S. 292 (1986), and Lehnert v. Ferris Faculty Assn., 500 U.S. 507 (1991)).

pay as dues.[3] Such an amount, however, represents more than just the *pro rata* costs of collective bargaining, contract administration, and grievance adjustment: it includes the costs of political contributions and other non-germane activities that have nothing to do with the collective bargaining process and that are not properly chargeable to nonmembers.

Nonmember employees of an agency shop previously could recover such non-chargeable portion of their agency fee only by periodically objecting in response to a so-called *Hudson* packet identifying the excess charges and giving the employees a limited opportunity to opt-out of such charges. That system effectively enabled the union automatically to take money to which it had no proper entitlement and then placed the burden on the nonmembers to seek a rebate of money that was rightfully theirs to begin with.

That opt-out approach regarding excess agency fees was changed in part when the people of Washington adopted by initiative a provision that forbids a union from using excess agency fees for political purposes without the affirmative consent of the nonmembers from whom the excess fees were taken. The relevant provision, RCW 42.17.760 ("§ 760"), provides:

> A labor organization may not use agency shop fees paid by an individual who is not a member of the organization to make contributions or expenditures to influence an election or to operate a political committee, unless affirmatively authorized by the individual.

Instead of the opt-out system previously in effect, the law thus requires an "opt-in" system in order for a union to convert excess fees taken without employee consent into voluntary political contributions to the union.

In litigation by the state of Washington and by nonunion employees to enforce § 760, the Washington Education Association ("WEA" or the "Union") challenged the opt-in requirement as being a violation of its supposed First Amendment right to use excess agency fees for non-chargeable purposes absent affirmative objection from the nonmember employees. When the case eventually reached the

[3] Wash. Rev. Code §§ 41.59.060, 41.59.100 (2007).

Washington Supreme Court, that court, over a vigorous dissent, agreed with the Union and struck down § 760.

The court below reached that conclusion based on the ill-conceived grounds that § 760 abridged the First Amendment rights of the Union to engage in political association with nonmembers who simply fail to respond to the periodic opt-out notice, and that any competing rights of dissenting nonmembers were adequately protected by the *Hudson* opt-out procedure, which served as a less restrictive means of protecting their rights without burdening the supposed First Amendment rights of the Union.[4] In reaching that rather bold conclusion, the court relied on language from an earlier U.S. Supreme Court case, *Machinists v. Street*, which held, in the context of a union shop (*i.e.*, mandatory union membership for all employees), that a union member's dissent from the use of union dues for political purposes unrelated to collective bargaining "should not be presumed."[5] The court also relied on the supposed association rights of the Union and employees who had not actually joined the Union but who might silently wish to make a contribution of their excess agency fees.[6]

II. The Supreme Court's Opinion

In a unanimous judgment (and partly unanimous opinion by Justice Antonin Scalia), the Supreme Court reversed and held that § 760's opt-in requirement did not violate the Union's First Amendment rights.

The unanimous portion of the opinion began by summarizing the constitutional distinction between chargeable and non-chargeable expenses under the Court's earlier cases and then suggested, without elaboration, that "[n]either *Hudson* nor any of our other cases, however, has held that the First Amendment mandates a public-sector union obtain affirmative consent before spending a nonmember's agency fees for purposes not chargeable under *Abood*."[7] The Court then assumed, for purposes of the consolidated cases, that

[4]State v. Washington Educ. Ass'n, 130 P.3d 352, 364 (Wash. 2006).

[5]*Id.* at 358–59, 364 (citing International Ass'n of Machinists v. Street, 367 U.S. 740, at 760–64 (1961)).

[6]*Id.* at 364 (citing Boy Scouts of America v. Dale, 530 U.S. 640 (2000)).

[7]Davenport v. Washington Education Association, 127 S. Ct. 2372,2377 (2007).

the opt-out procedures applied by the Union were consistent with the constitutional requirements of *Hudson* and *Abood* with regard to non-chargeable expenses.[8]

Having thus assumed that it was constitutionally permissible for the state to allow the Union to charge the excess fees in the first place, subject to a subsequent opt-out procedure, the Court nonetheless characterized as "unusual" and "extraordinary" the power granted the Union to exact agency fees at all, much less the power to tax fees beyond the amounts chargeable to collective bargaining and related activities. Viewing the entire power of the Union to charge agency fees as being merely a government-granted privilege that could be eliminated entirely without offending the Constitution, the Court held that the "far less restrictive limitation" on the use of such fees for election-related speech "is of no greater constitutional concern."[9]

The Court similarly rejected the lower court's purported balancing of First Amendment rights as between the Union and the nonmember employees "for the simple reason that unions have no constitutional entitlement to the fees of nonmember-employees" in the first place.[10] According to the Court, cases such as *Abood* and *Hudson,* which require unions to give nonmember employees the opportunity to object to allegedly non-chargeable portions of agency fees, establish a *minimum* set of procedures for such agency-shop arrangements in those cases, not a maximum set of safeguards beyond which a union gets to claim constitutional offense.[11]

As for the language from *Street* that dissent should not be presumed, relied upon by the court below, the Court explained that such language posed a limitation only on the power of the *courts* to enjoin the expenditure of funds collected from all employees, including those who had not objected. But while "courts have an obligation to interfere with a union's statutory entitlement no more than is necessary to vindicate the rights of nonmembers," said the Court, such restrictions do not apply to the legislatures or voters

[8] *Id.*

[9] *Id.* at 2379.

[10] *Id.*

[11] *Id.*

that have granted (and hence can limit) the scope of the entitlement to collect agency fees.[12]

The Court also quickly disposed of the lower court's odd reliance on *Boy Scouts of America v. Dale* as supporting the Union's right to associate with employees who had declined to join the Union but silently may have wished to contribute the excess agency fees taken from them to the Union for purposes of election-related speech. Needless to say, the Supreme Court found such reliance misplaced, noting that, unlike the compelled association at issue in *Dale*, § 760 neither compelled the Union to accept unwanted members nor otherwise made union membership less attractive.[13]

In a further portion of the opinion joined by only six of the justices, the Court rejected a number of alternative First Amendment arguments made by the Union though not raised in, or relied upon by, the court below.[14]

Rejecting the Union's argument that § 760 imposes a restriction on how the Union may spend "its" money for political purposes, and discriminates between certain political spending by unions and supposedly comparable spending by corporations, the Court found the campaign finance cases relied upon by the Union inapplicable because § 760 was not a restriction on the *Union's* money. Rather, it placed a condition "upon the Union's extraordinary *state* entitlement to acquire and spend *other people's* money."[15] The Court observed that it would have been a different matter if the restriction were on union spending of the voluntary dues from its members, rather than involuntary exactions from nonmembers.[16]

The Court then noted that the question thus became one of whether § 760 was a constitutional condition on the spending of the excess agency fees. Rejecting the Union's argument that § 760 drew unconstitutional content-based distinctions between spending excess

[12] *Id.*

[13] *Id.* at 2380 n.2 (second paragraph).

[14] The three justices not joining this part of the opinion—The Chief Justice, Justice Breyer, and Justice Alito—simply declined to reach the Union's further arguments, preferring that they instead be presented to and ruled upon by the lower courts in the first instance. *Id.* at 2383 (Breyer, J., concurring in part and concurring in the judgment).

[15] *Id.* at 2380.

[16] *Id.* n.2 (first paragraph)

agency fees on election-related speech and spending such excess on other non-chargeable speech, the Court instead declared that the content distinctions here were innocuous and permissible. The Court analogized the speech at issue in this case to obscenity or defamation—speech that itself is unprotected and of negligible First Amendment value—and noted that content discrimination within such "a class of proscribable speech does not pose a threat to the marketplace of ideas when the selected subclass is chosen for the very reason that the entire class can be proscribed."[17] Also particularly relevant, said the Court, are situations in which the government acts in a non-regulatory capacity—such as when it subsidizes speech or allows speech on government property that is a nonpublic forum—and is given greater leeway to use content-based distinctions.[18]

The Court held that § 760 was a reasonable and viewpoint–neutral limitation and did not impermissibly distort the marketplace of ideas. Addressing the objection that § 760 did not cover all union spending of agency fees for nonchargeable purposes, the Court argued that the purpose of § 760 was "to protect the integrity of the election process . . . which the voters evidently thought was being impaired by the infusion of money extracted from nonmembers of unions without their consent. The restriction on the state-bestowed entitlement was thus limited to the state-created harm that the voters sought to remedy."[19] The Court concluded finally that the content-based limitation at issue "[q]uite obviously" involved "no suppression of ideas . . . since the union remains as free as any other entity to participate in the electoral process with all available funds other than the state-coerced agency fees lacking affirmative permission."[20]

[17] *Id.* at 2381–82 (citing, R. A. V. v. St. Paul, 505 U.S. 377, 382 (1992)).

[18] *Id.* (citing Regan v. Taxation With Representation of Wash., 461 U.S. 540, 548–50 (1983), and Cornelius v. NAACP Legal Defense & Educ. Fund, Inc., 473 U.S. 788, 799–800, 806 (1985)).

[19] *Id.* at 2381. The Court expressly limited its holding to the application of § 760 to public-sector unions, taking no position on its lawfulness as applied to private-sector unions that receive agency-shop fees as a matter of contract and government non-interference rather than affirmative government compulsion. *Id.* at 2382. It declined to consider any overbreadth claim as such an argument was not raised by the Union. *Id.*

[20] *Id.*

III. Discussion

As I noted at the outset, I think *Davenport* was an easy case and that the Supreme Court reached the correct result. The reasons I think the case was easy, however, are not the reasons given by the Court in its opinion. Rather, I think the dispositive consideration is that not only did the Union lack any "right" to the excess fees, but in fact the First Amendment rights of the nonmember employees *precluded* the state from giving the Union the power to compel even the *initial* payment of such excess fees. Before defending that stricter application of the First Amendment, however, it is useful to consider some of the problems with the Supreme Court's reliance on state discretion, rather than employee rights, to reach its result.

A. Section 760's Content-Based Condition on the Union's Statutory Privilege Raises More Significant First Amendment Concerns than the Court Acknowledges

Regarding the unanimous portion of the Court's opinion, the holding that the collection of agency fees is an extraordinary privilege, rather than a right, is certainly correct as far as it goes, but it does not go far enough to resolve the First Amendment question. Even privileges may be subject to conditions that violate the First Amendment, as the Court implicitly recognizes in the latter (non-unanimous) portion of its opinion. That the privilege of collecting non-chargeable fees at issue in this case is unusual or extraordinary adds little to the analysis given the Court's *assumption* that Washington's system of collecting such excess fees subject to later objection satisfies *Abood* and *Hudson*.

The Court's further holding that *Abood* and *Hudson* establish *minimum* procedures rather than maximum safeguards that cannot be exceeded again is certainly correct as far as it goes, but once again does not resolve whether the imposition of more burdensome procedures—applied in a content-based manner to only a subset of the excess agency fees—imposes an unconstitutional condition regardless whether those same procedures would be innocuous if applied uniformly to all non-chargeable expenses covered by the excess agency fees.

Insofar as the Court's initial approach is offered as only a first step in an unconstitutional conditions analysis, it is not particularly troubling. Insofar as it is offered as the *end* of the analysis, it seems to slight the unconstitutional conditions doctrine and threatens to revive the discredited rights/privileges distinction and the mistaken notion that the greater power to eliminate agency fees entirely includes the lesser power to regulate them at will. Although the Court certainly does not go that far, the language of the opinion leans heavily in that direction, to the detriment of First Amendment doctrine generally.

As for the Court's treatment of the language from *Street* that dissent is not to be presumed, its reconciliation of that case is a bit more troubling. *Street*, of course, dealt with the very different situation of a *union* shop rather than an agency shop, where all employees were in fact members of the union, albeit some of those memberships were involuntary. Because a union and its voluntary members indeed have a First Amendment right to associate and to use their voluntary dues for expressive purposes (including purposes unrelated to collective bargaining), and because there is no facially obvious way to distinguish voluntary membership from involuntary membership, it is at least a fair notion that dissent is not to be presumed as to *all* union *members* and that such a presumption would indeed create an added burden on the free association of the union and its voluntary members.

In the agency-shop context, however, there is no possibility of mistakenly burdening the association of a union and its voluntary members, because any limitation on the use of excess agency fees by definition does not apply at all to the ordinary dues of voluntary union members. Agency fees, by their very nature, are exacted only from employees who have declined to join the union, for whatever reasons, and as to them not only can dissent from the exaction of excess fees be presumed, it in fact should be presumed and arguably must be presumed in order to protect the First Amendment rights of the nonmembers.

Rather than distinguish *Street* on such grounds, however, the Court seemed to suggest that *Street*'s language might well apply even in the agency-shop context, at least where the state legislature agreed that dissent should not be presumed. While state legislatures (or voters) enacting state law are not bound by *Street*'s presumptions concerning assent or dissent, the Court's suggestion that federal courts applying the First Amendment might indeed by bound even in the agency-shop context undermines the rights of nonmember employees who, unlike the union members in *Street*, certainly *can* be presumed, and in fact *should* be presumed, to dissent from a union's compulsory exaction of agency fees in excess of the amount germane to collective bargaining.

The Court's opinion becomes more troubling still when it moves on to the non-unanimous discussion of whether § 760 is an unconstitutional condition on the use of excess agency fees. Analogizing the Union's use of agency fees for non-chargeable political speech to a class of "proscribable" speech such as obscenity or defamation is a doubtful and dangerous stretch. Political speech in general, and the election-related political speech targeted by § 760 in particular, has ample First Amendment value quite unlike obscenity or defamation. The *value* of that speech is unrelated to the source of the funds or to whether the state could eliminate agency fees entirely. The State could just as easily increase my taxes, yet that does not make the speech I pay for with a tax refund any less valuable. (And if the state increased my taxes using content-based distinctions, that action would likewise raise a First Amendment problem, notwithstanding that non-content-based increases in taxes raise no First Amendment concerns regardless whether they decrease my available resources for speech.)

The analogy to proscribable speech further breaks down in that even assuming the class of agency fees, and speech resulting therefrom, to be proscribable in the manner suggested by the Court because it is involuntarily extracted from third-parties, the sub-class of money spent on election-related speech is no more or less involuntary than any other non-chargeable portion of the agency fee spent on speech, and hence the content-based burden imposed on funds for election-related speech is *not* imposed for the same reason that the entire class can be proscribed. Rather, the burden of § 760 is imposed out of concern for the integrity of elections in particular, an interest based either on a particular objection to unions as speakers in the election context—the usual concern in the campaign finance context—or else as merely a proxy for the rights of the employees whose funds may be used for speech contrary to their desires, at which point it is not a concern unique to election-related speech (*i.e.*, § 760 is underinclusive). The Court's casual acceptance of the undefined and amorphous "integrity" of elections as an interest sufficient to justify content-based restrictions on political speech should also cause concern among First Amendment opponents of so-called "campaign finance reform." While the Court's recent campaign finance cases have shown an increased willingness to scrutinize such laws critically under the First Amendment, the glib acceptance of the purported interest here is surprising and unsettling, particularly coming from Justice Scalia.

The analogy to government subsidies for speech, which can be content-based as long as they are not viewpoint discriminatory, also falls short in that this is not a government subsidy of speech using tax dollars but rather the direct transfer of funds from one private party to another. Treating agency fees as if they were government subsidies rather than the taking of private funds risks collapsing the distinctions between government speech, government–subsidized speech, and compelled private support for third-party speech. While those distinctions may indeed be thin to begin with (and I have argued that the *Abood* line of cases should apply even to government speech using general tax revenues), given that the Court has effectively taken the First Amendment out of consideration for government speech, building the analogy between government-authorized agency-fee collection and government-directed subsidies or speech only threatens to destroy the protections set out by the *Abood* line of cases. That should be of great concern to First Amendment advocates, particularly in states that are likely to be pro-union and have little concern for the rights of nonmember employees.

In any event, suffice it to say that none of this gets much attention in the opinion, and the entire matter is brushed aside in a few sentences. In fact, the Court's suggestion that there "obviously" is no suppression of ideas afoot is anything but obvious given both the content-based and speaker-based nature of § 760. Indeed, if anything, there seems to be a battle over whether to help or hinder the expression of union views in elections. The Washington *legislature* seemingly leans toward aiding the unions and their political speech by giving them a presumption of assent when collecting and spending non-chargeable fees in the first place, while the *people* of Washington seem to lean against the unions, thus partially repealing the union-favoring presumption of assent adopted by the legislature. The fact that unions remain free to spend their membership dues and other money as they see fit hardly rebuts the notion that the purpose behind § 760 is content or speaker driven. Such distinctions need not suppress all speech in order to run afoul of the First Amendment. (A tax on or subsidy for only a particular viewpoint in the election context would almost certainly violate the First Amendment, regardless whether it fully suppressed or overwhelmingly magnified the viewpoint at issue.)

Overall, because the Court *assumed* that the Washington system of exacting agency fees overtly in excess of chargeable expenses was consistent with *Abood* and *Hudson*, the Court was forced to find indirect ways of getting around the unconstitutional conditions doctrine. The means chosen by the Court were not entirely convincing, and in fact threaten to weaken First Amendment protections that in other contexts are important to achieving the proper constitutional result.

B. Finding that the First Amendment Precludes Granting Unions the "Privilege" of Exacting Fees for Non-Chargeable Expenses Yields the Same Result with Less Injury to Other First Amendment Doctrines

The far simpler means of resolving this case was to recognize the seemingly self-evident unconstitutionality of knowingly collecting excess agency fees in the first place. The notion (asserted by the lower court and simply assumed, *arguendo*, by the Supreme Court) that the First Amendment is satisfied by providing the opportunity for a rebate of that portion of the agency fee that the Union knows, *ex ante*, is attributable to non-chargeable expenses simply misreads the Supreme Court's cases, particularly *Hudson*.

This Court's long line of cases regarding compelled support for union activities has identified only two related government interests that can justify the First Amendment burdens created by such compelled support. The first interest is the promotion of labor peace that is thought to stem from an increased use of collective bargaining and related contract administration and grievance procedures that apply to all employees, regardless whether they are union members.[21] The second related interest is that of allowing unions to negotiate for a fair distribution of the *costs* of such collective bargaining and related procedures, which benefit all employees and hence should be

[21] See Teachers v.Hudson, 475 U.S. 292, 302 n. 8 (1977); Ellis v. Railway Clerks, 466 U.S. 435, 455–56 (1984); Abood v. Detroit Bd. Of Ed., 431 U.S. 209 (1977).

borne by members and nonmembers alike—often referred to as eliminating the "free-rider" problem.[22]

Those are the sole interests that support the imposition of agency fees, and any agency fee arrangement must be narrowly tailored to such interests.[23] Excess agency fees that do not support collective bargaining and related activities thus are not narrowly tailored to the state interests. In *Davenport*, therefore, the mere collection of that portion of the agency fee that represents expenditures for political activities rather than collective bargaining—the admittedly non-chargeable expenses—violates the First Amendment on its face, regardless whether employees are allowed to seek reimbursement by jumping through the formal procedural hoops for opting out each year. Indeed, the procedures for after-the-fact challenges in *Hudson* and other agency-shop cases were not intended as a means of permitting unions to collect and potentially keep what they *know* to be excess fees for non-chargeable expenses, but rather were intended as a means of testing the unions' good-faith calculation of *chargeable* expenses to determine if the agency fee was indeed valid.

In *Hudson*, the Illinois law under review allowed the union to charge only "proportionate share payments" as an agency fee from nonmembers, and specified that such payment amounts "could not exceed the members' dues."[24] Consistent with the cost-sharing and free-rider justifications for the agency fee, the union "identified expenditures unrelated to collective bargaining and contract administration," calculated the percentage of such unrelated expenditures relative to its total expenditures, and set the agency fee at 95% of

[22]See Hudson, 475 U.S. at 294–95; Abood, 431 U.S. at 221–22; Street, 367 U.S. at 761, 763.

[23]Abood, 431 U.S. at 220, 237; cf. Street, 367 U.S. at 767,768 ("[I]t is abundantly clear that Congress did not completely abandon the policy of full freedom of choice embodied in the 1934 Act, but rather made inroads on it for the *limited purpose* of eliminating the problems created by the 'free rider.'" The power given to unions to spend exacted money is not "unlimited," and "[i]ts use to support candidates for public office, and advance political programs, is not a use which helps defray the expenses of the negotiation or administration of collective agreements, or the expenses entailed in the adjustment of grievances and disputes. In other words, it is a use which falls *clearly outside the reasons* advanced by the unions and accepted by Congress *why authority to make unionshop agreements was justified.*") (emphasis added).

[24]475 U.S. at 295.

the amount of union dues.[25] Only *after* deducting all plainly nonchargeable amounts off the top did the union's procedure for objecting to the remaining, presumptively chargeable, fee kick in.[26] Furthermore, any subsequent successful objections to items included in the fee calculation resulted in "an immediate reduction in the amount of future [fees] for all nonmembers and a rebate for the objector."[27]

On a subsequent legal challenge to the procedures adopted by the union, the district court upheld those procedures in part because, *inter alia*, the fee charged "represented a good-faith effort by the Union" to calculate a proper fee.[28] The Seventh Circuit reversed and struck down the procedures as insufficiently protective of nonmember rights not to be compelled to subsidize union activities that were not germane to the collective bargaining process.[29]

The Supreme Court affirmed the Seventh Circuit, finding the procedures constitutionally inadequate. Based on its earlier decision in *Ellis v. Railway Clerks*, the Court held that a '"pure rebate approach is inadequate"' because the union was not entitled to an '"involuntary loan"' and there were '"readily available alternatives, such as *advance reduction of dues* and/or interest-bearing escrow accounts."'[30] The Court further held that '"the Union should not be permitted to exact a service fee from nonmembers without first establishing a procedure which will avoid the risk that their funds will be used, even temporarily, to finance ideological activities unrelated to collective bargaining."'[31]

Hudson concluded that even the advance reduction of dues, without the necessity of prior objection by nonmembers, was constitutionally inadequate because it did not provide nonmembers with sufficient information about what other charges were *included* in the

[25] *Id.*

[26] *Id.* at 296.

[27] *Id.*

[28] *Id.* at 298.

[29] *Id.* at 299.

[30] *Id.* at 303–04 (quoting Ellis v. Railway Clerks, 466 U.S. 435, 443–44 (1984)) (emphasis added).

[31] *Id.* at 304 (quoting Abood v. Detroit Bd. Of Ed., 431 U.S. 209 at 244 (1977) (Stevens, J., concurring)).

fee calculation as supposedly germane to collective bargaining.[32] The problem even with the advance reduction in fees thus was that it did not go *far enough* in that it only "identified the amount that it admittedly had expended for purposes that did not benefit dissenting nonmembers," and provided no information that would enable nonmembers to challenge allegedly germane expenditures that *were* included as part of the fee.[33] The Court thus concluded that the Constitution required, among other things, "an adequate explanation for the advance reduction of dues," and a prompt and impartial procedure for challenging the union's claims that the remaining *reduced* fee represents only properly chargeable expenses.[34]

In that context the Court's comment regarding the nonmember's "burden of raising an objection" takes on a very different meaning—it is a burden of challenging portions of the fee that the union in good faith claims are indeed chargeable, not the burden of challenging amounts that are indisputably *not* chargeable. Quoting *Abood*, the Court in *Hudson* reiterated

> "that the nonunion employee has the burden of raising an objection, but that the union retains the burden of proof: '"Since the unions possess the facts and records from which the proportion of political to total union expenditures can reasonably be calculated, basic considerations of fairness compel that they, not the individual employees, bear the burden of proving such proportion."' *Abood*, 431 U.S., at 239–240, n.40, quoting *Railway Clerks* v. *Allen*, 373 U.S. 113, 122 (1963)."[35]

"[B]ecause the agency shop itself impinges on the nonunion employees' First Amendment interests, and because the nonunion employee has the burden of objection," the "appropriately justified *advance*

[32] *Id.* at 306.

[33] *Id.* at 307; see *id.* n.20 (procedures failed to fulfill the union's front-end obligation "to minimize the risk that nonunion employees' contributions might be used for impermissible purposes," and "failed to provide adequate justification for the advance reduction of dues").

[34] *Id.* at 309; *id.* at 310 (describing "constitutional requirements" for collection of agency fee).

[35] *Id.* at 306 (footnote omitted).

reduction and the prompt, impartial decisionmaker are *necessary* to minimize both the impingement and the burden."[36]

Hudson thus makes clear that an advance reduction of the agency fee to exclude non-chargeable expenses was necessary, but not sufficient, and that the *nonmember's* burden of objection to an agency fee arises only *after* the initial deduction of expenses that are plainly not related to collective bargaining. While a nonmember may have the burden of initiating a challenge to parts of the fee included in good faith, it is the *union* that bears the initial burden of removing obviously non-chargeable amounts from the fee before it is even exacted.

The misnamed *Hudson* procedures that are used by the WEA in Washington, and that the Court assumed to be adequate to protect nonmember rights, do not even remotely satisfy *Hudson*'s constitutional requirements because they required no advance reduction of obviously non-chargeable amounts for political activities and placed the burden on nonmembers to object to such facially improper charges. Section 760's opt-in procedure does nothing more than partially restore the safeguards discussed in *Hudson* itself by requiring a deduction of non-chargeable amounts absent a voluntary and affirmative contribution of such amounts by the nonmembers.[37]

In the end, not only is an opt-in requirement, at a minimum, a *permissible* obligation to impose on the union relative to obviously non-germane fees, it is likely *insufficient* to protect nonmembers from paying such excess agency fees because the First Amendment forbids even the initial *collection* of such amounts in the first place.

[36] *Id.* at 309 (footnote omitted).

[37] As mentioned in Part III. A, *supra*, *Street*'s concern for the expressive interests of the union and its *voluntary members*, and its resulting statement that dissent should not be presumed, has no applicability in *this* case given that § 760 does not apply to the use of union membership dues, but only to the use of nonmember agency fees. Such nonmembers—persons who have not, by definition, voluntarily associated with the union—are easily and properly distinguished from union members whose associational rights *inter se* are entirely unaffected by § 760. Unlike in *Street*, there is no need here for involuntary payors to raise their hands and object in order to separate themselves from the majority of voluntary union members—they are readily distinguished by their nonmembership. A presumption that they object to associating with the union for political purposes is entirely justified by their decision not to join the union, and such a presumption in no way burdens those whose support for the union can be presumed by the fact of their voluntary membership.

IV. Conclusion

The result in *Davenport* was easy to reach, is easy to like, and is hard to argue with. The means by which that result was reached, however, are more problematic and disappointing to those who favor a strong First Amendment. There was certainly a more direct way of confirming that unions have no First Amendment right to collect fees from nonmembers in excess of amounts chargeable for collective bargaining. Confirming that it was the nonmember employees, not the Union, whose rights were being protected by the opt-in procedures of § 760 would have been consistent with the Court's precedent and would have added clarity to the law. Instead, the opinion erodes First Amendment protections in a variety of ways and elevates state discretion above individual rights. While it is typically the hard cases that are supposed to make bad law, here seems to be an example of an easy case making bad law because the result was sufficiently obvious that less attention was paid to the means of getting there. One hopes that the case will be remembered and relied on primarily for its result, not for its reasoning, and that future cases will apply First Amendment principles with greater vigor.

BONG HiTS 4 JESUS: The First Amendment Takes a Hit

*Hans Bader**

I. Introduction

In 1969, the Supreme Court observed that students do "not shed their constitutional rights to freedom of speech or expression at the schoolhouse gate."[1] But thirty eight years later, the Court gave school officials authority to ban speech even beyond the schoolhouse gate in *Morse v. Frederick*.[2]

In *Morse*, the Supreme Court held that a school may restrict student speech it reasonably views as promoting illegal drug use.[3] Creating a new exception to free speech in schools, the Court upheld disciplinary action against Joseph Frederick, a high school senior who was suspended after he displayed a banner reading "BONG HiTS 4 JESUS" across the street from his school in Juneau, Alaska, during the Winter Olympics Torch Relay. The Court for the first time countenanced viewpoint-based restrictions on speech that would clearly be protected from punishment if the speech occurred among citizens in society at large.

The Court failed to provide any clear test for when to carve out exceptions to free speech in school, beyond stating the general premise that school officials have broader power over student speech than the government has over speech in general. Moreover, in its zeal to give the government a win in the "War on Drugs," the Court upheld censorship of speech that posed little risk of causing drug use, and decided the case in a way that showed inadequate respect for procedural safeguards mandated by federal court rules. The

*Counsel for Special Projects, Competitive Enterprise Institute; J.D., Harvard Law School; B.A. in history and economics, University of Virginia.

[1] Tinker v. Des Moines School District, 393 U.S. 503, 506 (1969).

[2] 127 S. Ct. 2618 (2007).

[3] *Id.* at 2629.

Court's decision did nothing to make schools safer or more orderly, since it is other legal challenges, not the First Amendment, that have undermined school discipline.

There were two bright spots for free speech advocates. One was the justices' recognition that political speech advocating the legalization of drugs could not be banned under their ruling. Another was the Court's implicit rejection of some lower court rulings that students' speech must be on matter of "public concern" to enjoy any protection.

II. Background

On January 24, 2002, students and teachers were allowed to leave classes at Juneau-Douglas High School to watch the Olympic torch pass by. Frederick, who was late for school that day, joined some classmates on the sidewalk across from the high school, off school grounds. Frederick and his friends waited for the television cameras that accompanied the Olympic torch so they could unfurl a fourteen-foot banner reading "BONG HiTS 4 JESUS." When they displayed the banner, Principal Deborah Morse immediately crossed the street and seized it.[4]

Morse initially suspended Frederick for five days for violating the school district's policy against advocating drug use, but increased his suspension to ten days after he quoted Jefferson on free speech and refused to give the names of his fellow participants.[5] Frederick administratively appealed his suspension to the superintendent, who denied his appeal but limited his suspension to the time he had already spent out of school prior to his appeal (eight days). Frederick then appealed to the Juneau School Board, which upheld his suspension.[6] In April 2002, Frederick filed a lawsuit against the principal and the school board in federal court, claiming they violated his free speech rights.

III. The Lower Courts Rule In Favor of the Student

The federal district court in Alaska ruled in favor of the school board and Principal Morse, holding that Frederick's speech was

[4] *Id.* at 2622.

[5] David Savage, Free Speech on Campus Is Debated, Los Angeles Times, March 20, 2007, at A9, available at 2007 WLNR 5245985.

[6] Morse, 127 S. Ct. at 2622–23.

unprotected, and granting summary judgment against him.[7] On appeal, the Ninth Circuit Court of Appeals unanimously reversed the district court's decision in 2006. It held that Frederick's speech was protected, because it did not fall into any of three kinds of speech that the Supreme Court has held school officials can prohibit.

First, it held that Frederick's speech was not disruptive within the meaning of the Supreme Court's 1969 *Tinker* decision, which recognized that students enjoy free speech, provided the speech does not disrupt school activities, in ruling that students could wear black armbands to protest the Vietnam War.[8] Second, it held that the speech was not lewd or vulgar within the meaning of the Supreme Court's 1986 *Fraser* decision, which upheld a boy's discipline for an address to a school assembly laced with sexual innuendos.[9] Third, it held that the speech was not itself school-sponsored within the meaning of the Supreme Court's 1987 *Kuhlmeier* decision, which gives schools a free hand in controlling the content of school newspapers and other speech by the school.[10]

The Ninth Circuit held that even if Frederick's banner could be construed as a positive message about marijuana use, "in the absence of concern about disruption of educational activities," the school could not punish or censor his speech because it promoted a social message contrary to one favored by the school.[11]

IV. The Supreme Court Rules In Favor of the School

In 2007, the Supreme Court reversed the Ninth Circuit, and ruled that the school board did not violate Frederick's First Amendment rights by confiscating his "Bong Hits 4 Jesus" banner and suspending him for it.

A. The Majority Opinion

The Court, in an opinion by Chief Justice Roberts for five justices, recognized that Frederick's banner did not fall within the kinds of

[7] Frederick v. Morse, No. J 02-008 CV(JWS), 2003 WL 25274689 (D. Alaska May 27, 2003).

[8] Frederick v. Morse, 439 F.3d 1114, 1118 (9th Cir. 2006) (citing Tinker v. Des Moines Independent Community School District, 393 U.S. 503, 511 (1969)), rev'd, 127 S. Ct. 2618 (2007).

[9] *Id.* at 1119 (citing Bethel School District No. 403 v. Fraser, 478 U.S. 675 (1986)).

[10] *Id.* at 1119–20 (citing Hazelwood School District v. Kuhlmeier, 484 U.S. 260 (1988)).

[11] *Id.* at 1118–19.

school speech that the Court had previously held were unprotected in its *Hazelwood* and *Fraser* rulings. So the Court created a new exception to First Amendment protection for pro-drug speech that is not political in nature.

It conceded that although Frederick's speech occurred near the school it was not itself school-sponsored expression, and thus was not subject to restriction under *Kuhlmeier,* because "no one would reasonably believe that Frederick's banner bore the school's imprimatur."[12]

Similarly, the Court recognized that Frederick's speech was not lewd or vulgar like the speech the Court allowed schools to restrict in *Fraser*. The Court also recognized that the school's contrary argument for extending *Fraser* beyond lewd or vulgar speech to other "plainly 'offensive'" speech such as pro-drug speech "stretches *Fraser* too far" and if accepted, would endanger "much political and religious speech."[13]

But it noted that the Supreme Court had previously created a new, school-specific exception to free speech in *Fraser*, which itself involved a category of speech—vulgar or lewd speech—which is generally protected in society at large, showing that students have fewer free speech rights than citizens in society at large.[14] Based on its prior precedent creating free speech exceptions for students, the Court concluded that it could create yet another exception, this time for student speech that schools "reasonably regard as promoting illegal drug use."[15] The Court justified its new exception for drug-related speech by citing the government's "important—indeed, perhaps compelling interest" in deterring drug use by students, observing that "[d]rug abuse can cause severe and permanent damage to the health and well-being of young people."[16]

The Court then placed Frederick within its new exception for pro-drug speech in schools. Although the opinion admitted that the banner's message was "cryptic," and "probably means nothing at

[12] Morse v. Frederick, 127 S. Ct. 2618, 2627 (2007).

[13] *Id.* at 2639.

[14] *Id.* at 2626 (citing Cohen v. California, 403 U.S. 15 (1971) ("Fuck the Draft" T-shirt was protected)).

[15] *Id.* at 2629.

[16] *Id.* at 2628.

all'' to some people, it declared that it was nevertheless undeniably a ''reference to illegal drugs'' and the principal reasonably concluded that it ''advocated the use of illegal drugs.''[17] Although it conceded that Frederick was not on school grounds, it concluded that his ''Bong Hits'' banner was still displayed during a school event, since the Olympic Torch Relay occurred during normal school hours, attendance was encouraged by the school, and teachers, administrators, the school band, and cheerleaders were present. Thus, his speech qualified as ''school speech'' properly regulated by the school rather than a normal case of speech on a public street.[18] Finally, the Court emphasized the non-political nature of the speech, observing that ''not even Frederick argues that the banner conveys any sort of political or religious message.''[19]

B. Justice Thomas's Concurrence

Justice Thomas wrote a concurrence that argued that students in public schools do not have a right to free speech and that *Tinker*, which held to the contrary, should be overturned. He argued that schools stand in the shoes of parents, who voluntarily send their children to school, and thus should enjoy parental prerogatives in restricting speech,[20] even as to the 18-year old Frederick, who was not a minor:[21]

> Parents decide whether to send their children to public schools. . .If parents do not like the rules imposed by those schools, they can seek redress in school boards or legislatures; they can send their children to private schools or home school them; or they can simply move.[22]

He complained that ''*Tinker* has undermined the traditional authority of teachers to maintain order in public schools,'' resulting in ''defiance, disrespect, and disorder.''[23]

[17] *Id.* at 2629.

[18] *Id.* at 2624.

[19] *Id.* at 2625.

[20] *Id.* at 2631 (Thomas, J., concurring).

[21] *Id.* at 2631 n.3; see also Frederick v. Morse, 439 F.3d 1114, 1117 n.4 (9th Cir. 2006) (noting that Frederick was not a minor under Alaska law).

[22] Morse v. Frederick, 127 S. Ct. 2618, 2635 (2007) (Thomas, J., concurring).

[23] *Id.* at 2636 (citations omitted).

C. *Justice Alito's Concurrence*

By contrast, two other justices, who provided the deciding votes for the majority's holding that the school board had not violated the First Amendment, wrote a very different concurring opinion that attempted to limit the reach of the Court's decision. Justice Alito, joined by Justice Kennedy, wrote a concurrence indicating that he agreed with the majority opinion to the extent that:

> (a) it goes no further than to hold that a public school may restrict speech that a reasonable observer would interpret as advocating illegal drug use and (b) it provides no support for any restriction of speech that can plausibly be interpreted as commenting on any political or social issue, including speech on issues such as "the wisdom of the war on drugs or of legalizing marijuana for medicinal use."[24]

The concurrence rejected the school board's argument that "the First Amendment permits public school officials to censor any student speech that interferes with a school's 'educational mission,'" observing that that "argument can easily be manipulated in dangerous ways," because "some public schools have defined their educational missions as including the inculcation of whatever political and social views" are held by school officials.[25]

Justice Alito pointed out that under that broad reasoning, schools could ban whatever speech they choose:

> During the *Tinker* era, a public school could have defined its educational mission to include solidarity with our soldiers and their families and thus could have attempted to outlaw the wearing of black armbands on the ground that they undermined this mission. Alternatively, a school could have defined its educational mission to include the promotion of world peace and could have sought to ban the wearing of buttons expressing support for the troops on the ground that the buttons signified approval of war. The "educational mission" argument would give public school authorities a license to suppress speech on political and social issues based

[24] *Id.* at 2636 (Alito, J., concurring).

[25] *Id.* at 2637 (citing Brief for Petitioner at 6, Morse v. Frederick, 127 S. Ct. 2618 (2007) (filed Jan. 16, 2007), available at 2007 WL 118979).

> on disagreement with the viewpoint expressed. The argument, therefore, strikes at the very heart of the First Amendment.[26]

His concurrence also rejected, as a "dangerous fiction," Justice Thomas's argument that parents' act of sending their children to public schools constitutes a delegation, to public school educators, of parents' power to restrict their children's speech. He observed that "most parents, realistically, have no choice but to send their children to a public school and little ability to influence what occurs in the school."[27] Instead, he grounded his concurrence in a "health" rationale, arguing that "altering the usual free speech rules" is necessary because (a) "illegal drug use presents a grave and in many ways unique threat to the physical safety of students," and (b) students are rendered more vulnerable to such threats by the fact that they cannot leave school grounds or look to their parents for protection during school hours.[28]

D. Justice Breyer's Concurrence in Part and Dissent in Part

Justice Breyer concurred in the judgment in part and dissented in part, arguing that the Court should not have ruled on the First Amendment issue, but rather dismissed Frederick's claim based on qualified immunity. Qualified immunity protects individual government officials who violate the Constitution from being sued for damages if the law was not "clearly established" when they acted.[29] Because he felt that the Court's prior decisions did not make clear whether the principal's actions in taking down the banner violated the First Amendment, Breyer would have issued a narrow ruling that she was shielded by qualified immunity, without deciding whether Frederick's free speech rights were actually violated.[30]

[26] *Id.* at 2637 (Alito, J., concurring).

[27] *Id.* at 2637–38.

[28] *Id.* at 2638.

[29] *Id.* at 2640 (Breyer, J., concurring in the judgment in part and dissenting in part).

[30] *Id.* at 2638–42. Frederick also sought a court order that the school erase his suspension from his record, a remedy not subject to a qualified immunity defense, but Breyer doubted that such relief would be appropriate for reasons having nothing to do with the First Amendment. See *id.* at 2642–43.

E. The Dissent

Justice Stevens dissented in an opinion joined by Justices Souter and Ginsburg. Stevens criticized the majority decision for upholding "a punishment meted out on the basis of a listener's disagreement with her understanding (or, more likely, misunderstanding) of the speaker's viewpoint,"[31] flouting traditional First Amendment norms both by permitting viewpoint discrimination and by depriving speech of First Amendment protection based on the perceptions of listeners and speculation that the speech may cause harm.

Past First Amendment rulings, he noted, had recognized that "'viewpoint discrimination is . . . an egregious form of content discrimination'" forbidden by the First Amendment,[32] and that "'the Government may not prohibit the expression of an idea simply because society finds the idea itself offensive or disagreeable.'"[33] And under the Supreme Court's *Brandenburg* decision, "punishing someone for advocating illegal conduct is constitutional only when the advocacy is likely to provoke the harm that the government seeks to avoid."[34]

In light of that tradition, Stevens argued that "carving out pro-drug speech for uniquely harsh treatment finds no support in our case law and is inimical to the values protected by the First Amendment."[35] Indeed, Stevens argued, it would be "profoundly unwise to create special rules for speech about drug and alcohol use," citing the historical example of resistance to Prohibition in the 1920s.[36] Pointing to the current debate over medical marijuana (marijuana use is illegal under federal law, but permitted under Alaska state law), Stevens concluded, "[s]urely our national experience with alcohol should make us wary of dampening speech suggesting—however inarticulately—that it would be better to tax and regulate marijuana than to persevere in a futile effort to ban its use entirely."[37]

[31] *Id.* at 2645 (Stevens, J., dissenting).

[32] *Id.* at 2644 (quoting Rosenberger v. Rector of Univ. of Va., 515 U.S. 819, 828–829 (1995)).

[33] *Id.* at 2645 (quoting Texas v. Johnson, 491 U.S. 397, 414 (1989)).

[34] *Id.* (citing Brandenburg v. Ohio, 395 U.S. 444, 449 (1969) (distinguishing "mere advocacy" of illegal conduct from "incitement to imminent lawless action")).

[35] *Id.* at 2646.

[36] *Id.* at 2650.

[37] *Id.* at 2651.

Moreover, Stevens mocked the majority's interpretation of the banner, which merely contained an "ambiguous statement" that "contained an oblique reference to drugs,"[38] as being a dangerous incitement to drug use:

> Admittedly, some high school students (including those who use drugs) are dumb. Most students, however, do not shed their brains at the schoolhouse gate, and most students know dumb advocacy when they see it. The notion that the message on this banner would actually persuade either the average student or even the dumbest one to change his or her behavior is most implausible.[39]

Stevens noted the irony of the Court's decision to defer to school officials' perceptions about the ambiguous meaning of Frederick's banner and whether to punish him based on one possible interpretation of his speech. He noted that a decision the Supreme Court issued on the very same day had done just the opposite, enunciating the rule that when the "First Amendment is implicated, the tie goes to the speaker," and that "when it comes to defining what speech" is prohibited by campaign finance laws, "we give the benefit of the doubt to speech, not censorship."[40]

V. Discussion

The Court's opinion in *Morse* was disappointing in many respects. Its decision was a marked departure from its prior First Amendment rulings, in permitting viewpoint discrimination and censorship based on speculation about the consequences of speech. Justice Thomas's concurrence was still worse, advocating that school administrators receive blanket power to restrict student speech, based on constitutional theories he himself has rejected elsewhere as dangerous and unfounded.

Ironically, although the justices rejected the school district's arguments for restricting speech—the idea that any speech which interferes with a school's "basic educational mission" or is "plainly offensive" can be prohibited—as too broad, the Court's own justification

[38] *Id.* at 2643.

[39] *Id.* at 2649.

[40] *Id.* at 2650 (quoting Federal Election Commission v. Wisconsin Right to Life, Inc., 129 S. Ct. 2652, 2669, 2674 (2007)).

for restricting speech—that it would advance an important state interest—is almost as sweeping.

The Court's decision to adopt school officials' contested interpretation of Frederick's speech and claim that it occurred in a school-sponsored activity gave short shrift both to established summary judgment standards, by making factual findings that should have been made only after giving the plaintiff the opportunity to prove his case at trial, and to the Court's constitutional obligation under the First Amendment to make an independent judgment about the meaning of his speech after a full hearing of the evidence.

A. Morse *Wrongly Permits Viewpoint Discrimination*

Whatever other limits the Supreme Court had placed on students' free speech rights in the past, it had never countenanced viewpoint discrimination of student speech prior to *Morse*, as lower courts recognized.[41] "[A]bove all else, the First Amendment means that government has no power to restrict expression because of its message,"[42] and like others, "students are entitled to freedom of expression of their views."[43]

As the Supreme Court emphasized in its 1995 *Rosenberger* decision, "viewpoint discrimination is . . . an egregious form of content discrimination" that is forbidden even in contexts where content discrimination is permitted, such as a college's decisions about which student publications to fund.[44] Thus, even when a school's educational mission gives it extra leeway to restrict speech, it still cannot discriminate based on viewpoint.[45]

[41] See, e.g., Castorina v. Madison County School Board, 246 F.3d 536, 540 (6th Cir. 2001) (under *Tinker* and its progeny, "viewpoint-specific speech restrictions are an egregious violation of the First Amendment"); Pyle v. South Hadley School Committee, 861 F. Supp. 157, 170–74 (D. Mass. 1994) (upholding general ban on indecency, but striking down harassment code's restriction on certain views); East High Gay/Straight Alliance v. Bd. of Educ. of Salt Lake City, 81 F. Supp. 2d 1166, 1193 (D. Utah 1999).

[42] Police Dep't of Chicago v. Mosley, 408 U.S. 92, 95 (1972).

[43] Tinker v. Des Moines School District, 393 U.S. 503, 511 (1969).

[44] Rosenberger v. Rector and Visitors of Univ. of Va., 515 U.S. 819, 828–29 (1995).

[45] See Board of Regents v. Southworth, 529 U.S. 217, 229 (2000) (although university's educational mission enables it to use student activities fees for ideological purposes that would be forbidden in other contexts, it is nevertheless governed by the core "requirement of viewpoint neutrality").

Its 1943 *Barnette* decision holding that dissenting students could not be forced to salute the flag emphasized that "[i]f there is any fixed star in our constitutional constellation, it is that no official, high or petty, can prescribe what shall be orthodox in politics, nationalism, religion, or other matters of opinion or force citizens to confess by word or act their faith therein."[46]

Nor was there any reason to relax this rule against viewpoint discrimination in the schools, which form part of the "marketplace of ideas."[47] As the Supreme Court observed long ago in *Barnette,* that school boards "are educating the young for citizenship is a reason for scrupulous protection of constitutional freedoms of the individual, if we are not to strangle the free mind at its source, and teach youth to discount important principles of our government as mere platitudes."[48] Indeed, punishing views on drug legalization can undermine the educational process by stifling debate.[49]

When the justices upheld a student's discipline for making sexual innuendos in an address to a school assembly in their 1986 *Fraser* decision, which created an exception for lewd or vulgar speech, they did so precisely because "the penalties imposed in th[at] case were unrelated to any political viewpoint,"[50] and school officials did not "regulate [the student's] speech because they disagreed with the views he sought to express."[51] Indeed, the offensiveness of Fraser's speech, such as his claim that a student government candidate was "firm in his pants" and would "go to . . . the climax," was not based on his viewpoint.[52] If instead of calling the candidate "firm," he had called him "flaccid," it would have been just as vulgar, and just as punishable, even though it would have expressed the opposite view. *Fraser* drove this point home by likening the rules for appropriate

[46] West Virginia Board of Education v. Barnette, 319 U.S. 624, 642 (1943).

[47] See Tinker, 393 U.S. at 512 ("The classroom is peculiarly the 'marketplace of ideas'") (quoting Keyishian v. Board of Regents, 385 U.S. 589, 603 (1967)).

[48] Barnette, 319 U.S. at 637.

[49] Blum v. Schlegel, 18 F.3d 1005, 1011 (2d Cir. 1994) (professor's advocacy of marijuana legalization was protected, given need for "free and open debate" and harm from "excessive [speech] regulation of speech").

[50] Bethel School District No. 403 v. Fraser, 478 U.S. 675, 685 (1986).

[51] *Id.* at 689 (Brennan, J., concurring).

[52] See *id.* at 687 (quoting the speech).

communication in a school to the rules of conduct for debates promulgated in each house in Congress, where the broadest possible range of viewpoints can be discussed freely.[53]

B. Morse *Wrongly Strips Speech of Protection Based on a Small, Speculative Risk of Harm*

The Court's decision to allow viewpoint discrimination was bad enough. Perhaps even worse was its decision to allow speech to be banned based on sheer speculation that it would cause harm in the form of drug abuse. As Justice Stevens observed in his dissent, "most students . . . do not shed their brains at the schoolhouse gate," and "the notion that the message on [Frederick's] banner would actually persuade either the average student or even the dumbest one to change his or her behavior [to use drugs] is most implausible."[54]

Generally, even speech that expressly advocates illegal conduct cannot be prohibited unless the speaker deliberately incites imminent unlawful action.[55] Yet the Court permitted Frederick's banner to be banned based on its fear that it would somehow promote drug use—even though the Court itself admitted that Frederick's message was "cryptic," and "probably means nothing at all" to some people,[56] and even many of the school board's defenders admitted that it might simply be "'jabberwocky' or 'nonsense.'"[57] It did so even though scholars disagree about whether Frederick's banner endorsed drugs even obliquely.[58]

[53] *Id.* at 681–82.

[54] Morse v. Frederick, 127 S. Ct. 2618, 2649 (2007) (Stevens, J., dissenting).

[55] Brandenburg v. Ohio, 395 U.S. 444 (1969) (per curiam); Hess v. Indiana, 414 U.S. 105 (1973).

[56] Morse, 127 S. Ct. at 2629.

[57] Brief of Amici Curiae National School Boards Association, et al., in Support of Petitioners at 22–23, Morse v. Frederick, 127 S. Ct. 2618 (2007) (filed Jan. 16, 2007), available at 2007 WL 14099.

[58] Compare Bill Poser, The Supreme Court Fails Semantics, Language Log, July 7, 2007, at http://itre.cis.upenn.edu/~myl/languagelog/archives/004696.html (language expert concludes banner did not endorse drugs), with Eugene Volokh, The Morse v. Frederick Dissent, Volokh Conspiracy, June 26, 2007, at http://volokh.com/posts/1182873609.shtml (law professor concludes banner was plausibly interpreted as pro-drug, and its message was so interpreted by high school students he showed it to).

But as the Supreme Court has observed in its past school decisions, "censorship or suppression of expression is tolerated by our Constitution only when the expression presents a clear and present danger" of harm,[59] not just "undifferentiated fear or apprehension of disturbance" or other harm.[60] "Broad prophylactic rules in the area of free expression are suspect. Precision of regulation must be the touchstone," since First Amendment freedoms "need breathing space to survive."[61]

The Court's decision to allow Frederick's speech to be suppressed merely because it was viewed as obliquely encouraging drug use does not begin to comply with that standard, especially since students can be prevented from using drugs without any restrictions on speech.[62]

Moreover, in deferring to the principal's perception about the meaning of Frederick's banner, the Court also departed from its usual practice of basing First Amendment protection on speech's objective meaning, not subjective perceptions, no matter how reasonable, as Justice Stevens noted.[63] In past cases, the Court has warned that "deference to a legislative finding" that certain types of speech are harmful "cannot limit judicial inquiry when First Amendment rights are at stake,"[64] and that "an appellate court has an obligation to make an independent examination of the whole record"[65] without

[59] West Virginia Board of Education v. Barnette, 319 U.S. 624, 633 (1943).

[60] Tinker v. Des Moines School District, 393 U.S. 503, 508 (1969).

[61] NAACP v. Button, 371 U.S. 415, 438 (1963); see Shelton v. Tucker, 364 U.S. 479, 488 (1960); Perry Educational Ass'n v. Perry Local Educators' Ass'n, 460 U.S. 37, 45 (1983) ("For the state to enforce a content-based exclusion it must show that the regulation is necessary to serve a compelling state interest and that it is narrowly-drawn to achieve that end.").

[62] Compare Schneider v. State, 308 U.S. 147 (1939) (state could not ban distribution of handbills to prevent litter, since the state could simply punish littering itself, rather than restricting speech).

[63] Morse v. Frederick, 127 S. Ct. 2618, 2645 (2007) (Stevens, J., dissenting) (citing, e.g., Thomas v. Collins, 323 U.S. 516, 535 (1945) ("varied understanding of [speaker's] hearers" does not control)); Cox v. Louisiana, 379 U.S. 536, 543 (1965) (sheriff's view of speech as disturbance of peace not controlling); Bethel School District No. 403 v. Fraser, 478 U.S. 675, 683 (1986).

[64] Landmark Communications, Inc. v. Virginia, 435 U.S. 829, 843 (1978).

[65] Bose Corp. v. Consumers Union of United States, 466 U.S. 485, 486 (1984).

deference to prevent any "intrusion on the field of free expression."[66] And in a decision rendered the very same day as *Morse*, the Court had done just the opposite, declaring that when the "First Amendment is implicated, the tie goes to the speaker," and that "when it comes to defining what speech qualifies as the functional equivalent of express advocacy [regulated by the campaign finance laws], we give the benefit of the doubt to speech, not censorship."[67]

C. Morse *Disregarded Summary Judgment Rules*

Frederick denied that his banner was intended to promote drug use, claiming it was just a humorous nonsense message that was directed not at students, but at the TV cameras that followed the Olympic torch, and he submitted affidavits from students who said they did not view it as an endorsement of drug use.[68]

More importantly, he disputed whether his speech even occurred in a school-sponsored activity—an important fact, since Frederick's case had been dismissed before trial, on summary judgment, where federal rules require courts to resolve all factual disputes and draw all plausible inferences in Frederick's favor.[69]

Yet in squeezing Frederick into its exception for pro-drug speech in school-sponsored activities, the Court did nothing of the kind. Instead, it ignored record evidence that the Olympic Torch Relay at which Frederick displayed his banner was not a school event in any meaningful sense, since it was sponsored by Coca-Cola and local businesses, not the school; that his banner was aimed at the nationwide TV audience watching the Olympic Torch Relay, not students; and that students watching the event had no obligation to attend it or even remain at school, and were virtually unsupervised.[70]

[66] *Id.* at 509.

[67] Morse, 127 S. Ct. at 2650 (Stevens, J., dissenting) (quoting Federal Election Commission v. Wisconsin Right to Life, Inc., 129 S. Ct. 2652, 2669, 2674 (2007)).

[68] Joint Appendix ("J.A.") at 28, 33, 37–38, 66–68, Morse v. Frederick, 127 S. Ct. 2618 (2007), available at 2007 WL 119039 and http://www.lawmemo.com/sct/06/Morse/app.pdf (Jan. 16, 2007).

[69] See Anderson v. Liberty Lobby, 477 U.S. 242, 255–56 (1986) (citing Federal Rule of Civil Procedure 56); Eisenmann Corp. v. Sheet Metal Workers Int'l Ass'n Local No. 24, 323 F.3d 375, 380 (6th Cir. 2003).

[70] See, e.g., Morse v. Frederick, 127 S. Ct. 2618, 2643 (2007) (Stevens, J., dissenting) (citing record evidence that banner was addressed to "national television" audience, not "fellow students"); J.A. at 23, 27–28, 33, 36, 37–38, 66–68; Brief of Amicus Curiae Center for Individual Rights in Support of Respondents at 1–2, 18–20, Morse v.

D. Morse *Ignored Adults' Free Speech Rights*

The Court never explained why it was appropriate to apply school-based limits on free speech rights of minors to curb the speech of an adult (the eighteen-year-old Frederick) to a mostly adult audience (the nationwide TV viewers of the Olympic Torch Relay), simply because the banner's viewers also included some students.[71] The Court has traditionally rejected attempts to restrict speech in public, such as tobacco advertising, merely because it can be seen by children.[72]

E. Morse's *"Important Interest" Exception to Censorship Is Dangerously Broad*

Instead, the Supreme Court simply justified its newfound willingness to sanction viewpoint discrimination by citing the "important—indeed, perhaps compelling interest" in deterring drug use by students.[73] Its "important government interest" justification for restricting speech was inconsistent with the results of its past decisions, and set a dangerous precedent for future First Amendment cases, since the courts treat almost any state goal as an "important interest."

1. The Exception Is Inconsistent with Precedent

The Court's decision paved no new ground in recognizing that the government has a compelling interest in preventing adolescent drug use.[74] But its decision went much further by allowing a school to prohibit not just drug use itself, but speech that carries the remote possibility that it might induce students to use drugs.

Frederick, 127 S. Ct. 2618 (2007) (filed Feb. 20, 2007), available at 2007 WL 550933 (listing factual disputes between the parties).

[71] See Morse, 127 S. Ct. at 2631 n.3 (Thomas, J., concurring) (Frederick was "not a minor").

[72] Lorillard Tobacco v. Reilly, 533 U.S. 525, 561–62 (2000) (invalidating tobacco advertising ban); Erznoznik v. City of Jacksonville, 422 U.S. 205, 213 (1975) (nudity at drive-in theater protected); Reno v. ACLU, 521 U.S. 844 (1997) (indecent websites protected even though some viewers are minors).

[73] Morse, 127 S. Ct. at 2628 (quoting Vernonia School Dist. 47J v. Acton, 515 U.S. 646, 661 (1995)).

[74] See Vernonia Sch. Dist. 47J v. Acton, 515 U.S. 646, 661 (1995) (compelling interest in preventing school children from using drugs justifies random drug testing of student athletes); Board of Education v. Earls, 536 U.S. 822 (2002) (upholding random drug testing of students participating in extracurricular activities).

The Supreme Court's seminal school speech cases all involved speech restrictions that were struck down despite being designed to advance important state interests. The rule requiring students to salute the flag at issue in the Court's 1943 *Barnette* decision reflected an attempt to instill patriotism and a spirit of sacrifice in the midst of a terrible war against a Japanese Empire that had bombed Pearl Harbor and a Third Reich that was perpetrating the Holocaust.[75] And the black armbands the Supreme Court held were protected in its 1969 *Tinker* decision were worn in opposition to a war America was waging against a communist insurgency in the Vietnam War. That insurgency was backed by a totalitarian North Vietnamese regime that murdered or imprisoned millions of people after the United States withdrew from the conflict.

The idea that viewpoints can be restricted when they oppose or undercut important government policies is fundamentally at odds with the purpose of the First Amendment.[76] As the Court observed in *Barnette*, "freedom to differ is not limited to things that do not matter much. That would be a mere shadow of freedom. The test of its substance is the right to differ as to things that touch the heart of the existing order."[77] The whole point of free speech is "to assure the unfettered interchange of ideas for the bringing about of political and social changes desired by the people."[78]

2. *The "Important Interest" Justification for Censorship Is Too Broad, Since Countless "Important Interests" Exist*

Allowing viewpoint discrimination because it serves an important government interest sets a dangerous precedent, because of the vast range of interests that the courts have accepted as important, and the judiciary's concomitant unwillingness to second-guess the wisdom of just about any government objective or mission.

[75] See West Virginia Board of Education v. Barnette, 319 U.S. 624, 640–41 (1943); *id.* at 636 n.16 (rationale behind uniform application of rule).

[76] See Collin v. Smith, 578 F.2d 1197, 1205 (7th Cir. 1978) ("That the effective exercise of First Amendment rights may undercut a given government's policy on some issue is, indeed, one of the purposes of those rights.").

[77] Barnette, 319 U.S. at 642.

[78] New York Times v. Sullivan, 376 U.S. 254, 269 (1964) (quoting Roth v. United States, 354 U.S. 476, 484 (1957)).

A school board can make a plausible argument that it has an important government interest in doing almost everything—even if another school board is doing just the opposite. "Over the years, the Supreme Court has found an enormous range of government interests to be compelling," many of them quite mundane and commonplace.[79] The test for what is an important interest is almost standardless, since the Supreme Court itself has confessed that "we have never set forth a general test to determine what constitutes a compelling state interest."[80]

The net result is that even competing interests can qualify as compelling. For example, the Supreme Court has held that there is a compelling interest in eradicating racial discrimination in education, even purely private discrimination.[81] Yet at the same time, it has held that the courts will defer to a school's conclusion that it needs to discriminate based on race to promote "diversity," finding that, too, to be a compelling interest.[82] And the Court has managed to find important interests both in eradicating, and perpetuating, other forms of discrimination, such as sex discrimination, allowing states to ban discrimination by voluntary associations, while engaging in it themselves.[83] Moreover, judges have argued that the government has a compelling interest both in discriminating against gays (in the context of gay marriage)[84] and in banning discrimination against them, even in private associations.[85]

[79] David A. Strauss, Affirmative Action and the Public Interest, 1995 Sup. Ct. Rev. 1, 29, 30 n.78 (1995) (citing examples such as preventing splintered political parties and establishing professional standards).

[80] Waters v. Churchill, 511 U.S. 661, 671 (1994).

[81] Bob Jones University v. United States, 461 U.S. 574, 604 (1983) (school that banned interracial dating lost tax exemption).

[82] Grutter v. Bollinger, 539 U.S. 306, 328–33 (2003).

[83] Compare Roberts v. United States Jaycees, 468 U.S. 609, 626 (1984) (state had compelling interest in banning sex discrimination in public accommodations that did not violate federal law) with Rostker v. Goldberg, 453 U.S. 57 (1981) (upholding male-only draft registration); Michael M. v. Superior Court, 450 U.S. 437 (1981) (upholding sex-discriminatory statutory rape law); Vorcheimer v. School District of Philadelphia, 532 F.2d 880 (3d Cir. 1975) (upholding single-sex schools), aff'd, 430 U.S. 703 (1976).

[84] See, e.g., Andersen v. King County, 138 P.3d 963, 1007 (Wash. 2006) (Johnson, J., concurring) (citing Adams v. Howerton, 486 F. Supp. 1119, 1124 (D. Cal. 1980)).

[85] Boy Scouts of America v. Wyman, 335 F.3d 80, 92 n.5 (2d Cir. 2003) (state may have a compelling interest in banning sexual orientation discrimination, even though the First Amendment protects some such discrimination); Dale v. Boy Scouts of America, 734 A.2d 1196, 1228 (N.J. 1999) ("compelling interest in eliminating [sexual

The justices in the majority did not seem to recognize this fact. They rejected what they perceived as the school district's most sweeping arguments for restricting Frederick's speech. The majority rejected "the broader rule" advocated by the school district that speech could be restricted as "plainly 'offensive'" even if it is not lewd or indecent, observing that doing so would endanger "much political and religious speech."[86] But it is hard to imagine anything "plainly offensive" to public sensibilities that would not conflict with an important government interest under the Courts' indulgent interpretation of what interests are important.

F. Justice Alito's Concurrence

1. Alito Rightly Rejected the "Educational Mission" Justification for Censorship

Justice Alito's concurrence went out of its way to reject the school board's argument that it could ban any speech that conflicted with its "basic educational mission" because that "argument would give public school authorities a license to suppress speech on political and social issues based on disagreement with the viewpoint expressed" simply be defining their mission as "the inculcation of whatever political and social views are held by" school officials.[87]

Justice Alito's concern was well-founded. As the Ninth Circuit had observed, "All sorts of missions are undermined by legitimate and protected speech—a school's anti-gun mission would be undermined by a student passing around copies of John R. Lott's book, *More Guns, Less Crime* (1998) [and] . . . a school's anti-alcohol mission would be undermined by a student e-mailing links to a medical study showing less heart disease among moderate drinkers than teetotalers."[88]

Colleges and school districts make it their mission to take sides in a host of thorny social issues, and it cannot be the case that merely by injecting themselves into a controversy, they get license to suppress opposing viewpoints.

orientation] discrimination"), rev'd on other grounds, Boy Scouts of America v. Dale, 530 U.S. 640 (2000).

[86] Morse v. Frederick, 127 S. Ct. 2618, 2639 (2007).

[87] *Id.* at 2637 (Alito, J., concurring).

[88] Frederick v. Morse, 439 F.3d 1114, 1120 (9th Cir. 2006), rev'd, 127 S. Ct. 2618 (2007).

For example, the Seattle School District used race in student assignment to promote racial balance.[89] Using race was part of the school's "mission."[90] But students of that very same school district have criticized that policy, both in the schools and in letters to the editor of the *Seattle Times*.[91] Can they be punished for expressing their First Amendment rights in that time-honored fashion?

Schools rightly have a mission of teaching gender equality. Does that mean that they can punish a Catholic student for arguing that the priesthood should be reserved for men? Can a school district in a state that bans same-sex marriage silence a gay student who criticizes it? Many school districts seek to promote nondiscrimination based on sexual orientation. Does that mean that they can ban members of religious denominations from defending their denomination against criticism for not hiring gays as ministers? Or make them participate in gay pride events?

Under the school district's "basic educational mission" argument, schools could take just such draconian measures. Justices Alito and Kennedy went out of their way to reject that argument. Cases prior to *Morse v. Frederick* mostly rejected it as well, by protecting viewpoints that ran counter to school policies, practices, and positions.[92]

[89] Parents Involved in Community Schools v. Seattle School District No. 1, 127 S. Ct. 2738 (2007).

[90] *Id.* at 2758 n.14 (plurality opinion) (school district denounced colorblindness in public statements); *id.* at 2787 n.30 (Thomas, J., concurring) (same).

[91] See, e.g., Andrew Kaplan, letter, Reaching for Parity: Students' Dream Exclude Obstacles to Equal Opportunity, Seattle Times, Dec. 6, 2006, at B9, available at 2006 WLNR 21111614.

[92] E.g., Gay Alliance of Students v. Matthews, 544 F.2d 162 (4th Cir. 1976) (school could not bar gay student group based on its opposition to homosexuality, at a time when gay sex was illegal); Chambers v. Babbitt, 145 F. Supp. 2d 1068 (D. Minn. 2001) (student in state with gay rights law could wear anti-gay T-shirt); see also Seemuller v. Fairfax County School Board, 878 F.2d 1578 (4th Cir. 1989) (male chauvinist parody celebrating archaic sex roles was protected); UWM Post v. Board of Regents of Univ. of Wisconsin, 774 F. Supp. 1163 (E.D. Wis. 1991) (invalidating racial harassment code); Doe v. University of Michigan, 721 F. Supp. 852 (E.D. Mich. 1989) ("university could not . . . establish an anti-discrimination policy which had the effect of prohibiting certain speech [such as discussion of innate race and gender differences] because it disagreed with ideas or messages sought to be conveyed"); Thompson v. Board of Education, 711 F. Supp. 394, 398 (N.D. Ill. 1989) (criticism of schools' bilingual education program protected); but see Harper v. Poway Unified School District, 445 F.3d 1166 (9th Cir. 2006) (anti-gay T-shirt opposing school's gay-pride message unprotected), vacated as moot, 127 S. Ct. 1484 (2007).

It would be difficult to think of a mission that contemporary educators are more obsessed with than "diversity." Yet the courts have consistently blocked colleges' attempts to suppress speech that is at odds with "diversity," even though the Supreme Court has held that there is a compelling interest in promoting diversity.[93]

For example, Shippensburg University's restriction on speech was overturned even though it was a cornerstone of its diversity policy, under which "Shippensburg University is committed without qualification to all aspects—moral, legal, and administrative—of racial and cultural diversity," a "commitment" that "require[s] every member of [its student body] to ensure that the principles of these ideals be mirrored in their attitudes and behaviors."[94] Similarly, the courts overturned George Mason University's discipline of a fraternity for an offensive blackface "ugly woman" skit, where "punishment was meted out to the fraternity because its boorish message," which was "antithetical to the University's mission of promoting diversity and providing an educational environment free from racism and sexism."[95]

But the "important government interest" test that the Court adopted would (absent *Morse*'s caveats about political speech remaining protected) often lead to the opposite results in the K-12 context, since even most controversial "educational missions" would likely be deemed by judges to qualify as an important government interest.

2. *Alito's Dangerous "Health" Rationale for Censorship*

Justices Alito and Kennedy argued that an anti-drug exception was nevertheless justified because drug use threatens students' "physical health." But the connection between an ambiguous "Bong Hits 4 Jesus" banner and students' health is very attenuated, since it assumes that the banner will somehow persuade previously law-abiding students to start using drugs, even though it contains no express advocacy.

It would not be much more of a stretch to argue that a school could ban an invitation to a birthday party at which cake will be

[93] Grutter v. Bollinger, 539 U.S. 306, 328-33 (2003).

[94] Bair v. Shippensburg University, 280 F. Supp. 2d 357, 363, 370 (M.D. Pa. 2003).

[95] Iota Xi Chapter of Sigma Chi Fraternity v. George Mason University, 993 F.2d 386, 389, 392 (4th Cir. 1993).

consumed. After all, eating sweets contributes to obesity, a major health problem, and obesity in turn both affects students' health and reduces their energy and ability to learn.[96] And since fast driving can be dangerous, schools might similarly ban reference to the many movies that glorify it.[97]

Violence poses a far more direct threat to health than does drug use, yet courts have not allowed speech celebrating violence to be banned for health reasons. The Supreme Court upheld a deputy constable's right to applaud the assassination attempt on President Reagan, in which she said, "[i]f they go for him again, I hope they get him," even though that was obviously in tension with her employer's mission of preventing crime.[98]

The California Supreme Court reversed on First Amendment grounds the conviction of a high school student who wrote a poem saying, "I am dark, destructive, and dangerous" and "I can be the next kid to bring guns to kill students at school," since he did not intend the statements as a threat. Although the student's English teacher, and prosecutors, saw this as a threat, the California Supreme Court, applying its own independent judgment, found otherwise.[99] Similarly, a college's "workplace violence" policy was found to violate the First Amendment, as applied to a professor who celebrated imaginary violence against his college president, such as "dropping a two-ton slate of polished granite on his head," and made references to "go[ing] postal."[100]

Almost any controversial speech can take a psychological toll on those who passionately disagree with it. For example, the Ninth

[96]See, e.g., Child Nutrition and WIC Reauthorization Act of 2004, Pub. L. No. 108–265, § 401, 118 Stat. 729, 788 (2004) (congressional findings); Oregon School Boards Ass'n, The High Cost of Childhood Obesity, at http://www.osba.org/hotopics/atrisk/obesity/highcost.htm (obesity linked to poorer academic performance); Carol Torgan, Childhood Obesity on the Rise, The NIH Word on Health, June 2002, available at http://www.nih.gov/news/WordonHealth/jun2002/childhoodobesity.htm.

[97]Compare South Dakota v. Neville, 459 U.S. 553, 558–59 (1983) (highway safety is compelling interest).

[98]Rankin v. McPherson, 483 U.S. 378, 382–83 (1987). The Court did not defer to the government as to "whether the speech [was] protected," instead deciding the issue as a "question of law." See *id.* at 386 n.9.

[99]In re George T., 93 P.3d 1007 (Cal. 2004).

[100]Bauer v. Sampson, 261 F.3d 775, 780 (9th Cir. 2001).

Circuit, in a much criticized decision vacated by the Supreme Court, held that a student's anti-gay-pride T-shirt could be banned to protect the "psychological health" of a school's gay students, even though they were attending a school that celebrated gay pride.[101] As a lawyer who specializes in challenging college speech codes noted, "virtually all restrictive speech policies" challenged in court "are justified by the prevention of serious mental or physical harm to young people."[102]

G. *Justice Thomas's Concurrence Wrongly Claims Students Have No Free Speech Rights*

Justice Thomas, who joined in the majority opinion, nevertheless recognized that its test for carving out exceptions to free speech in the schools was essentially standardless. "Today, the Court creates another exception [to free speech for students]. In doing so, we continue to distance ourselves from *Tinker*, but we neither overrule it nor offer an explanation of when it operates and when it does not... I am afraid that our jurisprudence now says that students have a right to speak in schools except when they don't."[103]

To resolve this ambiguity, Thomas advocated ruling that "the Constitution does not afford students a right to free speech in public schools."[104] But to reach that conclusion, he had to misread legal history, embrace legal fictions, and ignore the logic of his own opinions in other First Amendment and constitutional cases.

1. *Justice Thomas Misreads Legal History*

Justice Thomas noted that state courts in the Nineteenth and early Twentieth centuries had declined to protect students from discipline by school officials for their speech.[105] From this, he drew the conclusion that the original intent of the First Amendment was not to place any restrictions on censorship in the schools.

[101] Harper v. Poway Unified School District, 445 F.3d 1166 (9th Cir. 2006) (student can be banned from wearing anti-gay T-shirt opposing school's gay-pride message), vacated as moot, 127 S. Ct. 1484 (2007).

[102] David French, A Bong Hit to Free Speech, National Review Online, June 25, 2007, available at http:// phibetacons.nationalreview.com/post/?q=ZDUxMjJkZWVmZTBhMjFkYjIwZWU2ZGZiZGRiMjdlM2Q=.

[103] Morse v. Frederick, 127 S. Ct. 2618, 2634 (2007) (Thomas, J., concurring).

[104] *Id.*

[105] *Id.* at 2632–33.

But in these cases, neither the First Amendment nor any state constitutional free speech argument was even raised, and many of them did not involve censorship at all.[106] It is black-letter law that "cases cannot be read as foreclosing an argument that they never dealt with"[107] and that "constitutional rights are not defined by inferences from" such cases.[108] Moreover, as Justice Thomas admitted, "the First Amendment did not [even] apply to the States until at least the ratification of the Fourteenth Amendment."[109] Indeed, the Supreme Court did not consider the First Amendment applicable to state or local governments at all until around 1930, long after almost all of the cases he cited for the proposition that students have no free speech rights.[110] So most of the cases he cited had nothing to do with the First Amendment.[111] Indeed, shortly after applying the First Amendment to the states, the Court applied it to the public schools and their students.[112]

[106] E.g., Stevens v. Fassett, 27 Me. 266 (1847) (student seized teacher's desk); Sheehan v. Sturges, 53 Conn. 481 (1885) (assault and stone possession); State v. Pendergrass, 19 N.C. 365 (1837); State v. Mizner, 45 Iowa 248 (1876); Patterson v. Nutter, 78 Me. 509 (1886).

[107] Waters v. Churchill, 511 U.S. 661, 678 (1994) (plurality opinion); see Plaut v. Spendthrift Farm, 514 U.S. 211 (1995) (striking down a law even though a similar law was previously upheld, in a case where the same constitutional attack was not made: "the unexplained silences of our decisions lack precedential weight.").

[108] Texas v. Cobb, 532 U.S. 162, 169 (2002).

[109] Morse v. Frederick, 127 S. Ct. 2618, 2630 n.1 (2007) (Thomas, J., concurring).

[110] See Near v. Minnesota, 283 U.S. 697 (1931) (striking down a state limit on speech for the first time; reasoning that the First Amendment, which once applied only to Congress, was extended against states by the Fourteenth Amendment's Due Process Clause).

[111] Justice Thomas justified his citation of these cases by noting that some states did have state constitutional free speech guarantees, which were presumably understood to be consistent with students having no free speech rights. Morse, 127 S. Ct. at 2630 n.1. But no state constitutional argument was raised in any of these cases, and Thomas has often rejected state court interpretations in interpreting the federal Constitution. Compare Parents Involved in Community Schools v. Seattle School District No. 1, 127 S. Ct. 2738, 2782–83 (2007) (Thomas, J., concurring) (using race in student assignment violates federal Constitution) with Parents Involved in Community Schools v. Seattle School District No. 1, 72 P.3d 151 (Wash. 2003) (contrary conclusion under Washington law); Roberts v. City of Boston, 5 Cush. 198 (Mass. 1849) (upholding segregation despite state constitution's "equality" and "exclusive privileges" provisions).

[112] West Virginia Board of Education v. Barnette, 319 U.S. 624, 637–38 (1943).

2. *Justice Thomas Relies on False Legal Fictions He Has Himself Rejected*

Thomas argued that parents consent to school rules, including speech rules, by sending their children to school, so courts should defer to schools' rulemaking authority under the doctrine of *in loco parentis*.[113] "Parents decide whether to send their children to public schools. If parents do not like the rules imposed by those schools, they can seek redress in school boards or legislatures; they can send their children to private schools or home school them; or they can simply move."[114]

But in a case decided just three days after *Morse*, Justice Thomas himself emphatically rejected the idea of "deference to local authorities" as a dangerous abdication of judges' "constitutional responsibilities," and held that parents could challenge the application of a school's rules to their children as a violation of the Constitution.[115] Right after voting to uphold the Juneau School Board's discipline of Frederick, Justice Thomas voted with a majority of the Supreme Court to strike down the Seattle and Louisville school boards' use of race in student assignment to promote "racial balance" and "diversity" in its schools.[116] To illustrate the risks of deferring to school boards, he pointed to the bizarre "racial theories endorsed by the Seattle school board," which defined "individualism" as a form of "cultural racism," and attacked the concept of a "melting pot" and colorblindness, on its website.[117]

Ironically, if Justice Thomas had approached the Seattle and Louisville cases the way he did *Morse*—by asking whether Nineteenth and early Twentieth century courts had historically permitted the

[113] Morse, 127 S. Ct. at 2635 (Thomas, J., concurring) (citing tradition in which "courts routinely deferred to schools authority to make rules," and "treated identically" both "speech rules and other school rules"); *id.* at 2631 (parents "delegate" their "parental authority" to schools under the doctrine of in loco parentis").

[114] *Id.* at 2635.

[115] Parents Involved in Community Schools v. Seattle School District No. 1, 127 S. Ct. 2738, 2783, 2788 n.30 (2007) (Thomas, J. concurring).

[116] *Id.*

[117] *Id.* at 2788 n.30. My brief in the Seattle case discussed these bizarre racial theories. Amicus Curiae Brief of Competitive Enterprise Institute in Support of Petitioner at 2–3, Parents Involved in Community Schools v. Seattle School District No. 1 127 S. Ct. 2738 (2007) (filed Aug. 17, 2006), available at http://www.cei.org/pdf/5482.pdf.

challenged school board practice, and deferring to the decisions of school officials—he would have had to reach the exact opposite result, since the use of race in student assignment was, unfortunately, consistently upheld by courts in the Nineteenth and early Twentieth centuries;[118] and remains a sadly common practice today by schools seeking to promote "racial balance."[119]

Justice Thomas's suggestion that parents agree with school policies if they send their children to school is belied by parents' frequent lawsuits against schools over values. For example, parents sued a Massachusetts school system for forcing their children to attend an "AIDS awareness" assembly at which they were barraged with crude remarks celebrating anal sex.[120]

3. *Justice Thomas Contradicts His Own Rulings*

Moreover, Justice Thomas himself has previously recognized that students have free speech rights, in ruling against viewpoint discrimination in the funding of student groups at the University of Virginia and the University of Wisconsin.[121] While his concurrence in *Morse* was "limited to elementary and secondary education,"[122] and free

[118] E.g., Plessy v. Ferguson, 163 U.S. 537 (1896); Berea College v. Kentucky, 211 U.S. 45 (1908); Lehew v. Brummell, 103 Mo. 546 (1890); People ex rel. King v. Gallagher, 93 N.Y. 438 (1883); Ward v. Flood, 48 Cal. 36 (1874); Cory v. Carter, 48 Ind. 327 (1874); State ex rel. Garnes v. McCann, 21 Ohio St. 198 (1871); Roberts v. Boston, 5 Cush. 198 (Mass. 1849); Parents Involved in Community Schools, 127 S. Ct. at 2782–83 (Thomas, J., concurring) ("My view of the Constitution is Justice Harlan's view in Plessy: 'Our Constitution is colorblind'" (quoting Plessy, 163 U.S. at 559 (Harlan, J., dissenting))).

[119] See Parents Involved in Community Schools, 127 S. Ct. at 2783 (Thomas, J., concurring) (rejecting use of race merely because it reflects "current societal practice" and "societal practice and expectation"); *id.* at 2800 (Breyer, J., dissenting) ("The school board plans before us resemble many others adopted in the last 50 years by primary and secondary schools throughout the nation").

[120] Brown v. Hot, Sexy & Safer Prods., 68 F.3d 525 (1st Cir. 1995) (rejecting parental rights claims).

[121] Rosenberger v. Rector & Visitors of the Univ. of Va., 515 U.S. 819 (1995) (university cannot discriminate against Christian magazine in student activities funding); Bd. of Regents v. Southworth, 529 U.S. 217, 235 (2000) (using referendum to dispense student funding to political popular groups constitutes impermissible viewpoint discrimination).

[122] Morse v. Frederick, 127 S. Ct. 2618, 2631 n.3 (2007) (Thomas, J., concurring).

speech is broader at the college level,[123] the logic of his argument cannot be so limited, since the state court rulings he cited denied the existence of free speech in colleges just as in K-12 schools, as Thomas candidly conceded.[124] Indeed, his argument that voluntary attendance at a school manifests consent to its rules was made most explicitly in a case involving a college.[125]

4. Thomas Wrongly Blames Free Speech for Disorderly Schools

Thomas's concurrence closed by attacking free speech as the cause of disorder in the schools, arguing that "*Tinker* has undermined the traditional authority of teachers to maintain order in public schools," resulting in "defiance, disrespect, and disorder."[126] But *Tinker* leaves teachers with plenty of authority to maintain order, making clear that "conduct by the student, in class or out of it, which for any reason . . . materially disrupts classwork or involves substantial disorder or invasion of the rights of others is, of course, not immunized by the constitutional guarantee of freedom of speech."[127]

Thomas cited no examples of how *Tinker* caused disorder. If free speech caused disorder, one would expect to see it most in states like Massachusetts that give students more free speech than they enjoy under Supreme Court decisions like *Fraser*.[128] But there is no

[123] See Thonen v. Jenkins, 491 F.2d 722 (4th Cir. 1973) (free speech in college is "coextensive" with society at large); compare Papish v. Curators of the Univ. of Missouri, 410 U.S. 667 (1973) (graduate student's vulgarities protected) with Fraser, *supra* (high school student's vulgar speech was not protected).

[124] Morse, 127 S. Ct. at 2631 n.2 (Thomas, J., concurring) (colleges required "strict obedience").

[125] *Id.* at 2635 (citing Hamilton v. Board of Regents of University of California, 293 U.S. 245, 262 (1934) (students who chose to attend university could not challenge its military training requirement under Due Process or Privileges or Immunities Clauses)). This was the only federal case Thomas cited for his claim that students lack free speech, and the only one that raised a constitutional argument.

[126] *Id.* at 2636 (Thomas, J., concurring) (citations omitted).

[127] Tinker v. Des Moines School District, 393 U.S. 503, 513 (1969).

[128] See, e.g., Pyle v. South Hadley School Comm., 667 N.E.2d 869, 872 (Mass. 1996) (rejecting *Fraser*'s limits on students' lewd T-shirts under Massachusetts law, which allows limits on speech "only where such expression creates a disruption or disorder within the school"); Smith v. Novato Unified School Dist., 59 Cal. Rptr. 3d 508, 516 (Cal. Ct. App. 2007) (state law protects speech unprotected under U.S. Supreme Court rulings, barring a school newspaper from censoring column on illegal immigration), citing Leeb v. DeLong, 198 Cal. App. 3d 47, 54 (Cal. Ct. App. 1988).

evidence of that. And the campus disorders of the 1960s began long before the 1969 *Tinker* decision.

Thomas's opinion reflected a misunderstanding of the challenges facing educators, which have little to do with free speech. Other legal changes—such as cumbersome disciplinary procedures mandated by state education codes and case law,[129] the Individuals with Disabilities Education Act, and disparate-impact regulations that make teachers reluctant to suspend "too many" disruptive minority students for fear of discrimination charges[130]—have created far more obstacles to discipline than free speech.

The worst example is the 1975 Individuals with Disabilities Education Act (IDEA).[131] It forces schools to provide schooling to all children with behavioral or other disabilities, even if they are dangerous and "have been suspended or expelled from school" for misconduct.[132] That is true even if the misconduct was unrelated to the student's disability, such as a murder committed by a student with a learning disability.[133]

Violent students cannot be suspended or expelled without the school first seeking a judicial hearing, if the violence supposedly

[129] See, e.g., Goss v. Lopez, 419 U.S. 565 (1975) (even though principal who suspended students for brawling in the school lunchroom personally witnessed the fight, the Court concluded he had failed to give the students an adequate hearing before suspending them).

[130] See, e.g., Edmund Janko, It Still Leaves a Bad Taste, City Journal (Summer 2006), available at http://www.city-journal.org/html/16_3_diarist.html (in response to inquiry from Office for Civil Rights, complaining that school "had suspended black students far out of proportion to their numbers in [its] student population," school decided "we needed to suspend fewer minorities or haul more white folks into the dean's office for our ultimate punishment." As a result, "obscenities directed at a teacher would mean, in cases involving minority students, a rebuke from the dean and a notation on the record or a letter home rather than [the] suspension" that white students would receive).

[131] 20 U.S.C. § 1400 et seq.

[132] 20 U.S.C. § 1412(a)(1)(A).

[133] See 20 U.S.C. §§ 1415(j), 1415(k)(4); Amos v. Maryland Department of Public Safety & Correctional Services, 126 F.3d 589, 603 n.8 (4th Cir. 1997) ("Congress amended the [IDEA] to ensure, contrary to our holding in [Virginia v.] Riley, [106 F.3d 559 (4th Cir. 1997) (en banc)], that states provide educational services to disabled children expelled from school for misconduct unrelated to their disabilities"); Riley, 106 F.3d at 562 (government said even murderers are entitled to schooling, such as being tutored in prison).

stems from a behavioral or emotional disability.[134] As a result, there are "'examples of kids who have sexually assaulted their teacher and are then returned to the classroom.'"[135] That has a big effect on school discipline, since "special education students account for a disproportionate share of school violence and disciplinary problems."[136] They account for about 12 percent of all children and adolescents,[137] but commit a far higher percentage of school violence.[138]

The IDEA also effectively requires school systems to "mainstream" many students with behavioral disabilities.[139] The "rush to mainstream" such children disrupts many of the classes into which they are thrust, "alienating teachers and driving some of the best from their profession."[140]

The IDEA has produced a flood of lawsuits. It is "reportedly the fourth most litigated federal statute,"[141] and "disagreements involving punishment" under the IDEA "often head to court."[142] By contrast, free speech lawsuits by students are fairly rare. Getting rid of

[134] Honig v. Doe, 484 U.S. 305, 312–15, 323 (1988) (school could not unilaterally expel students for "violent and disruptive conduct" arising from their disabilities, since "the removal of disabled students could be accomplished only with the permission of the parents or, as a last resort, the courts," and school officials could not "read a 'dangerousness' exception into" the IDEA); 20 U.S.C. § 1415(j).

[135] Kay S. Hymowitz, Who Killed School Discipline?, City Journal, Spring 2000 (quoting a school board attorney), available at http://www.city-journal.org/html/10_2_who_killed_school_dis.html.

[136] See, e.g., Robert Tansho, Educating Eric, Wall Street Journal, May 12, 2007, at A1, available at 2007 WLNR 9144018.

[137] Karen Berkowitz, Attorney: Disabilities Law Confusing, Contradictory, Buffalo Grove Countryside, June 14, 2007, abstract available at 2007 WLNR 11780215.

[138] See Boston Globe, Editorial, A Clash of Rights in Education, Feb. 1, 2007, at A8, available at 2007 WLNR 3934276, ("special education students issued threats at a significantly higher rate (33 per 1,000) than regular education students (6.9 per 1,000)," and their threats were more "serious").

[139] See Tansho, Educating Eric, Wall Street Journal, May 12, 2007, at A1; A Clash of Rights in Education, *supra* note 138, at n.136.

[140] See John Hechinger, 'Mainstreaming' Trend Tests Classroom Goals, Wall Street Journal, June 25, 2007, at A1, abstract available at 2007 WLNR 12072470.

[141] Walt Gardner, Letter, Special Education Abuses, New York Times, April 25, 2007, at A26, available at 2007 WLNR 7783903 (letter from veteran teacher); see 28 U.S.C. § 1415 (annotated code lists numerous court decisions involving just the IDEA section involving "procedural safeguards").

[142] Harriet Tramer, Awareness of Disability Law Up Among Lawyers, Families, Crain's Cleveland Business, April 16, 2007, at 15, available at 2007 WLNR 7386331.

free speech rights will do nothing about the impediment to discipline created by statutes like the IDEA. It will simply make censorship more glaring by allowing some students to be disciplined for harmless speech while other students are able to use the threat of lawsuits to avoid punishment for violence.

Indeed, censorship may actually promote disorder. Colleges with stringent speech codes often are not peaceful or harmonious places.[143] One of the cases that Justice Thomas cited with approval upheld discipline of a student for publicizing fire-safety problems.[144] Such discipline could easily cause unrest in a student body angry about school officials' indifference to their welfare. As Justice Brandeis observed, since "repression breeds hate," and "hate menaces stable government," "the path of safety lies in the opportunity to discuss freely supposed grievances and proposed remedies," not in censorship.[145]

H. The Justices Rightly Rejected Censorship of Political Speech

While the justices wrongly created a new "drug exception" to the First Amendment, they rightly declined to include political speech advocating drug legalization within that exception. In holding Frederick's speech was not protected, the Court emphasized the non-political nature of the speech, observing that "this is plainly not a case about political debate over the criminalization of drug use or possession" and that "not even Frederick argues that the banner conveys any sort of political or religious message."[146] And the day after its ruling, the Court refused to hear an appeal of a lower court decision holding that a student's anti-Bush T-shirt was protected despite containing drug and alcohol-related images.[147]

The two justices who provided the deciding votes in favor of the school district, Justices Alito and Kennedy, emphasized that their decision "provides no support for any restriction of speech that can

[143] See Alan Kors & Harvey Silverglate, The Shadow University (1998) (discussing speech codes).

[144] Morse v. Frederick, 127 S. Ct. 2618, 2632 (2007) (Thomas, J., concurring) (citing Wooster v. Sunderland, 27 Cal. App. 51, 52 (Cal. Ct. App. 1915)).

[145] Whitney v. California, 274 U.S. 357, 375 (1927) (Brandeis, J., concurring).

[146] Morse, 127 S. Ct. at 2625.

[147] See Guiles v. Marineau, 461 F.3d 320 (2d Cir. 2006), cert. denied, 75 USLW 3313 (2007).

plausibly be interpreted as commenting on any political or social issue, including speech on issues such as "the wisdom of the war on drugs or of legalizing marijuana for medicinal use."[148] Similarly, the three dissenters agreed on "the constitutional imperative to permit unfettered debate, even among high school students, about the wisdom of the war on drugs or of legalizing marijuana for medical use."[149]

As the dissenters observed, the case arose in Alaska, and "the legalization of marijuana is an issue of considerable public concern in Alaska," since the "State Supreme Court held in 1975 that Alaska's constitution protects the right of adults to possess less than four ounces of marijuana for personal use," a ruling the voters responded to both by voting (unsuccessfully) to ban marijuana possession in general, and by voting to decriminalize its use for medical purposes.[150] At least six other states have also held referenda on whether to legalize marijuana.[151]

Unlike Alaska state law, federal law bans marijuana possession.[152] But federal law apparently contains a religious exemption,[153] so not all marijuana use is illegal. The fact that not all marijuana use is illegal is an additional argument that Frederick could have made, but did not make, against banning pro-drug speech.[154]

[148] Morse, 127 S. Ct. at 2636 (Alito, J., concurring); see Marks v. United States, 430 U.S. 188, 193 (1977) (court's holding is "position taken by those . . . who concurred in the judgment on the narrowest grounds").

[149] Morse, 127 S. Ct. at 2649 (Stevens, J., dissenting); accord *id.* at 2651 (advocating protection for "speech suggesting" that drug war is "futile").

[150] *Id.* at 2649 n.8 (Stevens, J., dissenting) (citing Ravin v. State, 537 P.2d 494 (Alaska 1975)); Initiative Proposal No. 2, §§ 1–2 (effective Mar. 3, 1991), 11 Alaska Stat., p. 872 (Lexis 2006) (attempting to recriminalize marijuana) (invalidated under state law in Noy v. State, 83 P.3d 538 (Alaska App. 2003)); 1998 Ballot Measure No. 8 (approved Nov. 3, 1998), codified at Alaska Stat. §§ 11.71.090, 17.37.010–17.37.080 (medical marijuana initiative).

[151] See Brief for Respondents, Morse v. Frederick, 127 S. Ct. 2618 (2007) (filed Feb. 20, 2007), available 2007 WL 579230 at 17 (listing states).

[152] See Gonzales v. Raich, 545 U.S. 1 (2005) (federal law bans marijuana even when state law permits it).

[153] See Gonzales v. O Centro Espirita Beneficente Uniao Do Vegetal, 546 U.S. 418 (2006) (affirming preliminary injunction against prosecuting a sect for using a hallucinogen in communion, since the Religious Freedom Restoration Act created a probable exemption to federal drug laws).

Carving out an exception for speech of political or social importance was perfectly sensible and in accord with the Court's own past precedents. The Supreme Court frequently exempts speech on matters of public concern from regulations that prohibit speech of lesser importance, recognizing that state interests that are strong enough to justify restricting ordinary speech may be inadequate to justify restricting public debate or core political speech.[155] Society has a compelling interest in ensuring that "debate on public issues" like drug legalization is "uninhibited, robust, and wide open,"[156] which would be undermined by censorship.[157]

I. The Justices Rightly Did Not Apply a Threshold "Public Concern" Test to Student Speech

Another, smaller victory for students' rights came in the Court's tacit conclusion that students—unlike government employees—need not show that their speech addresses a matter of public concern for it to enjoy some degree of protection. The school district argued that Frederick's speech was not protected under the Supreme Court's *Tinker* decision because it was not—like the antiwar armband in *Tinker*—"political expression."[158]

[154] See This That & The Other Gift and Tobacco, Inc. v. Cobb County, 439 F.3d 1275 (11th Cir. 2006) (since state's ban on sex toys contained a medical exemption, sex toy advertising could not be banned).

[155] Compare Dunn & Bradstreet, Inc. v. Greenmoss Builders, Inc., 472 U.S. 749 (1985) (strict liability for defamation of private figure on matter of private concern) with Rosenbloom v. Metromedia, 403 U.S. 29 (1971) (negligence required for liability for defamation on matter of public concern); see also Connick v. Myers, 461 U.S. 138, 152 (1983) ("stronger showing" of disruption required "if the employee's speech more substantially addresses matters of public concern"); accord Hall v. Marion School District No. 2, 31 F.3d 183, 195 (4th Cir. 1994); Miller v. California, 413 U.S. 15, 34 (1973) (exempting speech with "serious literary, political, or scientific value" from obscenity).

[156] New York Times v. Sullivan, 376 U.S. 254, 271 (1964) (First Amendment reflects "profound national commitment to the principle that debate on public issues should be uninhibited, robust, and wide open"); cf. Belyeu v. Coosa County Bd. of Educ., 998 F.2d 925, 928 (11th Cir. 1993) ("compelling interest in the unrestrained discussion of racial problems").

[157] Blum v. Schlegel, 18 F.3d 1005, 1011 (2d Cir. 1994) (law professor's advocacy of marijuana legalization was protected, given need for "free and open debate" and harm to educational process from "excessive regulation of . . . speech").

[158] See, e.g., Petitioners' Brief, Morse v. Frederick, 127 S. Ct. 2618 (2007) (filed Jan. 16, 2007), available at 2007 WL 118979 (Frederick's "message lay far outside the province of Tinker-protected political expression").

In First Amendment cases in general, speech need not be political to be protected.[159] But some courts have held that students' speech must be on a matter of public concern to be protected, excluding speech deemed trivial.[160] By contrast, most courts have rejected the argument that student speech must be on a matter of "public concern" to be protected,[161] the way that public employees' speech must be.[162] These rulings have reasoned that the "public concern" limit on speech generally applies only to public employees, not First Amendment plaintiffs in general;[163] is justified by reasons that apply to employees, but not students;[164] and has never been applied by the Supreme Court in its rulings on student speech.[165]

None of the justices accepted the argument that student speech needs to be political or on a matter of public concern to be protected under *Tinker*. Indeed, three of the justices found his speech protected despite their conclusion that Frederick's banner contained nothing more than a "nonsense message."[166] And the majority, rather than issuing a short opinion finding Frederick's speech unprotected due to its lack of political content, subjected his banner to extended analysis before finding it unprotected due to the government's important interest in curbing drug use. The majority did, however, treat the lack of a political message as an important factor in finding that his free speech rights were outweighed by the school's interests.[167]

[159] E.g., United Mine Workers v. Illinois State Bar Ass'n, 389 U.S. 217, 223 (1967); Time, Inc. v. Hill, 385 U.S. 374, 388 (1967); NAACP v. Alabama, 357 U.S. 449, 460 (1958).

[160] Marcum v. Dahl, 658 F.2d 731, 734 (10th Cir. 1981); Richard v. Perkins, 373 F. Supp. 2d 1211, 1217 (D. Kan. 2005).

[161] E.g., Pinard v. Clatskanie School District, 467 F.3d 755, 765 (9th Cir. 2006); Garcia v. S.U.N.Y. Health Sciences Center, 280 F.3d 98, 106 (2d Cir. 2001); Qvyjt v. Lin, 953 F. Supp. 244, 247–48 (N.D. Ill. 1997).

[162] Connick v. Myers, 461 U.S. 138 (1983).

[163] Pinard, 467 F.3d at 765–66.

[164] Garcia, 280 F.3d at 106.

[165] Qvyjt, 953 F, Supp. at 247–48 (citing Papish v. Board of Curators of University of Missouri, 410 U.S. 667, 670–671 (1973)).

[166] Morse v. Frederick, 127 S. Ct. 2618, 2649 (2007) (Stevens, J., dissenting).

[167] *Id.* at 2625 (majority opinion); *id.* at 2636 (Alito, J., concurring).

VI. Conclusion

In creating a new "drug exception" to free speech in the public schools, the Supreme Court's decision in *Morse v. Frederick* undermined fundamental First Amendment protections against viewpoint discrimination, and censorship based on speculative fears of harm. It did nothing to make schools safer or more orderly, since it is other legal mandates, not free speech rights, that have made schools less safe. The justices did, however, rightly reject curbs on political speech about drug legalization.

Gonzales v. Carhart: An Alternate Opinion

*Brannon P. Denning**

SUPREME COURT OF THE UNITED STATES

Nos. 05-380 and 05-1382

ALBERTO R. GONZALES, ATTORNEY GENERAL,
PETITIONER

v.

LEROY CARHART ET AL.,
RESPONDENTS.

ON WRIT OF CERTIORARI TO THE UNITED STATES COURT OF APPEALS FOR THE EIGHTH CIRCUIT

ALBERTO R. GONZALES, ATTORNEY GENERAL,
PETITIONER

v.

PLANNED PARENTHOOD FEDERATION OF AMERICA, INC.
ET AL.,
RESPONDENTS.

ON WRIT OF CERTIORARI TO THE UNITED STATES COURT OF APPEALS FOR THE NINTH CIRCUIT

[April 18, 2007]

CHIEF JUSTICE ROBERTS delivered the opinion of the Court.

*Professor and Director of Faculty Development, Cumberland School of Law at Samford University. This article is fondly dedicated to the memory of Boris I. Bittker (1916–2005), who was a master at the article-as-judicial-opinion. See Boris I. Bittker, *The Case of the Fictitious Taxpayer: The Federal Taxpayer's Suit Twenty Years after* Flast v. Cohen, 36 U. Chi. L. Rev. 364 (1969); Boris I. Bittker, *The Case of the Checker-Board Ordinance: An Experiment in Race Relations*, 71 Yale L.J. 1387 (1962).

These cases require us to consider the constitutionality of 18 U.S.C. § 1531 (2000 ed., Supp. IV), the Partial-Birth Abortion Ban Act of 2003 (hereinafter the "Act"). After extensive trials and appeals in the two cases, the Court of Appeals for the Eighth Circuit and the Court of Appeals for the Ninth Circuit affirmed lower court decisions enjoining the enforcement of the Act. *See Planned Parenthood Federation of Am. v. Gonzales,* 435 F.3d 1163 (9th Cir. 2006); *Carhart v. Gonzales*, 413 F.3d 791 (8th Cir. 2005); *Planned Parenthood Federation of Am. v. Ashcroft,* 320 F. Supp. 2d 957 (N.D. Cal. 2004); *Carhart v. Ashcroft*, 331 F. Supp. 2d 805 (D. Neb. 2004). The Courts of Appeals based their rulings on our prior decision in *Stenberg v. Carhart*, 530 U.S. 914 (2000), which, in turn, employed the framework developed in *Planned Parenthood of Southeastern Pa. v. Casey*, 505 U.S. 833 (1992) grounding the right to abortion in the Due Process Clause of the Fourteenth Amendment. In addition to the due process issue, we granted certiorari on "whether 18 U.S.C. § 1531 is a valid exercise of congressional power under the Commerce Clause." We conclude that it is not, thus affirming the lower courts, but without reaching the respondents' due process claims.

I

Congress passed the Act in response to legislators' and constituents' disapproval of, indeed revulsion at, a particular method of late-term abortion termed "dilation and evacuation" ("D&E"), in which the physician dilates the woman and partially exposes the fetus outside the womb before piercing its brain and suctioning out the brain's contents. This so-called "intact" D&E differs from the standard D&E because the latter sometimes results in dismemberment of the fetus during the procedure. Further, though the evidence here is disputed, the intact D&E procedure may result in less risk to the mother in terms of scarring and bleeding than the standard D&E. Congress approved the Act in 1996 and 1997, but both times it was vetoed by President Clinton. The Act was then passed again in 2003, and signed by President Bush on November 5, 2003. Specifically, the Act reads, in relevant part:

> (a) Any physician who, in or affecting interstate or foreign commerce, knowingly performs a partial-birth abortion and thereby kills a human fetus shall be fined under this title or imprisoned not more than 2 years, or both. This subsection

> does not apply to a partial-birth abortion that is necessary to save the life of a mother whose life is endangered by a physical disorder, physical illness, or physical injury, including a life-endangering physical condition caused by or arising from the pregnancy itself. This subsection takes effect 1 day after the enactment.
> (b) As used in this section—
> (1) the term "partial-birth abortion" means an abortion in which the person performing the abortion—
> (A) deliberately and intentionally vaginally delivers a living fetus until, in the case of a head-first presentation, the entire fetal head is outside the body of the mother, or, in the case of breech presentation, any part of the fetal trunk past the navel is outside the body of the mother, for the purpose of performing an overt act that the person knows will kill the partially delivered living fetus; and
> (B) performs the overt act, other than completion of delivery, that kills the partially delivered living fetus; and
> (2) the term "physician" means a doctor of medicine or osteopathy legally authorized to practice medicine and surgery by the State in which the doctor performs such activity, or any other individual legally authorized by the State to perform abortions: Provided, however, that any individual who is not a physician or not otherwise legally authorized by the State to perform abortions, but who nevertheless directly performs a partial-birth abortion, shall be subject to the provisions of this section.
> . . .
> (d) (1) A defendant accused of an offense under this section may seek a hearing before the State Medical Board on whether the physician's conduct was necessary to save the life of the mother whose life was endangered by a physical disorder, physical illness, or physical injury, including a life-endangering physical condition caused by or arising from the pregnancy itself.
> (2) The findings on that issue are admissible on that issue at the trial of the defendant. Upon a motion of the defendant, the court shall delay the beginning of the trial for not more than 30 days to permit such a hearing to take place.
> (e) A woman upon whom a partial-birth abortion is performed may not be prosecuted under this section, for a conspiracy to violate this section, or for an offense under section 2, 3, or 4 of this title based on a violation of this section.

18 U.S.C. § 1531 (2000 ed., Supp. IV). Congress included extensive findings with the Act, which we discuss below, but a threshold

question is whether Congress has the power, under the Commerce Clause of Article I, section 8, to pass the Act in the first place.[1] For the answer to that question, we must review our recent Commerce Clause jurisprudence. *See Gonzales v. Raich*, 545 U.S. 1 (2005); *United States v. Morrison*, 529 U.S. 598 (2000); *United States v. Lopez*, 514 U.S. 549 (1995).

II

A

Time was, claims that a statute exceeded congressional power under the Commerce Clause had replaced equal protection claims as the "usual last resort of constitutional arguments. . . ." *Buck v. Bell*, 274 U.S. 200, 208 (1927). That changed in 1995 when this Court invalidated the Gun Free School Zones Act ("GFSZA"), which prohibited the knowing possession of "a firearm at a place that the individual knows, or has reasonable cause to believe, is a school zone." 18 U.S.C. § 922(q)(1)(A) (1988 ed., Supp. V). We concluded in *Lopez* that the GFSZA regulated activity—mere possession of a firearm—that could in no way "substantially affect" interstate commerce. *Lopez*, 514 U.S. at 552. Five years later, we similarly concluded that Congress did not have power under the Commerce Clause or the Fourteenth Amendment to create a federal civil cause of action for violence motivated by "gender-based animus." *Morrison*, 529 U.S. at 617-18 (striking down 42 U.S.C. § 13981). The activity in question, we held, did not constitute activity that had a substantial effect on interstate commerce. But two terms ago we upheld the application of the Controlled Substances Act, 21 U.S.C. §§ 801 *et seq.*, prohibiting the sale or possession of Schedule I drugs, like marijuana, to one who grows or uses marijuana pursuant to a state law permitting such growth or possession for medicinal use. *Raich*, 545 U.S. at 32–33. We concluded in *Raich* that if Congress could, as all the litigants conceded, eliminate a market in interstate commerce *in toto*, then it could regulate every single instance of that market, no matter

[1]We are aware that Congress also claimed authority to pass the statute under its "power to enforce, by appropriate legislation, the provisions of" the Fourteenth Amendment. U.S. Const. amend. XIV, § 5. Whether that basis for the Act is consistent with our interpretation of section 5 in *City of Boerne v. Flores*, 521 U.S. 507 (1997) is a question that we must leave for another time as it is not properly before this Court today.

how local or non-commercial the activity. *Id.* ("[T]he case for the exemption comes down to the claim that a locally cultivated product that is used domestically rather than sold on the open market is not subject to federal regulation. Given the findings in the [Controlled Substances Act ("CSA")] and the undisputed magnitude of the commercial market for marijuana, our decisions in *Wickard v. Filburn* and the later cases endorsing its reasoning foreclose that claim.")

The question in this case, thus, is whether the Act is more like those invalidated in *Lopez* and *Morrison*, or more like the application of the CSA upheld in *Raich*. We are aided somewhat by the nature of the respondents' claim: unlike the respondent in *Raich*, the parties here are challenging the Act on its face, just as the GFSZA and the civil-suit provision at issue in *Morrison* were. As was noted at the time, that difference was a significant one between *Lopez* and *Morrison* on the one hand, and *Raich* on the other. Randy E. Barnett, *Limiting* Raich, 9 Lewis & Clark L. Rev. 743, 744–45 (2005) ("In one important respect, the holdings of *Lopez* and *Morrison* survive completely intact: a statute that is on its face entirely outside the powers of Congress described by the Commerce and Necessary and Proper Clauses is unconstitutional") (footnote omitted). We will thus analyze the Act using the framework developed in *Lopez* and applied in *Morrison*, though, as will become apparent below, *Raich* is not without significance.

B

In *Lopez*, after an extensive survey of this Court's case law, Chief Justice Rehnquist concluded that Congress could regulate three broad classes of activities: (i) the channels of interstate commerce; (ii) instrumentalities of interstate commerce, including things and persons moving in interstate commerce; and (iii) intrastate activities that nevertheless "substantially affect" interstate commerce. *Lopez*, 514 U.S. at 558–59; *see also Morrison*, 529 U.S. at 608–09. No claim is made that the Act regulates the channels of interstate commerce, or its instrumentalities. The Act criminalizes a service performed in a single state usually on a person who resides in that state. Thus, we must analyze the Act under the third of *Lopez*'s categories—local activities that have a "substantial effect" on interstate commerce.

The Act uses the language "in or affecting interstate or foreign commerce" in section (a), thus signaling Congress's intent to exercise its power to the maximum. *See Allied-Bruce Terminix Cos. v. Dobson*, 513 U.S. 265, 273 (1995) (noting that the words "affecting commerce" "are broader than the often found words of art 'in commerce.' They therefore cover more than 'only persons or activities within the flow of interstate commerce'") (quoting *United States v. American Building Maintenance Industries*, 422 U.S. 271, 276 (1975), quoting *Gulf Oil Corp. v. Copp Paving Co.*, 419 U.S. 186, 195 (1974)); *see also Gulf Oil Corp.*, 419 U.S. at 195 (defining "in commerce" as related to the "flow" and defining the "flow" to include "the generation of goods and services for interstate markets and their transport and distribution to the consumer"). As we noted in *Allied-Bruce Terminix*, "[t]hat phrase—'affecting commerce'—normally signals a congressional intent to exercise its Commerce Clause powers to the full." *Allied-Bruce Terminix Cos.*, 513 U.S. at 273. Therefore, if the Act is to be upheld, it must satisfy the *Lopez* and *Morrison* factors used to determine whether intrastate activity nevertheless substantially affected commerce such that it could be reached by Congress.

C

In *Lopez*, the majority opinion listed criteria by which the impact on interstate commerce could be assessed: (i) whether the regulated activity was economic or non-economic; (ii) whether there was a jurisdictional element tying the regulated activity to interstate commerce so as to permit a case-by-case inquiry when the connection to interstate commerce was not apparent; (iii) whether the statute was accompanied by congressional findings describing the connection of the regulated activity to interstate commerce; (iv) whether the regulation was part of a nationwide regulatory scheme whose efficacy would be undermined if Congress could not reach the activity; and (v) whether accepting arguments regarding the connection of interstate activity would mean, as a practical matter, that the commerce power had no enforceable limit.[2] *Lopez*, 514 U.S. at 559–61. Justices Kennedy and O'Connor also urged the Court to consider

[2]This has been referred to as the "non-infinity principle," *i.e.*, no interpretation of the Commerce Clause that permits Congress infinite power under that clause can be the correct interpretation of it. *See* David B. Kopel & Glenn H. Reynolds, *Taking Federalism Seriously:* Lopez *and the Partial-Birth Abortion Ban Act*, 30 Conn. L. Rev. 59, 69 (1997). We think this term accurately—and more elegantly—captures the point that we were trying to make in *Lopez*.

whether this was an area of traditional state (as opposed to federal) concern. *Id.* at 577 (Kennedy, J., concurring) ("Were the Federal Government to take over the regulation of entire areas of traditional state concern, areas having nothing to do with the regulation of commercial activities, the boundaries between the spheres of federal and state authority would blur and political responsibility would become illusory"). The Court included this in its list of factors in *Morrison*, 529 U.S. at 618 (noting that in striking down the civil suit provision, "we preserve one of the few principles that has been consistent since the [Commerce] Clause was adopted. The regulation and punishment of intrastate violence that is not directed at the instrumentalities, channels, or goods involved in interstate commerce *has always been the province of the States*") (emphasis added).

Questions remained after *Lopez*. For example, it was unclear whether the presence of all factors was *required* to support a finding of "substantially affects" interstate commerce. If not, then which ones were more important? *See* Glenn H. Reynolds & Brannon P. Denning, *Lower Court Readings of* Lopez, or *What If the Supreme Court Held a Constitutional Revolution and Nobody Came?*, 2000 Wis. L. Rev. 369, 375–78 (discussing questions that remained after after *Lopez*). *Lopez* itself was not clear; we offered no rank ordering of the criteria, nor prescribed relative weights to be assigned to each factor.

Five years later, *Morrison* answered some, if not all of these questions. The Court clarified that the economic or non-economic nature of the regulated activity was "central to our decision in" *Lopez*. 529 U.S. at 610–11 ("[A] fair reading of *Lopez* shows that the noneconomic, criminal nature of the conduct at issue was central to our decision in that case"); we also stressed the importance of the jurisdictional element. 529 U.S. at 611–12 ("Although *Lopez* makes clear that such a jurisdictional element would lend support to the argument that [the statute] is sufficiently tied to interstate commerce, Congress elected to cast [its] remedy over a wider, and more purely intrastate, body of violent crime") (footnote omitted).

Further, though the civil suit provision in question was accompanied by extensive congressional findings, the Court emphasized that mere recitation of a connection between the regulated activity and interstate commerce would not suffice. In our opinion, the findings in *Morrison* were "substantially weakened by the fact that they rel[ied] so heavily on a method of reasoning that we have already rejected as unworkable if we are to maintain the Constitution's enumeration of powers." *Id.* at 615. Specifically, we rejected the rationale that would have permitted Congress "to regulate any crime as long as the nationwide, aggregate impact of that crime has substantial effects on employment, production, transit, or consumption." *Id.*

With these principles in mind, we turn to the question of the Act's constitutionality.

III

A

The first question concerns the nature of the regulated activity; the correct characterization of the regulated activity lies at the heart of our recent Commerce Clause jurisprudence. As commentators noted at the time, *Lopez* tended to use the terms "economic" and "commercial" interchangeably. Reynolds & Denning, *supra*, at 375 & n.39 (quoting *Lopez,* 514 U.S. at 560, 561, 566, 567). In *Morrison,* however, we focused on whether the regulated activity was, in some sense, "economic," even if it was not strictly "commercial." 529 U.S. at 610 ("[A] fair reading of *Lopez* shows that the noneconomic, criminal nature of the conduct at issue was central to our decision in that case"). While we declined to "adopt a categorical rule against aggregating the effects of any noneconomic activity" in *Morrison,* we noted that "our cases have upheld Commerce Clause regulation of intrastate activity only where that activity is economic in nature." 529 U.S. at 613.

Applying the teachings of *Lopez* and *Morrison,* we concluded in *Raich* that "[u]nlike those at issue in [our prior cases] the activities regulated by the [Controlled Substances Act] are quintessentially economic," which, the Court went on to define as "the production, distribution, and consumption of commodities." 545 U.S. at 25. Since the CSA regulated "the presumption, distribution, and consumption of commodities for which there is an established, and lucrative, interstate market," the Court had "no difficulty concluding that Congress acted rationally in determining that" locally-produced, consumed, or possessed marijuana—even for medicinal purposes—was covered by the CSA. *Id.* at 26–27. As Justice Scalia explained in his concurring opinion:

> In the CSA, Congress has undertaken to extinguish the interstate market in Schedule I controlled substances, including

> marijuana. The Commerce Clause unquestionably permits this. . . . To effectuate its objective, Congress has prohibited almost all intrastate activities related to Schedule I substances—both economic activities (manufacture, distribution, possession with intent to distribute) and noneconomic activities (simple possession). . . . That simple possession is a noneconomic activity is immaterial to whether it can be prohibited as a necessary part of a larger regulation. Rather, Congress's authority to enact all of these prohibitions of intrastate controlled-substance activities depends only upon whether they are appropriate means of achieving the legitimate end of eradicating Schedule I substances from interstate commerce.

Id. at 39–40 (Scalia, J., concurring).

Following our cases, then, the question presented by the Act is whether a prohibition on the provision of even a noncommercial, locally-rendered, medical service by a physician should be considered "economic"?

The government asserts vigorously that it is regulating the provision of medical services, an economic activity. In part, the government relies on the definition of "economic" activity adopted in *Raich*. Specifically, the Government urges us to view abortion merely as one class of activities within the broad field of "health care," which, because of its size, the Government argues, is surely amenable to congressional regulation. In its brief and at oral argument it quoted one expert who testified that

> The provision of abortion services is commerce . . . at least where payment is received from some source. . . . Abortion services would generally be classed with the broader category of medical and health care services for purposes of Commerce Clause analysis. Health care constitutes . . . a large and significant portion of the national economy, and it would seem absurd to hold that an industry comprising one-seventh of the national economy could not be regulated under the Commerce Clause.

Partial Birth Abortion: Hearing on H.R. 1833 Before the Subcomm. on the Constitution of the House Comm. on the Judiciary, 104th Cong. 102 (1995) (testimony of David M. Smolin, Professor of Law, Cumberland School of Law). Further, the Government cites our conclusion in

Raich that if Congress can eliminate the interstate market in a particular item or activity, it may apply its prohibition to even the most local, non-commercial instance, at least as long as Congress had a rational basis for concluding that leaving those local instances "outside federal control would . . . affect price and market conditions" generally. *Raich*, 545 U.S. at 19.

We begin our analysis with a couple of observations. First, our decision in *Raich* offers little guidance for deciding the present case. In it, the constitutionality of the Controlled Substances Act itself, as opposed to a particular application of it, was not at issue; plaintiffs conceded its constitutionality. *Id.* at 15 ("Respondents in this case do not dispute that the passage of the CSA, as part of the Comprehensive Drug Abuse Prevention and Control Act, was well within Congress' commerce power. . . . Nor do they contend that any provision or section of the CSA amounts to an unconstitutional exercise of congressional authority."). Here, by contrast, the very ability to regulation partial-birth abortions *at all* is the issue.

Second, Professor Smolin's testimony, on which the Government has heavily relied, is not helpful to its case for two reasons. Whatever the scope of Congress's power to regulate "health care" generally—a question that is not before us today—the fact is that the Act purports to regulate only one aspect of health care: partial-birth abortions. Further, the Act itself regulates *all* partial-birth abortions, not simply those in which the physician performing the procedure receives a fee.

As one commentator put it, the Act "regulates only the noneconomic part of the transaction, namely, the performance of the medical procedure." Allen Ides, *The Partial-Birth Abortion Ban Act of 2003 and the Commerce Clause*, 20 *Const. Comment.* 441, 446 (2003–2004). This is not surprising, of course, since "Congress prohibited partial-birth abortions on the ground that they are morally objectionable (like all crimes), not because they are commercial activity requiring uniform national regulation." Robert J. Pushaw, Jr., *Does Congress Have the Constitutional Power to Prohibit Partial-Birth Abortion?*, 42 Harv. J. on Legis. 319, 335 (2005).

In *Lopez* and *Morrison*, we declined to characterize as "economic" either simple possession of an item not otherwise connected to interstate commerce by the statute or violence committed against a victim because of their gender. *Lopez*, 514 U.S. at 516 (noting that the Act was "a criminal statute that by its terms has nothing to do with 'commerce' or any sort of economic enterprise, however broadly one might define those terms") (footnote omitted); *Morrison*, 529 U.S. at 613 ("Gender-motivated crimes of violence are not, in any sense of the phrase, economic activity"). In this case, we decline to find that a statute criminalizing the performance of a medical procedure on another is, without more, "economic" activity. One commentator put it succinctly:

> The performance of a partial-birth abortion bears a close resemblance to the noneconomic possession of a gun. Just as possession of a gun can occur without any commercial element, the performance of a partial-birth abortion—indeed, the performance of any medical procedure—can be accomplished without a commercial overlay. It may be that most medical procedures, including partial-birth abortions, are done for hire. But this does not alter the simple fact that the procedure itself, unadorned by any commercial exchange, is noneconomic in the same sense as gun possession.

Ides, *supra*, at 446.

The Government's argument rests on the premise that provision of a service, like a partial-birth abortion, involves some sort of wealth transfer from one person to another and, thus, in the broadest possible sense of the word could be understood to be "economic." We reject such a broad construction of that term for several reasons.

First, the Constitution speaks of the ability to regulate "commerce among the several states"; while we need not adopt a cramped construction of that phrase and limit Congress to regulating only that activity that could be considered "commercial," we hesitate to err in the other direction, and risk losing sight of Chief Justice Marshall's observation that the "enumeration" of powers "presupposes something *not* enumerated." *Gibbons v. Ogden*, 22 U.S. (9 Wheat.) 1, 74 (1824) (emphasis added). To forget Chief Justice Marshall's admonition would be to countenance what this Court has always denied: that the Federal Government possesses a general police power akin to that retained by state governments. *See Lopez*, 514 U.S. at 566 (responding to dissent's claim that decision produced "legal uncertainty" with observation that "[t]he Constitution mandates this uncertainty by withholding from Congress a plenary police power that would authorize enactment of every type of legislation").

Even were we to accept the Government's argument that performance of a partial-birth abortion is "economic," it is not sufficient for us to conclude that the Act is constitutional. At most such a conclusion merely renders the activity eligible for aggregation, which may demonstrate that the regulated activity "substantially affects" interstate commerce as our case law requires. Figures given for the number of partial birth abortions vary widely; some claim that 500 or fewer are performed each year, while others claim the number performed annually is closer to ten times that. Whatever number is correct, it is a tiny number of procedures compared to other fairly common medical procedures performed around the country. For example, in 1996, the last year comprehensive statistics are available, over 287,000 children under the age of 15 underwent tonsillectomies. Joseph Gigante, *Tonsillectomy and Adenoidectomy*, 26 Pediatrics in Review 199 (2005). According to the American Academy of Family Physicians, over one million caesarian sections are performed each year. American Academy of Family Physicians, *Caesarian Delivery in Family Medicine*, at http://www.aafp.org/online/en/home/policy/policies/c/cesarean.html (2003). Even when considered alongside the number of abortions generally performed in this country—nearly 750,000 of which were performed in 2003, according to the Centers for Disease Control—the number of partial-birth abortions are miniscule by comparison.

If one attempts to assess the monetary value represented by paid partial-birth abortions using the largest estimate of number of procedures performed, moreover, the total value, according to one estimate, was only $12 million.[3] If that number is small when compared to the fees generated by *all* abortions, estimated to "generate[] hundreds of millions of dollars in direct fees (and many more times that amount in overall economic activity)," Pushaw, *supra*, at 334 n.104, it is infinitesimal when compared to the $1.8 *trillion* spent on U.S. health care in 2004.[4]

Moreover, other factors support our conclusion that the Government fails to demonstrate that the activities regulated by the Act "substantially affect" interstate commerce.

[3]Pushaw, *supra*, at 334 & n.104. He notes that this is only a rough estimate, given the scarcity of "accurate financial statistics on partial-birth abortions. . . ." *Id.* n.104.

[4]Marc Kaufman & Rob Stein, *Record Share of Economy Spent on Health Care*, Wash. Post, Jan. 10, 2006, at A01.

B

The Government points to the presence of the Act's "jurisdictional hook," which, it argues, distinguishes it from the acts invalidated in both *Lopez* and *Morrison*, and insulates it from a facial challenge like that mounted here. It is true that we regarded the absence of the hook as an important factor in our previous decisions; however, we never intimated that the mere presence of such language would, in all cases, preclude a finding that a statute exceeded Congress's powers. To do otherwise would be to make "*Lopez* stand[] for nothing more than a drafting guide. . . ." *Raich*, 545 U.S. at 46 (O'Connor, J., dissenting).

The language of the Act reads: "Any physician who, *in or affecting interstate* or foreign commerce, knowingly performs a partial-birth abortion and thereby kills a human fetus shall be fined under this title or imprisoned not more than 2 years, or both." 18 U.S.C. § 1531 (emphasis added). As we noted above, the Act purports to do more than, for example, punish a physician or a patient who crosses state lines to perform or receive a partial-birth abortion. Moreover, it does not seek to prohibit the use of anything that *itself* has traveled in interstate commerce to perform a partial-birth abortion. *See, e.g.*, 18 U.S.C. § 2252(a)(4)(B) (prohibiting possession of child pornography produced with material that had traveled in interstate commerce); *United States v. Rodia*, 194 F.3d 465 (3d Cir. 1999) (upholding statute against constitutional challenge).

It is difficult to see how a physician could meaningfully perform a procedure "in" interstate commerce, unless the physician performed the procedure in a mobile unit that kept moving throughout the operation. Whether the performance of partial-birth abortions "affects" interstate commerce does not get us very far in our inquiry either, because it simply raises that question that we are considering: Do partial-birth abortions substantially affect the national economy?[5]

C

As we noted in *Lopez* and *Morrison*, where an effect on interstate commerce is not apparent, we can look to congressional findings to

[5] As one scholar put it, the Act's "jurisdictional element does not in any fashion resolve the critical question—namely, whether the performance of partial-birth abortions, either singly or in the aggregate, *substantially* affects interstate commerce." Ides, *supra*, at 458.

assist us in our inquiry. *Lopez*, 514 U.S. at 562 ("[A]s part of our independent evaluation of constitutionality under the Commerce Clause we of course consider legislative findings, and indeed even congressional committee findings, regarding effect on interstate commerce. . . ."), 563 (noting that "congressional findings [can] enable us to evaluate the legislative judgment that the activity in question substantially affected interstate commerce, even though no such substantial effect was visible to the naked eye"); *Morrison*, 529 U.S. at 612 (quoting *Lopez*).

The Act was accompanied by extensive findings—set forth in the Appendix— regarding the nature of the procedure, the frequency, and the lack of need for a health exception. Most of the findings detail the deference that this Court has claimed to show to congressional findings in particular cases. Other findings express Congress's opinion that partial-birth abortion is a morally repugnant procedure that ought never be performed, and need never be performed to protect a mother's health. Significantly, *none* of the findings address the connection between partial-birth abortions and the economy or interstate commerce, much less describing how, even in the aggregate, partial-birth abortions "substantially affect" the latter. Thus, we even lack evidence that Congress had a rational basis for concluding that substantial effects are present.

D

Further, the Act is not "part of a national regulatory scheme" whose efficacy would be undermined if the local activity is not reached. *See Lopez*, 514 U.S. at 561 ("Section 922(q) is not an essential part of a larger regulation of economic activity, in which the regulatory scheme could be undercut unless the intrastate activity were regulated"). This case is unlike *Raich* or *Wickard*, in which a goal clearly within federal power—the elimination of an interstate market in Schedule I drugs or raising the price of agricultural commodities through limits on production—would be compromised by individual evasions, no matter how minor or trivial each might be in and of itself. As we declared in *Raich*:

> *Wickard* . . . establishes that Congress can regulate purely intrastate activity that it not itself "commercial," in that it is not produced for sale, if it concludes that failure to regulate that class of activity would undercut the regulation of the

> interstate market in that commodity. . . . While the diversion of homegrown wheat tended to frustrate the federal interest in stabilizing prices by regulating the volume of commercial transactions in the interstate market, the diversion of homegrown marijuana tends to frustrate the federal interest in eliminating commercial transactions in the interstate market in their entirety. In both cases, the regulation is squarely within Congress's commerce power because production of the commodity meant for home consumption, be it wheat or marijuana, has a substantial effect on the supply and demand in the national market for that commodity.

545 U.S. at 18–19 (footnote omitted).

In contrast to those cases, the Act represents a stand-alone ban on a medical procedure that members of Congress found inhumane and immoral. The regulated activity thus looks more like the simple possession of a gun in a school zone or the creation of a civil remedy for gender-based violence invalidated in *Lopez* and *Morrison*. At the very least, this is not a case involving an attempt to carve out a class of regulated activities as too local or too noncommercial to be included within the class of activities Congress clearly has authority to regulate.

E

In *Lopez*, Justices Kennedy and O'Connor criticized the Gun Free School Zones Act for usurping the state role in both education and in the prevention and punishment of crime. Moreover, it noted that the federal law preempted state experimentation, depriving policymakers of the results from experiments in state "laboratories of democracy."

> The statute before us forecloses the States from experimenting and exercising their own judgment in an area to which States lay claim by right of history and expertise, and it does so by regulating an activity beyond the realm of commerce in the ordinary and usual sense of that term. The tendency of this statute to displace state regulation in areas of traditional state concern is evidence from its territorial operation. There are over 100,000 elementary and secondary schools in the United States.

Lopez, 514 U.S. at 583 (Kennedy, J., concurring).

Similarly, the licensing and regulation of the medical profession—and of most professions in general—is and has been the traditional province of states. If we concluded that Congress could, by exercising its commerce power, ban a procedure performed, at most, a few thousand times a year, then certainly Congress ban other procedures to which its membership objected on moral grounds. In 2004, for example, there were 11.9 million surgical and nonsurgical cosmetic procedures performed, including over 300,000 breast augmentations. The American Society for Aesthetic Plastic Surgery, Press Release, *11.9 Million Cosmetic Procedures in 2004, available at* http://www.surgery.org/press/news-release.php?iid=395 (Feb. 17, 2006). Were we to uphold the Act, we could see no reason Congress could not, on moral grounds, outlaw non-essential plastic surgery.

We are unwilling to start down this road, especially when there has been no showing that states are incapable of banning partial-birth abortions on their own, as long as they abide by this Court's decision in *Stenburg v. Carhart*, 530 U.S. 914 (2000) (invalidating Nebraska's partial-birth abortion statute based on the lack of a "health" exception). Thirty-one states have laws that ban partial-birth abortions in whole or in part. Guttmacher Institute, *State Policies in Brief: Bans on "Partial-Birth" Abortions,* available at http://www.guttmacher.org/statecenter/spibs/spib_BPBA.pdf (Aug. 1, 2007). This is not an area in which problems of coordination necessitate a uniform policy imposed by Congress, or where states are constitutionally barred from legislating at all.

F

This last point also implicates what others have termed the "non-infinity principle," i.e., that any interpretation of a constitutional power that, in essence, means that power has no judicially-enforceable limit is, perforce, incorrect. In *Lopez*, we rejected the Government's proffered arguments that a federal ban on gun possession in a school zone was justified because of the costs crime imposed on the national economy and because unsafe schools produced unproductive citizens who would eventually affect the national economy. We wrote:

> The Government admits, under its "costs of crime" reasoning, that Congress could regulate not only all violent crime, but all activities that might lead to violent crime, regardless

> of how tenuously they relate to interstate commerce. . . . Similarly, under the Government's "national productivity" reasoning, Congress could regulate any activity that it found was related to the economic productivity of individual citizens. . . . Thus, if we were to accept the Government's arguments, we are hard pressed to posit any activity by an individual that Congress is without power to regulate.

Lopez, 514 U.S. at 564. We declined "to pile inference upon inference in a manner that would bid fair to convert congressional authority under the Commerce Clause to a general police power. . . ." *Id.* at 567. In *Morrison,* we rejected a similar "costs of crime" argument contained in the congressional findings that accompanied the civil suit provision of the Violence Against Women Act:

> The reasoning that petitioners advance seeks to follow the but-for causal chain from the initial occurrence of violence crime (the suppression of which has always been the prime object of the States' police power) to every attenuated effect upon interstate commerce. If accepted, petitioners' reasoning would allow Congress to regulate any crime as long as the nationwide, aggregated impact of that crime has substantial effects on employment, production, transit or consumption.

529 U.S. at 615.

Unlike in *Morrison,* Congress appended no findings, and there is little meaningful testimony as to how partial-birth abortions affect, much less substantially affect interstate commerce—even when aggregated. Thus, we are left to speculate on why Congress might have concluded that partial-birth abortion substantially affects interstate commerce. Unfortunately, none of the reasons that we can even imagine are sufficient to render the Act constitutional.

First, there is the claim that, whether 500 or 5,000, the annual potential life eliminated by partial-birth abortions would, over time, generate productive citizens who, when employed, would substantially affect interstate commerce over their lifetimes. Not only is this precisely the sort of attenuated chain of causation that we rejected in *Lopez* and *Morrison,* its implications are fairly radical. It would, for example, potentially validate federal power to regulate regarding marriage, procreation, and childcare that even our dissenting colleagues in *Lopez* foreswore. *Lopez,* 514 U.S. at 624 (Breyer, J., dissenting) ("To hold this statute constitutional is not to 'obliterate' the 'distinction between what is national and what is local' . . . nor is it to hold that the Commerce Clause permits the Federal Government to 'regulate any activity that it found was related to the economic productivity of individual citizens,' to regulate 'marriage, divorce, and child custody,' or to regulate any and all aspects of education").

The other potential justification for the Act—that any medical procedure is "economic" and thus can be reached by Congress through the Commerce Clause—is equally problematic. For reasons articulated above, we decline to adopt such a broad definition of "commerce." To do so would fly in the face of the text of the clause itself, be inconsistent with what our case law has said about the effect the regulated activity must have on the national economy, and would convert the Commerce Clause into a federal police power. All human activity, after all, can be understood to be economic in some sense.

Thus, in order to accept that the Act regulates activity that substantially affects interstate commerce, we would again have to "pile inference upon inference" in ways we have previously declined to do. We decline to do so here, as well.

IV

We do not lightly invalidate an act of Congress, but our duty here is clear. Based on the record before us, we cannot conclude that the Act—regulating as it does local medical procedures, whether or not performed for a fee—"substantially affects" interstate commerce, as our cases require. The procedure regulated by the Act seems to us more akin to the simple possession or gender-motivated violence in *Lopez* and *Morrison*, than to either the local possession, production, or use of marijuana in *Raich* or the wheat quota enforced in *Wickard*, a case we have described as "the most far reaching example of Commerce Clause authority over intrastate activity. . . ." *Id.* at 560. Even assuming *arguendo* that partial-birth abortions constitute economic activity, thus subject to aggregation, we are unable to conclude that the aggregate effect on interstate commerce of *all* partial-birth abortions is "substantial."

The judgments of the United States Courts of Appeals for the Eighth and Ninth Circuits are affirmed.

It is so ordered.

APPENDIX TO OPINION OF ROBERTS, C.J.

SEC. 2 FINDINGS

The Congress finds and declares the following:

(1) A moral, medical, and ethical consensus exists that the practice of performing a partial-birth abortion—an abortion in which a physician delivers an unborn child's body until only the head remains inside the womb, punctures the back of the child's skull with a Sharp instrument, and sucks the child's brains out before completing delivery of the dead infant—is a gruesome and inhumane procedure that is never medically necessary and should be prohibited.

(2) Rather than being an abortion procedure that is embraced by the medical community, particularly among physicians who routinely perform other abortion procedures, partial-birth abortion remains a disfavored procedure that is not only unnecessary to preserve the health of the mother, but in fact poses serious risks to the long-term health of women and in some circumstances, their lives. As a result, at least 27 States banned the procedure as did the United States Congress which voted to ban the procedure during the 104th, 105th, and 106th Congresses.

(3) In *Stenberg v. Carhart*, 530 U.S. 914, 932 (2000), the United States Supreme Court opined "that significant medical authority supports the proposition that in some circumstances, [partial birth abortion] would be the safest procedure" for pregnant women who wish to undergo an abortion. Thus, the Court struck down the State of Nebraska's ban on partial-birth abortion procedures, concluding that it placed an "undue burden" on women seeking abortions because it failed to include an exception for partial-birth abortions deemed necessary to preserve the "health" of the mother.

(4) In reaching this conclusion, the Court deferred to the federal district court's factual findings that the partial-birth abortion procedure was statistically and medically as safe as, and in many circumstances safer than, alternative abortion procedures.

(5) However, the great weight of evidence presented at the *Stenberg* trial and other trials challenging partial-birth abortion bans, as well as at extensive congressional hearings, demonstrates that a partial-birth abortion is never necessary

to preserve the health of a woman, poses significant health risks to a woman upon whom the procedure is performed, and is outside of the standard of medical care.

(6) Despite the dearth of evidence in the *Stenberg* trial court record supporting the district court's findings, the United States Court of Appeals for the Eighth Circuit and the Supreme Court refused to set aside the district court's factual findings because, under the applicable standard of appellate review, they were not "clearly erroneous." A finding of fact is clearly erroneous "when although there is evidence to support it, the reviewing court on the entire evidence is left with the definite and firm conviction that a mistake has been committed." *Anderson v. City of Bessemer City, North Carolina*, 470 U.S. 564, 573 (1985). Under this standard, "if the district court's account of the evidence is plausible in light of the record viewed in its entirety, the court of appeals may not reverse it even though convinced that had it been sitting as the trier of fact, it would have weighed the evidence differently." *Id.* at 574.

(7) Thus, in *Stenberg*, the United States Supreme Court was required to accept the very questionable findings issued by the district court judge—the effect of which was to render null and void the reasoned factual findings and policy determinations of the United States Congress and at least 27 State legislatures.

(8) However, under well-settled Supreme Court jurisprudence, the United States Congress is not bound to accept the same factual findings that the Supreme Court was bound to accept in *Stenberg* under the "clearly erroneous" standard. Rather, the United States Congress is entitled to reach its own factual findings—findings that the Supreme Court accords great deference—and to enact legislation based upon these findings so long as it seeks to pursue a legitimate interest that is within the scope of the Constitution, and draws reasonable inferences based upon substantial evidence.

(9) In *Katzenbach v. Morgan*, 384 U.S. 641 (1966), the Supreme Court articulated its highly deferential review of Congressional factual findings when it addressed the constitutionality of section 4(e) of the Voting Rights Act of 1965. Regarding Congress' factual determination that section 4(e) would assist the Puerto Rican community in "gaining nondiscriminatory treatment in public services," the Court stated

that "[i]t was for Congress, as the branch that made this judgment, to assess and weigh the various conflicting considerations. . . . It is not for us to review the congressional resolution of these factors. It is enough that we be able to perceive a basis upon which the Congress might resolve the conflict as it did. There plainly was such a basis to support section 4(e) in the application in question in this case." *Id.* at 653.

(10) *Katzenbach*'s highly deferential review of Congress's factual conclusions was relied upon by the United States District Court for the District of Columbia when it upheld the "bail-out" provisions of the Voting Rights Act of 1965, 42 U.S.C. §1973c, stating that "congressional fact finding, to which we are inclined to pay great deference, strengthens the inference that, in those jurisdictions covered by the Act, state actions discriminatory in effect are discriminatory in purpose." *City of Rome, Georgia v. U.S.*, 472 F. Supp. 221 (D. Colo. 1979), *aff'd*, 46 U.S. 156 (1980).

(11) The Court continued its practice of deferring to congressional factual findings in reviewing the constitutionality of the must-carry provisions of the Cable Television Consumer Protection and Competition Act of 1992. *See Turner Broadcasting System, Inc. v. Federal Communications Commission*, 512 U.S. 622 (1994) (*Turner* I) and *Turner Broadcasting System, Inc. v. Federal Communications Commission*, 520 U.S. 180 (1997) (*Turner II*). At issue in the *Turner* cases was Congress' legislative finding that, absent mandatory carriage rules, the continued viability of local broadcast television would be "seriously jeopardized." The *Turner I* Court recognized that as an institution, "Congress is far better equipped than the judiciary to 'amass and evaluate the vast amounts of data' bearing upon an issue as complex and dynamic as that presented here." 512 U.S. at 665–66. Although the Court recognized that "the deference afforded to legislative findings does 'not foreclose our independent judgment of the facts bearing on an issue of constitutional law,'" its "obligation to exercise independent judgment when First Amendment rights are implicated is not a license to reweigh the evidence *de novo*, or to replace Congress' factual predictions with our own. Rather, it is to assure that, in formulating its judgments, Congress has drawn reasonable inferences based on substantial evidence." *Id.* at 666.

(12) Three years later in *Turner II*, the Court upheld the "must-carry" provisions based upon Congress' findings, stating the Court's "sole obligation is 'to assure that, in formulating its judgments, Congress has drawn reasonable inferences based on substantial evidence.'" 520 U.S. at 195. Citing its ruling in *Turner I*, the Court reiterated that "[w]e owe Congress' findings deference in part because the institution 'is far better equipped than the judiciary to "amass and evaluate the vast amounts of data" bearing upon' legislative questions," *id.* at 195, and added that it "owe[d] Congress' findings an additional measure of deference out of respect for its authority to exercise the legislative power." *Id.* at 196.

(13) There exists substantial record evidence upon which Congress has reached its conclusion that a ban on partial-birth abortion is not required to contain a "health" exception, because the facts indicate that a partial-birth abortion is never necessary to preserve the health of a woman, poses serious risks to a woman's health, and lies outside the standard of medical care. Congress was informed by extensive hearings held during the 104th, 105th, and 107th Congresses and passed a ban on partial-birth abortion in the 104th, 105th, and 106th Congresses. These findings reflect the very informed judgment of the Congress that a partial-birth abortion is never necessary to preserve the health of a woman, poses serious risks to a woman's health, and lies outside the standard of medical care, and should, therefore, be banned.

(14) Pursuant to the testimony received during extensive legislative hearings during the 104th, 105th, and 107th Congresses, Congress finds and declares that:

(A) Partial-birth abortion poses serious risks to the health of a woman undergoing the procedure. Those risks include, among other things: an increase in a woman's risk of suffering from cervical incompetence, a result of cervical dilation making it difficult or impossible for a woman to successfully carry a subsequent pregnancy to term; an increased risk of uterine rupture, abruption, amniotic fluid embolus, and trauma to the uterus as a result of converting the child to a footling breech position, a procedure which, according to a leading obstetrics textbook, "there are very few, if any, indications for . . . other than for delivery of a second twin"; and a risk of lacerations and secondary hemorrhaging due to the doctor blindly forcing a sharp instrument into the base of the unborn child's skull while he or she is lodged in the birth canal, an act which could result in severe bleeding, brings with it the threat of shock, and could ultimately result in maternal death.

(B) There is no credible medical evidence that partial-birth abortions are safe or are safer than other abortion procedures. No controlled studies of partial-birth abortions have been conducted nor have any comparative studies been conducted to demonstrate its safety and efficacy compared to other abortion methods. Furthermore, there have been no articles published in peer-reviewed journals that establish that partial-birth abortions are superior in any way to established abortion procedures. Indeed, unlike other more commonly used abortion procedures, there are currently no medical schools that provide instruction on abortions that include the instruction in partial-birth abortions in their curriculum.

(C) A prominent medical association has concluded that partial-birth abortion is "not an accepted medical practice," that it has "never been subject to even a minimal amount of the normal medical practice development," that "the relative advantages and disadvantages of the procedure in specific circumstances remain unknown," and that "there is no consensus among obstetricians about its use." The association has further noted that partial-birth abortion is broadly disfavored by both medical experts and the public, is "ethically wrong," and "is never the only appropriate procedure."

(D) Neither the plaintiff in *Stenberg v. Carhart*, nor the experts who testified on his behalf, have identified a single circumstance during which a partial-birth abortion was necessary to preserve the health of a woman.

(E) The physician credited with developing the partial-birth abortion procedure has testified that he has never encountered a situation where a partial-birth abortion was medically necessary to achieve the desired outcome and, thus, is never medically necessary to preserve the health of a woman.

(F) A ban on the partial-birth abortion procedure will therefore advance the health interests of pregnant women seeking to terminate a pregnancy.

(G) In light of this overwhelming evidence, Congress and the States have a compelling interest in prohibiting partial-birth abortions. In addition to promoting maternal health, such a prohibition will draw a bright line that clearly distinguishes abortion and infanticide, that preserves the integrity of the medical profession, and promotes respect for human life.

(H) Based upon *Roe v. Wade*, 410 U.S.113 (1973), and *Planned Parenthood v. Casey*, 505 U.S. 833 (1992), a governmental interest in protecting the life of a child during the delivery process arises by virtue of the fact that during a partial-birth abortion, labor is induced and the birth process has begun. This distinction was recognized in *Roe* when the Court noted, without comment that the Texas parturition statute, which prohibited one from killing a child "in a state of being born and before actual birth," was not under attack. This interest becomes compelling as the child emerges from the maternal body. A child that is completely born is a full, legal person entitled to constitutional protections afforded a "person" under the United States Constitution. Partial-birth abortions involve the killing of a child that is in the process, in fact mere inches away from, becoming a "person." Thus, the government has a heightened interest in protecting the life of the partially-born child.

(I) This, too, has not gone unnoticed in the medical community, where a prominent medical association has recognized that partial-birth abortions are "ethically different from other destructive abortion techniques because the fetus, normally twenty weeks or longer in gestation, is killed outside of the womb." According to this medical association, the "'partial birth' gives the fetus an autonomy which separates it from the right of the woman to choose treatments for her own body."

(J) Partial-birth abortion also confuses the medical, legal, and ethical duties of physicians to preserve and promote life, as the physician acts directly against the physical life of a child, whom he or she had just delivered, all but the head, out of the womb, in order to end that life. Partial-birth abortion thus appropriates the terminology and techniques used by obstetricians in the delivery of living children—obstetricians who preserve and protect the life of the mother and the child—and instead uses those techniques to end the life of the partially-born child.

(K) Thus, by aborting a child in the manner that purposefully seeks to kill the child after he or she has begun the process of birth, partial-birth abortion undermines the public's perception of the appropriate role of a physician during the delivery process, and perverts a process during which life is brought into the world, in order to destroy a partially-born child.

(L) The gruesome and inhumane nature of the partial-birth abortion procedure and its disturbing similarity to the killing of a newborn infant promotes a complete disregard for infant human life that can only be countered by a prohibition of the procedure.

(M) The vast majority of babies killed during partial-birth abortions are alive until the end of the procedure. It is a medical fact, however, that unborn infants at this stage can feel pain when subjected to painful stimuli and that their perception of this pain is even more intense than that of newborn infants and older children when subjected to the same stimuli. Thus, during a partial-birth abortion procedure, the child will fully experience the pain associated with piercing his or her skull and sucking out his or her brain.

(N) Implicitly approving such a brutal and inhumane procedure by choosing not to prohibit it will further coarsen society to the humanity of not only newborns, but all vulnerable and innocent human life, making it increasingly difficult to protect such life. Thus, Congress has a compelling interest in acting—indeed it must act—to prohibit this inhumane procedure.

(O) For these reasons, Congress finds that partial-birth abortion is never medically indicated to preserve the health of the mother; is in fact unrecognized as a valid abortion procedure by the mainstream medical community; poses additional health risks to the mother; blurs the line between abortion and infanticide in the killing of a partially-born child just inches from birth; and confuses the role of the physician in childbirth and should, therefore, be banned.

117 Stat. 1201 (2003).

Litigating to Regulate: *Massachusetts v. Environmental Protection Agency*

*Andrew P. Morriss**

I. Introduction

By a 5-4 vote in *Massachusetts v. Environmental Protection Agency,*[1] the Supreme Court took yet another significant step away from the Framers' vision of the judiciary and toward a politicized Supreme Court sitting as a super-legislature and super-regulator. The Court substituted its judgment for that of the politically accountable branches of the federal government. By dramatically loosening the rules of standing, the Court invited those unhappy with the federal government's failure to regulate in a particular manner in any substantive area to use the federal courts to force federal agencies to regulate. In short, the Court encouraged interest groups to seek to obtain from the courts what they could not from agencies or Congress. The Court rolled out the welcome mat for state governments unhappy with a federal agency's decision, creating from whole cloth a new rule of standing that allows states to gain a hearing in federal court with only the thinnest of allegations of harm. In doing so, the Court undermined the legal rules of standing. The majority also supported its decision with a one-sided and unsophisticated account of the scientific evidence for the petitioners' claims concerning climate change, needlessly inserting the courts into a scientific dispute that, as the majority's opinion demonstrated, they are woefully unprepared to handle.

Unfortunately *Massachusetts v. EPA* is but one piece of a broader trend toward regulation through litigation. A wide range of interest

*Professor of Law and Economics at Case Western Reserve University. Thanks to Jonathan H. Adler, Benjamin D. Cramer, and Roger E. Meiners for comments on an earlier draft. All errors remain, of course, my responsibility.

[1] 127 S. Ct. 1438 (2007).

groups, including state politicians, private interest groups, and federal regulators, is increasingly using the courts as a vehicle to impose regulatory measures the interest groups cannot obtain from legislatures and agencies.[2] The usual regulatory process has many flaws, but it at least incorporates a measure of political accountability. By shifting key aspects of regulatory decision-making to the courts, these interest groups are finding ways to deflect responsibility for the costs imposed by the regulatory state. By doing so in a way that provides only a means to increase regulatory agencies' activity and jurisdiction, the courts' acquiescence in regulation by litigation further erodes the constraints on regulators, giving them (and interest groups that favor increased regulation) a second chance on those occasions when they lose in the political process.

II. The Decision

The substantive dispute at the heart of *Massachusetts v. EPA* was straightforward. Section 202(a)(1) of the Clean Air Act requires that the administrator of the Environmental Protection Agency (EPA) "shall by regulation prescribe . . . standards applicable to the emission of any air pollutant from any class or classes of new motor vehicles or new motor vehicle engines, which in his judgment cause, or contribute to, air pollution which may reasonably be anticipated to endanger public health or welfare."[3] In October 1999, a group of nineteen organizations ranging from Greenpeace USA to the Network for Environmental and Economic Responsibility of the United Church of Christ filed a petition with EPA, requesting that the agency initiate rulemaking to regulate greenhouse gas emissions from new motor vehicles under that section. Before formulating the response required by law, EPA sought and received extensive public comment on the petition and obtained a report on the science of climate change from the National Research Council of the National

[2] See Andrew P. Morriss, Bruce Yandle & Andrew Dorchak, Regulation by Litigation (Yale University Press, forthcoming 2008); Andrew P. Morriss, Bruce Yandle & Andrew Dorchak, Choosing How to Regulate, 29 Harv. Env. L. Rev. 179 (2005); Andrew P. Morriss, Bruce Yandle & Andrew Dorchak, Regulation by Litigation: The EPA's Regulation of Heavy Duty Diesel Engines, 56 Admin. L. Rev. 403 (2004); Regulation Through Litigation (W. Kip Viscusi, ed. 2002).

[3] 42 U.S.C. § 7521(a)(1).

Academy of Sciences.[4] After considering the matter, the agency decided in 2003 against issuing a rule, concluding that it lacked statutory authority to do so.[5] In addition, EPA determined that even if it had authority to regulate mobile source emissions of greenhouse gases, rulemaking on motor vehicle greenhouse gas emissions alone would be imprudent because it would fragment government policy toward emissions and impede negotiations with other countries over a global approach to climate change.

The interest groups, now joined by twelve states[6] and local and territorial governments,[7] appealed EPA's decision to the D.C. Circuit. The three judge panel in that court produced three opinions, two of which supported upholding EPA's decision (albeit on different grounds) and one of which favored overturning the agency decision not to regulate motor vehicle greenhouse gas emissions as arbitrary and capricious.[8] Most of the unsuccessful petitioners then sought review of the decision in the Supreme Court. A variety of interest groups and ten states[9] supported EPA's position on one ground or another before the Supreme Court (including the Cato Institute).

The case presented two questions for the Supreme Court. First, did any of the organizations, states, or local governments complaining about EPA's failure to regulate have standing to seek review of the agency's decision in the courts? Standing is a component of Article III's limitation of the federal courts' jurisdiction to "Cases" and "Controversies."[10] Standing's requirement that a petitioner seeking to overturn an agency action must demonstrate that the agency's action "injures him in a concrete and personal way"[11] was a difficult hurdle to overcome for those who simply objected to an agency's

[4]National Research Council, Climate Change: An Analysis of Some Key Questions (2001).

[5]Control of Emissions from New Highway Vehicles and Engines, Notice of Denial of Petition for Rulemaking, 68 Fed. Reg. 52922 (Sept. 8, 2003).

[6]California, Connecticut, Illinois, Maine, Massachusetts, New Jersey, New Mexico, New York, Oregon, Rhode Island, Vermont, and Washington.

[7]The District of Columbia, American Samoa, New York City, and Baltimore.

[8]Massachusetts v. EPA, 415 F.3d 50 (D.C. Cir. 2005), rev'd 127 S. Ct. 1438 (2007).

[9]Alaska, Idaho, Kansas, Michigan, Nebraska, North Dakota, Ohio, South Dakota, Texas, and Utah.

[10]U.S. Const., Art. III.

[11]Lujan v. Defenders of Wildlife, 504 U.S. 555, 581 (1992) (Kennedy, J., concurring).

policy choices. And because global climate change is by definition a *global* phenomenon, standing posed a serious obstacle to the petitioners. Indeed, one of the opinions in the D.C. Circuit had rejected their claim on precisely this ground. To reach the merits of the case, the Supreme Court had to find that at least one of the petitioners who objected to EPA's decision had standing to object to EPA's refusal to regulate. Second, if at least one of the petitioners did have standing, there was a serious question about whether the Court should disturb the agency's decision not to regulate. Under the Supreme Court's decision in *Chevron USA, Inc. v. Natural Resources Defense Council*,[12] federal courts are to defer to an agency's reasonable interpretation of an ambiguous statute absent a clear congressional intent. In other words, if an agency interprets a statute in a reasonable way, the courts should not substitute their own construction for that of the agency. The petitioners were on firmer ground here than they were on standing. However, as a plausible decision could have upheld the agency's decision not to regulate, they were by no means assured of success even if they prevailed on the standing issue, if the Court applied *Chevron*.[13]

The Court divided 5-4 on both questions. The majority (Justices Breyer, Ginsburg, Kennedy, Souter, and Stevens), in an opinion by Justice Stevens, found in favor of the petitioners on both the standing issue (by holding that Massachusetts, at least, had standing) and the merits.[14] In dissent, Chief Justice Roberts, joined by the remaining three (Justices Alito, Scalia, and Thomas), rejected Massachusetts's claims on standing grounds. In a second dissenting opinion, joined in by the same four, Justice Scalia examined and rejected the petitioners' claims on the merits.

[12] 467 U.S. 837 (1984).

[13] The courts' application of *Chevron* has been uneven from the start. See Peter H. Schuck & E. Donald Elliott, To the Chevron Station: An Empirical Study of Federal Administrative Law, 1990 Duke L.J. 984 (1991); Orin S. Kerr, Shedding Light on Chevron: An Empirical Study on the Chevron Doctrine in the U.S. Courts of Appeals, 15 Yale J. on Reg. 1 (1998); Christopher H. Schroeder & Robert L. Glicksman, Chevron, State Farm, and EPA in the Courts of Appeals During the 1990s, 31 Envtl. L. Rep. 10376 (2001). Amici, including the Cato Institute, also offered non-*Chevron*-based arguments that supported the decision not to regulate.

[14] One of the ironies of the case is that Justice Stevens is the author of the *Chevron* opinion. Deference to agencies apparently only matters to him when he agrees with the results.

III. The Majority

Justice Stevens opened the majority opinion with a remarkably one-sided summary of the scientific evidence on climate change. From the first sentences—"A well-documented rise in global temperatures has coincided with a significant increase in the concentration of carbon dioxide in the atmosphere. Respected scientists believe the two trends are related."[15]—through the remainder of the opinion, a reader who was not acquainted with the debate over climate change would be hard pressed to realize that there is considerable disagreement over virtually every aspect of the issue.[16] And a reader of Justice Stevens's opinion could be forgiven for not knowing that there was debate over how to best approach climate change within the political branches. Stevens's summary of congressional and presidential attention to climate change issues barely mentioned the unanimous Senate resolution opposing the Kyoto Protocol from 1997.[17]

Stevens's selective account had a purpose. The petitioners' standing problem stemmed from the requirement, as articulated in the 1992 decision in *Lujan v. Defenders of Wildlife,* that a litigant must show a "concrete and particularized" injury that is "actual or imminent," that the injury is "fairly traceable" to the defendant, and that a favorable decision will redress the injury.[18] If climate change was less than certain, it would hamper the standing claim by making it hard to show an "actual or imminent" injury. By avoiding any of the uncertainties about the petitioners' claims concerning climate change, Stevens strengthened their claim to have standing.

The problem was not solved by assuming a resolution to the scientific debate, however. A global change in climate over decades,

[15] Massachusetts v. EPA, 127 S. Ct. 1438, 1446 (2007).

[16] See, e.g., Robert M. Carter, C. R. de Freitas, Indur M. Goklany, David Holland & Richard S. Lindzen, Climate Change: Climate Science and the Stern Review, 8 World Economics 161 (April–June 2007); Fraser Institute, Independent Summary for Policymakers: IPCC Fourth Assessment Report (2007).

[17] S. Res. 98, 105th Cong., 1st Sess. (1997). Even accepting the petitioners' scientific claims, Stevens's opinion is still inaccurate scientifically. See Jonathan H. Adler, Justice Stevens' Scientific Mistake, The Volokh Conspiracy (April 4, 2007), available at http://www.volokh.com/posts/1175698890.shtml (visited August 13, 2007). No doubt Stevens would have found standing even if he had not made this error, but the lack of scientific literacy in the opinion underscores the problematic nature of relying on courts to evaluate such claims.

[18] Lujan v. Defenders of Wildlife, 504 U.S. 555, 560–61 (1992).

caused by emissions of greenhouse gases from sources spanning the globe is difficult to characterize as a "particularized injury" that is "fairly traceable" to EPA's failure to regulate one source of emissions in the United States.[19] Stevens solved this piece of the standing problem with a clever move, one so clever none of the parties or amici had discussed it in their briefs.[20] He reached back to a 1907 case, *Georgia v. Tennessee Copper Co.*,[21] which involved a common law nuisance suit by the state of Georgia against a polluter in Tennessee. The decision in that case recognized Georgia's interest in protecting its citizens from the ill-effects of air pollution caused in Tennessee. Massachusetts's case was stronger than Georgia's, Justice Stevens concluded, because Massachusetts owned considerable coastal property it alleged was threatened by rising sea levels as a result of climate change. If Georgia could complain about the smelter in Tennessee harming Georgia's citizens' property, Stevens reasoned, surely Massachusetts could complain about EPA's failure to prevent greenhouse gas emissions from mobile sources from causing sea levels to rise and land owned by the state to flood. Stevens's interpretation of *Tennessee Copper* is wrong—the case has nothing to do with standing and Stevens's attempted analogy falls flat.

The final standing issue was whether the remedy sought by Massachusetts and the other states—regulation of mobile source greenhouse gas emissions—would "redress" the injury. In other words, if EPA regulated mobile source greenhouse gas emissions, what would happen? Would regulating mobile source emissions of greenhouse gases prevent the harms alleged by Massachusetts? Only if the state could show that EPA regulation would reduce the harm it suffered would the state have standing under *Lujan v. Defenders of Wildlife*. As U.S. mobile source emissions constitute less than a

[19] The Cato amicus brief argued that the "particularized injury" claimed by Massachusetts (the flooding of state coastal property) was not in "imminent" danger, as the flooding would not occur until far in the future. Relying on distant harms to make the alleged harm particular had the effect of eviscerating the imminent portion of the test. See Brief of the Cato Institute and Law Professors Jonathan H. Adler, James L. Huffman, and Andrew P. Morriss as Amici Curiae in Support of Respondents, 2006 WL 3043962, at *9–*12 (2006).

[20] Jonathan H. Adler, Warming Up to Climate Change Litigation, 93 Va. L. Rev. In Brief 61, 63 (2007).

[21] 206 U.S. 230 (1907).

third of total U.S. greenhouse gas emissions, which in turn constitute only a fraction of world emissions,[22] reducing emissions by American mobile sources would not seem likely to solve Massachusetts' problem since it would affect at most only six percent of total CO_2 emissions if *all* emissions from mobile sources ended, which no one claims would happen. Justice Stevens then simply concluded: "[j]udged by any standard, U.S. motor-vehicle emissions make a meaningful contribution to greenhouse gas concentrations and hence, according to petitioners, to global warming."[23] That any potential regulation would have such a small impact did not bother Stevens. For example, he concluded that even if China and India increased their emissions of greenhouse gases (as seems likely they will), reducing U.S. mobile source emissions would "slow the pace of global emissions increases."[24] He therefore declared that Massachusetts had standing. Unpacking Stevens's chain of reasoning reveals that the case held that a rise in sea level of a few inches over a century was sufficient to satisfy the requirement, effectively eliminating any substantive content in the standing analysis.

Stevens accorded Massachusetts "special solicitude" in his analysis of standing.[25] This weakening of standing rules for state governments is something new. The most limited government proponents can hope for from this case is that these new, looser rules are restricted to state governments and that there will be a return to more rigorous standing analysis for private parties. But even limited to state governments, the looser standing rules are problematic because the loosening benefits are almost entirely available only to those demanding additional regulation. Those who object to expanding a regulation for other than a purely philosophical reason could already challenge an agency's action because the harm caused by the regulatory expansion would suffice for standing. But the looser standard for standing is a benefit for those objecting to the absence of a regulation because it allows a state (and perhaps others) that can make a minimally plausible claim that a regulation would mitigate a harm to its interests to challenge the decision not to regulate.

[22] Massachusetts v. EPA, 127 S. Ct. 1438, 1468–69 (2007) (Roberts, C.J., dissenting).

[23] *Id.* at 1457–58.

[24] *Id.* at 1458.

[25] *Id.* at 1454–55.

Having found standing, Justice Stevens had little trouble finding that EPA was required to act. EPA had determined that CO_2 was not within the statutory definition of ''air pollutant'' and so it lacked authority to regulate under the statute. Even if it had had such authority, however, the agency had determined that it *should* not act, because doing so would likely impede reducing greenhouse gas emissions globally by hindering U.S. negotiations with other countries' over their emissions and by fragmenting the domestic approach to the issue.[26]

As it had on the standing issue, EPA appeared to be on firm ground here for two reasons. First, greenhouse gas emissions make a poor fit with the Clean Air Act's regulatory approach and history. The Act was adopted to address what were primarily local air pollution problems[27] and expanded in 1990 to deal more extensively with transboundary air pollution questions such as acid rain.[28] Nowhere in the legislative history of the Act is there any evidence that the statute was intended by Congress to address global air pollution issues like climate change. Further, Congress had repeatedly addressed climate change, both by authorizing and funding studies, by encouraging ''non-regulatory'' measures to address greenhouse gas emissions, and by the Senate's unanimous expression of disapproval of the Kyoto Accord in 1997.[29] In all the various resolutions, appropriations riders, and statutes on climate change issues passed by Congress over the years, there has never been any indication that anyone in Congress, for or against regulation of greenhouse gas emissions, thought that the Clean Air Act already authorized EPA to regulate those emissions. However, Justice Stevens rejected EPA's (and the Cato Institute's) argument that this history suggested that EPA was correctly interpreting Congress's intentions on its authority with respect to those substances. ''That subsequent Congresses have eschewed enacting binding emissions limitations to combat global warming tells us nothing about what Congress meant when it

[26] Control of Emissions from New Highway Vehicles and Engines, Notice of Denial of Petition for Rulemaking, 68 Fed. Reg. 52922, 52931 (Sept. 8, 2003).

[27] Adler, *supra* note 20, at 67.

[28] See Gary C. Bryner, Blue Skies, Green Politics: The Clean Air Act of 1990 and Its Implementation (1995).

[29] That history is well summarized in the Cato Institute's amicus brief, in which I participated. See Brief of the Cato Institute, *supra* note 19, at *17–*24.

amended [the relevant section] in 1970 and 1977."[30] Even if the Court thought that the statute was ambiguous on this point, however, under *Chevron* the courts are to defer to reasonable agency interpretations of an agency's organic statutes.

Apart from its impact in this case, Justice Stevens' action essentially limited an important recent Supreme Court precedent to its facts, eliminating a key constraint on regulatory agencies. In *Food & Drug Administration v. Brown & Williamson Tobacco Corp.*,[31] the Supreme Court had rejected the FDA's unilateral effort to assert regulatory authority over cigarettes despite nearly a century of congressional refusal to grant the agency such authority.[32] (The four dissenters in that case were joined in *Massachusetts v. EPA* by Justice Kennedy, who had disagreed with them in the earlier case, making clear Kennedy's pivotal role on the court.)[33]

Justice O'Connor wrote the majority opinion in *Brown & Williamson* and the parallels and distinctions from Justice Stevens's opinion in *Massachusetts v. EPA* are instructive. Like Stevens, O'Connor noted that there was a significant problem for which a regulatory solution was proposed. After examining the history of the regulatory statute in question, however, she concluded that Congress had precluded the agency from acting, in part because Congress had repeatedly

[30] Massachusetts v. EPA, 127 S. Ct. 1438, 1460 (2007). It seems likely that if Congress thought anything about greenhouse gases in either 1970 or 1977, it probably thought that they might be a good idea as the dominant climate change theory of the 1970s was that the earth was cooling rather than warming. See, e.g., The Cooling World, Newsweek (April 28, 1975) at 64 available at http://www.resiliencetv.fr/uploads/newsweek_coolingworld.pdf ("The central fact is that after three quarters of a century of extraordinarily mild conditions, the earth's climate seems to be cooling down. Meteorologists disagree about the cause and extent of the cooling trend, as well as over its specific impact on local weather conditions. But they are almost unanimous in the view that the trend will reduce agricultural productivity for the rest of the century.").

[31] 529 U.S. 120 (2000).

[32] For a detailed discussion of tobacco and regulation by litigation, see, Morriss, Yandle & Dorchak, Regulation by Litigation, *supra* note 2, at Chapter 7; Bruce Yandle, Joseph A. Rotondi, Andrew P. Morriss & Andrew Dorchak, Bootleggers, Baptists & Televangelists: Regulating Tobacco by Litigation, Univ. of Illinois Law and Economics Research Paper No. LE07-021 (2007).

[33] See Jonathan H. Adler, Massachusetts v. EPA Heats Up Climate Policy No Less than Administrative Law: A Comment on Profs. Watts and Wildermuth, Case Research Paper Series in Legal Studies Working Paper 07-20 (2007).

declined to provide the agency with the authority it now asserted. An important reason for O'Connor's conclusion was that if the FDA did have authority over tobacco under the Food, Drug and Cosmetic Act, it would have no choice but to ban tobacco products since they could not be considered "safe" under the statute.[34] Since Congress regularly enacted legislation that showed it accepted the legal sale of cigarettes, O'Connor interpreted this legislative history as precluding the FDA's broad reinterpretation of its statutory authority.

Justice Stevens found that this reasoning did not apply to greenhouse gas emissions and the Clean Air Act for two reasons. First, he suggested that the key to *Brown & Williamson* was that regulation by the FDA would have led to a ban of tobacco. Since EPA action in this case "would only *regulate* emissions" rather than ban vehicles, the earlier case did not apply.[35] Second, in the case of tobacco, the FDA had for decades explicitly denied it had authority over tobacco. Here, EPA had never formally addressed the issue of its authority over greenhouse gases but EPA's general counsel had previously claimed authority to regulate.[36] This assertion is particularly pernicious, because agencies rarely have an incentive to make "consistent and repeated" disclaimers of authority. In the case of tobacco, it was only the tobacco industry's extraordinary political clout that prompted such disclaimers. Stevens's reasoning thus protects only powerful political interests able to cajole or coerce an agency into disclaiming jurisdiction.

Worse, granting legal significance to self-serving statements by agency counsel about expansive authority undercuts political accountability. The public choice literature has long explained that agency staff have strong incentives to pursue their agency's mission, ranging from the personal (expanding their agency's jurisdiction enhances their own careers) to the publicly-minded (staff who want to further their agency's mission to help the public but are likely to experience "tunnel vision" and thus focus narrowly on the importance of their mission to the exclusion of the government's broader goals).[37] In short, principal-agent problems are rampant in the relationship between agency staff and elected officials, even within an

[34] FDA v. Brown & Williamson Tobacco Corp., 529 U.S. 120, 134–39 (2000).

[35] 127 S. Ct. at 1461.

[36] *Id.*

[37] See William A. Niskanen, Bureaucracy and Representative Government (1971).

administration. In this context, relying on staff statements concerning broadening agency authority creates a one-way ratchet for expanding agency regulatory authority.

Justice Stevens concluded with a touch of false modesty. On remand, EPA need not regulate greenhouse gases, it need merely "ground its reasons for action or inaction in the statute."[38] But Stevens actually left EPA with almost no room to avoid a decision to regulate mobile source greenhouse gas emissions, not just those to which Section 202 applied, for the logic of Stevens's analysis extends beyond that section. As Professor Adler noted earlier this year:

> Without any further action by Congress, the regulation of greenhouse gas emissions from new motor vehicles under Section 202 is a near absolute certainty, as is the regulation of industrial and utility emissions under Section 111. Litigation to force the listing of carbon dioxide as a criteria air pollutant, and requiring the establishment of a National Ambient Air Quality Standard, such as those that exist for ozone, particulates and other ambient pollutants, will not be far behind. At this point, if not before, Congress will be compelled to act.[39]

IV. The Roberts Dissent

Chief Justice Roberts authored a dissenting opinion contesting the majority's standing analysis, joined by Justices Alito, Scalia, and Thomas. Roberts noted the scale of the change in the rules of standing made by the majority. He also established that the majority's reliance on *Georgia v. Tennessee Copper Co.* was not consistent with prior treatment of that case or the opinion's facts. Rather than easing standing rules for states, Roberts explained, *Tennessee Copper* raised "an additional hurdle for a state litigant: the articulation of a 'quasi-sovereign interest' '*apart* from the interests of particular private parties.'"[40] As Roberts noted, the irrelevance of *Tennessee Copper* to the question presented in this case—prior to the majority's reinterpretation of it—is evidenced by the petitioners' failure to cite the case before the Supreme Court or D.C. Circuit and its absence from the

[38] Massachusetts v. EPA, 127 S. Ct. 1438, 1463 (2007).

[39] Adler, *supra* note 20, at 71.

[40] 127 S. Ct. at 1465 (Roberts, C.J., dissenting) (quoting Alfred L. Snapp & Son, Inc. v. Puerto Rico ex rel. Barez, 458 U.S. 592, 607 (1982) (emphasis added)).

briefs of the many amici and the three opinions below. The chief justice noted the irony in the majority's reformulation of standing, a doctrine whose purpose is in part to ensure that the issues are vigorously contested by parties with a real stake in the outcome, based on an interpretation of *Tennessee Copper* that was never briefed or argued by the parties.

Applying the "traditional" standing test, the chief justice argued Massachusetts's allegations of loss of coastal land to rising seas was not sufficient to satisfy the "particularized injury" portion of the test for at least three reasons. First, "[t]he very concept of global warming seems inconsistent with this particularization requirement" and "the redress petitioners seek is focused no more on them than on the public generally—it is literally to change the atmosphere around the world."[41] Second, the claim that Massachusetts is losing coastal land is based solely on a statement that rising sea levels have already occurred, without any supporting detail. Third, the declarations of experts on which the state relied also include evidence that Massachusetts's coast is gradually sinking anyway, an alternative explanation for any loss that might have occurred or be threatened that is not distinguished from the alleged loss from rising sea levels. The result is "pure conjecture."[42] All the state had to offer in addition to these conjectures were computer models with substantial error margins and timelines that placed much of the harm over the course of a century. None of this would have been sufficient under *Lujan v. Defenders of Wildlife.*

Further, the state's claim should have failed because of a lack of connection between the remedy sought (regulation of mobile source emissions) and the harm alleged (rising sea levels). Not only do domestic mobile source emissions constitute only four percent of global greenhouse gas emissions (six percent of CO2 emissions), but the regulations sought would apply only to new vehicles, reaching maximum effect only as the fleet of vehicles turned over. Any reductions would initially come from only a small proportion of mobile sources, and hence from a fraction of the four percent of total greenhouse gas emissions. "In light of the bit-part domestic new motor vehicle greenhouse gas emissions have played in what petitioners

[41] *Id.* at 1467.

[42] *Id.*

describe as a 150-year global phenomenon, and the myriad additional factors bearing on petitioners' alleged injury-the loss of Massachusetts coastal land-the connection is far too speculative to establish causation."[43]

Finally, the chief justice noted that eighty percent of greenhouse gas emissions come from outside the United States and developments in other countries are likely to have the major impact on overall greenhouse gas levels irrespective of U.S. controls. The majority had waved this problem away, essentially saying that any reduction in greenhouse gas emissions would mitigate the problem. Roberts was unwilling to do so, contending that Massachusetts should have been required to show that regulation by EPA would be likely to protect it from the loss of coastal land. Unfortunately for Massachusetts, he continued, there was an "evident mismatch between the source of their alleged injury-catastrophic global warming-and the narrow subject matter of the Clean Air Act provision at issue in this suit. The mismatch suggests that petitioners' true goal for this litigation may be more symbolic than anything else. The constitutional role of the courts, however, is to decide concrete cases-not to serve as a convenient forum for policy debates."[44]

Despite its failure to garner five votes, the chief justice's dissent is chiefly valuable as an example of how the traditional standing doctrine would have applied to the facts of this case. The contrast between its analysis and the more elastic standing test applied in the majority opinion make clear the substantial differences in the doctrine of standing that occurred as a result of *Massachusetts v. EPA.*

V. The Scalia Dissent

Justice Scalia joined the chief justice's dissent on standing but authored his own (joined by the other three dissenters as well) to address the merits of the claim. Here the dispute turned on the words "in his judgment" in Section 202(a)(1) of the Clean Air Act, which mandates that the EPA administrator "shall by regulation prescribe . . . standards applicable to the emission of any air pollutant from any class or classes of new motor vehicles or new motor vehicle engines, which in his judgment cause, or contribute to, air pollution

[43] *Id.* at 1469.

[44] *Id.* at 1470.

which may reasonably be anticipated to endanger public health or welfare.'' The majority focused on the public health and welfare language, arguing that the administrator could consider only such matters in making a decision about whether to regulate or not. Scalia saw the decision as two phase: The administrator first has to decide *whether* to make a decision about regulating a pollutant. Once he decides to do so, then he makes a regulatory decision on the basis of ''public health and welfare.'' In the first phase, the administrator may consider other factors, such as the impact on foreign policy and on other departments. Even under the majority's analysis, Scalia argued that EPA was justified in finding that the scientific uncertainty was too great to allow it to act now, pointing to extensive material in the record suggesting that such uncertainty existed.

Scalia also contested the majority's interpretation of the term ''air pollutant'' in the Clean Air Act. ''Air pollutant'' is defined as ''any air pollution agent or combination of such agents, including any physical, chemical, . . . substance or matter which is emitted into or otherwise enters the ambient air.''[45] Engaging in a close grammatical analysis of the statute's text, Scalia argued that this is a two part definition. To be an air pollutant, a substance must be ''an air pollutant agent or combination of such agents.'' The words after ''including'' do not define things that are air pollutants, they simply illustrate things that may be air pollutants if those things are also air pollutant agents. EPA had read the definition of ''air pollutant'' in this way and Justice Scalia argued that the agency's view deserved deference as a plausible interpretation of the statute under the *Chevron* doctrine.[46]

Justice Scalia's legal analysis of EPA's statutory position is the type of careful textual analysis that is too often lacking in regulatory matters. However, as Professor Adler has pointed out, EPA did not refuse to make a judgment about the dangers of climate change but instead made a judgment that it would not regulate.[47] Since that judgment was not based on the standard in Section 202, once the Court had decided that greenhouse gases were included under Section 202 EPA was left vulnerable to a complaint that it had not

[45] 42 U.S.C. § 7602(g).

[46] Chevron USA, Inc. v. Natural Resources Defense Council, 467 U.S. 837 (1984).

[47] Adler, *supra* note 20, at 71.

followed the statute. Why did EPA not make the more prudent declaration that it was refusing to make a judgment on climate change's risks? We can only speculate, but two explanations are plausible. First, the decision was made in 2003, during the run up to the 2004 election between President George W. Bush and Sen. John Kerry. One of the Democrats' more pointed attacks on the Bush Administration was that it was "anti-environment." A refusal by EPA to affirm the gospel of climate change would have reinforced this attack. If political considerations played any role in setting EPA's strategy, they likely were seen as supporting a nuanced decision that paid homage to climate change fears while avoiding regulation. Second, to the extent that the decision was driven by EPA's analysis, it seems likely that the agency's staff would have been concerned with both pushing the agency toward regulation and preserving the agency's powers. From their position, a disclaimer based on prudential grounds would have been preferable to a "we don't know" position as it would have allowed a later administration to make a different decision by claiming circumstances had changed rather than reversing a legal position. If the agency lost the lawsuit, as it surely anticipated it might, it would find itself in the position of having to regulate. Finding itself ordered to regulate was an outcome that it is difficult to imagine the agency staff finding unpleasant. Thus both the administration's and the agency's interests were served by the approach EPA took, even though it undercut the chances of the decision being upheld.

VI. Standing and Separation of Powers

For the Supreme Court, "[t]he principle of separation of powers was not simply an abstract generalization in the minds of the Framers: it was woven into the document that they drafted in Philadelphia in the summer of 1787."[48] Separation of powers does not *accidentally* make it harder to address serious problems, it *intentionally* makes it harder for the government to act in all cases *including* when there are serious problems that a group thinks need to be addressed. The point of deliberately making it harder for the government to act was to check abuse of power; the price of checking abuse of power was

[48] Buckley v. Valeo, 424 U.S. 1, 124 (1976).

that it became harder for the government to act even when there was not an abuse.

Standing is a crucial part of the separation of powers because it both protects the judiciary from being brought into disputes where it has no role and protects the political branches from the judiciary by limiting when the judiciary might interfere with decisions by the political branches. The requirement of standing derives from Article III's limitation of federal-court jurisdiction to "Cases" and "Controversies," which restricts "the business of federal courts to questions presented in an adversary context and in a form historically viewed as capable of resolution through the judicial process."[49] There are other important limits as well (e.g., the requirement that a matter appealed to the courts be a final agency action), but standing's role is critical to restricting the courts to their proper sphere.

Massachusetts v. EPA opens the door to many more suits by interest groups, and by states in particular, dissatisfied with the outcome of the political process. It opens a one way door toward expanding the role of the federal government. Any individual or state actually injured by a regulatory action already met the *Lujan v. Defenders of Wildlife* test. The only beneficiaries of this decision are those who object to government decisions *not* to regulate. The unequal nature of the relaxation of the standing rules undermines the independence of the political branches from the judiciary.

It is easy to understand why the Sierra Club or Greenpeace would want EPA to regulate more; lobbying for more regulations is what such groups do. It is less obvious why state governments would want more federal regulation. The answer lies in the incentives created by the Clean Air Act.

VII. The Politics of the Clean Air Act

The Clean Air Act's structure plays a key role in the politics behind the state efforts to push EPA to regulate mobile source emissions of greenhouse gases. Two features are important. First, with respect to the criteria pollutants, the federal government determines the overall levels of air pollution acceptable and selects the pollution control technologies required to be used by various industries. Once the EPA has set these standards, states get to figure out how to

[49] Flast v. Cohen, 392 U.S. 83, 95 (1968).

meet them and implement specific restrictions on stationary sources within their borders through state implementation plans (SIPs). SIPs are massive technical documents for which the operative unit of measurement is "filing cabinets."[50] Many states' SIPs lack indices; most portions of a SIP are incomprehensible to the non-specialist. The result is that the key details of air pollution control—how the burden of reducing pollution is allocated among sources—are opaque to the general public. Federal regulation thus creates valuable rights to be distributed by state environmental agencies through their SIPs. Of course, requiring regulation of greenhouse gas emissions from mobile sources under Section 202 would not by itself trigger the listing of those gases as criteria pollutants. As noted earlier, however, the Court's decision leaves little room for EPA to avoid such a listing and the victorious interest groups certainly see this decision as the first step in a broader assault on greenhouse gas emissions under existing provisions of the Clean Air Act.[51]

Further, EPA bases its analysis of states' compliance with the national standards using computer models of emissions.[52] The models contain important assumptions about the environment and about government regulation, assumptions that do not always match reality. In a conflict between model and reality, the model trumps—what matters from a state's point of view is what EPA *says* the state's emission levels are.[53] An important goal of the litigation in

[50]See Andrew P. Morriss, The Politics of the Clean Air Act in Political Environmentalism 263 (Terry L. Anderson, ed. 2000).

[51]See, e.g., EarthJustice, Press Release: High Court Rules Clean Air Act Gives EPA Authority to Fight Global Warming (April 2, 2007) ("To combat this most urgent environmental crisis, strong and comprehensive U.S. action is crucial. EPA must use its existing Clean Air Act authority to require control of greenhouse gas emissions—by motor vehicles (the subject of this case) as well as by other sources like power plants. The Act has successfully cut emissions of many pollutants, and it can do the same for greenhouse gases.").

[52]See Morriss, Yandle & Dorchak, Diesel, *supra* note 2, at 412–21 (discussing modeling issues).

[53]On greenhouse gases there will be many important assumptions necessary to make the models work. In particular, the relationship between greenhouse gas emissions and mobile sources is different than the relationship between many other pollutants and mobile sources. For example, many pollutants (e.g. particulates) are the result of incomplete combustion. Pollution sources can become cleaner with respect to these by increasing the efficiency of combustion or by preventing the pollutants from leaving the combustion system (as through the catalytic converters on U.S. automobiles). Greenhouse gases, however, are the product of combustion.

Massachusetts v. EPA was to gain states the ability to regulate greenhouse gases independently. To the extent they are able to do so before EPA acts—and everyone agrees that EPA will move slowly to implement the decision in this case and even more slowly to extend its regulatory reach to greenhouse gases in other areas—these states will establish "facts on the ground" that EPA will likely have to recognize in its modeling.

Second, the statute distinguishes between stationary and mobile sources in important ways. While state and federal governments share responsibility for regulating emissions from both, the federal government has most of the authority in the area of mobile sources. The federal government has the authority to mandate what technology auto and truck makers use to reduce pollution. States have only three means of affecting these: they can institute inspection and maintenance ("I&M") programs that ensure engines and exhaust systems are operating properly, restrict the use of mobile sources (i.e. tell people they can't drive as much), and require cars sold in their states to meet the California emissions standards rather than the federal standards.[54] The first two of these options are extremely unpopular. When EPA convinced Ohio to adopt an I&M program, it provoked a political backlash that led the state government to pay for the inspection costs rather than charging car owners as it had done.[55] Driving restrictions are a complete non-starter politically.

Not only are there relatively few ways to reduce their emission without replacing the internal combustion engine (and even alternatives like electric vehicles still produce greenhouse gas emissions at the powerplants that charge them), but the most important technology for reducing greenhouse gas emissions from an internal combustion engine is improving fuel efficiency. As fuel efficiency increases, however, the cost of operating a vehicle falls and so actual use may increase, reducing the net reduction in greenhouse gas emissions.

One additional option to control mobile source emissions is to regulate fuel formulation, something EPA, the states, and even some local governments are already doing. See Andrew P. Morriss & Nathaniel Stewart, Market Fragmenting Regulation: Why Gasoline Costs So Much (And Why It's Going to Cost More), 72 Brook. L. Rev. 939, 1021–35 (2007). We may already be reaching the limits of emissions gains possible through this means, however, and the costs of increasing the complexity of fuel formulation to consumers are starting to be recognized.

[54] California's emission control legislation predated the federal limits and so it was permitted to continue to have a separate set of standards. In 1990, the federal statute was amended to permit other states to adopt the California standards.

[55] Todd A. Stewart, E-Check: A Dirty Word in Ohio's Clean Air Debate—Ohio's Battle Over Automobile Emissions Testing, 29 Cap. U.L. Rev. 265 (2001); Tieran Lewis,

The result is that states can do little to affect their mobile source emissions. Once EPA's computer model analyzes both the stationary and mobile source emissions and makes a prediction of the pollution levels due to mobile sources, any reductions needed to meet the federally mandated ambient air quality standards are left to the states to discover.

For understanding *Massachusetts v. EPA,* the key points are that mobile sources are major sources of greenhouse gas emissions and that the politically feasible set of regulatory measures that can limit their emissions available to states is vanishingly small. What states interested in reducing greenhouse gas emissions need, therefore, is for EPA to impose a technological solution on greenhouse gas emissions on car and truck manufacturers and to give states plenty of credit in EPA's mobile source emission model for that technology (irrespective of whether the technology actually reduces emissions.)[56] States that want to address climate change need this because they have few other means of addressing mobile source emissions of greenhouse gases. The decision in this case moved them considerably closer to that goal.

VIII. The Politics of Climate Change and the Courts

The roster of states participating on both sides of *Massachusetts v. EPA* tells a great deal about the politics of climate change regulation. Joining Massachusetts in demanding that EPA address mobile source emissions of greenhouse gases were eleven states and the District of Columbia; opposing were ten states. Using federal Energy Information Administration data,[57] I calculated the ratio of fossil fuel energy production (coal, natural gas, and petroleum) in each jurisdiction to its total energy use. The ratio is evidence of a state's economic interest in continuing hydrocarbon energy use; a low (high) ratio suggests that a state would benefit (lose) economically relative to other states if greenhouse gas emissions were regulated,

Governor's E-Check Veto Concerns Some Residents, Daily Kent Stater (July 17, 2007) (elimination of fees).

[56]See Morriss, Yandle & Dorchak, Diesel, *supra* note 2, at 480–81 (discussing mobile source model problems in dealing with ozone levels and nitrogen oxide emissions).

[57]Energy Information Administration, Table S1—Energy Consumption Estimates by Source and End-Use Sector, 2004, available at http://www.eia.doe.gov/emeu/states/sep_sum/plain_html/sum_btu_1.html (last visited August 12, 2007).

since its energy sector would suffer a comparative advantage (disadvantage).

Of the states demanding that EPA regulate, all but one are at or below the median ratio of hydrocarbon energy use to total energy use and six are among the ten with the lowest ratios. New Mexico, the one exception, has a governor running for the Democratic nomination for president, a campaign in which demonstrating one's environmental credentials is important. Of the ten states opposing regulation, eight are above the median ratio; only Idaho and South Dakota are below it. If we examine the percentage of energy states produce from non-nuclear, non-hydrocarbon sources, we find a similar pattern. Eleven U.S. states produced ten percent or more of their energy from such sources in 2004 (thirty-three produced five percent or less). Of those eleven, five supported Massachusetts (California, Washington, Oregon, Maine, Vermont) and only two (Idaho and South Dakota) supported EPA.[58]

IX. Consequences for the Future

That states have different economic interests is true with respect to many dimensions of federal policy—and the potential for conflict over such differences was a concern of the Founders in their design of the Constitution. The Supreme Court was not the forum the Founders anticipated would resolve those differences; the political branches were. By weakening standing rules, the Court's decision in *Massachusetts v. EPA* threw the door wide open for states dissatisfied with the outcome of the political process to seek redress in the courts.

Whether or not the federal government should be regulating mobile source (or any other) emissions of greenhouse gases is fundamentally a political question. Unlike many of the air pollution issues of the past, regulating greenhouse gases would insert EPA into virtually every aspect of human activity. Indeed, it is hard to conceive of an economic activity that does not result in at least the production of greenhouse gases, whether from transportation of products and

[58] A similar division of interests among states existed in the federal nuisance suit (since dismissed) by primarily Northeastern states over power plant greenhouse gas emissions. The plaintiff states sued primarily utilities in the Midwest and South, not in their own states. See Connecticut et al. v. American Electric Power Co. et al., No. 04-cv-05569, 2005 WL 2249748 (S.D.N.Y. Sept. 15, 2005).

raw materials for manufacturing or air travel and electricity use for service industries. Climate change is thus the Holy Grail for those seeking to expand state authority over the economy as it justifies regulating everything.[59]

Perhaps most alarmingly, Justice Stevens's analysis essentially reduces to an assertion that the regulatory state must be able to respond to what he sees as a crisis of the magnitude of climate change because *somebody* needs to do *something*. Nowhere in Justice Stevens's opinion is there any sense that he believes that Congress can only act when it has been allocated the power to do so by the Constitution or that an agency's mandate might not include addressing a problem not known at the time the agency's authority was established. The reader is left with the impression that Justice Stevens cannot imagine that no one has the authority to address a problem if the problem is large enough.

Of course, it would be the height of folly to rely on Congress or a regulatory agency for the protection of liberty. That is why we have the separation of powers, among other features of the national government. But the political process does offer some protection from government over-reaching in circumstances like these. Regulating greenhouse gas emissions is likely to be extremely costly because of their ubiquity in economic activity.[60] In a debate over the costs and benefits of such regulations, it seems likely that imposing those costs on the American public generally would be the preference, intensely felt, of a minority of Americans, while the majority would be resistant to bearing the economic impact of action without greater assurance that other nations would also address the issue or that waiting for technological improvements would not substantially lower the costs. If that debate occurred in Congress, there would be an opportunity for those who see global warming as a crisis requiring immediate action and for those who think differently to make their respective cases. A vigorous debate over everything from the underlying science to the most cost-effective regulatory approaches would

[59] Politicians can benefit as well, since the threat of regulation alone is often remarkably lucrative. See Fred S. McChesney, Money for Nothing: Politicians, Rent Extraction, and Political Extortion (1997).

[60] See House of Lords, Select Committee on Economic Affairs, The Economics of Climate Change, vol. I, HL Paper 12-I (2005) (reviewing economic issues surrounding climate change).

ensue. The result might not be less regulation, indeed it could be more,[61] but the prospect of being held accountable at the polls for either refusing to act or imposing unnecessary costs would give individual members of Congress a reason to consider their actions carefully. While far from perfect, the political process would force the choices into the public eye.

Both directly (by giving EPA little choice but to enter the greenhouse gas regulation arena) and indirectly (by making it easier for states and interest groups to push the regulatory state to expand through the relaxation of the requirements for standing), *Massachusetts v. EPA* is a major step away from limited government. As a result of this shift to a world where regulatory policy is determined by and through litigation, economic freedoms are likely to become increasingly scarce.

[61] See David Schoenbrod, Remarks to the National Resource Defense Council, 20 Cardozo L. Rev. 767 (1999).

Narrow Issue of Taxpayer Standing Highlights Wide Divisions Among the Justices

*Robert Corn-Revere**

Not everyone can sue in federal court claiming that a government action is unconstitutional. Among other requirements, the plaintiff must assert personal injury caused by the government's alleged misbehavior. Ordinarily, federal taxpayers are not granted standing to sue merely because they profess injury when their taxes are spent in a way that they believe offends the Constitution. But the Supreme Court has fashioned a narrow exception to the general rule against taxpayer standing. If Congress has exercised its taxing and spending power in a manner that might have violated the First Amendment's prohibition against "laws respecting an establishment of religion," taxpayers can challenge the expenditure. This term, the Court grappled with the following question: Does the taxpayer standing exception in Establishment Clause cases apply only to specific congressional enactments, or does it extend to general appropriations for the executive branch which uses the money to fund its own programs? The Court's answer to that seemingly arcane question could have profound implications for executive branch support of religious institutions.

In *Hein v. Freedom From Religion Foundation, Inc.* the U.S. Supreme Court held, on a 5-4 vote, that taxpayers lacked standing to challenge a decision by the executive branch to finance religiously oriented conferences in support of programs established by the White House Office of Faith-Based Initiatives.[1] The decision produced no majority

*Robert Corn-Revere is a partner at Davis Wright Tremaine LLP in Washington, D.C., where he practices First Amendment law. He and Davis Wright Tremaine associate David M. Shapiro filed an amicus brief supporting the respondent in *Hein v. Freedom From Religion Foundation, Inc.* on behalf of American Atheists, Inc.

[1] 127 S. Ct. 2553 (2007).

opinion. Instead, it revealed a gulf between members of the Court's conservative majority on both the Establishment Clause question at issue and on the value of adhering to precedents established by past decisions. Moreover, seven of the nine justices voted to preserve the ability of taxpayers in certain narrowly prescribed circumstances to challenge governmental expenditures in support of religion as a violation of the First Amendment's Establishment Clause.

Justice Samuel Alito wrote the plurality opinion, reversing a decision written by Judge Richard Posner of the U.S. Court of Appeals for the Seventh Circuit, which had found that taxpayers have standing to challenge executive branch expenditures that were made to assist religious organizations in applying for and receiving federal grants. Justice Alito was joined by Chief Justice John Roberts and Justice Anthony Kennedy. Justices Antonin Scalia and Clarence Thomas agreed with the result, but Justice Scalia's concurring opinion, reading more like an unusually tart dissent, would have disposed of the concept of taxpayer standing altogether by overruling the controlling precedent established in *Flast v. Cohen*.[2] Justice David Souter's dissenting opinion, which would have found taxpayer standing in this case, was joined by Justices John Paul Stevens, Ruth Bader Ginsburg, and Steven Breyer.

The plurality and dissenting opinions appeared to have more in common with one another than with the two-justice concurrence that rounded out the majority vote. That fact, plus Justice Scalia's particularly blunt rhetoric, appear to undermine the promise of the Roberts Court to emphasize collegiality and reach broader consensus. *Hein* is one of 24 cases decided by a 5-4 vote during the 2006–07 term—representing fully a third of the Court's docket—and most of these decisions appeared to split along ideological lines.[3]

In this respect, the decision in *Hein* says far less about the narrow issue of taxpayer standing in Establishment Clause cases than it does about the makeup of the current Supreme Court and the prospects for radical doctrinal change. Although the Court has become more conservative since Chief Justice Roberts was confirmed, a

[2] 392 U.S. 83 (1968).

[3] See, e.g., Linda Greenhouse, In Steps Big and Small, Supreme Court Moved Right, New York Times, July 1, 2007 at p. 1; Robert Barnes, A Rightward Turn and Dissention Define Court This Term, Washington Post, July 1, 2007 at A7.

majority of justices appear committed to preserving existing precedent with only incremental change. The decision in *Hein* illustrates this right-of-middle course. At the same time, the doctrinal importance of the Court's decision to preserve taxpayer standing in Establishment Clause cases as articulated in *Flast v. Cohen* may be overshadowed by its practical effect. That is, the doctrine survived *Hein*, but it may have little real world impact where financial support for religion is initiated by executive action rather than congressional mandate. Accordingly, *Flast* will likely have a much diminished importance.

I. Background

Hein focused solely on the narrow question of when taxpayers are considered to have standing to challenge in court governmental expenditures made in support of religion. The First Amendment to the United States Constitution provides, among other things, that "Congress shall make no law respecting an establishment of religion, or prohibiting the free exercise thereof. . . ."[4] This has long been held to prohibit direct or indirect financial support of religion as a violation of the Establishment Clause.[5] However, this constitutional restriction does not automatically authorize any citizen who disputes a particular spending program to bring a judicial challenge. Article III of the Constitution limits the judicial power of the United States to the resolution of "Cases" and "Controversies."[6]

The constitutional limitation of federal court jurisdiction to actual cases or controversies is governed to a large degree by the concept of "standing." That is, federal judicial power is not to be exercised to provide advisory opinions about generalized grievances. A more concrete harm is required. As a consequence, in order to have standing, a plaintiff "must allege personal injury fairly traceable to the defendant's allegedly unlawful conduct and likely to be redressed

[4]U.S. Const., amend. I.

[5]E.g., Everson v. Board of Education, 330 U.S. 1, 11 (1947) ("The imposition of taxes to pay ministers' salaries and to build and maintain churches and church property aroused [the colonists'] indignation. It was these feelings which found expression in the First Amendment.").

[6]U.S. Const., art. III, § 2.

by the requested relief."[7] As the Supreme Court explained in *Frothingham v. Mellon*,

> We have no power *per se* to review and annul acts of Congress on the ground that they are unconstitutional. The question may be considered only when the justification for some direct injury suffered or threatened, presenting a justiciable issue, is made to rest upon such an act. . . . The party who invokes the power must be able to show not only that the statute is invalid but that he has sustained or is immediately in danger of sustaining some direct injury as the result of its enforcement, and not merely that he suffers in some indefinite way in common with people generally.[8]

The Court in *Frothingham* held that paying taxes alone was insufficient to confer standing on an individual who wanted to challenge the legality of a spending program. A federal taxpayer had sought to challenge federal appropriations for mothers' and children's health, arguing that federal involvement in this area intruded on the rights reserved to the states under the Tenth Amendment. With respect to standing, the plaintiff argued that the program would "increase the burden of future taxation and thereby take [the plaintiff's] property without due process of law."[9] However, the Court held that the general payment of taxes was not the kind of particularized injury required for Article III standing. It explained that the added tax burden was "essentially a matter of public and not of individual concern" because it "is shared with millions of others; is comparatively minute and indeterminable; and the effect upon future taxation, of any payment out of the funds, [is] so remote, fluctuating and uncertain, that no basis is afforded for an appeal to the preventive powers of a court of equity."[10] Thus, although an individual clearly has standing to challenge a specific tax imposed directly on his exercise of a constitutional right,[11] no such "particularized injury"

[7] Allen v. Wright, 468 U.S. 737, 751 (1984).

[8] 262 U.S. 447, 488 (1923).

[9] *Id.* at 486.

[10] *Id.* at 487.

[11] See, e.g., Follett v. Town of McCormick, 321 U.S. 573 (1944) (invalidating tax on preaching on First Amendment grounds).

is associated with paying taxes generally, even when some portion of the collections is spent illegally.

In *Flast v. Cohen,* the Supreme Court carved out a narrow exception to the general constitutional prohibition against taxpayer standing. The taxpayer-plaintiff in that case challenged the distribution of federal funds to religious schools under the Elementary and Secondary Education Act of 1965, alleging that such aid violated the Establishment Clause. The Court set out a two-part test for determining whether a federal taxpayer has standing to challenge an allegedly unconstitutional expenditure. First, the taxpayer must establish "a logical link between that status and the type of legislative enactment attacked. Thus, a taxpayer will be a proper party to allege the unconstitutionality only of exercises of congressional power under the taxing and spending clause of Art. I, § 8, of the Constitution." Second, the taxpayer must establish

> a nexus between that status and the precise nature of the constitutional infringement alleged. Under this requirement, the taxpayer must show that the challenged enactment exceeds specific constitutional limitations imposed upon the exercise of the congressional taxing and spending power and not simply that the enactment is generally beyond the powers delegated to Congress by Art. I, § 8.[12]

The Court recognized this exception to the prevailing rule with respect to taxpayer standing because the use of tax dollars to support religion is the very type of injury the Establishment Clause was designed to prevent. Although "[a] large proportion of the early settlers of this country came here from Europe to escape the bondage of laws which compelled them to support . . . government favored churches," many settlers suffered from the "practices of the old world" even in the colonies.[13] Such abuses of the power to tax and spend "aroused . . . indignation" and engendered "the conviction that individual religious liberty could be achieved best under a government which was stripped of all power to tax, to support, or otherwise to assist any or all religions." In the Virginia Assembly, "Thomas Jefferson and James Madison led the fight" against taxation

[12] Flast v. Cohen, 392 U.S. 83, 102–03 (1968).

[13] Everson v. Board of Educ., 330 U.S. 1, 8–9 (1947).

that supported Virginia's established church.[14] In his *Memorial and Remonstrance Against Religious Assessments*, James Madison, who is generally recognized as the leading architect of the religion clauses of the First Amendment, stated that the taxing and spending power has the potential to injure taxpayers because '"the same authority which can force a citizen to contribute three pence only of his property for the support of any one establishment, may force him to conform to any other establishment in all cases whatsoever."'[15] Renewal of the tax was defeated in committee, and the Virginia Assembly squarely condemned taxation that supports religion by enacting Thomas Jefferson's Virginia Bill for Religious Liberty, which proclaimed that "to compel a man to furnish contributions of money for the propagation of opinions which he disbelieves, is sinful and tyrannical."[16]

Like the Virginia Bill for Religious Liberty, the Establishment Clause "reflected in the minds of early Americans a vivid mental picture of conditions and practices which they fervently wished to stamp out."[17] Animated by concern that "religious liberty ultimately would be the victim if government could employ its taxing and spending powers to aid one religion over another or to aid religion in general," the Establishment Clause was "designed as a specific bulwark against such potential abuses of governmental power."[18] It exists to ensure that "[n]o tax in any amount, large or small, can be levied to support any religious activities or institutions."[19]

Nevertheless, the *Flast* exception to the rule against taxpayer standing has been construed narrowly. For example, in *Valley Forge College v. Americans United for Separation of Church and State*, the Court held that there was no taxpayer "injury" (and, therefore, no standing) where the Department of Health, Education, and Welfare donated property to a Christian college under the Federal Property and Administrative Services Act of 1949, which allows the federal

[14] *Id.* at 11–12.

[15] Flast, 392 U.S. at 103. (quoting 2 Writings of James Madison 183, 186 (Hunt ed. 1901)).

[16] Everson, 330 U.S. at 12.

[17] *Id.* at 8.

[18] Flast, 392 U.S. at 103–04.

[19] Everson, 330 U.S. at 16.

government to dispose of "surplus property" that has "outlived its usefulness."[20] The Court observed that the only direct expenditure even remotely related to the case was the money the government originally spent to acquire the property approximately 30 years before the transfer at issue. Moreover, if the government had not donated the "surplus property" to a religious organization, it might well have donated the property to some other non-profit entity, in which case taxpayers would not have benefited.[21] In other words, there was no reason to believe that the government would have sold the property, realized a financial windfall, and used the proceeds to reduce taxes. Years later, in a 2006 case, the Court again drew a line that separates *Valley Forge* from *Flast*: In cases that do not involve direct expenditures, "a litigant may not assume a particular disposition of government funds in establishing standing."[22]

By contrast, when direct expenditures appropriated by Congress are at issue, the injury may consist of the "'very extract[ion] and spen[ding]' of 'tax money,'" and that injury can suffice to confer standing.[23] Thus, in *Bowen v. Kendrick*, the Court held that taxpayers had standing to challenge the Adolescent Family Life Act, which authorized federal grants to private community service groups, including religious organizations. Although the funds were administered by executive branch officials, the Court focused on the disbursement of funds flowing from Congress' taxing and spending power and the fact that the legislature contemplated a partnership between governmental and religious institutions.[24]

Hein presented the further question of whether discretionary spending by executive departments to fund religious activities may independently support taxpayer standing to bring an Establishment Clause claim. The Court was asked to decide whether a series of conferences funded by the federal government in support of the White House program of faith-based initiatives is more akin to the spending program in *Kendrick* than to the property giveaway in *Valley Forge*.

[20] 454 U.S. 464, 466 (1982).

[21] *Id.* at 480 n.17.

[22] DaimlerChrysler Corp. v. Cuno, 126 S.Ct. 1854, 1865 (2006).

[23] *Id.* (quoting Flast, 392 U.S. at 106).

[24] Bowen v. Kendrick, 487 U.S. 589, 595–96, 619–20 (1988).

II. Faith-Based Initiatives and Taxpayer Standing in *Hein*

On January 29, 2001, nine days after his inauguration as president of the United States, George W. Bush issued an executive order that created the White House Office of Faith-Based and Community Initiatives ("OFBCI") for the express purpose of using federal funds to "expand the role" of religious organizations and "increase their capacity."[25] The executive order directed OFBCI to "coordinate a national effort to expand opportunities" for religious organizations and undertake "a comprehensive effort to enlist, equip, enable, empower and expand the work" of religious organizations.[26] That same day, in a separate executive order, President Bush directed five federal agencies to establish Executive Department Centers for Faith-Based and Community Initiatives ("Faith-Based Agency Centers"), and instructed the Faith-Based Agency Centers to incorporate religious organizations "in department programs and initiatives to the greatest extent possible."[27] On December 12, 2002, President Bush signed Executive Order 13,279, which reduced the separation between federally-funded services and inherently religious activities, allowing religious organizations to provide federally-funded services in facilities adorned with "religious art, icons, scriptures, or other symbols."[28]

In 2002, OFBCI began to orchestrate a series of faith-based conferences and by the end of 2006 had held 28 such events.[29] The stated goal of the conferences was to promote community organizations whether secular or religious.[30] However, the conferences were operated as training and recruiting grounds primarily to support religious applicants for government grants that give such groups an

[25] Exec. Order No. 13,199, § 3(a), 66 Fed. Reg. 8,499 (2001).

[26] *Id.* at Preamble & § 2.

[27] Exec. Order No. 13,198, § 3(b), 66 Fed. Reg. 8,497 (2001). In subsequent executive orders, President Bush directed other federal agencies to establish similar Faith-Based Agency Centers. Exec. Order No. 13,280, 67 Fed. Reg. 77,145 (2002); Exec. Order No. 13,342, 69 Fed. Reg. 31,509 (2004).

[28] Exec. Order No. 13,279, § 2(f), 67 Fed. Reg. 77,141 (2002).

[29] White House, WHOFBCI Accomplishments in 2006 ("White House, WHOFBCI Accomplishments"), http://www.whitehouse.gov/government/fbci/2006_accomplishments.html (last visited July 5, 2007); White House, Logistics, Washington, D.C., September 24, 2007 ("White House, Logistics"), http://www.dtiassociates.com/FBCI/logisticsDC.cfm?location=DC (last visited July 5, 2007).

[30] See White House Conferences on Faith-Based and Community Initiatives, www.dtiassociates.com/FBCI/ (last visited July 5, 2007).

advantage over secular organizations in the application process. The conferences generate federal grant applications from religious groups by "provid[ing] participants with information about the government grants process and available funding opportunities" and offering "various grant writing tutorials."[31] Thousands of individuals attended the conferences,[32] which have trained 26,000 "new and potential federal grantees" since 2002.[33]

Apart from the grants themselves, the conferences require substantial expenditures of government funds entirely separate from any costs attributable to the salaried time of executive branch officials who organize, manage, and attend.[34] Expenses include renting ballrooms, meeting rooms, and overflow space for the massive conferences at hotels across the nation;[35] sending mailings prior to the conferences "to every church, synagogue, mosque, and social service organization within two hundred miles [of the conference location], about 20,000 invitations" per conference;[36] and allowing thousands of individuals to attend each conference. Attendance at the conferences is without charge to the participants, so that taxpayers and the public fisc bear the full financial burden of the events.[37]

The faith-based conferences tend to promote religious messages, which include prayer and performances of "All Hail, King Jesus" by religious choirs.[38] At one typical conference, for example, President Bush opened his remarks by assuming that there was not a single atheist or agnostic in an audience of over one thousand: "You love God with all your heart and all your soul and all your

[31] White House, Faith-Based & Community Initiative, www.whitehouse.gov/government/fbci/president-initiative.html (last visited Jan. 29, 2007).

[32] David Kuo, Tempting Faith 209 (2006); United States Department of Justice, E-Alert, www.ojp.usdoj.gov/fbci/newsletters/ealert002.htm (last visited Jan. 29, 2007).

[33] White House, WHOFBCI Accomplishments.

[34] Kuo, Tempting Faith, at 231.

[35] *Id.* at 211; Amy Sullivan, "Patron Feint," New Republic, Apr. 3, 2006.

[36] Kuo, Tempting Faith, at 209.

[37] White House, Logistics (stating that the conferences are free for attendees).

[38] Adelle M. Banks, "Bush Touts His Faith-Based Initiative Despite Congressional Foot-Dragging," Religion News Service, June 2, 2004, pewforum.org/news/display.php?NewsID=3481 (last visited Jan. 29, 2007).

strength."[39] The president's assumption evidently was correct, for the audience responded enthusiastically to his speech by shouting "Preach on, brother!"[40] In remarks at another such conference, then–Attorney General John Ashcroft, after identifying "faith" as a "fundamental value[ ] that define[s] our nation," made the same assumption as had the president, telling the audience "through the message of faith, you uphold our values."[41]

The overall religious focus of the faith-based initiative has had a predictable impact on the ways in which grants have been awarded and implemented. According to David Kuo, a former special assistant to President George W. Bush for faith-based programs, the grants process has been infused with religious discrimination.[42] For example, in awarding grants from the Compassion Capital Fund, a grants program created by Congress in 2002, the Department of Health and Human Services convened "an overwhelmingly Christian group of wonks, ministers, and well-meaning types" whose "biases were transparent." The group was tasked with rating organizations on a scale from 1 to 100, and these ratings determined which organizations would receive grants.[43] According to Kuo, "[i]t was obvious that the ratings were a farce." In fact, one of the raters stated that "when [she] saw one of those non-Christian groups in the set [she] was reviewing," she "just stopped looking at them and gave them a zero." She further stated that such behavior was typical among the raters. Under this rating system, "Jesus and Friends Ministry from California, a group with little more than a post office box" scored much higher than Big Brothers/Big Sisters of America and other leading national charities.[44]

Not surprisingly, the combination of using faith-based conferences to instruct religious organizations in applying for grants and then

[39] George W. Bush, Remarks at the White House Conference on Faith-Based and Community Initiatives, Philadelphia, Pennsylvania (Dec. 12, 2002).

[40] *Id.*

[41] Prepared Remarks of Attorney General John Ashcroft, White House Faith-Based Conference, Tampa, Florida (Dec. 5, 2003).

[42] Kuo, Tempting Faith, *supra* note 32, at 212–16.

[43] *Id.* at 213–15. See also Government Accountability Office, Faith-Based and Community Initiative 6 (June 2006) (GAO Report) (stating that the decisions to award grants "were generally based on applicants' scores" assigned by raters).

[44] Kuo, Tempting Faith, *supra* note 32, at 213–16.

selecting grantees on the basis of religion vastly increased the flow of federal funds to sectarian organizations. According to the congressional testimony of the Department of Housing and Urban Development (HUD), the conferences contributed to a major increase in HUD funding for religious organizations between fiscal years 2002 and 2004.[45] In fiscal year 2005, religious organizations received $2.1 billion in federal grants, nearly twice what they received in fiscal year 2003.[46] The White House announced that ''[d]ue to the President's leadership, more faith-based organizations are participating in the Federal grants process,'' and that the Department of Health and Human Services has nearly doubled the number of grants to religious organizations since fiscal year 2002.[47]

In addition to channeling unprecedented levels of monetary aid to religious organizations, the executive branch was less than vigilant when recipients diverted funds to inherently religious activities. According to the grant conditions, a religious organization is not allowed to misuse federal funds by conducting religious activities during government-funded services, such as counseling.[48] However, the Government Accountability Office (GAO) has found that religious organizations often ignore such restrictions.[49] It found that in many cases federal agencies fail to monitor the use of grant money and neglect even to inform religious organizations of their legal obligations.[50] In this regard, most federal agencies that provide grants to religious organizations do not even tell grant recipients that they

[45] See Federal Agencies and Conference Spending, Hearings Before the Subcomm. on Federal Financial Management, Government Information and International Security of the S. Comm. on Homeland Security and Government Affairs, 109th Cong. 58 (2006) (statement of James M. Martin, Acting Deputy Chief Financial Officer, HUD).

[46] White House, Fact Sheet: Compassion in Action (March 2005) (''White House, Fact Sheet''), www.whitehouse.gov/news/releases/2005/03/20050301-1.html (last visited July 5, 2007); White House, WHOFBCI Accomplishments.

[47] White House, Fact Sheet, *supra* note 46.

[48] See Exec. Order No. 13,279, § 2(e) (''[O]rganizations that engage in inherently religious activities, such as worship, religious instruction, and proselytization, must offer those services separately in time or location from any programs or services supported with direct Federal financial assistance . . .'').

[49] GAO Report, *supra* note 43, at 6–7, 34–36.

[50] *Id.* at 30–34.

cannot discriminate on the basis of religion in providing social services.[51]

According to GAO, several federal agencies fail to visit more than five to ten percent of grant recipients in a given year.[52] GAO further stated that "[f]ew government agencies administering [grant] programs monitor organizations to ensure compliance with [ ] safeguards" regarding inherently religious activities.[53] GAO reviewed financial and performance reports submitted to federal agencies by religious organizations that received federal grants, but "none of the reports . . . contained any questions related to compliance with the safeguards" that prohibit the use of government funds in inherently religious activities.[54] GAO also reported that the Department of Justice's Community Corrections Contracting program contained "no reference to the prohibition on inherently religious activities," which "could be read as allowing all providers of social services in [correctional] settings to engage in worship, religious instruction, or proselytization."[55] In sum, GAO concluded that "the government has little assurance" that safeguards surrounding the use of federal funds are enforced.[56]

As a consequence, compliance with funding restrictions has been haphazard. After surveying thirteen organizations that receive federal grants and offer voluntary religious services, GAO found that four "did not appear to understand the requirement to separate [inherently religious] activities in time or location from their program services funded with federal funds." One official of a religious organization told GAO "that she discusses religious issues while providing federal funded services," and others stated that they "pray with beneficiaries during program time." Another official acknowledged that she began government-funded social services for children by reading from the Bible.[57]

[51] *Id.* at 29.

[52] *Id.* at 37.

[53] *Id.* at 6–7, 29.

[54] *Id.* at 36.

[55] *Id.* at 32. See also 28 C.F.R. § 38.2(b)(2).

[56] GAO Report, *supra* note 43, at 52.

[57] *Id.* at 7, 35.

III. Judicial Challenge to the Faith-Based Conferences

Freedom From Religion Foundation, Inc. and three of its members filed suit in their capacity as federal taxpayers, alleging that the faith-based conferences violated the First Amendment's Establishment Clause. The government filed a motion to dismiss, which the United States District Court for the Western District of Wisconsin granted, concluding that the plaintiffs lacked standing because the conferences were established by discretionary executive action, not by congressional enactment. The United States Court of Appeals for the Seventh Circuit reversed this decision by a vote of 2-1 in a decision written by Judge Richard Posner.[58]

Although he found that many of the allegations in the complaint lacked merit, Judge Posner concluded that it was "not entirely frivolous, for it portrays the conferences organized by the various Centers as propaganda vehicles for religion." If this allegation were proven, he noted, "one could not dismiss the possibility that the defendants are violating the establishment clause." He acknowledged that money to fund the conferences came from appropriations for general administrative expenses, over which the president and other executive branch officials have a degree of discretionary power, rather than from directed congressional appropriations. But Judge Posner concluded that the lack of a specific congressional spending mandate was not dispositive on the question of taxpayer standing. Otherwise, he reasoned, the executive branch would have unfettered authority to use discretionary funds appropriated by Congress to aid religion, even to the point of allowing "the Secretary of Homeland Security . . . to build a mosque and pay an Imam a salary to preach in it."[59]

At the same time, Judge Posner explained that "the fact that almost all executive branch activity is funded by appropriations does not confer standing to challenge violations of the establishment clause that do not involve expenditures." Rather, in order for government action to "involve expenditures," there must be a "marginal or incremental cost to the taxpaying public of the alleged violation of the establishment clause." Although a speech by the president entails "preparations, security arrangements, etc.," and although "an accountant could doubtless estimate the cost," the court of appeals

[58] Freedom from Religion v. Chao, 433 F.3d 989, 994 (7th Cir. 2006).

[59] *Id.* at 994.

held that such expenses, without more, do not confer taxpayer standing. The court reasoned that such costs, like official salaries, would be incurred regardless of whether the president "mentioned Moses rather than John Stuart Mill," and hence, the decision to mention Moses would inflict no injury on taxpayers.[60] Judge Kenneth Ripple dissented, describing the majority opinion as "a dramatic expansion of current standing doctrine." He disagreed with Judge Posner's opinion, which he believed would make "virtually any executive action subject to a taxpayer suit.[61]

IV. The Supreme Court's Decision

Without issuing a majority opinion, the Supreme Court voted 5-4 to reverse the Seventh Circuit, holding that the plaintiffs lacked standing to challenge the faith-based conferences. Justice Alito's plurality opinion, joined by Justice Kennedy and Chief Justice Roberts, focused on the fact that the conferences were not established by a specific congressional spending program, and therefore the matter did not fall within the narrow exception for taxpayer standing established in *Flast v. Cohen*. The plurality observed that "[t]he Court of Appeals did not apply *Flast*; it extended *Flast*." Noting that "*Flast* focused on congressional action," the Court "decline[d] this invitation to extend its holding to encompass discretionary Executive Branch expenditures."[62]

Justice Alito's opinion started from the premise that a federal taxpayer may have standing to challenge the collection of a specific tax as being unconstitutional—*e.g.*, a tax on a particular exercise of free speech—but that a general interest in ensuring that treasury funds are spent in accordance with the Constitution is not the type of redressable "personal injury" necessary to establish Article III standing.[63] Because the interests of the taxpayer are identical to those of the public at large, he reasoned, deciding a constitutional claim with standing based solely on the plaintiffs' status as taxpayers would not decide a judicial case or controversy, but instead would

[60] *Id.* at 945.

[61] *Id.* at 997, 1000 (Ripple, J., dissenting).

[62] Hein v. Freedom From Religion Foundation, Inc., 127 S. Ct. 2553, 2568, 2571–72 (2007).

[63] *Id.* at 2563. Compare Follett v. Town of McCormick, 321 U.S. 573 (1944) (invalidation tax against preaching on First Amendment grounds).

extend judicial power generally over acts of the legislative branch. Where the interests of the taxpayer are so indeterminable, remote, uncertain, and indirect, they cannot serve as the basis of the Court's jurisdiction.[64]

The plurality opinion emphasized that the expenditures at issue in *Flast* were made pursuant to an express congressional mandate and a specific congressional appropriation. By contrast, the expenditures in *Hein* were not made pursuant to a specific act of Congress, but were drawn from general appropriations for the executive branch to fund its day-to-day activities. As a consequence, Justice Alito concluded that the funding for the faith-based conferences came from discretionary executive spending, not congressional action, notwithstanding the fact that Congress appropriated the general funds.[65] Tracing the Court's case law regarding taxpayer standing, the plurality noted that the plaintiffs could "cite no statute whose application they challenge." To emphasize that point, Justice Alito observed that "[w]hen a criminal defendant charges that a federal agent carried out an unreasonable search and seizure, we do not view that claim as [a] challenge to the constitutionality of the statute appropriating funds for the Federal Bureau of Investigation." Accordingly, he was unwilling to permit a taxpayer challenge to executive programs "funded by no-strings, lump-sum appropriations."[66]

The plurality opinion essentially limited the *Flast* exception to its facts where Congress exercised its taxing and spending power. To do otherwise, Justice Alito wrote, would give too little weight to concerns over the proper allocation of power among the branches of government. He noted that "almost all Executive Branch activity is ultimately funded by some congressional appropriation [and that] extending the *Flast* exception to purely executive expenditures would effectively subject every federal action—be it a conference, a proclamation or a speech—to Establishment Clause challenge by any taxpayer in federal court."[67] Accordingly, the plurality declined to "deputize federal courts as 'virtually continuing monitors of the

[64] *Id.*

[65] *Id.* at 2565–66.

[66] *Id.* at 2567–68.

[67] *Id.* at 2569.

wisdom and soundness of Executive action.'"[68] In addition, Justice Alito faulted the Seventh Circuit for failing to articulate a workable test for determining when the cost of an executive action could reasonably be identified as a harm to taxpayers.

At the same time, the plurality discounted the example, set forth by Judge Posner, that "a federal agency could use its discretionary funds to build a house of worship or to hire clergy of one denomination and send them out to spread their faith." It noted that neither this, nor other examples in a "parade of horribles" had occurred, notwithstanding the fact that *Flast* had not been extended to cover discretionary executive spending. But if such things happened, wrote Justice Alito, "Congress could quickly step in" or such improbable abuses could be "challenged in federal court by plaintiffs who would possess standing based on grounds other than taxpayer standing." Accordingly, the plurality decided neither to extend nor to overrule the taxpayer standing exception of *Flast*, but instead to "leave *Flast* as we found it."[69]

Although he joined the plurality opinion, Justice Kennedy wrote separately to stress the danger to separation of powers principles that an expansion of *Flast* would entail. "The Executive Branch should be free, as a general matter, to discover new ideas, to understand pressing public demands, and to find creative new responses to address governmental concerns," he wrote, and if more extensive judicial intervention and supervision were permitted based on taxpayer suits arising from general appropriations, "the courts would soon assume the role of speech editors for communications issued by executive officials and event planners for meetings they hold." Nevertheless, Justice Kennedy cautioned against executive and legislative actions that strain Establishment Clause concerns. He stressed that government officials are obligated to obey the Constitution whether or not their acts can be challenged in court. Finally, Justice Kennedy stressed that "the result reached in *Flast* is correct and should not be called into question."[70]

[68] *Id.* at 2570 (quoting Allen, 468 U.S. at 760, quoting Laird v. Tatum, 408 U.S. 1, 15 (1972)).

[69] *Id.* at 2571–72.

[70] *Id.* at 2572–73 (Kennedy, J., concurring).

Contrasting sharply with the plurality's promise to "leave *Flast* as we found it," and Justice Kennedy's amplification of that pledge, Justice Scalia's concurring opinion argued strenuously that *Flast* should be overruled and the taxpayer standing exception eliminated. Joined by Justice Thomas, the opinion disparaged the Court's taxpayer standing cases as part of a "shameful tradition" based on "utterly meaningless distinctions" that lack "coherence and candor" and that lead to "demonstrably absurd results."[71] Justice Scalia wrote that attempts to apply such unprincipled doctrine "deaden the soul of the law, which is logic and reason."[72] As a consequence, he argued that "[i]f this Court is to decide cases by rule of law rather than show of hands, we must surrender to logic and choose sides: Either *Flast* . . . should be applied to (at a minimum) all challenges to the government expenditure of general tax revenues in a manner alleged to violate a constitutional provision specifically limiting the taxing and spending power, or *Flast* should be repudiated."[73]

For Justice Scalia and Thomas, at least, "the choice is easy." Describing *Flast* as "damaged goods," a "blot on our jurisprudence," and a "jurisprudential disaster," they argued that the Court should have seized the opportunity to "erase" it, but instead "simply smudged it."[74] Justice Scalia blamed this outcome on "the plurality's pose of minimalism" as shown by its disinclination to overrule established precedent. In this regard, he used Justice Alito's plurality opinion as a vehicle for mocking Chief Justice John Roberts' announced goal of judicial restraint. "Minimalism is an admirable judicial trait," Justice Scalia wrote, "but not when it comes at the cost of meaningless and disingenuous distinctions that hold the sure promise of engendering further meaningless and disingenuous distinctions in the future."[75]

In analyzing whether there is a showing of some concrete and particularized "injury in fact" in taxpayer standing cases, Justice Scalia observed that the Court alternately has relied on two entirely distinct conceptions of harm, which he characterized as "Wallet

[71] *Id.* at 2573, 2577–78, 2580 (Scalia, J., concurring).

[72] *Id.* at 2582.

[73] *Id.* at 2573.

[74] *Id.* at 2583–84.

[75] *Id.* at 2580, 2582.

Injury" and "Psychic Injury." He reasoned that "Wallet Injury" is the only legitimate basis for standing, since "Psychic Injury" stems solely from "the taxpayer's *mental displeasure* that money extracted from him is being spent in an unlawful manner."[76] In this regard, Justice Scalia noted that taxpayer standing in *Flast* was based in fact on "Psychic Injury," whether or not the Court was willing to acknowledge it. But he found that the approach in *Flast* was "peculiarly restricted" because it permitted "taxpayer displeasure over unconstitutional spending to support standing *only if* the constitutional provision allegedly violated is a specific limitation on the taxing and spending power."[77] In his view, logic requires that the Court either permit standing in all cases in which "Psychic Injury" is alleged, or limit standing to cases in which there is a concrete showing of "Wallet Injury."

Justice Scalia chided the majority for being "unwilling to acknowledge that the logic of *Flast* (its Psychic Injury rationale) is simply wrong." And he agreed with the four dissenters, that "*Flast* is *indistinguishable* from this case for purposes of Article III."[78] Justice Scalia explained that the plurality's decision "flatly contradicts *Kendrick*," and confessed to "shar[ing] the dissent's bewilderment" as to the plurality's explanation.[79] Unlike the dissent, however, he would confront "*Flast's* adoption of Psychic Injury . . . head-on." *Flast* should either "be accorded the wide application that it logically dictates," according to Justice Scalia, or it "must be abandoned in its entirety."[80]

He did not hesitate to embrace the latter course, regardless of the fact "that it is the alleged violation of a specific constitutional limit on the taxing and spending power that produces the taxpayer's mental angst." Justice Scalia found it to be "of no conceivable relevance to this issue whether the Establishment Clause was originally conceived of as a specific limitation on the taxing and spending power."[81] To find otherwise, he reasoned, would transform courts into "ombudsmen of the general welfare" in Establishment Clause

[76] *Id.* at 2574 (emphasis in original).

[77] *Id.* (emphasis in original).

[78] *Id.* at 2580 (emphasis in original).

[79] *Id.* at 2580–81.

[80] *Id.* at 2582.

[81] *Id.* at 2583.

cases.[82] To apply the logical consequence of *Flast* in this case, he explained, would permit any taxpayer to sue whenever tax funds were used in an alleged violation of the Establishment Clause. "So, for example, any taxpayer could challenge the fact that the Marshall of our Court is paid, in part, to call the courtroom to order by proclaiming 'God Save the United States and this Honorable Court.'"[83] Such generalized grievances affecting the public at large should only have a remedy in the political process, he concluded, and not in the courts.

Justice Souter dissented, joined by Justices Stevens, Ginsburg, and Breyer. He identified the injury in Establishment Clause cases as "the very 'extract[ion] and spen[ding]' of 'tax money' in aid of religion."[84] Citing the deep historical roots underlying the concept that imposing taxes in support of religion conflicted with individual freedom of conscience, Justice Souter disputed the characterization that it could be dismissed as a mere "Psychic Injury" whenever "a congressional appropriation or executive expenditure raises hackles of disagreement with the policy supported." He distinguished this from a "generalized grievance," and noted that "[w]hen executive agencies spend identifiable sums of tax money for religious purposes, no less than when Congress authorizes the same thing, taxpayers suffer injury."[85]

Echoing the hypothetical situation initially described by Judge Posner, the dissent posited that

> [i]t would surely violate the Establishment Clause for the Department of Health and Human Services to draw on a general appropriation to build a chapel for weekly church services (no less than if a statute required it), and for good reason: if the Executive could accomplish through the exercise of discretion exactly what Congress cannot do through legislation, Establishment Clause protection would melt away.[86]

[82] *Id.* at 2582 (quoting *Valley Forge*, 454 U.S. at 487).

[83] *Id.*

[84] *Id.* at 2584–85 (Souter, J., dissenting) (quoting *DaimlerChrysler Corp. v. Cuno*, 126 S. Ct. 1854, 1865 (2006)).

[85] *Id.* at 2585.

[86] *Id.* at 2586.

Accordingly, Justice Souter wrote that the injury raised by the case was not too abstract to be judicially cognizable.

V. Implications of the Decision

Hein represents a unique situation where a majority of six justices stated their belief that current Establishment Clause jurisprudence supports a ruling against the government, yet five justices rejected the taxpayer challenge to the expenditure of tax dollars to support religious activities. The primary casualties of this decision include not just the unsuccessful challengers in *Hein*, but also Chief Justice Roberts' stated goal of presiding over a less polarized Court. Justice Scalia's caustic dissent shattered such aspirations and directly challenged the chief justice's judicial philosophy of adhering to precedent and making only incremental changes. Joined by Justice Thomas, Justice Scalia would have seized the opportunity to overrule *Flast* and to eliminate taxpayer standing in Establishment Clause challenges, claiming that there are "few cases less warranting of *stare decisis* respect"[87]—that is, the Court's tendency not to disturb settled points of law.

Even though Justice Alito's plurality opinion took the more moderate course of "leav[ing] *Flast* as we found it," the decision as a practical matter will further marginalize the concept of taxpayer standing in Establishment Clause cases.[88] To the extent standing may still be found in cases where Congress enacts a program to support religious activities pursuant to its taxing and spending power, judicial oversight may easily be avoided using the road map articulated in *Hein*. As in this case, general appropriations can be provided to executive departments that, in their exercise of discretion, may be used to support religious programs. Accordingly, the Court may have decided not to plow *Flast* under, but it constructed a convenient bypass that routes around it.

The plurality stopped short of embracing Justice Scalia's premise that the Court should "apply *Flast* to *all* challenges to government expenditures in violation of constitutional provisions that specifically limit the taxing and spending power" or else it "should overturn *Flast*."[89] But it accepted his reasoning that to allow taxpayer

[87] *Id.* at 2584 (Scalia, J., concurring).

[88] *Id.* at 2572 (plurality op.).

[89] *Id.* at 2579–80 (Scalia, J., concurring) (emphasis in original). See also *id.* at 2582 ("Either *Flast* was correct, and must be accorded the wide application that it logically dictates, or it was not, and must be abandoned in its entirety.").

standing in this case would permit virtually any citizen to "challenge the fact that the Marshall of our Court is paid, in part, to call the courtroom to order by proclaiming 'God Save the United States and this Honorable Court.'"[90] The plurality agreed that permitting taxpayer standing would effectively subject every federal action to Establishment Clause challenges, including conferences, proclamations or speeches.[91] Thus, although it rejected Justice Scalia's "all or nothing" proposition with respect to *Flast*, the plurality accepted an "all or very little" resolution of the matter.

In doing so, it dismissed the Seventh Circuit's reasoning regarding how broadly to apply taxpayer standing under *Flast*. Judge Posner rejected the claim that permitting a challenge in this case would open the courthouse door to anyone who disagreed with even the smallest expenditures in support of religion. He wrote that incidental executive expenditures—such as the costs associated with giving a speech—without more, do not confer taxpayer standing. The Seventh Circuit reasoned that such costs, like official salaries, would be incurred regardless of whether the president discussed religious or secular topics. However, Judge Posner's opinion would have permitted taxpayer standing where the alleged Establishment Clause violation resulted in a marginal or incremental cost to the taxpaying public even when funds were the product of discretionary executive expenditures.[92]

It undoubtedly would create a difficult line-drawing exercise to determine when an expenditure would involve a "marginal or incremental cost to the taxpaying public," as both the Supreme Court plurality and concurring opinions noted. But doing so on the facts presented by *Hein*—where a series of expensive conferences was organized specifically to support a massive executive program dedicated to funneling grants to religious organizations with scant oversight—seems less problematic. The controversy the Court was asked to decide is far removed from hypothetical scenarios involving a potential challenge to the clerk invoking a deity while calling the Court to order or the president's stray reference to a supreme being. Accordingly, recognizing taxpayer standing in this case would have

[90] *Id.* at 2581.

[91] *Id.* at 2569 (plurality op.).

[92] Freedom From Religion v. Chao, 433 F.3d 989, 995 (7th Cir. 2006).

been unlikely to open the floodgates to challenges for all other conceivable expenditures.

At the same time, the Court's decision to deny taxpayer standing lacks a good answer to Judge Posner's concern that the executive branch would be able to use discretionary funds appropriated by Congress to aid religion, even to the point of allowing the secretary of homeland security to build and fund a church or mosque.[93] No such thing has happened, the plurality explained, and if it did, Congress could quickly intervene. Additionally, Justice Alito noted that the respondents had failed to show that other plaintiffs would lack standing based on grounds other than as taxpayers.[94] Justice Kennedy, by contrast, simply chose to hope for the best. Explaining his vote against standing so as to avoid "constant intrusion upon the executive realm," he observed that "[g]overnment officials must make a conscious decision to obey the Constitution whether or not their acts can be challenged in a court of law and then must conform their actions to these principled determinations."[95]

Justice Kennedy did not explain what, in his experience, justified the optimistic belief that executive officials would carefully identify, much less assiduously adhere to, the constitutional limitations of the Establishment Clause. Similarly, Justice Alito neglected to describe the real-world circumstances in which Congress might "step in" to block an executive program designed to fund religious enterprises. Neither the plurality, nor Justice Kennedy's concurring opinion, offered any assurance that courts would have jurisdiction to address such executive abuses. For his part, Justice Scalia seemed quite comfortable with the notion that no judicial remedy would be available, finding it to be entirely irrelevant that the Establishment Clause was enacted as a specific limitation on the taxing and spending power.[96] He brushed aside Madison's *Memorial and Remonstrance Against Religious Assessments* and instead relied on Alexis de Tocqueville's observation that some laws "*can never give rise to the sort of clearly formulated dispute that one calls a case.*"[97] Thus, in the name of

[93] *Id.* at 944.

[94] Hein, 127 S. Ct. at 2571 (plurality op.).

[95] *Id.* at 2573 (Kennedy, J., concurring).

[96] *Id.* at 2583 (Scalia, J., concurring).

[97] *Id.* (quoting and adding emphasis to A. de Tocqueville, Democracy in America 97 (H. Mansfield & D. Winthrop transls. and eds. 2000).

divining original intent, Justice Scalia found the views of a French tourist to be more authoritative than those of the Framers themselves.

Justice Scalia may well be correct—particularly following *Hein*—that no judicial remedy exists to challenge an Establishment Clause violation predicated on the misuse of discretionary funds by an executive official. Contrary to the plurality's assumption, no one else but a taxpayer may be in a position to assert standing in such a case. As Judge Ripple explained in his dissent to the Seventh Circuit panel decision, in such cases "[b]eneficiaries of such spending have no incentive to sue, and non-beneficiary outsiders cannot show direct injury." He described this vacuum in jurisdiction as the very reason that taxpayer standing exists in Establishment Clause cases. Judge Ripple took note of a specific grant program that had been created by congressional enactment (that had been a part of an earlier phase of *Hein*) and noted that "the district court, quite properly, allowed taxpayer standing to challenge the grant." Judge Ripple further acknowledged that "[w]ithout the *Flast* exception, it is unlikely that anyone would have had standing to sue in such a situation." However, he declined to join the Seventh Circuit's majority opinion in extending this reasoning to discretionary executive spending because, in his view, it "simply cuts the concept of taxpayer standing loose from its moorings."[98] According to this logic, no one would have standing to challenge a grant program created and funded by the executive, even if it is otherwise identical to an unconstitutional program created by Congress.

In the end, the Court in *Hein* left *Flast* "as we found it," but with a significant reservation. It created a road map by which the executive may circumnavigate judicial standing in Establishment Clause cases altogether, simply by supporting religious institutions on its own initiative. *Flast* may yet be good law, but there likely will be few occasions to apply it in the future.

[98] Chao, 433 F.3d at 998–99 (Ripple, J., dissenting).

The Non-Preferment Principle and the "Racial Tiebreaker" Cases

*Samuel Estreicher**

> Preferment by race, when resorted to by the State, can be the most divisive of policies, containing within it the potential to destroy confidence in the Constitution and the idea of equality.
>
> —Justice Anthony Kennedy, dissenting in *Grutter v. Bollinger*, 539 U.S. 306, 388 (2003)

I. Introduction: "The Racial Tiebreaker" Decision

In the Supreme Court's recent pass at "affirmative action," the justices again divided 5-4, offering impassioned disagreements over the extent to which public schools may invoke "diversity" as a "compelling purpose" for the use of racial classifications when making certain admissions and transfer decisions, and whether the plans under challenge were "narrowly tailored" to serve that purpose.

In companion cases decided in late June 2007—*Parents Involved in Community Schools v. Seattle School District No. 1*[1]—the Court struck down the use of race as an admissions and transfer "tiebreaker" by the public school systems of Seattle, Washington, and the greater Louisville area, Jefferson County, Kentucky. The plans of both systems were tied to the district-wide racial demographics; in Seattle, race was used to determine who would fill open slots at oversubscribed schools,[2] and in Jefferson County, race helped determine

*Dwight D. Opperman Professor of Law, New York University School of Law.

[1] 127 S. Ct. 2738 (2007).

[2] For the 2000–01 school year, five of the Seattle schools were oversubscribed in that 82 percent of students ranked them as one of their first choices. "Three of the oversubscribed schools were 'integration positive' because the school's white enrollment the previous school year was greater than 51 percent. . . . Thus, more nonwhite students (107, 27, and 82, respectively) who selected one of these three schools as a top choice received placement at the school than would have been the case had race not been considered, and [geographic] proximity been the next tiebreaker." *Id.* at 2747.

who could attend particular elementary schools within a geographic "cluster."[3] Writing for the majority, Chief Justice John Roberts insisted that all official racial classifications trigger strict judicial scrutiny and that neither a remedial purpose nor the diversity rationale accepted in *Grutter v. Bollinger*[4]—the 2003 decision sustaining the University of Michigan Law School's preferential racial admissions program—justified the racial tiebreaker used by Seattle and Jefferson County. The tiebreaker could not be viewed as a remedy for official discrimination, the Court reasoned, because Seattle had never been found by a court to have maintained a racially segregated school system; and, while Jefferson County had maintained such a system, it successfully argued in 2000 for release from a court desegregation order on the ground that it had achieved unitary status and had eliminated "[t]o the greatest extent practicable" the vestiges of its prior policy of segregation.[5] *Grutter*'s diversity rationale was found unavailing because *Grutter* "relied upon considerations unique to institutions of higher education";[6] and, in this case, "race, for some students, is determinative standing alone."[7] Here, the school districts used "racial classifications in a 'nonindividualized, mechanical' way,"[8] unlike the one-factor-among-many "highly individualized, holistic review"[9] engaged in by the University of Michigan Law School. Moreover, the plans under challenge used a racially

[3]Jefferson County required "all nonmagnet schools to maintain a minimum black enrollment of 15 percent, and a maximum black enrollment of 50 percent." *Id.* at 2749. Students were assigned within geographic clusters: "'Decisions to assign students to schools within each cluster are based on available space within the schools and the racial guidelines in the District's current student assignment plan.' If a school has reached the 'extremes of the racial guidelines,' a student whose race would contribute to the school's racial imbalance will not be assigned there. . . . Transfers [between nonmagnet schools in the district] may be requested for any number of reasons, and may be denied because of lack of available space or on the basis of the racial guidelines." *Id.* at 2749–50.

[4]539 U.S. 306 (2003).

[5]See Hampton v. Jefferson County Bd. of Educ., 102 F. Supp. 2d 358, 360 (2000).

[6]Parents Involved in Cmty. Sch. v. Seattle Sch. Dist. No. 1, 127 S. Ct. 2738, 2754 (2007).

[7]*Id.* at 2753.

[8]*Id.* at 2754 (quoting Gratz v. Bollinger, 539 U.S. 244, 276, 280 (2003) (O'Connor, J., concurring)).

[9]*Id.* at 2753 (quoting Grutter, 539 U.S. at 337).

binary "limited notion of diversity."[10] Five justices also agreed that the school districts failed the "narrow tailoring" prong of strict-scrutiny analysis because they had not seriously considered race-neutral alternatives;[11] and any claimed necessity for the use of race was further undermined by the minimal number of students affected by the racial preference.[12]

Chief Justice Roberts wrote only for himself and three colleagues in Parts III-B and IV of the opinion. Part IV consisted of a series of rejoinders to Justice Stephen Breyer's dissenting opinion. In Part III-B the plurality questioned whether the plans were narrowly tailored to meet the school districts' stated justification of reducing racially concentrated schools and taking advantage of the pedagogic benefits of educating students in a racially integrated environment. The school systems had made no effort to show how the claimed diversity benefits were tied to the racial demographics that governed use of

[10] "Even when it comes to race, the plans here employ only a limited notion of diversity, viewing race exclusively in white/nonwhite terms in Seattle and black/ 'other' terms in Jefferson County. . . . [U]nder the Seattle plan, a school with 50 percent Asian-American students and 50 percent white students but no African-American, Native-American, or Latino students would qualify as balanced, while a school with 30 percent Asian-American, 25 percent African-American, 25 percent Latino, and 20 percent white students would not. It is hard to understand how a plan that could allow these results can be viewed as being concerned with achieving enrollment that is 'broadly diverse.'" *Id.* at 2754 (quoting Grutter, 539 U.S. at 329).

[11] Consider the reasoning given in the Ninth Circuit's en banc decision: "The record demonstrates that the School Board considered using a poverty tiebreaker in place of the race-based tiebreaker. It concluded, however, that this proxy device would not achieve its compelling interest in achieving racial diversity, and had other adverse effects. Although there was no formal study of the proposal by District staff, Board members' testimony revealed two legitimate reasons why the Board rejected the use of poverty to reach its goal of racial diversity. First, the Board concluded that it is insulting to minorities and often inaccurate to assume that poverty correlates with minority status. Second, for the group of students for whom poverty would correlate with minority status, the implementation would have been thwarted by high school students' understandable reluctance to reveal their socioeconomic status to their peers." Parents Involved in Cmty. Sch. v. Seattle Sch. Dist. No. 1, 426 F.3d 1162, 1188–89 (9th Cir. 2005) (en banc).

[12] *Id.* at 2759–61. It is interesting to note, moreover, that two of the less popular Seattle schools, at least one with a student body that had been predominantly African-American, became in the late 1990s *oversubscribed* schools not because of the racial tiebreaker—which did not apply to selection of undersubscribed schools—but because of a change in principals and a change in location of one of the schools. *Id.* at 1169 n.5.

the racial tiebreakers. Unlike in *Grutter,* Roberts noted, the school districts were "working backward to achieve a particular type of racial balance, rather than working forward from some demonstration of the level of diversity that provides the purported benefits. . . ."[13] The challenged plans were constitutionally flawed because they sought, at bottom, to achieve racial balance rather than pedagogic diversity.

Justice Anthony Kennedy, who had dissented in *Grutter*[14] and joined the majority opinion in *Gratz v. Bollinger,*[15] which struck down the rigid racial preferences used for University of Michigan undergraduate admissions, wrote a separate concurrence in *Parents Involved.* The challenged plans, he agreed, failed to satisfy "narrow tailoring" review, but the chief justice's opinion was too sweeping in its condemnation of nearly all use of race. In Kennedy's view, government can be legitimately concerned with preventing "de facto resegregation"[16] of the public schools and is "free to devise race-conscious measures to address the problem in a general way and without treating each student in a different fashion solely on the basis of a systematic, individual typing by race."[17]

Justice Breyer penned the principal dissent for himself and three colleagues. For the dissent, the plans were easily justified as remedial measures: Jefferson County could not be faulted for continuing measures that were considered constitutionally *required* before 2000; and Seattle had voluntarily addressed racial segregation to head off a lawsuit. In any event, strict scrutiny was not appropriate as the government's purpose in both cases was to derive advantage from the pedagogic benefits of an integrated education rather than to make invidious judgments on the basis of race.

II. The Non-Preferment Principle

As long as analysis of racial classification cases turns on the familiar two-prong inquiry into whether government has asserted a "compelling interest" and, if so, whether the challenged program reflects

[13] *Id.* at 2757 (plurality opinion).

[14] Grutter v. Bollinger, 539 U.S. 306 (2003).

[15] 539 U.S. 244 (2003).

[16] Parents Involved in Cmty. Sch. v. Seattle Sch. Dist. No. 1, 127 S. Ct. 2738, 2791 (2007) (Kennedy, J., concurring in part and concurring in the judgment).

[17] *Id.* at 2792.

"narrow tailoring," the Supreme Court jurisprudence in this area will prove deeply unsatisfying and difficult to predict. Both prongs have an "in-the-eye-of-the-beholder" quality, particularly after the *Grutter* Court (at least on some accounts) accepted as a compelling interest race-based viewpoint diversity, and the concomitant necessity of maintaining a "critical mass" of the under-represented racial viewpoint. Once that hurdle was cleared, insistence on narrow tailoring seems almost churlish; Justice Breyer certainly has a point in stressing that the program sustained in *Grutter* was a lot less narrowly tailored than the racial-tiebreakers invalidated in *Parents Involved*.[18] Indeed, narrow tailoring appears paradoxical because if racial diversity is what the state is seeking (and can lawfully seek), racial preferences may be the best way to get there—hence, the lament of Circuit Judges Michael Boudin[19] and Alex Kozinski,[20] highlighted in the Breyer dissent, that it is simply incoherent to require the state to get to a valid goal by the most circuitous route possible.

Much ink has been spilled in this area, but perhaps it is time to fish or cut bait: the Court should either articulate a clear, compelling principle or it should give up altogether the effort to place constitutional limits on government use of race or ethnicity to benefit minorities. I suggest a return to first principles: Why bar use of racial preferences at all when many well-intentioned people would agree with Justice Breyer and others that such preferences are an important part of the social arsenal for achieving equality? Indeed, one might ask, as do Justices Breyer and John Paul Stevens in their dissents: Why engage in strict scrutiny at all when the state is acting from such a beneficent wellspring of motivation?

[18] "[B]road-range limits on voluntary school choice plans are less burdensome, and hence more narrowly tailored, than other race-conscious restrictions this Court has previously approved. Indeed, the plans before are *more narrowly tailored* than the race-conscious admission plans that this Court approved in *Grutter*. Here, race becomes a factor only in a fraction of students' non-merit based assignments—not in large numbers of students' merit-based applications. Moreover, the effect of applying race-conscious criteria here affects potentially disadvantaged students *less severely*, not more severely than the criteria at issue in *Grutter*." Parents Involved, 127 S. Ct. at 2825 (Breyer, J., dissenting) (emphasis in original and citations omitted).

[19] See Comfort v. Lynn School Comm., 418 F.3d 1, 27–29 (1st Cir. 2005) (Boudin, C.J., concurring).

[20] See Parents Involved in Cmty. Sch. v. Seattle Sch. Dist. No. 1, 426 F.3d 1162, 1993–96 (9th Cir. 2005) (Kozinski, J., concurring).

The answer lies, of course, in the constitutional guarantee that "No State shall . . . deny to any person within its jurisdiction the equal protection of the laws." We customarily think of "equal protection" from the stand-point of preventing the state from visiting physical harm either directly through its instrumentalities or indirectly by withholding the customary protective force of the law and law enforcement authorities. But because the state can also violate equal protection by distributing goods and services or other valuable benefits or opportunities to members of a favored group rather than to those of a disfavored one—and, indeed, the classic concern over withholding of law enforcement resources is itself a form of discriminatory distribution of a government benefit—a better conceptual approach might be to think of equal protection as based on a principle of state neutrality or state non-preferment of members of one racial group over those of another.

Why care about state neutrality or non-preferment? Because we ("any person within its jurisdiction") are at the state's mercy when it acts. We are at the state's mercy because the state enjoys monopoly power. The state's principal responsibility is to produce public goods like highways, police, fire and schools-goods that are likely to be under-produced in private markets because of the natural or rational reluctance to fund goods and services that will be available to all comers, including those unwilling to pay for them. The state accomplishes this responsibility through politics (a process of identifying and aggregating individual preferences) and law (a process of coercing unconsenting minorities in the production of the public good by taxing those within its jurisdiction).

We can imagine a world where racial groups live in their own separate societies, each with its own highways, police and fire departments, and school systems. In such a world, there might have been no need for a non-preferment principle: each society would take care of its own. But when the separatist option is neither available nor unattractive, and racial groups must and do live together and function within the same polity, the non-preferment principle is essential to avoid the injustice of forcing everyone to pay for a public good that only some enjoy. It is, put simply, a denial of equal protection for the state to deny equal access to public services or opportunities to any person within its jurisdiction.

The history of African Americans in the post-bellum South illustrates the double jeopardy they faced when the state, having a monopoly on the use of force, denied them public protection or the means of protecting themselves against racial violence. Or the pain endured when the state, having run its own transportation systems or funded and otherwise facilitated the construction of private railways, insisted that blacks use only crowded, poorly maintained rail cars or sections of cars. If you deny people the ability to act on their own or, through use of public monies, privilege the production or delivery of particular goods and services, you may not force them to subsidize their own disadvantage. If they are an equal part of the polity for the purpose of funding public goods and services, they are an equal part of the polity for the purpose of receiving the benefits of those goods and services.

At this level of generality it might still be possible to argue that what the majority racial group does to itself should be of no constitutional moment, for after all it is only the "discrete and insular" minority that needs constitutional protection. This, however, is both bad political science and flawed constitutional law. It is bad political science because "discrete and insular" minorities, if they are passionately committed to a political issue, may be more effective in a political struggle than a diffuse numerically dominant majority, each member of which would derive only a miniscule benefit if the political goal were achieved.[21] And it is bad sociology, especially in America, because whites sort themselves more along ethnic, religious, geographic, economic and perhaps ideological grounds and form their political alliances more along those lines than along the broader line of skin color. In addition, despite the binary (black vs. white) use of race by the school districts in the racial-tiebreaker cases,[22] it makes very little historical or political sense to group Hispanics and Asian-Americans with whites or with blacks.

It is also problematic constitutional law. The equal protection guarantee extends to "any person" within the state's jurisdiction. The constitutional injury is to the individual, even though the basis

[21] See generally Bruce A. Ackerman, Beyond Carolene Products, 98 Harv. L. Rev. 713 (1985); Mancur Olson, The Logic of Collective Action: Public Goods and the Theory of Groups (1962).

[22] See *supra* note 10.

for the problematic official preferment is a group characteristic.[23] If government rewards or services are allocated on the basis of race, the injury is to the person disfavored because of his race, whether or not the individual "belongs" to a numerically predominant racial group that in some way "allowed" the racial allocation by not marshalling political forces against it. One's skin color need not denote "membership" in a racial group, such that one can assume an almost tribal allegiance to group interests and political agenda. Few will be found to have given a decision-making proxy to "their" racial group.

The question might also be raised why the constitutional duty of non-preferment is triggered only by use of race, ethnicity, religious affiliation, and the like rather than by a host of other classifications like geography, occupation, or income informing government actions that are readily permitted. For the thorough-going libertarian, the answer might be that nearly all government action should be subject to strict scrutiny by the courts—and also by conscientious legislators, administrators, and citizens zealously preserving their liberty.

My answer would be a bit different: We know from history that certain governmental classifications, most especially race, are likely to generate intense social division and undermine commitment to national values, including the very "idea of equality." That proposition has not been seriously contested among the justices or, in recent decades, the legal culture.

III. Accounting for Supreme Court Precedent

The non-preferment principle does a fairly good job of explaining the course of Supreme Court decision-making in this area. To begin, take the two "compelling" interests the justices have recognized in the course of implementing strict scrutiny. The first is the remedial use of race. Beneficiaries of such remedies are victims of official racial discrimination. When they receive restoration of a job opportunity they should have received but for discrimination or are transported to a majority-white school because majority-black schools continue to suffer the effects of prior official segregation, government

[23] See, e.g., Adarand Constructors, Inc. v. Pena, 515 U.S. 200, 224 (1995) ("any person, of whatever race, has the right to demand that any governmental actor subject to the Constitution justify any racial classification subjecting that person to unequal treatment under the strictest of judicial scrutiny").

does not violate the duty of non-preferment. These victims are being made whole; they are being restored to the position they would have occupied had there been no prior official racial preferment. That is the justification for remedial preferment, even if applications do not always limit preferences to victims of past discrimination or confine burdens to those who have benefited from past discrimination.

So, too, with Justice Lewis Powell's conception of diversity in *Regents of the University of California v. Bakke*.[24] The duty of neutrality or non-preferment does not require the state to ignore relevant differences about individuals. Thus, when a university is pursuing the goal of a diverse student body, it can take into account the whole range of skills and perspectives that a particular student will bring to the educational experience. In that multi-factored, individualized inquiry, the individual's race is a relevant factor. The state is taking a full account of the individual applicant; no racial preference is being given; no racial spoils are being divided up. Thus, the Court in *Grutter* stated:

> As Justice Powell recognized in *Bakke*, so long as a race-conscious admissions program uses race as a "plus" factor in the context of individualized consideration, a rejected applicant
>
> > "will not have been foreclosed from all consideration for that seat because he was not the right color or had the wrong surname. . . . His qualifications would have been weighed fairly and competitively, and he would have no basis to complain of unequal treatment under the Fourteenth Amendment."[25]

The problem emerges—as arguably was the case in the University of Michigan Law School admission process at issue in *Grutter*—when the state seemingly moves away from Justice Powell's individualized conception of diversity to a pursuit of group-based viewpoint diversity through the use of racial preferences. If racial groups represent different viewpoints and a state university can act to ensure representation of diverse viewpoints through racial preferences, then individuals are being treated as members of racial groups and differential

[24] 438 U.S. 265 (1978).

[25] Grutter v. Bollinger, 539 U.S. 306, 341 (2003) (quoting Bakke, 438 U.S. at 318).

access to a valuable educational opportunity is being differentially allocated on the basis of race.

Yet, it is possible to read *Grutter* as adopting no broader a conception of diversity or no greater latitude in using race to achieve diversity than in the position staked out by Justice Powell in his separate opinion in *Bakke*. Justice Sandra Day O'Connor's majority opinion in *Grutter* is careful to identify the relevant diversity interest as the law school's "compelling interest in attaining a diverse student body,"[26] rather than an interest in racial diversity or group viewpoint diversity as such. Moreover, the Court repeatedly insisted that the University of Michigan's Law School admissions program was no different than the Harvard plan discussed approvingly by Justice Powell in *Bakke*:

> Here, the Law School engages in a highly individualized, holistic review of each applicant's file, giving serious consideration to all the ways an applicant might contribute to a diverse educational environment. The Law School affords this individualized consideration to applicants of all races. There is no policy, either *de jure* or *de facto*, of automatic acceptance or rejection based on any single "soft" variable. . . . Like the Harvard plan, the Law School's admissions policy "is flexible enough to consider all pertinent elements of diversity in light of the particular qualifications of each applicant, and to place them on the same footing for consideration, although not necessarily according them the same weight."[27]
>
> We find that the Law School's admissions program bears the hallmarks of a narrowly tailored plan. As Justice Powell made clear in *Bakke*, truly individualized consideration demands that race be used in a flexible, nonmechanical way. It follows from this mandate that universities cannot establish quotas for members of certain racial groups or put members of those groups on separate admissions tracks. Nor can universities insulate applicants who belong to certain racial or ethnic groups from the competition for admission. Universities can, however, consider race or ethnicity more flexibly as a "plus" factor in the context of individualized consideration of each and every applicant.[28]

[26] *Id.* at 328.

[27] *Id.* at 334 (quoting Bakke, 438 U.S. at 315).

[28] *Id.* at 334 (quoting Bakke, 438 U.S. at 315–16).

This may all be difficult to square with the *Grutter* Court's approval of the Law School's goal of enrolling "a 'critical mass' of minority students,"[29] but even here Justice O'Connor is careful to draw the line at "outright racial balancing, which is patently unconstitutional. Rather, the Law School's concept of critical mass is defined by reference to the educational benefits that diversity is designed to produce."[30] It must also be remembered that while *Grutter* establishes certain general propositions—most particularly, "whether the use of race as a factor in student admissions by the University of Michigan Law School . . . is unlawful"[31]—it is not clear that the Court was predeterming the outcome of as-applied challenges to the law school's admissions process.

In *Parents Involved,* however, there was no pretense of "holistic" or "individualized" review. Once the racial-balance guidelines were triggered, the racial tiebreaker operated automatically—in Seattle, as a second screen after considering whether there were siblings in the oversubscribed school, and in Jefferson County in determining student assignments within a geographic cluster. Given the Court's adoption of the *Bakke* approach in *Grutter,* to uphold the Seattle and Jefferson County plans the diversity rationale would have to be significantly extended to include pursuit of racial diversity through racial preferences. Such an extension would plainly have triggered the non-preferment objection: Individuals would be placed in preferred schools or denied placement in preferred schools because of their race.

IV. Race-Conscious Objectives Through Non Racial Means

Justice Kennedy wrote separately in *Parents Involved* to make clear his view that government can seek to accomplish "race-conscious" ends—eliminating racially homogenuous schools, bringing students of different races together—by race-neutral means without offending the Equal Protection Clause:

> School boards may pursue the goal of bringing together students of diverse backgrounds and races through other means, including strategic site selection of new schools;

[29] *Id.* at 329.

[30] *Id.* at 330.

[31] *Id.* at 311.

> drawing attendance zones with general recognition of the demographics of neighborhoods; allocating resources for special programs; recruiting students and faculty in a targeted fashion; and tracking enrollments, performance and other statistics by race. These mechanisms are race conscious but do not lead to different treatment based on a classification that tells each student he or she is to be defined by race, so it is unlikely that any of them would demand strict scrutiny to be found permissible.[32]

The non-preferment principle helps explain Justice Kennedy's view. Where the state acts through racially neutral means, there is no preferential allocation of government goods and services on the basis of one's race. There is no racial division of the spoils, no basis for constitutional concern when a "magnet school" is created in a minority-dense neighborhood; the top 10 percent of every high school class is automatically granted admission to the state university system; or active recruiting for students takes place in economically disadvantaged neighborhoods—as long as the opportunity is not allocated on the basis of race and is available on equal terms to all races.[33]

Under the non-preferment principle, there is also no warrant for strict scrutiny because the government classification is not based on race. Hence, one can avoid the conceptual awkwardness of recognizing an interest as "compelling" and yet declaring off-limits all direct means of pursuing the objective. One can deal affirmatively with the problem of equality through means that are consistent with government neutrality on matters of race.

[32] Parents Involved in Cmty. Sch. v. Seattle Sch. Dist. No. 1, 127 S. Ct. 2738, 2792 (2007).

[33] Facts can of course arise where what is avowedly a race-neutral program emerges over time as a race-based preferential program.

Protecting Consumers From Consumer Protection: *Watters v. Wachovia Bank*

*G. Marcus Cole**

I. Introduction

Watters v. Wachovia Bank[1] posed a perplexing dilemma for anyone interested in limited government, particularly libertarians and conservatives. On the one hand, the Court's slow but steady crawl back toward federalism holds the future promise of checking the otherwise unchecked growth of the federal government. On the other hand, the very real and present threat to liberty, prosperity, and advancement posed by the recent explosion of state consumer protection legislation might itself go unchecked without the shelter afforded by federal regulation and preemption. Put simply, the choice was one between form and function, federalism and freedom. Should the Commerce Clause and federal banking regulation be read so broadly as to preempt state regulation of banking activity, thereby weakening federalism and the concept of dual regulation? Or should the states maintain significant power to regulate state chartered subsidiaries of national banks, even if that meant the occasional enforcement of misguided and debilitating state consumer protection laws? This difficult choice divides not just the Court but libertarians from conservatives.

As difficult as this choice might be, it is equally difficult to see that this choice is being posed within the record of *Watters v. Wachovia Bank*. While the case nominally pitted the State of Michigan's Office of Insurance and Financial Services (''the OIFS'') against the

*Professor of Law, the Helen L. Crocker Faculty Scholar, and Associate Dean, Stanford Law School. I would like to thank Paul Brest, Richard Craswell, Larry Kramer, Mark Kelman, Ken Scott, and Jeff Strnad for comments at an early stage of this project.

[1] 127 S. Ct. 1559 (2007).

Wachovia National Bank, it was really a duel between the state regulator and the United States Office of the Comptroller of the Currency ("the OCC"). The central issue was whether federalism demanded that a state be permitted to continue to impose regulations on a state mortgage lender, including visitation, when a national bank acquires the state mortgage lender, or whether such state regulation was now preempted by federal law.

Although the Court long ago held in *McCulloch v. Maryland* that federal law trumps state law in the regulation of national banks, both federal and state regulators have shared the regulation of the banking industry. Federal regulation of national banks is vested in the OCC by virtue of the National Bank Act of 1864 ("the NBA").[2] States have maintained a parallel regulatory authority over state banks. This system of dual regulation, referred to by the Court as "equalization," preserves the federalist balance between the states and the federal government with respect to banks operating within their respective spheres.[3] As long as state chartered banks operate wholly within a state, their operations are entirely subject to state regulation.[4] Even when a national bank operates within a state, it is not exempt from the application of state laws of general application.[5] State law of property, contract, and tort apply to nationally chartered banks as much as they apply to any other individual or entity within the state. State regulation is preempted by federal law, however, if it encroaches on a national bank's exercise of a function essential or incidental to banking.[6] The central question in *Watters v. Wachovia Bank*, then, was whether the state's enforcement of its inspection prerogative touched banking operations of a national bank's state subsidiary in a way preempted by federal law. In this setting, as in many others, this seemingly straightforward doctrinal question is not entirely straightforward.

[2] 12 U.S.C. § 371.

[3] Lewis v. Fidelity & Deposit Co. of Md., 292 U.S. 559, 564 (1934) (recognizing "[t]he policy of equalization was adopted in the National Bank Act of 1964').

[4] See Kenneth Scott, The Dual Banking System: A Model of Competition in Regulation, 30 Stan. L. Rev. 1, 8–13 (1978) (describing the benefits of the dual banking system).

[5] *Id.*

[6] *Id.*

This article will attempt to show that the issue in *Watters v. Wachovia Bank* is actually a policy choice disguised as a doctrinal one. The real issue is whether, given our national credit markets, states should have extensive authority to impose cumbersome, expensive, and, indeed, irrational regulation on operating subsidiaries of national banks. While the decision to extend preemption will affect many forms of state banking regulation, some of its most important consequences will be to limit the reach of state consumer protection legislation. Such state measures, while rhetorically pleasing and politically popular, are increasingly shown by economists and determined by judges to be irrational since they often actually harm the very people they purport to help.

This article proceeds in five parts. After this Introduction, Part II provides a summary of the background of *Watters v. Wachovia Bank.* Part III discusses the conflicting policy choices confronting the Court, as well as libertarians and conservatives interested in limited government and economic prosperity. Part IV explains why, given this dilemma, the interests of freedom and prosperity are advanced with federal control of banking regulation and its concomitant limitations on state consumer protection laws. The pernicious effects of consumer protection laws, particularly in mortgage lending, may be ameliorated in the long run with federal preemption. The recent wave of short-sighted and misguided state consumer protection laws in other areas of consumer credit and commercial finance, unfortunately, will remain unaddressed by the application of preemption in *Watters v. Wachovia Bank.* Part V concludes with a brief look at the forecast for mortgage lending and consumer protection.

II. Background

Wachovia Mortgage, like many other mortgage lenders in the State of Michigan, operated in Michigan and elsewhere as a state-chartered financial institution lending to first-time and repeat home-buyers.[7] Like other state mortgage lenders in the state of Michigan, Wachovia Mortgage's operations were subject to regulation by the Michigan Office of Insurance and Financial Services.[8] Among its supervisory functions, the OIFS requires mortgage brokers, lenders,

[7] Wachovia Mortgage was and is actually chartered in North Carolina.

[8] Watters v. Wachovia Bank, 127 S. Ct. 1559, 1565 (2007).

and service entities to register with it. Registrants are required, among other things, to pay an annual operating fee, file annual reports, and open their books and records for inspection by OIFS examiners.[9]

Linda Watters, commissioner of the OIFS, exercises "general supervision and control" over registrants and administers the state of Michigan's lending laws. As commissioner, she has authority to exercise the agency's visitorial powers, including the power to conduct bank investigations, audits, and examinations.[10] The commissioner also bears the responsibility of enforcing the state's requirements against registered lenders.[11] In addition to these duties, the commissioner was charged with investigating consumer complaints and to take appropriate enforcement action should she find that a particular complaint was not "being adequately pursued by the appropriate federal regulatory authority."[12]

From 1997 to 2003, Wachovia Mortgage was registered with the OIFS to engage in mortgage lending. Then, on January 1, 2003, Wachovia Mortgage became a wholly owned subsidiary of Wachovia Bank, a national bank federally chartered under the National Bank Act.[13] Under the NBA, national banks like Wachovia are authorized "[t]o exercise . . . all such incidental powers as shall be necessary to carry on the business of banking."[14] Among these powers, the NBA specifically authorizes national banks to engage in real estate lending.[15] The statute also expressly permits banks to conduct its banking activities through "operating subsidiaries."[16] An operating subsidiary may engage solely in activities the bank itself could undertake, subject to the same limitations, terms, and conditions as the bank.[17]

[9] *Id.* at 1566.

[10] *Id.* See Mich. Comp. Laws Ann. §§ 445.1656(1), 445.1679(1)(a) (West 2002).

[11] Watters, 127 S. Ct. at 1565.

[12] Mich. Comp. Laws Ann. §§ 445.1663(2) (West 2002).

[13] 12 U.S.C. § 1 et seq.

[14] 12 U.S.C. § 24.

[15] 12 U.S.C. § 371.

[16] 12 U.S.C. § 24a(g)(3)(A).

[17] 12 C.F.R. § 5.34(e) (2006).

As a wholly owned subsidiary of a national bank, Wachovia Mortgage's management believed it was no longer subject to Michigan banking regulations, including the registration requirement. In March 2003, Wachovia Mortgage informed the state of Michigan that it was surrendering its registration to engage in mortgage lending.[18] Wachovia Mortgage management was of the opinion that Michigan law with respect to mortgage lending registration and oversight, as applied to a wholly owned subsidiary of a national bank like itself, was preempted by federal law.[19]

Commissioner Watters responded to the surrender of Wachovia Mortgage's registration by informing Wachovia Mortgage that it would no longer be permitted to engage in mortgage lending activity in the State of Michigan.[20] The commissioner's position was that all state chartered mortgage lenders had to comply with Michigan's registration requirements. While Michigan law exempts subsidiaries of national banks that maintain main or branch offices in Michigan, the company had no such offices in Michigan, and therefore did not fall within the law's exemption.[21] From the commissioner's perspective, she had no choice but to deny Wachovia Mortgage access to Michigan mortgage markets.

Wachovia Bank and Wachovia Mortgage ("the Banks") filed suit against Watters in her official capacity as commissioner of the OIFS, seeking declaratory and injunctive relief to prevent her from enforcing Michigan's registration requirements against Wachovia Mortgage.[22] The Banks asserted that two state statutes, the Michigan Mortgage Brokers, Lenders, and Services Licensing Act, and the Michigan Secondary Mortgage Loan Act, were preempted by the NBA and the supervisory authority it vests in the OCC.[23]

In response, the commissioner acknowledged that if the real estate lending activity were conducted by the parent company, Wachovia Bank, rather than the subsidiary, Wachovia Mortgage, the parent

[18] Watters v. Wachovia Bank, 127 S. Ct. 1559, 1565 (2007).

[19] *Id.* at 1565–66.

[20] *Id.* at 1566.

[21] Mich. Comp. Law. Ann. §§ 445.1652(1)(b) (West Supp. 2006), 445.1675(m) (West 2002), 493.53a(d) (West 1998).

[22] Watters, 127 S. Ct. at 1565.

[23] *Id.* at 1565–66.

Wachovia Bank and the activity would not be subject to Michigan banking laws and its registration requirements.[24] But because the subsidiary, Wachovia Mortgage, was not itself a national bank, it could not evade applicable Michigan controls by becoming a wholly owned subsidiary of a national bank.[25] Watters further asserted that her position was supported by the Tenth Amendment to the Constitution of the United States, which she claimed prohibits the OCC from exercising exclusive regulatory authority over lending activities conducted through operating subsidiaries of national banks.[26]

The United States District Court for the Western District of Michigan granted the Banks' motion for summary judgment on the preemption claim, and rejected the commissioner's Tenth Amendment argument.[27] The United States Court of Appeals for the Sixth Circuit affirmed, making it the fourth such circuit court to hold that state bank regulations are preempted, where applied to wholly owned operating subsidiaries of national banks, by federal law and the superintendence vested in the OCC.[28]

By a narrow five to three decision, the Supreme Court of the United States held that the National Bank Act of 1864, as amended, vests the power to regulate national banks and their wholly owned operating subsidiaries in the Office of the Comptroller of the Currency and therefore preempts state regulation of these entities.[29] Writing for the Court, Justice Ginsburg pointed to the Graham-Leach-Bliley Act of 1999,[30] amending the National Bank Act, as extending federal regulatory authority to "subsidiaries . . . which may engage only in activities national banks may engage in directly, 'subject to the same terms and conditions that govern the conduct of such activities by national banks.'"[31] Justice Ginsburg was joined by Justices Kennedy, Souter, Breyer, and Alito.

[24] *Id.* at 1566.

[25] *Id.*

[26] *Id.*

[27] 334 F. Supp. 2d 957, 965–66 (W.D. Mich. 2004).

[28] 431 F.3d 556 (6th Cir. 2005).

[29] Watters, 127 S. Ct at 1568. Justice Thomas took no part in the consideration or decision of the case.

[30] 12 U.S.C. § 24a(g)(3)(A).

[31] Watters v. Wachovia Bank, 127 S. Ct. 1559, 1570 (2007) (Ginsburg, J.) (quoting Graham-Leach-Bliley Act, 12 U.S.C. §24a(g)(3)(A)).

In dissent, Justice John Paul Stevens, joined by the chief justice and Justice Antonin Scalia, argued that the National Bank Act does not itself expressly extend OCC authority to subsidiaries of national banks, and in the absence of such statutory authority the Court should not substantially undermine the delicate balance between state and federal authority and the benefits made possible through the dual banking system.[32] According to Justice Stevens, the Court's decision in this case ignores the fact that Congress never expressly mentioned "operating subsidiaries" in Graham-Leach-Bliley, and indeed used that Act to curtail the OCC's definition of such entities by placing restrictions on "financial subsidiaries," thereby distinguishing them, by negative implication, from what the OCC had termed "operating subsidiaries."[33] But the OCC had determined that "operating subsidiaries" could engage in activities that national banks could not engage in directly, a position expressly rejected by Graham-Leach-Bliley.[34] Reading the NBA and Graham-Leach-Bliley together to effect preemption where subsidiaries of national banks are concerned, Stevens argued, undermines an important federalist structure in our economy and our traditional understanding of federalism.

Nevertheless, the Court affirmed the lower court determinations that state banking regulation was preempted when applied to state chartered operating subsidiaries of nationally chartered banks.

III. Federalism Versus Freedom? The Policy Choice of *Watters v. Wachovia Bank*

At first glance, *Watters v. Wachovia Bank* appears to have realigned the Court into chambers comprised of strange bedfellows. This first impression gives way to a more nuanced perception of the justices, however, once the underlying and unmentioned (except by *amici*) implications of the case are laid bare. This case posed an important dilemma for those interested in limited government and expanded economic freedom. Should a strict notion of federalism, which was conceived by the Framers as an essential check on the aggregation of power by the central government, be relaxed in order to permit

[32] *Id.* at 1578 (Stevens, J. dissenting).

[33] *Id.* at 1577.

[34] *Id.*

commercial entities to seek refuge from irrational local laws under the shelter of a potentially unchecked federal regulator? Libertarians might pose the general question more broadly as one of form versus function. "What's more important, federalism, or the liberty that federalism was designed to protect?" Conservatives, on the other hand, might view the choice differently. "Can structures like federalism, so essential to the preservation of freedom, be abandoned any time we dislike state decision-making?"

It would have been nice if the choice were one of doctrine and not of policy. Had the Court been confronted with a simple matter of statutory interpretation, the policy issue would have been moot, and the decision likely unanimous. The doctrinal dilemma was no simpler than the policy one, however. Under the National Bank Act, "[n]o national bank shall be subject to any visitorial powers except as authorized by Federal law."[35] The NBA specifically confers exclusive authority to exercise these powers in the Office of the Comptroller of the Currency.[36] "Visitation" has long been recognized by the Court to mean "the act of a superior or superintending officer, who visits a corporation to examine into its manner of conducting business, and enforce an observance of its laws and regulations."[37] The difficult question, however, was whether the NBA and the powers it conferred on the OCC extended to state-chartered but wholly owned subsidiaries of national banks.

The reason why this question is important is because of the implications with regard to a decision either way. As the American Association for Retired Persons ("the AARP") noted in its *amicus* brief, a decision holding that wholly owned subsidiaries are exempt from state banking regulation because of preemption would mean that these lenders are also exempt from state consumer protection laws.[38]

[35] 12 U.S.C. § 484(a).

[36] *Id.*

[37] Guthrie v. Harkness, 199 U.S. 148, 158 (1905).

[38] See AARP Brief at 3, Watters v. Wachovia Bank, 127 S. Ct. 1559 (2007) ("At issue in this case is whether the states will be able to protect their citizens from abuses by national banks operating subsidiaries under the states own charters"). See also Brief of Amicus The Center for State Enforcement of Antitrust and Consumer Protection Laws at 1, Watters v. Wachovia Bank, 127 S. Ct. 1559 (2007) ("preemption of state banking laws by the Office of the Comptroller of the Currency will result in inadequate protection of consumers against predatory lending practices and other abuses. . . .").

Such a holding could also provide an avenue for lenders seeking to escape the application of state consumer protection statutes, like predatory lending laws. Lenders could immunize themselves from these regimes by becoming wholly owned subsidiaries of national banks. Indeed, this is not a new fear; it was originally expressed when the NBA was passed nearly 140 years ago.[39]

From the perspective of lenders, a holding that subjected wholly owned subsidiaries of national banks to state banking regulation would deprive national banks of the ability to partition their assets and reduce overall risk exposure. By requiring national banks to either submit to state banking regulation, on top of federal regulation, or expand their activity by engaging in operations through divisions rather than separate corporate subsidiaries, such a holding would expose national bank assets to variant and disparate risks associated with disparate regulatory and economic conditions in each state. Add to this the exposure to irrational economic regulation at the state level, often under the banner of consumer protection, and the risks associated with state law become a major cost, perhaps a prohibitive cost in some circumstances, of national banking.

Yet, if those were the policy considerations confronted by Congress, why not let Congress choose? The circumstances of *Watters v. Wachovia Bank* and cases like it required courts to determine, given the statutory framework Congress had established and the regulatory regime flowing from it, which choice Congress actually made. In short, it was the business of the Court to make sense of the framework Congress imposed on these and similarly situated parties.

The majority's approach was to consider the implications of the statutory framework established by the NBA and subsequent amendments. It started with *McCulloch v. Maryland*, to establish the uncontested point that "federal law [is] supreme over state law with respect to national banking."[40] Supreme federal banking law is rooted, then, in the NBA. This statute, enacted in 1864, created a national banking system, which "shields national banking from

[39] See B. Hammond, Banks and Politics in America: From the Revolution to the Civil War 728 (1957) (it was feared that "existing banks would surrender their state charters and re-incorporate under the terms of the new law with national charters").

[40] Watters v. Wachovia Bank, 127 S. Ct. 1559, 1566 (2007).

unduly burdensome and duplicative state regulation."[41] Federally chartered banks are not, however, shielded from state laws of general application to the extent that such laws do not conflict with the letter and purpose of the NBA.[42] The Court cited "state usury laws" that "govern the maximum rate of interest national banks can charge on loans," as well as contracts, which are governed by state contract law, as examples of laws of general application.[43]

"States are permitted," according to the Court, "to regulate the activities of national banks where doing so does not prevent or significantly interfere with the national bank's or the national bank regulator's exercise of its powers."[44] Those "powers" include not just those enumerated by the NBA and other federal statutes but also those "incidental" to a national bank's powers under those federal laws.[45]

The NBA also specifically enumerates mortgage lending among the powers conferred upon national banks:

> Any national banking association may make, arrange, purchase or sell loans or extensions of credit secured by liens on interests in real estate, subject to 1828(o) of this title, and such restrictions and requirements as the Comptroller of the Currency may prescribe by regulation or order.[46]

What the NBA does not make clear expressly is that a national bank may engage in this activity through a subsidiary. In fact, Depression Era legislation expressly prohibited national banks from investing in other corporations.[47] The Glass-Steagall Act was crafted in 1933 to prevent banks from exposing their depositors to speculative activities, such as stock speculation in other companies, which was believed to have led to widespread bank failures.[48] Two years

[41] *Id.* at 1567.

[42] *Id.*

[43] *Id.*

[44] *Id.*

[45] *Id.*

[46] 12 U.S.C. § 371(a).

[47] See Jonathan R. Macey, Geoffrey P. Miller, and Richard Scott Carnell, Banking Law and Regulation 21 (3d ed. 2001).

[48] *Id.*

later, in 1935, Congress prohibited national banks from owning shares of any company.[49] That prohibition persists to this very day.[50]

Despite the prohibition on bank ownership of shares in other companies, the OCC in 1966 determined "that a national bank may acquire and hold the controlling stock interest in a subsidiary operations corporation" as long as that subsidiary engaged in "functions or activities that a national bank is authorized to carry on."[51] It was the position of the Comptroller that the categorical prohibition on national bank ownership of corporate stock did not prevent ownership of "operating subsidiaries," authority for which it found in the "incidental powers" provision of the National Bank Act.[52]

In 1996, the OCC attempted to expand the ownership powers of national banks, issuing a regulation permitting national bank operating subsidiaries to undertake activities that even the national bank itself was not permitted to engage in directly.[53] The passage of the Gramm-Leach-Bliley Act in 1999 directly overruled this particular OCC regulation.[54] Gramm-Leach-Bliley effectively repealed the Glass-Steagall Act's ban on affiliations between commercial banks and investment banks.[55] It also acknowledged the power of national banks to own subsidiary corporations. The Act provided, however, that any national bank subsidiary engaging in activities forbidden to the parent bank would be considered a "financial subsidiary" and would be subject to heightened regulatory obligations.[56] By implication, then, Gramm-Leach-Bliley, while never mentioning "operating subsidiaries" directly, acknowledges them only to the extent that they engage in activities falling within the enumerated or incidental powers granted to national banks under the National Bank Act.

The next question confronted by the Court, was whether a state-chartered operating subsidiary, which is never mentioned by any

[49] Banking Act of 1935 § 308(b), 49 Stat. 709; see also 31 Fed. Reg. 11459 (1966).

[50] See 12 U.S.C. § 24 (Seventh).

[51] 31 Fed. Reg. 11459 (1966).

[52] 12 U.S.C. § 24 (Seventh).

[53] 12 C.F.R. §§ 5.34(d)(f) (1997).

[54] 12 U.S.C. § 371c-1(a)(1).

[55] 12 U.S.C. § 101.

[56] See 12 U.S.C. § 371c-1(a)(1).

federal statute (except Glass-Steagall's blanket prohibition of them), could nevertheless invoke the sanctuary of federal preemption when a state attempts to enforce state banking regulations on it. That is the very question that served as the point of disagreement between the majority and the dissent. The dissent, finding no express statutory authority for operating subsidiaries, could not countenance the extension of federal preemption to such unmentioned entities. The majority found the statutory recognition of a national bank's power to own subsidiaries, coupled with the Comptroller's prescriptions regarding operating subsidiaries, as necessarily implying both the authority for their existence and the concomitant protection of federal law.

But why is this implication necessary? According to the majority, it follows naturally from the policy considerations of the alternative outcomes. Should the Court deny preemption in cases involving operating subsidiaries of national banks, the result would be, according to the Court, "significant interference by state regulators,"[57] with the imposition of "the burdens and undue duplication state controls could produce."[58]

Justice Stevens, in dissent, rejects this policy justification and advances his own as the basis for rejecting the extension of preemption to operating subsidiaries of national banks. He argues that the regulatory competition between state and federal bank regulation, referred to as "competitive equality," is severely undermined with the extension of preemption to such subsidiaries. According to the dissent, "the policy of competitive equality is . . . firmly embedded in the statutes governing the national banking system . . . , [s]o firmly embedded, in fact, that 'the congressional policy of competitive equality with its deference to state standards' is not 'open to modification by the Comptroller of the Currency.'"[59]

Those two dueling policy concerns—confusion and burdensome duplication so worrisome to the majority, and the loss of competitive regulatory federalism mourned by the dissent—served as the explicit basis for resolution of the doctrinal dilemma. Beneath the surface,

[57]Watters v. Wachovia Bank, 127 S. Ct. 1559, 1571 (2007).

[58]*Id.* at 1568.

[59]*Id.* at 1575 (Stevens, J., dissenting) (quoting First Nat. Bank in Plant City v. Dickinson, 396 U.S. 122, 138 (1969)).

however, a different policy debate was brewing. The dissent accurately identifies the risks to federalism posed by the Court's holding.

The Court, however, fails even to mention a policy concern raised by Commissioner Watters and several of the *amici*, namely, that of consumer protection. The commissioner cites her responsibility "to protect consumers from unfair, unsound, and abusive lending practices" as compelling a decision favoring state regulation of state chartered operating subsidiaries like Wachovia Mortgage.[60] According to Watters, "[s]tates have a substantial interest in protecting their citizens from abusive mortgage practices."[61] Similarly, the Center for State Enforcement of Antitrust and Consumer Protection Laws argues in its amicus brief that "preemption of state banking laws by the Office of the Comptroller of the Currency will result in inadequate protection of consumers against predatory lending practices and other abuses. . . ."[62] A joint amicus brief by the American Association of Retired Persons, eleven other consumer groups, and seventeen law professors (collectively "AARP") argues that consumer protection was *the* issue before the Court: "At issue in this case is whether the states will be able to protect their citizens from abuses by national bank operating subsidiaries established under the states' own charters."[63] AARP contends that states and localities "are much more likely than the federal government to appreciate the impact of abusive lending practices" and that "empirical studies have demonstrated" that state mortgage lending laws "are effective in reducing predatory lending without reducing consumers' access to legitimate credit."[64]

The dissent acknowledges this policy issue in a footnote when it notes that "Michigan laws focus on consumer protection, whereas the OCC regulations quoted by the Court focus on protection of depositors."[65] Justice Stevens expresses alarm at the fact that federal

[60] Petitioner's Brief at 5, Watters v. Wachovia Bank, 127 S. Ct. 1559 (2007).

[61] *Id.* at 11.

[62] Brief of Amicus Center for State Enforcement of Antitrust and Consumer Protection Laws at 1, Watters v. Wachovia Bank, 127 S. Ct. 1559 (2007).

[63] Brief of Amici AARP et al. at 3, Watters v. Wachovia Bank, 127 S. Ct. 1559 (2007).

[64] *Id.* at 8, 10.

[65] Watters, 127 S. Ct. at 1580 n.18 (Stevens, J., dissenting).

preemption is now being extended to "nonbank companies incorporated under state law."[66] This concern arises because, in Justice Stevens's view, such companies are not even "engaged in the core banking business of accepting deposits."[67] It is unclear why he defines "the core banking business" in this way; he does not, for example, explain the business model under which a bank engaged only in accepting deposits can sustain profitability. But with this particular vision of banking in mind, he makes clear his view that consumer protection is being sacrificed to an agency designed to protect banks and their depositors, not consumers.

If consumer protection is such an important state interest, did the Court make the right choice? Can the economy and society withstand both the impairment to federalism and the loss of state enforcement of consumer protection laws in mortgage lending? Had the court addressed this particular question directly, it should have found even more support for extension of preemption to state chartered mortgage lenders like Wachovia Mortgage.

IV. Protecting Consumers from Consumer Protection

A choice between federalism and consumer protection on the one hand, and duplicative state laws on the other, appears to be no real choice at all. Protection of federalism and consumers would seem to justify substantial additional burdens on large national banks and their corporate subsidiaries. But is this the real choice? Do the interests of states in the enforcement of consumer protection laws tip the balance in favor of federalism and state banking controls?

Both the majority and the dissent in *Watters v. Wachovia Bank* wisely avoided this policy issue, albeit for different reasons. While the rhetoric of consumer protection enflames passions in favor of more and expansive regulation, the economics of consumer protection law counsels precisely the opposite. As a result of the rhetoric, consumer protection laws are politically popular, and such measures are increasing in number and scope. Both economists and courts, however, have reached a consensus that consumer protection laws actually hurt those they purport to help.

[66] *Id.* at 1580.

[67] *Id.*

A. The Economics of Consumer Protection Laws

Economists have long understood the counterproductive, and indeed counterintuitive, effects of consumer protection laws. Decades of economic studies have demonstrated that consumers suffer as a result of consumer credit regulations. There is a consensus that, in "the longer run, the costs of [consumer credit] regulation are passed on to consumers in one way or another."[68] When consumer protection laws make the extension of credit more costly or unprofitable for providers of credit, credit dries up for those who need it most.

A recent "predatory lending" law in Illinois provides a ready example of the inverse relationship between the passage of consumer protection statutes and the welfare of their intended beneficiaries. In July, 2005, Illinois Governor Rod Blagojevich signed into law Illinois House Bill 4050, the "Illinois Fairness in Lending Act."[69] The law authorizes the Illinois Department of Financial and Professional Regulation to assemble a database of mortgage applications for nine zip-codes in Cook County, Illinois.[70] Most of the nine zip-codes are associated with poor to modest income households on the South and Southwest sides of the City of Chicago.[71] Under the new law, the Department of Financial and Professional Services reviews all new mortgage applications in these nine zip-codes, and determines from the terms of the loan agreement whether the applicant needs credit counseling. If so, then the lender must pay the costs of the counseling, which, according to some sources can add as much as $500 to $700 to the cost of a loan, and can add as much as 27 days

[68] Richard L. Peterson, The Costs of Consumer Credit Regulation at 3 (Credit Research Center Reprint #13, 1979), available at www.business.gwu.edu/research/centers/fsrp/pdf/Reprint13.pdf. See, e.g., Mark Meador, The Effects of Mortgagee Laws on Home Mortgage Rates, 34 J. Econ. & Bus. 143 (1981) (concluding that borrower protection laws place upward pressure on the interest rates charged by lenders).

[69] 765 ILCS 77/70 new §70(c) (West 2007), available at http://www.ilga.gov/legislation/publicacts/fulltext.asp?Name=094-0280.

[70] Illinois Office of the Governor Press Release, July 21, 2005, available at: http://www.illinois.gov/PressReleases/ShowPressRelease.cfm?SubjectID=3&RecNum=4166.

[71] Steve Daniels, New Lending Law Outlines Zip Codes for Credit Counseling, Crains Chicago Business, (January 30, 2006), available at http://www.illinois.gov/PressReleases/ShowPressRelease.cfm?SubjectID=3&RecNum=4166

to the loan approval process.[72] The law also expressly provides that the borrower "may not waive credit counseling."[73] The purpose of the law was "to protect homebuyers from predatory lending in Cook County's at-risk communities and reduce the incidence of foreclosures."[74]

As any economist (or economics student) might predict, the Illinois Fairness in Lending Act became the victim of another law, namely, the law of unintended consequences. Instead of protecting hard-working would-be homeowners from predatory lending, the new law protected them from credit. Within just a few months more than 30 mortgage lenders refused to lend on homes purchased in the targeted zip-codes.[75] Those lenders determined to service these communities saw a rise in their costs, which translated into higher interest rates on their loans.[76] The poor and moderate income homeowners were not left out of the suffering either: home sales in the designated zip-codes dropped an average of 45 percent in just one month after the bill took effect.[77] Home prices plummeted, draining relatively poor but hardworking people of what little equity they had in their homes.[78]

It is true that the program that inspired this new law, the Illinois High Risk Home Loan Act of 2003, saw foreclosures drop by 10 percent from 2003 to 2004.[79] Unfortunately, this statistic reflects the fact that fewer home loans were extended, and those denied happened to be in the lowest income, riskiest categories, for which sub-prime mortgages are the difference between home ownership and renting. The more important statistic, which the State of Illinois had not measured, was the number of *successful* sub-prime loans

[72] See Letter to Illinois Assembly at: http://www.themortgagereports.com/illinois_house_bill_4050/.

[73] 765 ILCS 77/70 new §70(c) (West 2007) ("The borrower may not waive credit counseling.").

[74] Illinois Office of the Governor Press Release, July 21, 2005, available at: http://www.illinois.gov/PressReleases/ShowPressRelease.cfm?SubjectID=3&RecNum=4166.

[75] See http://www.themortgagereports.com/illinois_house_bill_4050/.

[76] *Id.*

[77] Some neighborhoods (zip code 60629) saw sales drop by as much as 70 percent. *Id.*

[78] *Id.*

[79] Illinois Office of the Governor Press Release, July 21, 2005, available at: http://www.illinois.gov/PressReleases/ShowPressRelease.cfm?SubjectID=3&RecNum=4166.

(ones resulting in a home purchase that did not end in foreclosure) forgone because of the new law. In one fell swoop, hardworking, responsible homeowners were made instantly poorer, and hard-working, responsible homebuyers were instantly denied the American dream of homeownership, all because of where they lived and their elected representatives desire to "protect" them.[80]

Illinois politicians are not alone in employing misguided "predatory lending" laws. Other states have increased both the costs and risks to lenders and borrowers in the sub-prime mortgage market, resulting in many of the same unfortunate side-effects as Illinois currently experiences.[81] Georgia's predatory lending law, for example, "caused secondary market participants to cease purchasing certain Georgia mortgages and many mortgage lenders to stop making mortgage loans in Georgia," dramatically reducing the availability of credit.[82]

[80] See *id.* at 144–45; Office of the Comptroller of the Currency, Preemption Determination & Order, 68 Fed. Reg. 46264, 46271 n.26 (Aug. 5, 2003) ("a growing body of evidence indicates that state anti-predatory lending laws are likely to restrict the availability of credit to subprime borrowers"); OCC Working Paper, Economic Issues in Predatory Lending at 2 (July 30, 2003), available at www.occc.treas.gov/workingpaper.pdf ("there is substantial empirical evidence that anti-predatory statutes can impede the flow of mortgage credit, especially to low-income and higher-risk borrowers, and that any reduction in predatory abuses resulting from these measures is probably achieved at the expense of many legitimate loans"). See also Gregory Elliehausen & Michael Staten, Regulation of Subprime Mortgage Products: An Analysis of North Carolina's Predatory Lending Law (CRC Working Paper #66) (2002), available at www.business.gwu.edu/research/centers/fsrp/pdf/RevisedWP66.pdf; Robert E. Litan, Unintended Consequences: The Risks of Premature State Regulation of Predatory Lending at 15 (American Bankers Association, 2002), available at www.aba.com/NR/rdonlyres/D881716A-1C75-11D5-AB7B-00508B95258D/28871/PredReport200991.pdf) ("State and local laws [on predatory lending] threaten to dry up credit for the very same population about which critics of predatory lending are most concerned," and risk "discouraging the supply of credit to higher risk borrowers" and "to reduce overall lending to subprime borrowers."); OCC Working Paper, Economic Issues in Predatory Lending *supra* note 81, at 20 ("There is a good deal of empirical evidence to suggest that anti-predatory statutes impede the flow of mortgage credit, especially to low-income and higher-risk borrowers, and any reductions in predatory abuses resulting from these measures are probably achieved at the expense of many legitimate loans.").

[81] See Donald Lampe, Wrong from the Start? North Carolina's "Predatory Lending" Law and the Practice vs. Product Debate, 7 Chap. L. Rev. 135, 145 (2004) (studies show that "the North Carolina [predatory lending] law's 'triggers' form usury ceilings on residential mortgage loans made after the effective date of the law").

Other states, like North Carolina, have opted for what was thought to be less draconian predatory lending protection. But consumers have not fared better under these laws, which dry up the availability of credit for those least likely to afford it. Studies of sub-prime mortgage lending in North Carolina before and after enactment of that state's anti-predatory lending law have shown a 15 percent post-enactment decline in sub-prime mortgage placements.[83] As a result of its passage, "creditors appear to have sharply restricted lending to higher-risk customers in North Carolina—but not to customers in neighboring states or to lower risk customers in North Carolina—after passage of the law."[84] After enactment of the law, "significant declines [in mortgage loans] occurred only in North Carolina and only among the lower-income borrowers. Neither the higher-income borrowers in North Carolina nor borrowers in other states experienced significant declines."[85] In the end, "the North Carolina statute did impede the flow of mortgage credit to higher-risk borrowers . . . at the expense of many legitimate loans."[86] In the words of one analyst, studies suggest "that the North Carolina

[82] Office of the Comptroller of the Currency, Bank Activities and Operations: Real Estate Lending and Appraisals, 69 Fed. Reg. 1904, 1908 (Jan. 13, 2004); OCC Working Paper, Economic Issues in Predatory Lending, *supra* note 81, at 3, 20 (Fannie Mae and Freddie Mac stopped buying "high cost home loans" after the Georgia Fair Lending Act passed, and the law caused "the nation's seventh largest subprime originator to stop making all subprime loans in Georgia").

[83] Office of the Comptroller of the Currency, Preemption Determination & Order, 68 Fed. Reg. at 46271 n.26 (citing Keith Harvey & Peter Nigro, Do Predatory Lending Laws Influence Mortgage Lending? An Analysis of the North Carolina Predatory Lending Law, Paper Presented at the Credit Research Conference on Subprime Lending (September 2002)); Elliehausen & Staten, Regulation of Subprime Mortgage Products: An Analysis of North Carolina's Predatory Lending Law, Credit Research Center Working Paper #66 (November 2002); see also OCC Working Paper, Economic Issues in Predatory Lending, *supra* note 81, at 22 (Philadelphia predatory lending ordinance also found to have likely resulted in reduction in legitimate loans).

[84] Elliehausen & Staten, *supra* note 84, at 1.

[85] *Id.* at 15; see also OCC Working Paper, Economic Issues in Predatory Lending *supra* note 81, at 25 (declines were significant and "were found only in the higher-risk segment of the market").

[86] Elliehausen & Staten, *supra* note 84, at 15; see also OCC Working Paper, Economic Issues in Predatory Lending *supra* note 81, at 2, 20 (any putative benefits of the law likely came "at the expense of many legitimate loans"); Keith D. Harvey & Peter J. Nigro, Do Predatory Lending Laws Influence Mortgage Lending?, An Analysis of the North Carolina Predatory Lending Law, 29 J. Real Est. Fin. & Econ. 435 (2004).

'predatory lending' law has led to a reduction in the availability of higher cost or 'subprime' mortgage loan credit in the State."[87]

"Due–on–sale" clauses provide yet another handy example. A due-on-sale clause is a term in a mortgage agreement requiring the balance of the loan to be due and paid upon sale of the underlying real estate.[88] The sale of the property securing the loan acts to accelerate the loan. In the words of one real estate investment professional, many people . . .

> . . . who are not too bright tend to believe lenders want due-on-sale clauses because they are greedy. They then use that notion to rationalize illegal or immoral behavior toward the lender. In fact, the main reasons for due-on-sale clauses is lenders want and need to know to whom they are loaning money and they need to be able to predict roughly when a mortgage will be paid off. If you loaned your car to a friend, who agreed in writing not to let anyone else use it, then you saw it going down the street with some stranger at the wheel, you'd be upset, and rightly so. By the same token, lenders do not like to loan one guy $100,000 to buy a house then find that someone else now has the house, especially when the new guy has lousy credit and/or inadequate equity or income.[89]

The contractual due-on-sale clauses upheld against state regulation by the Supreme Court in *Fidelity Federal Savings and Loan Association v. de la Cuesta et al.,*[90] in the words of one commentator, "contribute economic benefit to borrower and lender alike" by keeping interest rates down, fostering the "flow of funds" into state mortgage markets, and helping "to ensure the continued availability of the fixed-rate mortgage, a popular instrument from the borrower's perspective." Fortunately, federal preemption of state "restrictions on

[87] Lampe, *supra* note 82, at 144.

[88] Investorwords.com provides the following definition of "due-on-sale" clause: "A provision in a mortgage enabling the lender to demand full repayment if the borrower sells the mortgaged property." See http://www.investorwords.com/1597/due_on_sale_clause.html.

[89] http://www.johntreed.com/dueonsale.html

[90] 458 U.S. 156 (1982).

the enforcement of due-on-sale clauses benefits both lenders and borrowers.''[91]

The same effects can be seen in the area of state usury laws with their interest rate ceilings. In the words of former Federal Reserve Governor Thomas Durkin, ''[t]he unanimous or near unanimous view of the profession'' of economists is that ''ceilings or controls of interest rates have been a bad idea for a long time and will continue to be a bad idea in the future.''[92] ''Nobel Laureate Milton Friedman spoke well for the entire profession in 1970 when he reported, 'I know of no economist of any standing . . . who has favored a legal limit on the rate of interest that borrowers could pay or lenders receive.'''[93]

Interest rate ceilings are offered to the voting public as a way to keep the cost of credit under control. Although interest rate ceilings

[91] Eric J. Murdock, The Due-on-Sale Controversy: Beneficial Effects of the Garn-St. Germain Depository Institution Act of 1982, 1984 Duke L.J. 121, 137, 140 (1984); see also Richard T. Pratt & Tim S. Campbell, An Economic Analysis of the ''Due on Sale'' Clause in California Mortgage Markets 5 (Credit Research Center (CRC) Working Paper #14, Jan. 1979), available at www.business.gwu.edu/research/centers/fsrp/pdf/ Mono14.pdf (''economic analysis of the 'due on sale' clause . . . demonstrates why unrestricted use of the clause is in the interest of both borrowers and lenders''). See also Grant S. Nelson & Dale A. Whitman, Congressional Preemption of Mortgage Due-on-Sale Law: An Analysis of the Garn-St. Germain Act, 35 Hastings L.J. 241, 310 (1983) (arguments for restricting due-on-sale clauses are ''not logical''); Thomas Kinzler, Due on Sale Clauses: The Economic and Legal Issues, 43 U. Pitt. L. Rev. 441, 460 (1982) (''mortgagors as a whole will benefit through enforcement of [the due on sale clause] because lenders will continue to offer a fixed rate mortgage'' and ''will be able to charge lower interest rates,'' and because enforcing them ''insures a supply of mortgage funds for tomorrow's mortgages''); Alan J. Blocher, Due-on-Sale in the Secondary Mortgage Market, 31 Cath. U.L. Rev. 49, 95, 99 (1981) (barring enforcement of due-on-sale clause will drive up interest rates for future borrowers, and ''the costs will be borne most heavily by those on relatively fixed incomes, such as the elderly or low-income groups,'' and the patchwork of state laws in this area restricting such clauses reduces ''the supply of conventional mortgage funding''); Bartke & Tagaropulos, Michigan's Looking Glass World of Due-on-Sale Clauses, 24 Wayne L. Rev. 971, 1002 (1978) (''A question legitimately may be asked whether a consumer, who is protected to the point that he or she can no longer get home financing because the sources of funds have dried out, is that much better off than before.'').

[92] Thomas Durkin, An Economic Perspective on Interest Rate Regulation, 9 Ga. St. U.L. Rev. 821, 837 (1993), available at www.business.gwu.edu/research/centers/fsrp/pdf/Reprint22.pdf.

[93] *Id.* at 821 (quoting Milton Friedman, Defense of Usury, Newsweek, Apr. 6, 1970, at 79).

are intended to help borrowers, they actually harm them. Interest rate "controls create credit shortages, they impede competition, they waste resources, and probably most tellingly, they do not work anyway."[94] Interest rate ceilings actually shut off the flow of credit to the very low-income and high-risk borrowers they seek to help, since these borrowers are precisely the ones for whom the higher risk premium at higher interest rates covers the cost of lending to higher risk consumers. These laws actually promote and fund criminal activity, since rate ceilings make credit unavailable from legitimate lenders, and force high-risk borrowers to turn to loan-sharks. They also victimize the poor by forcing them to purchase goods and services through installment sales, which are merely loan transactions camouflaged as sales transactions, but at inflated prices that reflect the risk associated with the loan.[95]

Consumers have actually benefited when the Supreme Court protected them from consumer protection.[96] The Court's decision in *Marquette National Bank v. First Omaha Serv. Corp.*, provides an apt example. In *Marquette National Bank,* the Court held that the National Bank Act preempted state credit card interest rate ceilings except for those imposed by the national bank's home state.[97] Likewise,

[94] *Id.* at 837. See also Crafton, An Empirical Test of the Effect of Usury Laws, 23 J.L. & Econ. 135, 140 (1980) (Usury laws lead to a decrease in mortgage loan origination.); Nathan, Economic Analysis of Usury Laws, 10 J. Bank Res. 200, 204 (1980) ("[R]esearch indicates that usury restrictions have limited the flow of credit to mortgage markets."); Ostas, Effects of Usury Ceilings in the Mortgage Market, 21 J. Fin. 821, 831 (1976) (usury laws reduced mortgage loan volume.).

[95] See, e.g., Christopher DeMuth, The Case Against Credit Card Interest Rate Regulation, 3 Yale J. of Reg. 201, 221 (1986) ("By effectively segmenting the supply of credit and reducing the competition faced by the firms who are superior repricers, usury controls raise net costs of credit. This was the conclusion of one recent study which found that usury controls significantly reduced price competition between finance companies and banks.") (citing A. Sullivan, Effects of Consumer Loan Rate Ceilings on Competition Between Banks and Finance Companies 20–22 (1981) (CRC Working Paper No. 38)); see also Michael E. Staten & Robert W. Johnson, The Case for Deregulating Interest Rates in Consumer Credit 7, 38, 48, 50 (CRC Monograph #31, 1995), available at www.business.gwu.edu/research/centers/fsrp/pdf/Mono31.pdf.

[96] 439 U.S. 299 (1978).

[97] *Id.* See, e.g., Todd Zywicki, The Economics of Credit Cards, 3 Chap. L. Rev. 79, 147 (2000) ("by eliminating archaic and largely ineffective usury restrictions, *Marquette* increased efficiency and competition in the credit card industry, made the market more responsive to consumer demand, and provided large benefits to consumers").

state laws limiting creditor remedies against debtors, such as garnishment, increase interest rates, drive up the cost of credit, and reduce its availability to the very consumers "protected" by those limits.[98]

B. Judicial Recognition of the Economics of Consumer Protection Laws

Economists are not alone in their understanding of the counterintuitive, inverse relationship between consumer protection laws and the well-being of consumers. Judges have long since come to the same conclusion. Many courts have recognized that protecting a

[98]See, e.g., Richard L. Peterson & James R. Frew, Creditor Remedy Restrictions and Interstate Differences in Personal Loan Rates and Availability: A Supplementary Analysis 1, 8 (CRC Working Paper #14, 1977), available at www.business.gwu.edu/research/centers/fsrp/pdf/WP14.pdf ("many restrictions on creditors' remedies are likely to reduce personal loan availability (per capita) and, to a lesser extent, increase personal loan finance rates"; for example, "restrictions on garnishment significantly affected the price and availability of consumer credit," leading to "significantly elevated finance company personal loan rates," while "prohibitions against confession of judgment clauses" were linked to "significant increases in loan rates" and "significant reductions in bank personal loan credit availability"); Richard L. Peterson, The Impact of Creditors' Remedies on Consumer Loan Charges 4, 7 (CRC Working Paper #15, 1977), available at www.business.gwu.edu/ research/centers/fsrp/pdf/WP15.pdf ("bank auto loan rates [were] significantly higher in states with the most restrictive creditor remedies," and "in every case a lack of restriction on (or prohibition against) a particular creditors' remedy was associated with lower loan rates"; for example, "State restrictions on attorney fee clauses are associated with 90 basis point increased in bank consumer loan rates," and restrictions on garnishment increase "consumer finance charges"; moreover, "restrictions on creditors' remedies also induce lenders to reduce their supplies of consumer credit—both in the aggregate . . . and to the most risky borrower groups"). See also Norman Geis, Escape from the 15th Century: The Uniform Land Security Act, 30 Real Prop. Prob. & Tr. J. 289, 300 (1995) ("Economists have predicted . . . that the increased cost of lending in the judicial foreclosure states will be reflected in an increased cost of mortgage borrowing"); accord Durham, In Defense of Strict Foreclosure: A Legal and Economic Analysis, 36 S.C. L. Rev. 461, 495–506 (1985) (increasing obstacles to foreclosure hurts rather than helps consumers); Anne Bradner, The Secondary Mortgage Market and State Regulation of Real Estate Financing, 36 Emory L.J. 971, 997 (1987) ("costs are largely a function of delays built into the system, and the delays [in foreclosure] harm both mortgagor and mortgagee") (citing Bauer, Judicial Foreclosure and Statutory Redemption: The Soundness of Iowa's Traditional Preference for Protection Over Credit, 71 Iowa L. Rev. 1, 9–10, 11–12 (1985)); Note, Foreclosures, Redemptions, and Homeowners, 1975 U. Ill. L.F. 335, 358–61; Pedowitz, Mortgage Foreclosure Under the Uniform Land Transactions Act (As Amended), 6 Real. Est. L.J. 179, 195 (1978); Madway & Pearlman, Mortgage Forms and Foreclosure Practices: Time for Reform, 9 Real Prop. Prob. & Tr. J. 560, 565 (1974).

particular individual consumer from loan provisions designed to protect the interests of a creditor may actually harm similarly situated consumers in the long run. In *Fidelity Federal Savings & Loan Ass'n v. De la Cuesta*, the Supreme Court upheld a Federal Home Loan Bank Board ("the FHLBB") regulation preempting state laws restricting the enforcement of "due-on-sale" clauses.[99] In doing so, the Court noted that the FHLBB had reasonably concluded, after economic analysis, that state laws restricting enforcement of due-on-sale clauses "'will reduce the amount of home-financing funds available to potential home buyers, and generally cause a rise in home loan interest rates'" at borrowers' expense.[100] Although the Court did not exercise its own independent judgment about whether enforcement of due-on-sale clauses was good for consumers, in deferring to the FHLBB it noted that there was nothing "arbitrary or capricious" about the FHLBB's conclusion, which was supported by both analysis and rulings from a number of courts.[101]

In fact, many other courts agreed with the FHLBB that imposing restrictions on the enforcement of due-on-sale clauses would hurt the very consumers such restrictions purport to help, mortgage borrowers. The United States Court of Appeals for the Fourth Circuit, for example, in *Williams v. First Federal Savings & Loan Ass'n of Arlington*, rejected challenges to the enforceability of a mortgage's due-on-sale clause without proof of impairment of security under Virginia's antitrust and common law.[102] The Court noted that such challenges might immediately benefit "a relative few" homeowners, but that they would cause far more harm to similarly situated prospective homeowners in the future. According to the court, invalidation of the due-on-sale clause in that case would "inexorably lead

[99] Fidelity Federal Savings and Loan Ass'n v. de la Cuesta, 458 U.S. 141 (1982).

[100] *Id.* at 168 (quoting the FHLBB's Schott Advisory Opinion); accord *id.* at 169 (citing risk that "flow of home loan funds . . . will be reduced" and savings and loans' very solvency will be endangered). Similarly, analysts have found that this Court's decision in Marquette National Bank v. First Omaha Serv. Corp., 439 U.S. 299 (1978), which held that the National Bank Act preempted state credit card interest rate ceilings except for those imposed by a national bank's home state, had clearly positive results for consumers and resulted in the democratization of credit markets in the United States. See *infra* at 14; Todd Zywicki, The Economics of Credit Cards, 3 Chap. L. Rev. 79, 147 (2000).

[101] *Id.* at 169.

[102] 651 F.2d 910, 930 n.47 (4th Cir. 1981).

to an increase in interest rates" and "all future purchasers of homes in the end would suffer." The Court noted that the purported "'beneficence'" of protecting borrowers from the clause is "'short-sighted,'' since this would "necessarily restrict, if not dry up, mortgage funds available to the next generation of borrowers.'"[103]

The Massachusetts Supreme Judicial Court, in a similar case, observed that enforcement of a due-on-sale clause was good for consumers, since it "lowers the interest rate at which the bank is willing to loan money" by reducing the lenders risks associated with interest rate fluctuations.[104] The court concluded that "[e]limination of the [due-on-sale] clause 'will cause widespread hardship to the general home-buying public.'"[105] Other state courts reached similar conclusions.[106] A majority of jurisdictions routinely enforce due-on-sale clauses, while only a minority bars their enforcement under state common law.[107]

[103] *Id.* (quoting Wellenkamp v. Bank of America, 21 Cal.3d 943, 954, 148 Cal. Rptr. 379, 386 (Cal. 1978) (Clark, J., dissenting)).

[104] Dunware v. Ware Savings Bank, 423 N.E.2d 998, 1001–02 (Mass. 1981).

[105] *Id.* at 1004 (quoting Federal Home Loan Bank Board Advisory Opinion No. 75-647, at 37 (July 30, 1975)).

[106] United Savings Bank Mut. v. Barnette, 695 P.2d 73, 76 (Or. App. 1981) (noting "the substantial benefits that due-on-sale clauses have on interest rates and loan availability"); Income Realty & Mortgage Inc. v. Columbia Savings & Loan Ass'n, 661 P.2d 257, 261–63 (Colo. 1983) (restricting enforcement of due-on-sale clauses will "necessitate an increase in the interest rate of new loans"; "The due-on-sale clause was of benefit to both" lender and borrower, since "the borrowers received a lower interest rate than they would have, if there had been no such clause."); Martin v. Peoples Mutual Savings & Loan Ass'n, 319 N.W.2d 220, 226–28 (Iowa 1982) ("economic and social consequences of nullifying the due-on-sale provisions" include "charging new borrowers a higher rate of interest than they would otherwise be required to pay"; Occidental Savings & Loan Ass'n v. Venco Partnership, 293 N.W.2d 843, 847, 849 (Neb. 1980) (if such clauses are not enforced, "ultimately, no one will be able secure satisfactory financing"; accordingly, "a 'due on sale' clause is not repugnant to public policy but, to the contrary . . . the clauses may favor the public interest"); Lake v. Equitable Sav. & Loan Ass'n, 674 P.2d 419, 422 (Idaho 1983) ("less money available to potential borrowers" if borrowers shielded from enforcement of such clauses); Weiman v. McHaffie, 470 So.2d 682, 684 (Fla. 1985) (restricting enforcement of the clause causes "shortage of mortgage money" for buyers); Malouff v. Midland Federal Savings & Loan Ass'n, 509 P.2d 1240, 1244–45 (Colo. 1973) (barring such clauses would "increase monthly payments and make the obtaining of such [mortgage] loans prohibitive to many people") (citation omitted).

[107] Lake, 674 P.2d at 423.

In short, it is well-recognized by both economists and jurists that credit regulations aimed at protecting consumers often actually hurt them. But just because consumer protection laws are at best ill-advised, and at worst irrational, should courts impose preemption to protect consumers from consumer protection?

While the public choice analysis of the costs and benefits of state versus federal regulation of banking and preemption of consumer protection laws is a question for another article, the immediate policy question for the Court demands an immediate answer. The proliferation of state consumer protection measures, with an absence of the very same measures at the federal level, seems to suggest that federal legislation is less likely than its state counterpart to take the form of irrational, inefficient, and harmful consumer protection laws. Given this likelihood, federal regulation of banking appears to be superior to state regulation. But employment of federal preemption as a check on runaway state consumer protection legislation is a blunt instrument. The purpose of the present discussion is to lay bare the unsubstantiated claim that deference to federalism and state regulation of banks brings with it advantages for consumers through state consumer protection laws. A long line of economic analysis has demonstrated that this claim is far from the truth.

V. Conclusion: The End of the Dual Banking System?

If preemption removes a number of lenders and their customers from the reach of state predatory lending laws, the harmful effects of such state statutes might be mitigated. But the demise of federalism can be exaggerated. First, only wholly owned subsidiaries of national banks are sheltered from state regulation by NBA preemption. Many state chartered institutions will continue to be regulated by state banking and consumer protection laws, and many will have very little choice about it.

Second, the opportunity for state chartered lending institutions to "flee the jurisdiction" by becoming acquired by a nationally chartered bank is not "forum shopping" in the pernicious meaning of the phrase. Forum shopping is bad when it occurs *ex post*, when parties to a transaction seek a favorable outcome by seeking a biased arbiter. On the contrary, *ex ante* forum shopping is what federalism is all about. Parties should exercise their constitutional right to interstate travel, for example, and "vote with their feet" when encountering an inhospitable legal or regulatory climate. Debtors do this all the time.[108] Why should creditors be different? In other words, preemption of state banking law in the narrow case of wholly owned operating subsidiaries of national banks may actually *promote and enhance* federalism, by providing lenders with an *ex ante* choice of legal regime, one that forces regulators to compete for their "business." In the end, federalism, the system of dual banking, and consumer welfare may all actually be enhanced, not threatened, by the Court's decision in *Watters v. Wachovia Bank.*

[108] See, for example, G. Marcus Cole, The Federalist Cost of Bankruptcy Exemption Reform, 74 Am. Bankr. L.J. 227, 229 (2000) (discussing "the market for deadbeats" by considering how variations in laws can facilitate exit strategies for certain kinds of debtors); see also Frank H. Buckley and Margaret F. Brinig, The Market for Deadbeats, 25 J. Legal Stud. 201 (1996) (analyzing the factors that cause debtors to migrate to more favorable jurisdictions).

Weyerhaeuser and the Search for Antitrust's Holy Grail

*Thomas A. Lambert**

I. Introduction

It's not often that the U.S. Supreme Court overrules a 96-year-old precedent. For that reason, the Court's decision in *Leegin Creative Leather Products, Inc. v. PSKS, Inc.*,[1] which quite properly overruled the much-maligned 1911 *Dr. Miles* decision,[2] must be deemed the most noteworthy antitrust decision of October Term 2006.[3] In the long run, though, another antitrust decision from the term may turn out to be more important. That decision is *Weyerhaeuser Co. v. Ross-Simmons Hardwood Lumber Co.*,[4] in which the Court addressed the legal standard applicable to predatory bidding claims (i.e., claims that buyers of inputs have driven prices up higher than necessary in an attempt to drive rival input-buyers from the market and thereby enhance monopsony power).[5]

On first glance, the matter addressed by the *Weyerhaeuser* Court looks quite narrow: Must a plaintiff complaining of predatory bidding make the same two-part showing as a predatory pricing plaintiff?[6]

*Associate Professor of Law, University of Missouri-Columbia.

[1] 127 S. Ct. 2705 (2007).

[2] Dr. Miles Med. Co. v. John D. Park & Sons, 220 U.S. 373 (1911).

[3] For an account of why the *Dr. Miles* decision was wrong and *Leegin* is right, see Thom Lambert, Dr. Miles (1911–2007), available at http://www.truthonthemarket.com/2007/06/29/dr-miles-1911-2007.

[4] 127 S. Ct. 1069 (2007).

[5] See *id* at 1075–76. Monopsony power is the flip-side of monopoly power; it is "market power on the buy side of the market." *Id.* at 1075.

[6] *Id.* at 1074. The Supreme Court laid down its two part test for predatory pricing in *Brooke Group Ltd. v. Brown & Williamson Tobacco Corp.*, 509 U.S. 209 (1993), in which it held that a plaintiff complaining of predatory pricing must show (1) "that the prices complained of are below an appropriate measure of [the defendant's] costs," *Id.* at 222, and (2) that "the [defendant] had . . . a dangerous probabilit[y] of recouping its investment in below-cost prices" by charging supra-competitive prices once its rivals were extinguished. *Id.* at 224.

In answering that narrow question in the affirmative,[7] however, the Supreme Court may have unwittingly weighed in on one of the most hotly disputed matters in antitrust—how to define "exclusionary conduct" under Section 2 of the Sherman Act.[8]

This article advances two primary claims, one descriptive and one normative. As a descriptive matter, it contends that *Weyerhaeuser* implicitly adopts one proposed definition of exclusionary conduct under Section 2 and implicitly rejects three others. As a normative matter, it argues that this is a salutary development.

The article proceeds as follows. Part II summarizes the ongoing debate over how to define exclusionary conduct under Section 2. Part III then describes *Weyerhaeuser* and explains, as a descriptive matter, why it constitutes an implicit endorsement of the "exclusion of an equally efficient rival" definition of exclusionary conduct. Part IV defends that endorsement.

II. Proposed Definitions of "Exclusionary Conduct" Under Section 2

Section 2 of the Sherman Act, the primary antitrust provision governing unilateral conduct by dominant firms, prohibits (among other offenses) "monopolization."[9] The Supreme Court has defined the monopolization offense to consist of two elements: (1) the possession of monopoly power in a relevant market, and (2) exclusionary conduct designed to attain, protect, or expand such power.[10] For quite some time now, courts and commentators have struggled to articulate a workable definition of exclusionary conduct.[11] The difficulty arises because all sorts of pro-competitive behavior is literally

[7] Weyerhaeuser, 127 S. Ct. at 1078 ("The general theoretical similarities of monopoly and monopsony combined with the theoretical and practical similarities of predatory pricing and predatory bidding convince us that our two-pronged *Brooke Group* test should apply to predatory bidding claims.").

[8] 15 U.S.C. § 2.

[9] *Id.* ("Every person who shall monopolize, or attempt to monopolize, or combine or conspire with any other person or persons, to monopolize any part of the trade or commerce among the several States, or with foreign nations, shall be deemed guilty of a felony. . . .").

[10] United States v. Grinnell Corp., 384 U.S. 563, 570–71 (1966) (listing elements of monopolization under Section 2 of Sherman Act).

[11] See generally Herbert Hovenkamp, Exclusion and the Sherman Act, 72 U. Chi. L. Rev. 147 (2005).

exclusionary. For example, if Acme Inc. usurps business from its rivals by lowering its price or building a better mousetrap, it has literally excluded its rivals from some marketing opportunities, making it more difficult for them to stay in business. Yet it would be perverse to forbid price-cuts and quality enhancements. The trick for courts, then, has been to articulate some test for identifying conduct that is *unreasonably* exclusionary.

The prevailing definition of unreasonably exclusionary conduct in the case law comes from the Supreme Court's *Grinnell* decision, which defined exclusionary conduct as "the willful acquisition or maintenance of [monopoly] power as distinguished from growth or development as a consequence of a superior product, business acumen, or historic accident."[12] But what is "willful" acquisition of monopoly power? Practically every firm "wills" to beat out its rivals and thereby attain monopoly power.[13] Recognizing as much, courts have sometimes referred to exclusionary conduct as conduct other than "competition on the merits."[14] But what exactly is *that*? These verbal formulae are not very helpful. In the words of Professor Einer Elhauge, the judicial definitions of exclusionary conduct are "not just vague but vacuous."[15]

Accordingly, a generalized definition of exclusionary conduct has become the Holy Grail for antitrust scholars. Last year, the American Bar Association's *Antitrust Law Journal* published a symposium issue

[12] Grinnell, 384 U.S. at 570–71.

[13] Ortho Diagnostic Sys., Inc. v. Abbott Labs., Inc., 920 F. Supp. 455, 465 (S.D.N.Y. 1996) ("Unfortunately, the *Grinnell* test is not of much assistance in resolving particular cases. Every competitor seeks to capture as much business as possible. If *Grinnell* condemns all such behavior by actual and threatened monopolists, it would condemn the proverbial inventor of the better mousetrap as well as the storied trusts of the nineteenth century.").

[14] See, e.g., Monsanto Co. v. Scruggs, 459 F.3d 1328, 1338–39 (Fed. Cir. 2006) ("To establish a section 2 violation, one must prove that the party charged had monopoly power in a relevant market and acquired or maintained that power by anti-competitive practices instead of by competition on the merits."); LePage's Inc. v. 3M, 324 F.3d 141 (3d Cir. 2003) (en banc) ("Exclusionary conduct . . . not only, one, tends to impair the opportunities of . . . rivals, but also, number two, either does not further competition on the merits, or does so in an unnecessarily restrictive way.").

[15] Einer Elhauge, Defining Better Monopolization Standards, 56 Stan. L. Rev. 253, 255 (2003).

on the matter,[16] and the topic emerged repeatedly during recent joint Federal Trade Commission-Department of Justice hearings on Section 2 of the Sherman Act. Indeed, at the introductory session of those hearings, Federal Trade Commission Chairman Deborah Platt Majoras characterized the issue of how unilateral conduct should be evaluated as having "dominated our antitrust debate for several years" and as "the most heavily discussed and debated area of competition policy in the international arena."[17]

At this point, four proposed definitions of exclusionary conduct appear most promising.[18] They are: (1) conduct that could exclude from the defendant's market an equally efficient rival, (2) conduct that raises rivals' costs unjustifiably, (3) conduct that enhances market power and does not create enough consumer benefit to offset that harm, and (4) conduct that would involve a sacrifice of profits (or would make "no economic sense") but for its ability to exclude rivals.

A. Excluding An Equally Efficient Rival

Judge Posner is responsible for popularizing the first definition. In the second edition of his book, *Antitrust Law*, he defined exclusionary conduct as that which is "likely in the circumstances to exclude from the defendant's market an equally or more efficient competitor."[19] This definition comports with the typical understanding of vigorous but fair competition. A competitive race is one in which (1) each runner does his best and (2) the fastest runner wins. Any conduct that could result in a winner other than the fastest runner is literally anti-competitive. At the same time, conduct that helps a competitor

[16] Symposium: Identifying Exclusionary Conduct Under Section 2, 73 Antitrust L.J. 311 (2006).

[17] Transcript of Hearing, Federal Trade Commission and Department of Justice Hearings on Section 2 of the Sherman Act: Single-Firm Conduct as Related to Competition (June 20, 2006) at 10 (available at http://ftc.gov./os/sectiontwohearings/docs/60620FTC.pdf.).

[18] See generally Hovenkamp, *supra* note 11, at 148–62. A fifth approach rejects the notion of a single generalized definition. See, e.g., Marina Lao, Defining Exclusionary Conduct Under Section 2: The Case for Non-Universal Standards, in International Antitrust Law and Policy 433 (2006) (Barry Hawk, ed.) (advocating different evaluative approaches for different types of potentially exclusionary conduct); Mark S. Popofsky, Defining Exclusionary Conduct: Section 2, the Rule of Reason, and the Unifying Principle Underlying Antitrust Rules, 73 Antitrust L. J. 435 (2006) (applying an overarching rule of reason to select distinct tests for different conduct).

[19] Richard A. Posner, Antitrust Law 194–95 (2000).

along—but could not push him ahead of his more deserving rivals—is expected. Under Posner's definition, competitors would be motivated to take all actions that would push them forward, except for those actions that could push them ahead of superior or equally competent and aggressive rivals. Each competitor would work his hardest, free from fear that he would be beaten by a less capable rival.

The definition has some support in the case law, most obviously in the law governing predatory pricing.[20] Under governing precedents, a plaintiff complaining of predatory pricing must prove that the defendant set its price below its cost.[21] Because any equally (or more) efficient rival could meet a discount that resulted in above-cost pricing, this requirement has the effect of punishing only those price cuts that could exclude equally efficient rivals. As explained below, though, the equally efficient rival test has been criticized as being under-deterrent.[22]

B. Raising Rivals' Costs Unjustifiably

The second prominent exclusionary conduct definition is significantly broader. That definition arises from so-called "post-Chicago" economic theories that purport to explain how dominant firms may use contracts, product innovations, or other means to impose disproportionately higher costs on their rivals.[23] By imposing such costs, dominant firms enable themselves to charge higher prices even if they do not completely exclude their rivals. They may do so because their competitors have become less efficient and thus less able to check higher prices.[24]

[20] The definition has also achieved some traction in the case law governing bundled discounts. See *infra* note 159 and accompanying text.

[21] See *supra* note 6 (summarizing two-part predatory pricing test outlined in *Brooke Group Ltd. v. Brown & Williamson Tobacco Corp.*, 509 U.S. 209, 222–24 (1993)).

[22] See *infra* notes 108–15 and accompanying text.

[23] Hovenkamp, *supra* note 11, at 159–60. For a lucid discussion of "post-Chicago" antitrust, see Herbert Hovenkamp, Post-Chicago Antitrust: A Review and Critique, 2001 Colum. Bus. L. Rev. 257.

[24] See Steven C. Salop, Exclusionary Conduct, Effect on Consumers, and the Flawed Profit-Sacrifice Standard, 73 Antitrust L.J. 311, 315 (2006) ("[Raising Rivals' Costs] generally describes conduct to raise the costs of competitors with the purpose and effect of causing them to raise their prices or reduce their output, thereby allowing the excluding firm to profit by setting a supracompetitive price.").

In light of these post-Chicago theories, a number of scholars advocate a definition that deems conduct exclusionary if it raises rivals' costs unjustifiably. The cost-raising must be "unjustifiable" because much pro-competitive, efficient conduct raises rivals' costs.[25] For example, offering a superior product or charging a lower price may usurp business from rivals, thereby reducing their scale and increasing their per-unit costs. Yet consumer-friendly design enhancements and price reductions should not be deemed exclusionary. The $64,000 question, then, is "When is cost-raising conduct unjustifiable?"

One option is to answer that question case-by-case, based on the competitive effects of the conduct at issue.[26] But that approach begs the question of *which* competitive effects will render a cost-raising practice unjustifiable. In light of that difficulty, Professor Elhauge, a leading proponent of the "raising rivals' costs" approach, has proposed a more structured test that essentially defines "justifiable" increases of rivals' costs as those that result as a byproduct of the defendant's enhanced efficiency. In other words, if the defendant's conduct raises rivals' costs because it makes the defendant more efficient, the cost-raising is justifiable; if the conduct raises rivals' costs *even without* making the defendant more efficient, the cost-raising is unjustifiable.[27]

[25] See, e.g., Posner, *supra* note 19, at 196 (contending that raising rivals' costs is "not a happy formula" and observing that a primary means of raising rivals' costs is by becoming so efficient as to make one's rivals "unable to reach a level of output at which to exploit the available economies of scale").

[26] See, e.g., Willard K. Tom, David A. Balto & Neil W. Averitt, Anticompetitive Aspects of Market-Share Discounts and Other Incentives to Exclusive Dealing, 67 Antitrust L.J. 615 (2000). The authors contend that loyalty discounts may raise rivals' costs by denying them economies of scale. *Id.* at 627–30. The authors then conclude that loyalty discounts should not be governed by straightforward predatory pricing rules but should instead by judged on a case-by-case basis. *Id.* at 638 ("Where the pricing structure, rather than the price level, is used to secure an anticompetitive result, the cost test of predatory pricing does not automatically apply. Instead, one must conduct a case-by-case analysis of the actual effects of the particular practice to determine whether anticompetitive outcomes are likely.").

[27] Elhauge, *supra* note 15, at 330. Professor Elhauge maintains that antitrust law should eschew "an open-ended rule of reason balancing test" for determining when cost-raising conduct is justifiable and should instead

> employ[] two rules to sort out when to condemn conduct that helps acquire or maintain monopoly power. One rule makes such conduct per se legal if its exclusionary effect on rivals depends on enhancing the defendant's efficiency. The other rule makes such conduct per se illegal if its exclusionary effect on rivals will enhance monopoly power regardless of any improvement in defendant efficiency.

As explained below, even the more structured versions of the raising rivals' costs approach are likely to be exceedingly difficult to administer and intolerably indeterminate.[28]

C. The Consumer Welfare Effect Test (A "Market-Wide Balancing" Approach)

A third set of tests for exclusionary conduct focuses on the challenged act's net effect on consumer welfare.[29] The most prominent version of this sort of test appears in the Areeda-Hovenkamp treatise, the leading antitrust treatise, which defines exclusionary conduct as acts that:

(1) are reasonably capable of creating, enlarging or prolonging monopoly power by impairing the opportunities of rivals; and

(2) that either (2a) do not benefit consumers at all, or (2b) are unnecessary for the particular consumer benefits that the acts produce, or (2c) produce harms disproportionate to the resulting benefits.[30]

Some commentators have referred to this sort of test as a "market-wide balancing" approach, for all the "action," from a practical standpoint, occurs in part 2c.[31] Challenges to conduct that failed to meet the first element would be immediately dismissed, and parts 2a and 2b deal with easy cases involving harm without benefit.[32] Because generalized definitions of exclusionary conduct are likely to be invoked only when the conduct at issue involves a mixed bag of pro-competitive benefits and anti-competitive harms, application of the test will almost always come down to balancing harms and benefits.

[28] See *infra* notes 125–29 and accompanying text.

[29] See, e.g., Salop, *supra* note 24, at 329–57 (arguing for a "consumer welfare effect test"); Hovenkamp, *supra* note 11, at 148–51 (arguing for test that similarly focuses on a practice's net effects on consumers).

[30] Phillip E. Areeda & Herbert Hovenkamp, 3 Antitrust Law: An Analysis of Antitrust Principles and Their Application ¶ 651a at 72 (2d ed. 2002).

[31] See, e.g., A. Douglas Melamed, Exclusive Dealing Agreements and Other Exclusionary Conduct—Are There Unifying Principles?, 73 Antitrust L.J. 375, 379 (2006).

[32] *Id.* at 380 (explaining why the Areeda-Hovenkamp test requires market-wide balancing in all cases in which a generalized test for exclusionary conduct would be helpful—i.e., those cases that involve "conduct that creates both efficiency benefits and exclusionary harm").

So construed, the Areeda-Hovenkamp definition is troubling for a couple of reasons. First, market-wide balancing of the various effects of mixed bag conduct is extremely difficult and would likely exceed the competence of courts and enforcement agencies. As Douglas Melamed recently observed, balancing the benefits and harms of efficiency-creating but exclusion-causing conduct would require courts to (1) "quantify[] both welfare effects by estimating price, cost, and quantity of output under two conditions—before and after exclusion of rivals"; (2) "deal[] with the time dimension (both duration and discounting to present value) of each"; and (3) "compare[] both to a hypothetical but-for world in which the conduct did not take place."[33] Such an inquiry would be next to impossible. In addition, a consumer welfare effect test would provide businesses with little *ex ante* guidance regarding the legality of proposed courses of conduct and is therefore likely to deter efficiency-enhancing, but novel, practices.[34]

D. The "No Economic Sense" Test

Whereas the approaches discussed above attempt to *define* exclusionary conduct—that is, to specify what it is about challenged conduct that makes it unreasonably exclusionary—the final approach seeks merely to *identify* such conduct. In other words, the approach abandons the Platonic quest for the essence of "unreasonable exclusionariness" and instead merely posits a test that will

[33] *Id.* at 381; see also Gregory J. Werden, Identifying Exclusionary Conduct Under Section 2: The "No Economic Sense" Test, 73 Antitrust L.J. 413, 431 (2006) ("Even if economists could perfectly sort out the relatively short-run economic consequences of all marketplace conduct, they still could not accurately account for the important long-term effects of any remedial action on incentives for innovation and risk taking—the twin engines of our prosperity.").

[34] As Douglas Melamed recently argued:

> The balancing test would require a firm to determine, before it embraces new competitive strategies, not just the impact of the strategies on its business, but also the impact on rivals and to weigh the benefits to its consumers against the long-run harm to consumers if the firm's less-inventive rivals are weakened or driven from the market as a result. Assessing the long-run harm would require, among other things, calculating the duration of the harm in light of responses by competitors, new entry, and future innovation.

Melamed, *supra* note 31, at 381. Given the near impossibility of this inquiry and the high cost of making a mistake (i.e., an adverse treble damages judgment), firms would likely forgo aggressive new methods of competition to the detriment of consumers.

identify conduct that is unreasonably exclusionary without saying what it is about the conduct that makes it so.

Early versions of this identifying (as opposed to defining) approach focused on profit sacrifice: conduct was tagged as unreasonably exclusionary if (but not because) it involved a sacrifice of immediate profits as part of a strategy whose profitability depended on the exclusion of rivals.[35] A purported benefit of a sacrifice-based approach is its administrability; proponents maintain that it can be easily applied both by courts and regulators analyzing past conduct and by firms and antitrust counselors analyzing proposed conduct.[36]

Despite this virtue, Professor Hovenkamp has criticized the traditional profit sacrifice test for being both over- and under-inclusive.[37] It is over-inclusive, he argues, because it would condemn some clearly pro-competitive conduct, such as new product development.[38] Hovenkamp offers the example of a firm that invests heavily in designing a new mousetrap that, when marketed, will drive out the competition. Such innovation, which would appear to involve an immediate profit sacrifice that leads to monopoly, obviously should not be condemned under the antitrust laws.[39] On the other hand, Hovenkamp maintains, the test is under-inclusive because it would fail to condemn various acts of monopoly maintenance (such as certain tying and exclusive contracts) that "may be profitable the instant they are in place yet also anticompetitive."[40]

[35] See, e.g., Janusz A. Ordover & Robert D. Willig, An Economic Definition of Predation: Pricing and Product Innovation, 91 Yale L.J. 8 (1981); Robert H. Bork, The Antitrust Paradox: A Policy at War With Itself 144 (1978).

[36] See, e.g., Melamed, *supra* note 31, at 393 ("Perhaps most important, the sacrifice test provides simple, effective, and meaningful guidance to firms so that they will know how to avoid antitrust liability without steering clear of procompetitive conduct."); Werden, *supra* note 33, at 415 ("Application of the no economic sense [variant of the profit sacrifice] test is conceptually straightforward.").

[37] See Herbert Hovenkamp, The Antitrust Enterprise: Principle and Execution 152–54 (2005); Hovenkamp, *supra* note 11, at 155–58.

[38] Hovenkamp, *supra* note 11, at 158 ("All innovation is costly, and many successful innovations succeed only because consumers substitute away from rivals' older versions and toward the innovator's version. . . . As a result, willingness to 'sacrifice' short-term profits in anticipation of later monopoly profits does not distinguish anticompetitive from procompetitive uses of innovation.").

[39] Hovenkamp, *supra* note 37, at 152.

[40] *Id.* As an example of immediately profitable exclusionary devices, Hovenkamp points to "tying and exclusive dealing contracts, such as Microsoft's insistence that Windows users also take Internet Explorer." *Id.*

Perhaps seeking to avoid these sorts of criticisms, some proponents of a sacrifice-based test for identifying exclusionary conduct have refined the test a bit.[41] The version of the test advocated by the U.S. Department of Justice, for example, provides that "conduct is not exclusionary or predatory unless it would make no economic sense for the defendant but for its tendency to eliminate or lessen competition."[42] So construed, the test avoids Hovenkamp's concerns about its over- and under-inclusivity. The argument that the test is "too broad" because it would condemn investments in innovation assumes that it is sufficient to ask whether the defendant's conduct entails a short run profit sacrifice. The "no economic sense" test, though, would require more: upon finding a short-run sacrifice, one must ask why it would be rational to make that sacrifice.[43] If there's a profit-enhancing rationale (some "economic sense") besides a lessening of competition, then the test is not satisfied.[44]

Hovenkamp's argument that the test is "too narrow" because it would fail to condemn immediately profitable anticompetitive acts similarly dissolves if the test is "no economic sense." Whereas the profit sacrifice test seemed to require two time periods—a short run period in which there are losses followed by a later period in which there is monopoly recoupment—the "no economic sense" test focuses on the nature of the conduct and asks merely whether it would reduce profits but for its tendency to eliminate competition. The key question is not when the conduct will be profitable but why it is (or is expected to be) profitable.[45] So construed, the test condemns

[41] See generally Melamed, *supra* note 31; Werden, *supra* note 33.

[42] See, e.g., Brief for the United States and the FTC as Amici Curiae Supporting Petitioner at 15, Verizon Commc'ns, Inc. v. Law Offices of Curtis V. Trinko, 540 U.S. 398 (2004) (No. 02-682), available at http://www.ftc.gov/os/2003/05/trinkof.pdf (emphasis omitted).

[43] See Werden, *supra* note 33, at 424 ("When the defendant's conduct entails a short-run profit sacrifice, the no economic sense test further asks why it is rational to make that sacrifice.").

[44] Hovenkamp's mousetrap example, see *supra* note 39 and accompanying text, would therefore fail. While "invest[ing] heavily in designing a better mousetrap" may entail a short run profit sacrifice, the rationality of that sacrifice does not depend on the elimination of rivals; the sacrifice would be economically rational if it were expected to result in a superior mousetrap for which consumers would be willing to pay a higher price.

[45] See Melamed, *supra* note 31, at 391 (observing that it is "incorrect" to interpret the profit-sacrifice test as holding that "conduct is anticompetitive only if it entails losses in the short run followed by monopoly recoupment in some later period"; rather, "the test depends, not on the timeline, but rather on the nature of the conduct—on whether it would make no business or economic sense but for its likelihood of harming competition").

practices that, in Hovenkamp's words, ''may be profitable the instant they are in place, yet also anticompetitive.''[46]

III. The *Weyerhaeuser* Decision and Its Implications for the Definitional Debate

When one considers the *Weyerhaeuser* decision in light of this ongoing debate over how to define exclusionary conduct, the decision's importance becomes apparent. The Supreme Court, it seems, has weighed in on the definitional question.

A. The Weyerhaeuser *Decision*[47]

The plaintiff in *Weyerhaeuser*, Ross-Simmons, operated a hardwood lumber sawmill in Longview, Washington. It purchased many of the red alder sawlogs it processed on the open bidding market, competing for such purchases with Weyerhaeuser, the defendant. Weyerhaeuser eventually grew to be substantially larger than Ross-Simmons and by 2001 was acquiring about 65% of the alder logs available for sale in the region.[48]

Ross-Simmons accused Weyerhaeuser of ''predatory bidding.'' Specifically, claimed Ross-Simmons, Weyerhaeuser bought more alder sawlogs than it needed and bid up the price for alder sawlogs higher than necessary to attain the quantity it required.[49] This had the effect of raising the cost of Ross-Simmons' key input. At the same time, Weyerhaeuser did not increase the price of its output; market prices for finished hardwood lumber actually fell.[50] This created a revenue squeeze: the sawmills' revenues (reflecting market prices of finished hardwood) fell, even as the sawmills' costs (reflecting the unnecessarily high price of the most important input) were rising. After enduring this squeeze for several years, Ross-Simmons shut down its mill completely in 2001.[51] Blaming Weyerhaeuser for

[46] Hovenkamp, *supra* note 37, at 152.

[47] Weyerhaeuser Co. v. Ross-Simmons Hardwood Lumber Co., 127 S. Ct. 1069 (2007).

[48] *Id.* at 1072.

[49] *Id.* at 1073.

[50] *Id.*

[51] *Id.*

its failure, Ross-Simmons sued the company for monopolization and attempted monopolization under Sherman Act Section 2.[52]

Weyerhaeuser unsuccessfully moved for summary judgment, and then, after trial, sought judgment as a matter of law or, alternatively, a new trial.[53] The district court denied both requests.[54] It also rejected Weyerhaeuser's proposed "predatory bidding" jury instruction, which incorporated the predatory pricing elements set forth in the Supreme Court's *Brooke Group* decision.[55] That decision held that a plaintiff complaining of predatory pricing must establish that (1) "the prices complained of are below an appropriate measure of its rival's costs,"[56] and (2) "a dangerous probability" existed that the rival would later "recoup[] its investment in below-cost prices" once it stopped such pricing.[57] Weyerhaeuser argued that the jury should be instructed that overbidding for sawlogs could be anticompetitive conduct only if it resulted in Weyerhaeuser's operating at a loss and a dangerous probability of its recoupment of losses existed.[58] The district court rejected Weyerhaeuser's proposed instruction and instead told the jury it could find an anticompetitive act if it concluded that Weyerhaeuser "purchased more logs than it needed or paid a higher price for logs than necessary, in order to prevent [Ross-Simmons] from obtaining the logs they needed at a fair price."[59]

[52] 15 U.S.C. § 2. Specifically, Ross-Simmons maintained that Weyerhaeuser had used "its dominant position in the alder sawlog market to drive up the prices for alder sawlogs to levels that severely reduced or eliminated the profit margins of Weyerhaeuser's alder sawmill competition." Weyerhaeuser, 127 S. Ct. at 1073.

[53] Weyerhaeuser, 127 S. Ct. at 1073.

[54] *Id.*

[55] *Id.*

[56] Brooke Group Ltd. v. Brown & Williamson Tobacco Corp., 509 U.S. 209, 222 (1993).

[57] *Id.* at 224.

[58] Weyerhaeuser, 127 S. Ct. at 1073.

[59] *Id.* The district court gave the following instruction regarding anticompetitive conduct:

> Anti-competitive conduct is conduct that has the effect of wrongly preventing or excluding competition, or frustrating or impairing the efforts of other firms to compete for customers within the relevant market, making it very difficult or impossible for competitors to engage in fair competition. Not everything that enables a company to gain or maintain a monopoly is anti-competitive.
>
> In deciding whether conduct is anti-competitive, you should consider whether the conduct lacks a valid business purpose, or unreasonably or unnecessarily impedes the efforts of other firms to compete for raw materials

Concluding that Ross-Simmons had proven monopolization, the jury returned a $26 million verdict, which was trebled to approximately $79 million.[60]

Weyerhaeuser appealed to the U.S. Court of Appeals for the Ninth Circuit, arguing that *Brooke Group*'s requirements for predatory pricing should similarly apply to predatory bidding claims.[61] The Ninth Circuit disagreed.[62] It reasoned that predatory bidding, while conceptually similar to predatory pricing, does not necessarily produce the same consumer benefit—lower prices for at least the short-term.[63] The court concluded that "the concerns that led the *Brooke Group* Court to establish a high standard of liability in the predatory pricing context do not carry over to this predatory bidding context with the same force," so the *Brooke Group* standards for predatory pricing liability should not apply to claims of predatory bidding.[64]

In an 8-0 decision authored by Justice Thomas, the Supreme Court reversed the Ninth Circuit and held that *Brooke Group*'s standard of liability does apply to predatory bidding claims.[65] The Court's holding was based on the similarity between predatory pricing and predatory bidding.[66] Both practices involve an attempt to attain market power—i.e., the power to enhance one's profits by affecting

> or customers, or if the anticipated benefits of the conduct flow primarily from its tendency to hinder or eliminate competition. Anti-competitive conduct does not include ordinary means of competition, such as offering better products or services, exercising superior skill or business judgment, utilizing more efficient technology, better marketing, or exercising natural competitive advantages such as unique geographic access to raw materials or markets.
>
> ....
>
> One of Plaintiffs' contentions in this case is that the Defendant purchased more logs than it needed or paid a higher price for logs than necessary, in order to prevent the Plaintiffs from obtaining the logs they needed at a fair price. If you find this to be true, you may regard it as an anti-competitive act.

Confederated Tribes of Siletz Indians of Ore. v. Weyerhaeuser Co., 411 F.3d 1030, 1039 n.30 (9th Cir. 2005), vacated by Weyerhaeuser Co. v. Ross-Simmons Hardwood Lumber Co., 127 S. Ct. 1069 (2007).

[60] Weyerhaeuser, 127 S. Ct. at 1073.

[61] *Id.*

[62] Weyerhaeuser, 411 F.3d at 1035–36.

[63] *Id.* at 1037.

[64] *Id.* at 1038.

[65] Weyerhaeuser, 127 S. Ct. at 1074.

[66] *Id.* at 1078.

prices.[67] Whereas predatory pricing may permit a firm to attain monopoly power (the power to drive output prices upward by withholding one's production), predatory bidding may enable a firm to attain monopsony power—the power to drive input prices (and thus the firm's costs) downward by cutting back on one's purchases.[68] Exercises of both types of market power result in allocative inefficiency—the wealth loss that occurs when resources, because of price distortions, are not directed toward their highest and best uses.[69] Thus, the Court concluded, "[p]redatory-pricing and predatory-bidding are analytically similar."[70]

Moreover, claims of predatory-pricing and predatory-bidding involve "strikingly similar allegations."[71] A predatory-pricing plaintiff alleges that the defendant reduced the price of its product in order to drive competing sellers out of business so that the defendant, insulated from selling competition, could then raise its prices above competitive levels. A predatory-bidding plaintiff alleges that the defendant deliberately bid up the price of a key input in order to drive competing buyers out of business so that the defendant, insulated from buying competition, could then cut back on its input purchases and thereby drive down the price of inputs. Both strategies "logically require firms to incur short-term losses on the chance that they might reap supracompetitive profits in the future."[72]

Finally, the Court observed, "predatory bidding mirrors predatory pricing in respects that [the Court] deemed significant to [its] analysis in *Brooke Group*."[73] First, because both schemes require certain losses and provide only speculative chances of future supracompetitive profits, each is "rarely tried, and even more rarely successful."[74] In addition, the specific activities taken in connection with the two schemes—output-discounting and input-stockpiling—may each

[67] *Id.* at 1075.

[68] *Id.*

[69] *Id.*

[70] *Id.* at 1076.

[71] *Id.*

[72] *Id.*

[73] *Id.* at 1077.

[74] *Id.* (quoting Brooke Group Ltd. v. Brown & Williamson Tobacco Corp., 509 U.S. 209, 226 (1993) (quoting Matsushita Elec. Industrial Co. v. Zenith Radio Corp., 475 U.S. 574, 589 (1986))).

have pro-competitive effects.[75] Discounting benefits consumers and wins business for the discounter, and stockpiling inputs may provide "a hedge against the risk of future rises in input costs or future input shortages."[76] Finally, both practices *may* benefit consumers in the long-term: predatory pricing may do so if recoupment attempts fail because of entry, and predatory bidding may do so if "the acquisition of more inputs leads to the manufacture of more outputs."[77]

Thus, the Court concluded, the similarities of predatory-pricing and predatory-bidding warrant an identical liability standard—the *Brooke Group* standard—for both types of conduct.[78] Applied in the predatory bidding context, the first prong of that standard requires a plaintiff to prove that "the predator's bidding on the buy side . . . caused the cost of the relevant output to rise above the revenues generated in the sale of those outputs."[79] To satisfy the second prong, the plaintiff must establish "that the defendant has a dangerous probability of recouping the losses incurred in bidding up input prices through the exercise of monopsony power."[80] Because Ross-Simmons had conceded that it could not satisfy these standards, its monopolization claim failed.[81]

B. *Implications of* Weyerhaeuser *for a Generalized Definition of Exclusionary Conduct*

On first glance, *Weyerhaeuser* would seem to be of little practical significance. As the Supreme Court noted, the specific practice to which the decision speaks is rarely attempted.[82] The apparent narrowness of the *Weyerhaeuser* decision, though, is likely deceiving. In

[75] Weyerhaeuser, 127 S. Ct. at 1077 ("Just as sellers use output prices to compete for purchasers, buyers use bid prices to compete for scarce inputs. There are myriad legitimate reasons—ranging from benign to affirmatively procompetitive—why a buyer might bid up input prices.").

[76] *Id.*

[77] *Id.*

[78] *Id.* at 1078.

[79] *Id.*

[80] *Id.*

[81] *Id.* ("Ross-Simmons has conceded that it has not satisfied the *Brooke Group* standard.").

[82] *Id.* at 1077.

its reasoning, if not its precise holding, the *Weyerhaeuser* Court took sides in what is perhaps the greatest debate in contemporary antitrust—how to define exclusionary conduct. By holding that Ross-Simmons' evidence could not, as a matter of law, establish exclusionary conduct, the Court implicitly rejected the sacrifice-based, consumer welfare effect, and raising rivals' costs tests for exclusionary conduct and implicitly endorsed Judge Posner's equally efficient rival test. That's because the first three tests, but not the last, would have deemed Weyerhaeuser's conduct exclusionary.

1. *Sacrifice-Based Tests*

First consider how Weyerhaeuser would have fared under the profit sacrifice test and its "no economic sense" variant. Under that test, the relevant question would have been whether there was sufficient evidence to uphold a conclusion that Weyerhaeuser's conduct would have been unprofitable—i.e., would have made "no economic sense"—but for an enhancement in Weyerhaeuser's market power. Thus, the jury would have been required to compare Weyerhaeuser's pre-overbidding profits with what its profits would have been had it engaged in overbidding without experiencing an enhancement of monopsony power; if the former figure were found to exceed the latter, the conduct would have been exclusionary.[83]

Without doubt, the record supported a conclusion that Weyerhaeuser's conduct would not have been profit-enhancing but for the fact that it enhanced the firm's monopsony power. As the Ninth Circuit emphasized,

[83] Professor Salop explains how the sacrifice-based tests operate as follows:

> The profit-sacrifice test examines the profitability of the defendant's conduct relative to a hypothetical market outcome that is used as the non-exclusionary benchmark. The hypothetical "but for" marketplace is one in which it is impossible to raise prices following the exclusionary conduct. When exclusionary conduct potentially raises barriers to competition in some way, a defendant's exclusionary conduct can be said to sacrifice profits if the conduct would have been unprofitable (and, thus, likely not undertaken) in the absence of those enhanced barriers to competition.

Salop, *supra* note 24, at 319. Professor Salop notes that the traditional profit sacrifice test and its no economic sense variant both involve this inquiry. The primary difference between the two is that the latter "does not require a showing that there is a period of time in which the defendant's profits are lower than they were before the exclusionary conduct was undertaken"; thus, "[t]he reduction in profits can be conceptual rather than temporal." *Id.* at 319–20.

> One of Weyerhaeuser's former senior analysts, Eugene Novak . . . authored a memorandum regarding the costs of sawlogs and lumber in which he stated that the increase in sawlog prices despite Weyerhaeuser's predominant market share made no sense. Novak estimated that, due to the excessive prices Weyerhaeuser paid for sawlogs, it "had given up some $40 to $60 million dollars in the last three years." He testified that his boss, Vicki McInnally, who was a member of the senior management team, told him that "that was the strategy that [Weyerhaeuser] designed."[84]

Given such evidence, a reasonable jury certainly could have concluded that Weyerhaeuser's conduct was exclusionary under a profit sacrifice or no economic sense tests.

This point was emphasized to the Supreme Court. For example, the American Antitrust Institute's amicus brief in support of Ross-Simmons observed that

> [Weyerhaeuser's] purchase of "more logs than it needed" and paying "a higher price for logs than necessary" are, as the jury found, practices that satisfy both the sacrifice test and the no economic sense test. Indeed, how could buying more than necessary ever be sensible, efficient or otherwise legitimate profit-maximizing conduct? Again, as the court of appeals recognized, evidence from petitioner's own officials and documents precluded any finding of a valid business purpose for this overbuying and overpaying.[85]

This no doubt overstates things a bit. As an amicus brief by a group of economists emphasized, "overbidding" of the sort Weyerhaeuser engaged in could be a profit-enhancing move.[86] But under the Supreme Court's ruling, Ross-Simmons' claim would have failed *even if* Ross-Simmons had proven that Weyerhaeuser's conduct could

[84] Confederated Tribes of Siletz Indians of Ore. v. Weyerhaeuser Co., 411 F.3d 1030, 1042 (9th Cir. 2005), vacated and remanded by Weyerhaeuser Co. v. Ross-Simmons Hardwood Lumber Co., Inc., 127 S. Ct. 1069 (2007) (alteration in orig.).

[85] Brief for the American Antitrust Institute as Amicus Curiae in Support of Respondent at 8, Weyerhaeuser Co. v. Ross-Simmons Hardwood Lumber Co., Inc., 127 S. Ct. 1069 (2007) (No. 05-381), available at 2006 WL 2950593.

[86] See Brief of Economists as Amici Curiae in Support of Petitioner at 9–11, Weyerhaeuser Co. v. Ross-Simmons Hardwood Lumber Co., Inc., 127 S. Ct. 1069 (2007) (No. 05-381), available at 2006 WL 2459522.

not have been calculated to enhance the company's profits. Even if there were no possible way the overbidding could have benefited Weyerhaeuser but for its ability to exclude rivals, the overbidding would not have been exclusionary unless it resulted in below-cost pricing in the output market.[87]

2. *The Consumer Welfare Effect Test*

The consumer welfare effect test similarly would have resulted in a decision for Ross-Simmons. Under the Areeda-Hovenkamp version of that test, a factfinder first determines whether a challenged practice is "reasonably capable of creating, enlarging, or prolonging monopoly [or monopsony] power by impairing the opportunities of rivals."[88] Without doubt, the sort of overbidding with which Weyerhaeuser was charged was "reasonably capable" of enhancing the firm's monopsony power by impairing its competitors in the input market.[89] The second step of the Areeda-Hovenkamp test, then, is designed to ensure that this enhancement of market power is not offset by some benefit to consumers: the plaintiff must show that the challenged practice either "do[es] not benefit consumers at all," or is "unnecessary for the particular consumer benefits that the act[] produce[s]," or "produce[s] harms disproportionate to the resulting benefits."[90] There was almost certainly evidence in the record to support a jury conclusion that one of these three prongs (most likely, the second or third) was satisfied. While overbidding may provide

[87] Weyerhaeuser, 127 S. Ct. at 1078 ("A plaintiff must prove that the alleged predatory overbidding led to below-cost pricing of the predator's outputs.").

[88] 3 Areeda & Hovenkamp, *supra* note 30, ¶ 651a, at 72.

[89] The Supreme Court conceded as much:

> A predatory bidder ultimately aims to exercise the monopsony power gained from bidding up input prices. To that end, once the predatory bidder has caused competing buyers to exit the market for purchasing inputs, it will seek to "restrict its input purchases below the competitive level," thus "reduc[ing] the unit price for the remaining inputs it purchases." . . . The reduction in input prices will lead to "a significant cost saving that more than offsets the profit[s] that would have been earned on the output." If all goes as planned, the predatory bidder will reap monopsonistic profits that will offset any losses suffered in bidding up input prices.

Weyerhaeuser, 127 S. Ct. at 1075–76 (quoting Steven C. Salop, Anticompetitive Overbuying by Power Buyers, 72 Antitrust L. J. 669, 672 (2005)).

[90] 3 Areeda & Hovenkamp, *supra* note 30, ¶ 651a, at 72.

benefits for consumers, a point emphasized in the economists' brief,[91] the jury apparently concluded that any such benefits were minor and incidental. Indeed, it was instructed that it should consider whether the conduct had "a valid business purpose," that "offering better products or services" could not be anti-competitive, and that the overbidding could be anti-competitive if it was done "in order to prevent the Plaintiffs from obtaining the logs they needed at a fair price."[92] It seems, then, that the jury determined that the harms from Weyerhaeuser's monopsony-enhancing conduct were disproportionate to the resulting consumer benefits.[93]

In any event, there can be no doubt that the Supreme Court's ruling rejects the consumer welfare effect test. Under the test laid down by the Court, *even if* Ross-Simmons had shown that Weyerhaeuser's overbidding drove rivals out of business, was not calculated to benefit consumers in any way whatsoever, and in fact did not produce an iota of consumer benefit, Ross-Simmons still would have lost unless it had also shown that the input overbidding resulted in a below-cost price for Weyerhaeuser's finished product.[94]

3. *Raising Rivals' Costs Unjustifiably*

If the Supreme Court believed exclusionary conduct is that which unjustifiably raises rivals' costs, then it surely would have sustained

[91] See Brief of Economists as Amici Curiae, *supra* note 86, at 9–11.

[92] See Confederated Tribes of Siletz Indians of Ore. v. Weyerhaeuser Co., 411 F.3d 1030, 1039 n.30 (9th Cir. 2005) (quoting jury instruction), (vacated by Weyerhaeuser Co. v. Ross-Simmons Hardwood Lumber Co., 127 S. Ct. 1069 (2007)).

[93] Again, the American Antitrust Institute emphasized this point to the Weyerhaeuser Court:

> [T]he jury was required to *rule out* such theoretical procompetitive explanations for petitioner's conduct before it could find against petitioner. More specifically, the jury was instructed to determine (a) whether petitioner purchased more logs than necessary "in order to prevent" plaintiffs from meeting their input needs; and (b) whether petitioner's conduct "lacks a valid business purpose." . . . Given these instructions, the jury plainly rejected petitioner's contention that it bid up prices or increased its purchases for procompetitive reasons.

Brief of American Antitrust Institute as Amicus Curiae, *supra* note 85, at 3 (emphasis in orig.).

[94] Weyerhaeuser, 127 S. Ct. at 1078 (to create liability, "the predator's bidding on the buy side must have caused the cost of the relevant output to rise above the revenues generated in the sale of those outputs.").

the jury verdict in favor of Ross-Simmons. Weyerhaeuser's overbidding obviously drove up the price of an input its rivals used and thereby raised their costs.[95] The key question is whether that cost-raising was justifiable. If justifiability were determined on a case-by-case basis,[96] the jury verdict would seem unassailable—the Supreme Court would not question a jury's decision on an "all things considered" matter. Affirmation would also have been required under the more structured approach proposed by Professor Elhauge.[97] He would define exclusionary conduct as that which "would further monopoly [here, monopsony] power by impairing the efficiency of rivals *even if the defendant did not successfully enhance its own efficiency*."[98] In other words, if the impairment of rivals' efficiency is not an inevitable byproduct of the perpetrator's improvement of its own efficiency, then the cost-raising is unjustified.[99] Here, Ross-Simmons' costs would have been raised by Weyerhaeuser's over-bidding even if that over-bidding did not enhance Weyerhaeuser's efficiency. Thus, the cost-raising would have been unjustified, and the over-bidding would have been exclusionary.[100]

Regardless of whether the jury actually found that Weyerhaeuser's raising of rivals' costs was unjustified, it is clear that even an express and fully supported jury finding that Weyerhaeuser had *no* pro-competitive justification for its rival-impairing conduct would not have helped Ross-Simmons. The Court essentially said that even if the jury found that Weyerhaeuser had raised its rivals costs for no good reason whatsoever, Ross-Simmons still would have lost unless

[95] *Id.* at 1073 (citing record evidence showing that Weyerhaeuser's bidding activity had raised rivals' costs).

[96] See *supra* note 26 and accompanying text (discussing approach that would determine justifiability of raising rivals' costs on a case-by-case basis).

[97] See *supra* notes 27 and accompanying text (discussing Professor Elhauge's test for determining when raising rivals' costs is justifiable).

[98] Elhauge, *supra* note 15, at 256 (emphasis supplied).

[99] *Id.* (arguing that the only tolerable conduct that raises rivals' costs is that which "successfully impair[s] rival efficiency only as a byproduct of the defendant improving its own efficiency").

[100] The jury was instructed that it could find an anti-competitive act if it concluded that Weyerhaeuser engaged in overbidding "in order to" hurt Ross-Simmons by raising its input costs. See *supra* notes 59. The jury thus appeared to find that the cost-raising was not an incidental result of otherwise efficiency-enhancing conduct; it was the intended result of the conduct. See *supra* note 93. Surely that could not be a "justifiable" instance of raising rivals' costs.

it could have shown that Weyerhaeuser's conduct resulted in below-cost prices for its finished product.[101]

4. Modus tollendo tollens[102]

A straightforward *modus tollens* argument therefore demonstrates the Court's rejection of the sacrifice-based, consumer welfare effect, and raising rivals' costs tests for exclusionary conduct:[103]

- If the essence of "exclusionariness" is either (1) failure to enhance profits but for an enhancement of market power, or (2) a reduction in consumer welfare occasioned by enhanced market power, or (3) raising rivals' costs unjustifiably, then Weyerhaeuser's conduct was unreasonably exclusionary.
- Weyerhaeuser's conduct was not unreasonably exclusionary.
- Therefore, neither the sacrifice-based tests, nor the consumer welfare effect standard, nor the raising rivals' costs approach determines whether conduct is unreasonably exclusionary for purposes of Section 2.

5. Equally Efficient Rival

Weyerhaeuser is fully consistent, though, with a test that determines whether conduct is exclusionary for purposes of Section 2 by asking whether the conduct could exclude an equally efficient rival. If a defendant who pays more for an input than the amount necessary to obtain it still charges an above-cost price for whatever output he sells, then any equally efficient seller of the same output could afford to pay the same price for the input. Such a seller would not be driven out of business by the overbidding. By contrast, if a defendant's overbidding results in a below-cost price for his product, then an equally efficient rival could not meet the discount without similarly pricing below cost and might thus be driven out of business by the overbidding. If the defendant's overbidding results in an output price equal to its cost of producing the output, then all equally or more efficient rivals could afford to pay the input price (and would

[101] Weyerhaeuser, 127 S. Ct. at 1078 (holding that there can be no antitrust liability based on predatory overbidding absent proof that the defendant's overbidding resulted in a below-cost price for its finished products).

[102] "Mode that denies by denying."

[103] A modus tollens argument follows the following form: If P, then Q; not Q; therefore, not P.

thus stay in business) and all less efficient rivals could not afford to do so (and would be excluded). Because *Weyerhaeuser*'s line of illegality appears at precisely the point at which the conduct at issue could exclude an equally efficient rival, the decision is consistent with Judge Posner's proposed test for exclusionary conduct.

IV. Should Exclusion of an Equally Efficient Rival Be Required for Section 2 Liability?

So far, this article's analysis has been entirely descriptive—I have shown simply that *Weyerhaeuser*'s reasoning implicitly rejects the sacrifice-based, consumer welfare balancing, and raising rivals' costs tests for exclusionary conduct under Sherman Act Section 2 and implicitly endorses Judge Posner's equally efficient rival approach. I turn now to the normative question of whether this development is a good one.

On the whole, it is. While a rule requiring proof that a practice could exclude an equally efficient rival is somewhat underdeterrent,[104] it is also much easier to apply in the context of litigation and far less likely to result in false positives.[105] Such a rule is therefore less likely to deter "mixed bag" conduct that is, on balance, procompetitive.[106] The key question, then, is whether the losses from the rule's relative under-deterrence are outweighed by the benefits the rule offers in terms of lower administrative costs and reduced losses from the over-deterrence of pro-competitive conduct. While a detailed accounting of those various costs and benefits is beyond the scope of this Article, there are sound reasons for believing that the losses from the rule's under-deterrence will be outweighed by gains from lower administrative costs and reduced over-deterrence.[107]

[104] See *infra* notes 108–15 and accompanying text.

[105] See *infra* notes 116–29 and accompanying text.

[106] "Mixed bag" conduct refers to practices that may create some market power (and may thus pose anticompetitive risks) but may also create efficiencies (and may thus confer procompetitive benefits). Evaluating mixed bag, single-firm conduct is, of course, the purpose of a generalized test for exclusionary conduct under Sherman Act Section 2.

[107] See *infra* notes 129–50 and accompanying text.

A. The Equally Efficient Rival Approach's Under-Deterrence

The equally efficient rival rule is almost certainly somewhat under-deterrent.[108] Critics of the rule point to three sources of under-deterrence. While one of those sources is probably illusory, the other two seem genuine.

First, critics of the rule maintain that it under-deters because it would approve exclusion-causing conduct of no social utility as long as that conduct could not exclude an equally efficient rival.[109] Professor Hovenkamp, for example, offers the example of a fraudulent patent suit that could be successfully defended by a rival with equivalent efficiencies (and thus equivalent per unit profits) but not by a less efficient upstart. Because the filing of such a lawsuit would create no social value and could exclude some competition, the law should sanction such behavior regardless of whether it could exclude an equally efficient rival.[110]

While that point seems correct, it does not discredit the equally efficient rival test. A general test for exclusionary conduct is needed only for evaluating mixed bag conduct that creates some efficiencies but also may enhance market power. "Naked" exclusionary practices—those that exclude competition without providing any efficiency benefits—can be easily condemned without reference to any test for exclusionary conduct. Thus, the fact that the equally efficient rival test would not condemn some instances of naked exclusion is not troubling.[111]

The other two criticisms of the equally efficient rival test are more potent. First, critics have observed that some acts of exclusion can

[108] See generally Lao, *supra* note 18, at 446–47; Hovenkamp, *supra* note 37, at 153–54; Salop, *supra* note 24, at 328–29; Melamed, *supra* note 31, at 388–89; Hovenkamp, *supra* note 11, at 153–55.

[109] See, e.g., Lao, *supra* note 18, at 447 (noting that under the rule "[a] dominant firm would be free to use *any* conduct, including those of no social utility, to exclude the only competitors that it would likely ever face"); Hovenkamp, *supra* note 37, at 154 (arguing that there is value in prohibiting socially useless conduct that could exclude less efficient rivals even if it could not exclude an equally efficient rival).

[110] Hovenkamp, *supra* note 11, at 154.

[111] Cf. Melamed, supra note 31, at 399 (observing that "conduct [that] has no efficiency properties and serves only to harm rivals . . . can be readily condemned without application of either a balancing test or a sacrifice test," for such conduct "does not raise the issue at which these tests are directed: what to do about conduct that both has efficiency benefits and excludes rivals").

prevent rivals from attaining equivalent efficiencies.[112] For example, conduct that forecloses marketing opportunities and thus impedes a rival's growth may prevent that rival from achieving minimum efficient scale so that it never becomes as efficient as the perpetrator.[113] The equally efficient rival test under-deters in that it would sanction this sort of efficiency-precluding conduct. In addition, critics of the test assert, there is significant social value in protecting even those rivals who are not as efficient as the perpetrator if they are the only ones likely to arrive on the scene.[114] For example, suppose a dominant firm had costs of $10 per unit but charged a profit-maximizing price of $20. The existence or potential entry of a rival with costs of, say, $13 could be beneficial for consumers. If that rival were to charge $15 per unit, the dominant firm would be forced to reduce its price or improve its quality.[115] Thus, consumer welfare may be harmed by an exclusionary conduct test that protects only equally or more efficient rivals.

B. The Other Approaches' Over-Deterrence

While the equally efficient rival test may fail to condemn some instances of anti-competitive unilateral conduct, the competing tests for exclusionary conduct are likely to over-deter if applied *ex post* in the context of litigation. Each of the competing tests requires a

[112] See, e.g., Lao, *supra* note 18, at 447 ("[E]xclusionary practices are often designed specifically to prevent a challenger from gaining scale efficiencies."); Melamed, *supra* note 31, at 388 ("[A] rival that is less efficient today might become equally or more efficient if permitted time to develop learning-by-doing economies or if its sales grew and enabled it to gain scale economies.").

[113] See, e.g., Einer Elhauge, The Exclusion of Competition for Hospital Sales Through Group Purchasing Organizations 24 n.68, 33–34 (2002) (report to U.S. Senate), available at http://www.law.harvard.edu/faculty/elhauge/pdf/gpo_report_june_02.pdf (arguing that it is not sufficient to ask whether a bundled discount could exclude an equally efficient competitor, for such discounts may be used to prevent rivals from growing and thereby attaining scale efficiencies).

[114] Lao, *supra* note 18, at 447 ("The existence, or even the potential entry, of a less efficient rival can, in fact, constrain a monopolist, thereby benefiting consumers, and its exclusion would harm consumer welfare."); Salop, *supra* note 24, at 328–29 (noting that "unencumbered (potential) entry of less-efficient competitors often raises consumer welfare"); Hovenkamp, *supra* note 11, at 154 (noting that equally efficient rival test "can underdeter in situations where the rival that is most likely to emerge is less efficient than the dominant firm").

[115] Lao, *supra* note 18, at 447; see also Salop, *supra* note 24, at 328–29 (offering similar example).

detailed factual inquiry that would likely have to be resolved at trial by a finder of fact—usually a jury. That is troubling, because antitrust issues are notoriously difficult for juries to comprehend,[116] and the risk of an arbitrary damages award—automatically trebled[117]—is quite significant. Business firms, recognizing this risk, may forego conduct that is pro-competitive on the whole but might not be recognized as such by a bunch of overwhelmed jurors.[118]

First consider the consumer welfare effect test set forth in the Areeda-Hovenkamp treatise.[119] That test deems conduct exclusionary if it is "reasonably capable of creating, enlarging or prolonging monopoly power by impairing the opportunities of rivals" and either does not benefit consumers at all or is not necessary for the claimed consumer benefits or produces harms disproportionate to the benefits produced.[120] Under that test, practically all mixed bag conduct would have to be evaluated by a jury. A court could grant summary judgment only if the conduct at issue was not "reasonably capable of creating, enlarging or prolonging monopoly power by impairing the opportunities of rivals" (in which case the defendant would be entitled to summary judgment) or if the conduct caused exclusion

[116] Consider, for example, Professor Arthur Austin's account of his post-trial interviews of the *Brooke Group* jurors. Austin concluded that "the jurors were overwhelmed, frustrated, and confused by testimony well beyond their comprehension" and that "at no time did any juror grasp—even at the margins—the law, the economics or any other testimony relating to the allegations or defense." Arthur Austin, The Jury System at Risk from Complexity, the New Media, and Deviancy, 73 Denv. U. L. Rev. 51 (1995).

[117] See 15 U.S.C. § 15 (providing for automatic trebling of damages in most civil antitrust suits).

[118] Professor Elhauge, for example, observes that

> firms must operate under the risk that the actual criteria by which their conduct will be judged will depend largely on the happenstance of which judge and jurors will be selected in a trial a great number of years later that will retroactively decide whether to assess multimillion or even multibillion dollar treble damages. Further, firms run the risk that different judges or juries will reach inconsistent conclusions about the legality of their conduct based on different implicit normative criteria. These sorts of risks cannot help but chill investments to create product offerings with a sufficient quality or cost advantage over preexisting market options. . . .

Elhauge, *supra* note 15, at 266–67.

[119] 3 Areeda & Hovenkamp, *supra* note 30, ¶ 651a at 72 (discussed *supra* in notes 30–34 and accompanying text).

[120] See *Id.*

but created no consumer benefit (in which case the plaintiff would be entitled to summary judgment on the exclusionary conduct element). All other cases would raise fact issues regarding the necessity of the conduct for the claimed consumer benefit and the degree to which the benefits of the conduct exceeded the costs thereof.[121] Given the prospects of an adverse verdict awarding treble damages, firms would do well to avoid any conduct—even efficiency-enhancing conduct—that could impair rivals' opportunities and thereby create, enlarge, or prolong monopoly or monopsony power.

On first glance, the sacrifice-based tests would seem to avoid this problem, for they call for a much more focused inquiry and create an apparent safe harbor for conduct that would enhance profits apart from an increase in market power. In actual practice, however, the sacrifice-based tests are likely to be similarly indeterminate and thus susceptible to arbitrary jury verdicts and the over-deterrence they generate. To apply the profit sacrifice or no economic sense test, a court would compare the defendant's expected profits without the allegedly exclusionary practice to what its profits would have been with the practice if there were no price-raising (or input cost-lowering) resulting from enhanced monopoly (or monopsony) power.[122] This gets quite complicated when the conduct at issue is likely to result in some efficiency enhancements and some increase in market power.[123] Because the key question is whether the conduct would be profitable but for the enhancement of market power, the fact-finder must: (1) determine the cost to the defendant of engaging in the conduct at issue, (2) ascertain the incremental revenue gain resulting from the conduct at issue, (3) estimate the portion of that revenue gain attributable to an increase in market power, (4) subtract

[121] In *Weyerhaeuser*, for example, plaintiff Ross-Simmons could easily have shown that defendant Weyerhaeuser's overbidding was reasonably capable of creating or enlarging monopsony power, see *supra* note 89 and accompanying text, so the case would have had to go to a jury to determine whether the conduct produced harms disproportionate to any consumer benefits.

[122] Salop, *supra* note 24, at 319 (discussing implementation of profit sacrifice test and its no economic sense variant).

[123] Indeed, Gregory Werden, an advocate of the no economic sense version of the test, admits as much. Werden, *supra* note 33, at 415–16 ("The application of the test can be difficult . . . if the defendant benefits from the conduct absent any tendency to eliminate competition, because the test may then require an analysis of a competitive environment quite different from that which currently exists.").

that amount from the total incremental revenue gain, and (5) compare the remaining incremental revenue gain to the cost of engaging in the conduct at issue. Only if the nonmarket power-induced revenue enhancement exceeds the cost of engaging in the conduct is such conduct non-exclusionary.[124]

An approach that asked whether challenged conduct raised rivals' costs unjustifiably would almost always send challenged conduct to the jury for an open-ended, unpredictable evaluation. If justifiability were assessed on a case-by-case basis, jurors would be called on to conduct a highly indeterminate "totality of the circumstances" inquiry. Even under the more structured approach advocated by Professor Elhauge, who has acknowledged the need to provide determinate standards,[125] arbitrary jury decisions would be inevitable. Elhauge defines "justifiable" cost-raising as that which occurs because of an enhancement in the defendant's efficiency; cost-raising occurring *regardless* of an increase in the defendant's efficiency is per se unjustifiable.[126] On first glance, the fact-finder's task appears simple: determine whether the increase in rivals' costs is a byproduct of an enhancement in the defendant's efficiency.[127] In actual practice, though, that inquiry gets quite messy.

Consider, for example, a challenge to a firm's 12% loyalty rebate on purchases over 1,000 units. Suppose that a rival firm claimed that this structured discount usurped so much business from the rival that it fell below minimum efficient scale (i.e., its per-unit costs were raised). The jury, then, would have to determine whether that cost-raising was justifiable. Suppose that the defendant demonstrated that it was running its factories at 70% capacity prior to

[124] In *Weyerhaeuser*, for example, the fact-finder would have had to (1) determine what it cost Weyerhaeuser to overbid, (2) predict how much Weyerhaeuser's total revenues were expected to increase because of the overbidding, (3) figure what percentage of that expected increase would be due to monopsony power, and (4) compare the remaining expected revenue enhancement to the cost of the overbidding to determine whether the overbidding would have made economic sense but for the enhancement in monopsony power.

[125] See *supra* note 118.

[126] See *supra* note 27.

[127] Elhauge, *supra* note 15, at 256 (arguing that the only tolerable conduct that raises rivals' costs is that which "successfully impair[s] rival efficiency only as a byproduct of the defendant improving its own efficiency").

offering the discount and that the discount increased sales so that the factories were run at 90% capacity, creating apparent economies of scale. If the plaintiff could show (1) that all available efficiencies could be exploited at 80% capacity because incremental scale economies above that level of production were offset by diseconomies occasioned by excessive wear and tear, and (2) that an 8% loyalty rebate would drive production to 80% capacity, then the "excessive" loyalty discount (the additional four percentage points) would appear unjustifiable—i.e., it would raise rivals' costs "regardless of any improvement in defendant efficiency."[128] Of course, it would be a Herculean task to determine the level of production at which economies of scale are maximized and the size of any structured discount necessary to achieve that level. But that is precisely the task a jury would confront under a raising rivals' cost test. Arbitrary verdicts—and the chilling effect they inspire—would inevitably result.

C. *Why the Equally Efficient Rival's Under-Deterrence Is of Less Concern than Other Approaches' Over-Deterrence*

We have seen that a liability rule requiring a plaintiff to establish exclusion of an equally efficient rival is somewhat under-deterrent but that the other proposed tests for exclusionary conduct are likely to over-deter. The key question, then, is whether the social loss resulting from the equally efficient rival test's under-deterrence is likely to outweigh that stemming from the other tests' over-deterrence, or vice-versa. While a detailed accounting of the welfare losses occasioned by the various tests is beyond the scope of this article, there are good reasons to suspect that the equally efficient rival test's under-deterrence is the better poison.

As noted above, the equally efficient rival test may produce false negatives for two reasons: it does not condemn practices that prevent rivals from becoming as efficient as the defendant, and it may permit exclusion of the only competition a dominant firm is likely to face if that competition is less efficient than the dominant firm.[129] The

[128] Elhauge, *supra* note 15, at 330.

[129] See *supra* notes 108–14 and accompanying text. (As noted, it is of no concern that the equally efficient rival test could approve socially useless conduct that would exclude less efficient rivals. A generalized test for exclusionary conduct is needed only when the challenged conduct presents a "mixed bag" of pro-competitive benefits and anti-competitive harms. See *supra* note 111 and accompanying text.)

first concern is not that great, for a broader definition of exclusionary conduct under Section 2—a definition that would capture conduct that could prevent rivals from achieving equivalent efficiency—would not provide much benefit in terms of *added* deterrence. That is because most of the means by which a defendant might attempt to prevent rivals from attaining equivalent efficiency either (1) are already regulated by another legal provision; (2) would be permitted, regardless of the governing test for exclusionary conduct, by immunities or safe harbors; or (3) could not succeed against a smaller rival that is both aggressive and competent.

To see this point, consider the various means by which a defendant could prevent rivals from achieving equivalent efficiencies. Most obviously, the defendant could engage in practices that would prevent rivals from reaching minimum efficient scale. For example, the defendant could engage in exclusive dealing or tying, both of which have the effect of foreclosing rivals from marketing opportunities.[130] It could also achieve foreclosure by offering discounts that have the effect of usurping business from rivals.[131] Alternatively, it might engage in more direct means of foreclosure by, for example, paying dealers not to carry rivals' products. If the defendant controlled an asset that rivals needed to access in order to grow to minimum efficient scale, it could deny access to that asset.[132]

In addition to denying rivals scale, a defendant might prevent rivals from attaining equivalent efficiency by taking steps to drive up the price of an input. Of course, the defendant would have to ensure that the price of the input rose for rivals only and not for itself; otherwise, the strategy would not render rivals *relatively* inefficient.[133]

[130] See Hovenkamp, *supra* note 37, at 199–201 (explaining how both exclusive dealing and tying, while often procompetitive, can lead to market foreclosure).

[131] *Id.* at 171–74 (explaining how structured discounts such as loyalty or bundled discounts can lead to market foreclosure); *Id.* at 161–62 (discussing foreclosure effects of predatory and limit pricing).

[132] See generally Phillip Areeda & Herbert Hovenkamp, 3A Antitrust Law ¶ 772a, at 174 (2d ed. 2002) (explaining "intuitive appeal" of essential facilities doctrine, which may reach either concerted or unilateral refusals to share).

[133] Thus, Weyerhaeuser-type overbidding, which drives up input prices for all competitors, could not preclude rivals from attaining equivalent efficiencies.

The defendant would therefore need to convince input-suppliers to charge a higher price to rivals than to the defendant.[134]

A third means of preventing equivalent efficiencies could be exploited by defendants who sell a product that must be used in conjunction with the competitive product. By redesigning the complementary product so that it would work with the defendant's version of the competitive product but not with that of rivals, the defendant could force rivals to engage in costly product re-design, thereby reducing their efficiencies relative to the defendant's.[135]

Finally, a defendant might render rivals less efficient by convincing the government to impose some restriction that would raise rivals' costs relative to those of the defendant.[136] For example, a defendant might lobby regulators to require all competitors to adopt design specifications the defendant was already utilizing.

While all of these strategies could plausibly prevent less efficient rivals from becoming as efficient as a defendant and therefore would not be condemned as exclusionary under the equally efficient rival test, that possibility does not provide a compelling reason for rejecting the test in Section 2 cases. Expanding Section 2 liability to reach the aforementioned practices would provide little in the way of additional deterrence. First, many of the practices are already adequately regulated. Any exclusionary practice involving concerted conduct—an agreement—is covered by Section 1 of the Sherman Act.[137] Thus, tying, exclusive dealing, concerted refusals to deal,

[134]This would require some sort of agreement between the defendant and input suppliers.

[135]See Phillip E. Areeda, Herbert Hovenkamp & Einer Elhauge, 10 Antitrust Law ¶ 1757a, at 317 (2d ed. 2004) (recognizing that "if a defendant has market power in a primary product that works better with his complementary product than with rival versions, this technological interdependence may have the 'practical effect' of foreclosing rivals in the complementary market" and proposing liability in very limited circumstances that would include, inter alia, redesign to create incompatibility).

[136]Phillip E. Areeda & Herbert Hovenkamp, 1 Antitrust Law ¶ 201, at 145 (2d ed. 2002) ("Collaborators or a single firm might use the machinery of government to obtain, maintain, or strengthen market power. Such a use could thus restrain trade or be an exclusionary practice if the behavior is improper, unlawful, not privileged, appropriate for inquiry by the antitrust court (or agency), and significant in result.").

[137]15 U.S.C. § 1 (prohibiting every "contract, combination . . . , or conspiracy" that unreasonably restrains trade).

agreements with dealers not to carry a rival's products, and agreements with the other owners or controllers of a jointly owned/controlled essential facility—behaviors that could reduce a rival's scale and render it relatively less efficient—are all regulated subject to well-established liability tests implementing Section 1's prohibition of unreasonable restraints of trade. The same would be true for any agreement with input suppliers that caused them to charge a higher price to rivals.

Of the remaining practices that might reduce rivals' efficiencies, many would be permissible—even if they were deemed "exclusionary" under the governing test—by immunities or safe harbors. Most exclusionary practices involving the procurement of government regulations, for example, would be permitted by the Noerr-Pennington doctrine, which removes most governmental petitioning from antitrust scrutiny.[138] Re-design of a complementary product would likely be protected under safe harbors that have been proposed as part of the other tests for exclusionary conduct.[139] And the Supreme Court has recently hinted that there can be no antitrust liability based on denial of access to an essential facility controlled exclusively by the defendant.[140]

The remaining practices on the laundry list of acts that could prevent rivals from attaining efficiencies involve discounting. While below-cost discounting and some above-cost "bundled" discounting would run afoul of the equally efficient rival test,[141] even some above-cost, single product discounting may prevent rivals from attaining

[138] See generally 1 Areeda & Hovenkamp, *supra* note 136, at ¶¶ 200–12 (summarizing Noerr-Pennington petitioning immunity and its "sham" exception).

[139] See, e.g., Werden, *supra* note 33, at 419 (proposing that no economic sense test include a safe harbor for new product introduction, improved product quality, and cost-reducing innovations because "the tools of antitrust are too blunt to make it worthwhile to attempt to the identification of rare exceptions" to the general rule that such conduct benefits consumers); 3 Areeda & Hovenkamp, *supra* note 30, ¶ 651b, (proposing that consumer welfare effect test include a safe harbor for "improved product quality, energetic market penetration, successful research and development, cost-reducing innovations, and the like").

[140] See Verizon Communications, Inc. v. Law Offices of Curtis V. Trinko, LLP, 540 U.S. 398, 410–11 & n.3 (2004) (declining to recognize or repudiate an "essential facilities" doctrine in case involving unilateral denial of access and taking pains to distinguish cases imposing liability for concerted denial of access).

[141] To compete with a defendant's below-cost price, a rival with equivalent efficiencies would have to price below its own costs. If it lacked the financial reserves to weather such a money-losing strategy, it could be driven out of business. With respect

equivalent efficiencies. For example, commentators have argued that so-called "limit pricing" (discounting from the profit-maximizing price level to a level that is below competitors' costs but still above one's own costs) and above-cost "loyalty discounts" (discounts or rebates that are conditioned upon meeting a certain purchase target) may be used to prevent rivals from growing to minimum efficient scale and thereby attaining equivalent efficiencies.[142] It seems, though, that an aggressive and competent rival confronting these sorts of practices would not be prevented from attaining equivalent efficiencies. If the disadvantaged rival's product was as good as the discounter's and could be produced as cheaply at minimum efficient scale, the rival should be able to raise enough capital to fund any discount necessary to grow its market share to the point necessary to achieve minimum efficient scale.[143] Its below-cost pricing for the period required to achieve such a scale would not amount to predation because there would be no likelihood of recoupment via supra-competitive pricing.[144]

It seems, then, that most of the practices that would prevent rivals from achieving minimum efficient scale are either regulated by other

to "bundled" discounts (i.e., discounts conditioned upon purchasing products from multiple product markets), even some discounts that are above-cost—in that the discounted price exceeds the aggregate cost of the products in the bundle—may exclude equally efficient competitors that do not produce as broad a line of products. See Thomas A. Lambert, Evaluating Bundled Discounts, 89 Minn. L. Rev. 1688, 1695–97 (2005).(explaining how bundled discount could exclude equally efficient, but less diversified, rival).

[142] Hovenkamp, *supra* note 37, at 162 (limit pricing); Tom et al., *supra* note 26, at 627–29 (loyalty discounts).

[143] See Phillip E. Areeda & Herbert Hovenkamp, Antitrust Law ¶ 421b, at 67 (2d ed. 2002) ("If capital markets are working well, new investment will be made in any market earning anything above competitive returns—a term defined to include sufficient profit to attract new capital—regardless of the absolute cost of entry."); George J. Stigler, The Organization of Industry 67–69 (1968); Harold Demsetz, Barriers to Entry, 72 Am. Econ. Rev. 47, 49–53 (1982); Harold Demsetz, Industry Structure, Market Rivalry, and Public Policy, 16 J. L. & Econ. 1, 4 (1973). But see Richard R. Nelson, Comments on a Paper by Posner, 127 U. Pa. L. Rev. 949, 950 (1979) ("The Chicago proposition that scale economies don't serve as a barrier to entry hinges on explicit or implicit assumptions about perfect capital markets and no adjustment lags or costs.").

[144] See Brooke Group Ltd. v. Brown & Williamson Tobacco Corp., 509 U.S. 209, 222–24 (1993) (positing the likelihood of recoupment via future monopoly pricing as prerequisite to a valid predation claim).

prohibitions besides Section 2, or subject to immunities or safe harbors that would prevent condemnation under Section 2, or unlikely to succeed against aggressive and competent rivals. Accordingly, the first source of the equally efficient rival test's under-deterrence is of little concern.

That leaves the second source of under-deterrence and raises the following question: In order to preserve rivals that are less efficient than the dominant firm but may constrain its exercise of market power, does it make sense to adopt a broader definition of exclusionary conduct under Section 2? Probably not. Monopoly profits provide a powerful incentive to enter monopolized markets, and it is quite difficult for monopolists to continually fight off new entrants.[145] For that reason, there are very few "real" monopolies—i.e., markets in which a single seller faces no meaningful competition. By contrast, mixed bag business practices that are pro-competitive on the whole are ubiquitous and are conceived of all the time. A broader, harder to apply test for exclusionary conduct would stymie those efficiency-enhancing practices, and since they are far more common than unchecked monopolies, it is more important to avoid thwarting them than to insure against the uncommon and unstable case of unchecked monopoly.[146]

In addition, a somewhat under-deterrent definition for exclusionary conduct is appropriate because significant over-deterrence is already built into Section 2. Successful antitrust plaintiffs are generally entitled to treble damages.[147] This damages multiplier, designed to account for the chance that a violation may go undetected or may

[145] Frank H. Easterbrook, The Limits of Antitrust, 63 Tex. L. Rev. 1, 2 (1984).

[146] As Judge Easterbrook has explained, the harms related to false positives and false negatives are incommensurate:

> If the court errs by condemning a beneficial practice, the benefits may be lost for good. Any other firm that uses the condemned practice faces sanctions in the name of stare decisis, no matter the benefits. If the court errs by permitting a deleterious practice, though, the welfare loss decreases over time. Monopoly is self-destructive. Monopoly prices eventually attract entry. True, this long run may be a long time coming, with loss to society in the interim. The central purpose of antitrust is to speed up the arrival of the long run. But this should not obscure the point: judicial errors that tolerate baleful practices are self-correcting while erroneous condemnations are not.

Id. at 2–3.

[147] 15 U.S.C. § 15.

not be successfully prosecuted, makes sense for clandestine practices that are unquestionably bad, such as price-fixing conspiracies. Trebling seems inappropriate, though, when the challenged conduct is a mixed bag practice that is conducted out in the open.[148] Awarding treble damages to plaintiffs who successfully challenge such conduct will invite lawsuits of little merit (it's easy to bring the lawsuit, and the payoff could be huge) and will thus tend to deter candid business practices that are pro-competitive on the whole but difficult to characterize and might, if challenged, be deemed to violate some provision of the antitrust laws.[149] The practices to be evaluated under a generalized definition of exclusionary conduct are precisely the sorts of practices for which trebling is overly deterrent: they are mixed bag practices and they are conducted unilaterally (so they do not involve secret collusion). For that reason, a somewhat under-deterrent liability standard may function as a salutary corrective.

D. Some Examples: Loyalty and Bundled Discounts

Brief consideration of two business practices that have recently been challenged as exclusionary demonstrates the superiority of the equally efficient rival test in Section 2 cases. Both loyalty discounts and bundled discounts[150] offer some pro-competitive benefits (most obviously, consumer-friendly price competition) but may tend to exclude rivals from the discounter's market.[151] They are precisely the sort of mixed bag, unilateral practice for which a general exclusionary conduct test is useful. It is thus helpful to compare how challenges to the practices would proceed under the various approaches.

Under each of the rejected approaches, challenges to either practice would almost automatically require jury consideration. Under sacrifice-based tests, the jury would have to determine whether some

[148] See Hovenkamp, *supra* note 37, at 66–68; Posner, *supra* note 19, at 271–73.

[149] Hovenkamp, *supra* note 37, at 67.

[150] Loyalty discounts are discounts or rebates on all purchases of some product once the purchaser meets a certain purchase target, such as *x* percent of its requirements. Bundled discounts are discounts or rebates conditioned on purchasing multiple goods from different product markets. See Lambert, *supra* note 144, at 1693–95, 1706–08 (describing bundled and loyalty, or "single-product purchase target," discounts).

[151] *Id.* at 1706–07 (explaining how loyalty rebates could exclude); *Id.* at 1695–97 (explaining how bundled discounts could exclude).

increment of the discount or rebate made no economic sense but for its ability to exclude rivals. (For example, if the discount were 10%, would the discounter, absent an exercise of market power, have been better off offering a 7% discount? If so, the incremental three percentage points of discount would make no economic sense but for the market power it created and would thus be exclusionary.) The consumer welfare effect test would require the jury to balance the consumer benefits of the discount against the consumer harms that could result if the discount impaired rivals and enhanced the discounter's market power. Raising rivals' costs approaches would require the jury to determine whether any impairment of rivals' efficiencies resulting from reduced scale was justified. Under Professor Elhauge's test for justifiability, the jury would have to determine whether the discount was greater than necessary to achieve whatever productive or distributional efficiencies it created; if so, the excess discount would raise rivals costs "regardless of any improvement in defendant efficiency" and would thus be unreasonably exclusionary.[152] Given the near inevitability that a challenge to loyalty or bundled discounting would result in jury consideration and a potential adverse treble damages verdict under these three approaches, the approaches would likely deter many consumer-friendly discounts. Indeed, two decisions that gave juries great leeway to evaluate the legality of structured discounts—the district court decision in *Concord Boat*[153] and the en banc Third Circuit decision in *LePage's*[154]—created significant concern for firms contemplating such discounts.[155]

By contrast, if loyalty or bundled discounts were evaluated under the equally efficient rival test, firms considering such discount programs could rely on genuine safe harbors. With respect to loyalty

[152] Elhauge, *supra* note 15, at 330.

[153] Concord Boat Corp. v. Brunswick Corp., 21 F. Supp. 2d 923, 929–30 (E.D. Ark. 1998) (denying defendant's motion for judgment as a matter of law in case involving above-cost loyalty discounts), rev'd 207 F.3d 1039 (8th Cir. 2000).

[154] LePage's Inc. v. 3M, 324 F.3d 141 (3d Cir. 2003) (en banc) (upholding jury verdict imposing Section 2 liability based on above-cost bundled discounts), cert. denied, 542 U.S. 953 (2004).

[155] Cf. Antitrust Modernization Commission, Report and Recommendations 94 (2007), available at http://www.amc.gov/report_recommendation/amc_final_report.pdf ("[T]he Third Circuit's [LePage's] decision is likely to discourage firms from offering procompetitive bundled discounts and rebates to consumers.").

discounts, firms would not need to worry about any discount that resulted in a discounted price that was still above the discounter's cost; any such discount could be met by, and thus would not exclude, an equally efficient rival.[156] Bundled discounts are a different competitive animal, for they may drive equally efficient rivals from the market even if they result in an above-cost price for the collection of items in the bundle.[157] Still, if such discounts were evaluated under the equally efficient rival test for exclusionary conduct, genuine safe harbors would exist. I have elsewhere detailed one safe harbor—i.e., a set of circumstances in which no equally efficient rival would be excluded by a bundled discount.[158] In addition, the *Ortho* court, implicitly relying on the equally efficient rival approach to identifying exclusionary conduct, created a safe harbor for bundled discounts by requiring that plaintiffs challenging such discounts prove either that the discounts resulted in a below-cost price for the bundle or that they were as efficient as the discounter but were not able to compete because of the discount.[159] Under that rule, a firm that knew it was the most efficient competitor could offer bundled discounts without fear of liability. Thus, the equally efficient rival test creates clear safe harbors. In light of the realities of antitrust litigation and the limited abilities of juries to resolve complicated economic questions, the test is therefore less likely than the rejected approaches to deter above-cost loyalty and bundled discounts, as well as other mixed bag practices that are pro-competitive on the whole but that might be deemed exclusionary by perplexed jurors.

V. Conclusion

Just last year, Professor Steven Salop curtly dismissed "the *Brooke Group* standard," which ultimately focuses on whether the conduct at issue could exclude an equally efficient rival, by observing that

[156] In reversing the district court and holding that the *Concord Boat* defendant's conduct could not give rise to antitrust liability absent proof that the discount resulted in below-cost pricing, the Eighth Circuit created this sort of safe harbor for above-cost loyalty discounts. See Concord Boat Corp. v. Brunswick Corp., 207 F.3d 1039, 1061–63 (8th Cir. 2000).

[157] See Lambert, *supra* note 141, at 1695–96.

[158] See *id.* at 1742–53.

[159] Ortho Diagnostic Sys., Inc. v. Abbott Labs., Inc., 920 F. Supp. 455, 469 (S.D.N.Y. 1996) (setting forth test for evaluating legality of bundled discount).

it "is not generally proposed as the liability standard for exclusionary conduct other than predatory pricing."[160] After *Weyerhaeuser*, the equally efficient rival standard cannot be so limited. Indeed, the other proposed definitions of exclusionary conduct would have mandated a different outcome in *Weyerhaeuser*, and the Supreme Court thus appears to have implicitly rejected those standards in favor of the equally efficient rival standard.

In doing so, the Court adhered to Voltaire's prudent maxim, "The perfect is the enemy of the good."[161] The equally efficient rival standard, while good, is admittedly imperfect: it is under-deterrent. On the other hand, its more "perfect" competitors—those that would more exhaustively condemn practices that could be anti-competitive in the long run—would entail administrative difficulties that would almost certainly result in the over-deterrence of practices that are, on the whole, pro-competitive. Because the welfare loss from such over-deterrence would likely outweigh that occasioned by the equally efficient rival test's under-deterrence, the *Weyerhaeuser* Court was wise to forego the perfect in favor of the good.

[160] Salop, *supra* note 24, at 318.

[161] Le mieux est ennemi du bien, Voltaire, La Begueule, 3 Recueil des Meilleurs Contes en vers 77, 77 (1778).

Punitive Damages and the Supreme Court: A Tragedy in Five Acts

Michael I. Krauss[1]*

The United States Supreme Court has had a stormy relationship with punitive damages over the last twenty years. The Court had largely ignored this issue before then—but as we will see, that is because punitive damages were not "company-busters" until relatively recently. Our Supreme Court is not a legislature, of course: its constitutional role is *not* to reform ill-advised state law (almost all punitive damage awards arise from state law), but rather only to strike down lower court decisions grounded in a rule or a process that violates the federal Constitution. Now that the punitive component of a single tort award can bankrupt a corporation, with of course repercussions on third parties (shareholders and employees), the constitutional implications of such awards are different than they used to be.

To understand and evaluate the Supreme Court's recent constitutional analyses of the punitives, it is necessary to understand how tort law fits in our legal system. That is where this brief essay will begin.

I. Tort Law and Private Ordering

Political-legal philosophers conventionally distinguish aspects of law that regulate *private ordering* from those that regulate *public ordering*.[2]

- *Private ordering* describes juridical regulation of interactions between citizens: property law, contracts, torts, and family law

*Professor of Law, George Mason University School of Law.

[1]An earlier version of this article appeared in *Engage*, the scholarly publication of the Federalist Society.

[2]See generally Michael I. Krauss, Tort Law and Private Ordering, 35 St. Louis U. L.J. 623 (1991).

essentially regulate this ordering. These areas of the law provide the rules we need to self-determine, in a way, to live our lives as free and responsible human beings.

- *Public ordering* describes the juridical regulation of interactions between a citizen and the state. Criminal law, administrative law, tax law, and welfare law are all part of public ordering, which provides us with the rules we need to know our rights and obligations vis-à-vis government.

Public ordering is the *only* kind of legal order in a totalitarian society, where citizens are not trusted to self-regulate their affairs. In a totalitarian society, even one governed by legal processes, there's no such thing as *property*, as we know it—rather, there are (provisional) grants from the state, returnable to the state *via* administrative law. Nor is there *contract* law between consenting adults, since private contracts would allow a form of self-governance without state authorization—incompatible with totalitarianism. Finally, totalitarian societies can have no true *tort* law—there's no such thing as a private wrong if only the state can be wronged. If one does something the state considers wrong, criminal law takes over. In a totalitarian society, therefore, administrative law and criminal law take the place of contract, property, and tort.

Tort law may be maligned by demagogic politicians, but it is an essential component of our freedom. Tort law is contract law's flip side—tort privately regulates *non-contractual* behavior among humans, obliging them to make good harm wrongfully caused to others. In a free society, criminal law is accompanied by myriad constitutional protections (such as the constitutional protection against self-incrimination, the double jeopardy rule, and the strong presumption of innocence) precisely because its threat to liberty is so different from that of tort law.

When property becomes a loan from the state, when all contracts are with the state, when tort law gives way to crimes, then private ordering will have been dissolved and only public ordering left standing. A monopoly of public ordering is incompatible with a society of free and responsible individuals.

II. Introduction to Tort Damages

A. Punitive Damages

In my view the moral foundation of tort law, seen as a component of private ordering, is *corrective justice*. When one citizen wrongs another, the wrongdoer must correct the (private) injustice he has caused. Tort law, under the doctrine of "sovereign immunity," did not originally cover injustices caused by wrongful state behavior; rather, the right of revolution was originally the only remedy for state torts. Today that is no longer the case, and many state wrongs are subject to private tort recovery.

Without a wrong there is no corrective justice requirement. An efficient businessman who, through acceptable practices, out-competes his competitor owes that competitor nothing as a matter of corrective justice, even though the competitor has suffered possibly devastating losses. Causing a loss incurs no tort liability. *Wrongfully* causing a loss creates the corrective justice requirement of compensation.

Analogously, wrongful behavior *that causes no damages* creates no corrective justice requirement. Driving home while drunk may be criminal (public ordering requires no victims—the affront is to "society" or "the state") and is also quite negligent (wrongful), if it exposes others on the road to excessive danger. Nonetheless, if a drunk driver gets home without hitting anyone, he has no tort liability. He may well have committed a *crime*—a matter for public ordering, with all the protections provided when the might of the state is directed at an individual. But he owes compensation to no one because his conduct, though wrongful, did no private harm.

It is the *conjunction of wrongfulness and the harm caused thereby* that creates the tort obligation. Typically, that obligation consists of compensation, that is, righting the wrong and making good the loss—no more, no less.

Compensation, by definition, must be full to be integral. This means that compensation is not a function of the extent of wrongdoing. A tortfeasor who negligently burns down a $50,000 house is liable in tort to pay $50,000 to compensate for the loss of the house.[3] If the tortfeasor just as negligently burns down a $1 million house, he is liable in tort to pay $1 million to its owner. This is not because tort favors the rich, but because tort *equally respects* poor and rich. Each tort victim has the right to be returned to her former state—that far and no farther—when she is wrongfully harmed. Similarly, rich tortfeasors owe no more to their victims in compensation than

[3] In addition to the cost of temporary lodging, etc.

do poor tortfeasors.[4] *Public* ordering may distinguish between the rich and the poor in sentencing, but private law is blind to wealth—only one's rights "count" with regard to private ordering.

As has likely already been seen, punitive damages do not fit into this scheme of tort law because, by definition, punitive damages are overcompensatory.

Nevertheless, in one deceptive and in one symbolic form, something called punitive damages was present at tort law's inception. Both of these forms can be usefully summarized here:

B. The Deceptive Historic Role of Punitives

In medieval days criminal and tort trials were combined. After all, what we today call *intentional torts*, such as battery and trespass, typically constituted both a crime (a breach of the peace punishable by the state) and a tort (some kind of harm wrongfully caused to a citizen). Both were adjudicated in the same judicial proceeding. For instance, a battery may have caused $10 in injury, payable to the plaintiff. In the days before police forces, this plaintiff was also the only one who had a strong incentive to track down and arrest the batterer. This plaintiff could also pursue the equivalent of a criminal fine (the amounts were tiny by today's monetary standards). The plaintiff was in a sense a private attorney general, prosecuting the criminal case, so the fine went into his coffers.

Today we have paid attorneys general and prosecutors, and fines are collected in public ordering settings. Those fines are subject to cherished American constitutional protections, as I noted above:

- The Double Jeopardy prohibition against multiple fines for the same offense;
- The Fifth Amendment protection against self-incrimination;
- The Eighth Amendment protection against excessive fines.

A tort trial today offers none of those protections: compulsory "discovery" may lead to involuntary inculpation of a tortfeasor, one tort committed may lead to several successful lawsuits, etc.

[4]Of course, if the tortfeasor is so poor that he has insufficient assets to compensate (and insufficient insurance to make him solvent), then he cannot be adequately reached in tort. We used to have debtors' prisons to take care of this issue—making tortfeasors "work off" their indebtedness—but that solution is now seen as inhumane. Thus, destitute people cannot be reached in tort. Many people in prison are destitute, of course.

In its deceptive form, punitive damages are an anachronism with no place in tort today. Criminal law with all its apparatus has essentially swept aside the combined tort/criminal suits, and anyway the Constitution doesn't allow them. But there is still a symbolic role for punitives in common law tort.

C. A Symbolic Place for Punitives

Punitive damages were also granted as symbolic damages in common law cases, when there was deliberate wrongdoing and real but unknowable or *de minimis* harm. For example, if A slandered B, but B could not prove exactly how much business he had lost because of the slander, A might be condemned to pay B $1. If A deliberately and flagrantly trespassed on B's land, but didn't trample any of B's crops, B could still sue A for $1.

The damages in such cases were symbolic: they recognized that one party was in the right, had been intentionally wronged by the other party, and had been damaged in a non-obviously quantifiable way. Suits like these might be filed because victory was itself a vindication of one's rights, and also because a "loser-pays rule" (in effect outside America) means that the tortfeasor would have to pay both his and his victim's lawyer's costs.

Thus, classical punitives were either (when substantial) disguised criminal fines (before the state criminal apparatus was organized and constitutional protections were enacted), or symbolic sums meant to vindicate intentional but hard-to-quantify violations of a plaintiff's rights. Since constitutional protections exist today, all that should remain are the small symbolic "vindication" awards.

The growth of substantial modern punitive damages is, I submit, a product of confusion between private and public ordering. Happily, four states' (Louisiana, Nebraska, Washington, and Massachusetts) supreme courts have declared that their common law of tort does not permit these punitive damages.[5] A fifth state (New Hampshire) abolished modern punitives by statute.[6] Any state in the union could

[5]See, e.g., Int'l Harvester Credit Corp. v. Seale, 518 So.2d 1039, 1041 (La. 1988); Distinctive Printing & Packaging Co. v. Cox, 443 N.W.2d 566, 574 (Neb. 1989); Dailey v. North Coast Life Ins. Co., 919 P.2d 589, 590–91 (Wash. 1996); Fleshner v. Technical Communications Corp., 575 N.E.2d 1107, 1112 (Mass. 1991).

[6]N.H. Rev. Stat. Ann. § 507:16 (1997).

abolish substantial punitive damages if it chose to, without federal constitutional impediment.

III. The Supreme Court and Punitive Damages: A Play in Six Parts (So Far . . .)

States vary tremendously in their rules about punitive damages. As just stated, a handful have no punitives at all. Quite a few other states allow punitive damages for intentional torts and gross negligence, but with a global monetary cap.[7] Other states have partial limitations on punitives, some of which may be unconstitutional.[8] Finally, many states have no limitation on punitives at all.

Yet, in all states punitive damages were mostly symbolic until the 1980s. *Up to 1976, the highest punitive damages award in the entire country was $250,000, a sobering observation in light of recent multibillion-dollar punitive awards.*

Starting in the late 1980s, though, some punitive awards in amounts, heretofore unheard of, were handed down. Defendants naturally protested that their constitutional rights were abridged by these new, non-compensatory awards. After all, these awards were for amounts that did not correspond to any harm they had wrongfully caused; they could be repeated many times for the same wrongdoing, if different persons sued them; they resulted from the compelled production of "self-incriminating" evidence through discovery; they could be granted if the fact finder believed them warranted "by a preponderance of the evidence," not "beyond a reasonable doubt"; and there seemed to be no limit on the amount that could be assessed. Imagine a criminal law in which violations are punishable by a fine, the amount of which will be determined by the ruler, at his discretion, with no presumption of innocence and after a forced confession. Such a law might lead us to dump tea in the nearest harbor. Analogously, modern punitive damages developments were shocking and seemed contrary to the basic nature of private ordering.

No small wonder that constitutional appeals to our nation's highest court followed. Obviously, every time one of these challenges

[7] In the case of Virginia, for example, the cap on punitive awards is $350,000. Va. Code Ann. §§ 8.01–38.1 (2000).

[8] See, e.g., Reynolds v Porter, 760 P.2d 816 (Okla. 1988) (holding that a state statute eliminating punitive damages only in medical malpractice cases violates the state constitution).

happened, by definition the complaining party was usually a pretty bad guy—not an "attractive client," as lawyers say . . .

Anyway, our Supreme Court play begins in 1989, with the case of *Browning-Ferris Industries.*[9]

A. Browning-Ferris Indus., Inc. v. Kelco Disposal, Inc. *(Vermont 1989)*

Browning-Ferris International (BFI) operates a nationwide commercial waste-collection and disposal business. In 1973, BFI entered the Burlington, Vermont area trash-collection market, and in 1976, began to offer "roll-off" collection services, which had not previously been available heretofore in the area.[10] Until 1980, BFI was the sole provider of "roll-off" services in Burlington. That year respondent Joseph Kelley, who, since 1973, had been BFI's local district manager, went into business for himself, starting Kelco Disposal, Inc. Within a year Kelco had obtained nearly 40 percent of the Burlington roll-off market. During 1982 BFI reacted to this competition, first by offering to buy Kelco Disposal and then, when Kelly refused to sell his company, by cutting BFI's own prices by 40 percent or more on new business. The orders given to the Burlington BFI office by its regional vice president were clear: one memo read, "Put [Kelco] out of business. . . .if it mean[s] giv[ing] the [service] away, give it away."[11]

Of course in most American jurisdictions, in England, and in economic theory, price competition is not a tort. So-called "predatory pricing" cannot succeed in the long run, as a matter of economic theory, and it didn't work in Burlington, either. BFI kept losing market share as Kelco matched its prices, and BFI threw in the towel when Kelco increased its market share to 56 percent. BFI then left Vermont. Turning the knife in the wound, Kelco sued BFI for the tort of unfair competition. A Vermont jury awarded Kelco $51,000 in lost profits due to BFI's futile effort at predatory pricing.

[9] Browning-Ferris Indus., Inc. v. Kelco Disposal, Inc., 492 U.S. 257 (1989).

[10] Roll-off service alludes to the bin used to store garbage before pickup. They are called "roll-off" bins because they are typically configured with small back wheels. The garbage truck uses a hoist and a tipping bed to roll the bin on and off the use site to and from the truck.

[11] *Id.* at 260–61 (emphasis added).

Normally this would merely be a legally questionable and economically silly decision, of which there are many. What distinguished it, however, was that Kelco's attorney urged the Vermont jury to return an award of punitive damages, asking the jurors to "*deliver a message to Houston* [BFI's headquarters]."[12] The attorney pointed to BFI's world revenues of $1.3 billion, "noting that this figure broke down to $25 million a week."[13] BFI urged that punitive damages were not appropriate at all (of course, BFI believed *no* damages, even compensatory, were due). But the jury socked it to this Texas company that had already left the state—$6 million in punitive damages.[14]

BFI, shell-shocked, asked the trial judge to reverse the punitives award, and when this motion was denied appealed this award to the Vermont Supreme Court and ultimately to the United States Supreme Court. At each level BFI claimed that the award was an excessive fine for the degree of its wrongdoing (which it claimed was zero), and therefore was imposed in violation of BFI's Fourteenth Amendment rights. The Supreme Court, in an 8-1 decision, rejected BFI's claim. Because the $6 million went to Mr. Kelly and not to the State of Vermont, it was not a fine, the majority ruled, and since it was not a fine it could not be an *excessive* fine.

Since BFI had not made a timely Fourteenth Amendment claim, the Supreme Court expressly reserved ruling on any due process argument. In fact, Justices Brennan and Marshall hinted strongly that they thought this kind of punitives award *did* violate BFI's right to due process of law. But these justices would both soon leave the Court.

Justice O'Connor's dissent in this case detailed the history of fines, and showed how substantial punitive damages had, in fact, always been treated as fines.

Note, by the way, that current events put into question even the dubious majority decision. Subsequent to the BFI decision, several states modified their statutes to provide that a certain percentage

[12] *Id.* at 261.

[13] *Id.*

[14] Note the combination of individual, local plaintiff, local jurors, and *out-of-state* corporate defendant with few in-state employees. This turns out to be the common denominator of crazy punitive damages—let's bring some money in state, boys.

of punitive damages (up to 60 percent in some instances) must henceforth be payable to the state government, not to the plaintiffs. This is how Illinois recently received a $3 billion punitive award against Philip Morris in a recent class action tobacco decision from notorious Madison County—30 percent of the total award to the plaintiff is payable to the state under Illinois law. This makes the state an explicit accomplice in the increasing acceleration of punitive awards.

So, Act I ends with a crushing defeat for those who, like me, claimed that tort law prohibits large punitive awards, since they cross the line to become public ordering and are therefore excessive fines.

But the BFI case did hold out the hope that punitives might violate due process of law, because they are not accompanied by the procedural guarantees of public ordering.

This set the stage for Act II:

B. Pacific Mutual Life Ins. Co. v. Haslip *(Alabama 1991)*[15]

Lemmie Ruffin was an insurance agent. He represented many insurance companies, including Pacific Mutual Life.

As Pacific Mutual's agent, Ruffin sold "major medical" health insurance policies to a group of civic employees in Alabama. The employees paid monthly premiums to Ruffin, which he was to forward to the company. The employees kept up with their premiums and thought they had health coverage. In reality, Ruffin had stopped sending money to Pacific Mutual Life, and converted the funds to his own use. The insurance company, thinking the policies were in arrears, gave Ruffin warning letters to deliver to the women (to pay their overdue premiums or have their policies cancelled)—of course Ruffin never transmitted those letters. Finally, when one employee (Ms. Haslip) got very sick, she found she was not covered. Needless to say, she sued Pacific Mutual Insurance for its "bad faith."

An Alabama jury found bad faith and inadequate supervision of Ruffin by the (out-of-state) insurance company. The jury held that Pacific Mutual was liable to Haslip in the amount of $230,000 to cover her hospital bills—a perfectly just tort award, given that Ruffin was Pacific Mutual's agent. But Haslip was not yet done with Pacific

[15] Pacific Mut. Life Ins. Co. v. Haslip, 499 U.S. 1 (1991).

Mutual—she asked for punitive damages. Alabama's punitive damages scheme gave a jury virtually complete discretion in this area. It provided no standard for deciding whether to impose punitives, and no method for calculating them. On the threshold question of whether to impose punitive damages, the trial court instructed the jury as follows: "Imposition of punitive damages is *entirely discretionary* with the jury, that means you don't have to award it unless this jury *feels* that you should do so."[16]

Thus instructed that there was no applicable *law* about the matter, the jury condemned Pacific Mutual to $1 million in punitives.[17] The company appealed all the way to the U.S. Supreme Court, on the grounds that it was deprived of due process by the standardless discretion invested in the local jury and by the huge amount of punitives. Clearly, by the way, the company had had no malice—it was just as defrauded by Ruffin as had been the plaintiff. It had no knowledge of the actions of Ruffin, who was not even its legal employee in any traditional sense.

Pacific Mutual lost its appeal, 7-1. Again only Justice O'Connor dissented. The due process claim that many had thought so promising after the BFI case foundered, as the justices who had espoused it had left the Court. The vague Alabama jury instruction was deemed precise enough to provide legal guidance to the jury.[18] The punitive award of four times compensatory damages was not so exorbitant as to violate due process standards, said the majority.[19] They did say it was "close to the line," however.[20]

Defendants were reeling after this case. (Local) juries seemed to have unfettered discretion to whack (invariably out-of-state) corporations for minor transgressions, though it was felt that the Supreme Court would henceforth at least require some legal standard for the calculation of punitives.

Haslip was disappointing, but the darkest hour had not yet been reached. It would come, in 1993, and Act III.

[16] *Id.* at 6 n.1 (emphasis added).

[17] *Id.*

[18] See *id.* at 19–20.

[19] See *id.* at 23–24. The punitives were "much in excess of the fine that could be imposed for insurance fraud" under Alabama criminal law. *Id.* at 23.

[20] *Id.*

C. *TXO Production Corp. v. Alliance Resources Corp.* (West Virginia, 1993)[21]

TXO and Alliance were engaged in a complex series of negotiations so that TXO could get oil and gas rights to West Virginia land owned by Alliance. They were bickering back and forth on what royalty rate would be paid to Alliance. During these negotiations, a third party claimed that in fact it, not Alliance, owned the rights to the land, by virtue of an obscure deed. TXO then expressed concern that any title it might get to the oil and gas rights was vulnerable to this claim; because of this, it asked for a reduction in its royalty rate to cover against possible precariousness. After more complex and ambiguous declarations on both sides, TXO declared that a deal with Alliance had been reached. Alliance disagreed. TXO then sought, at the West Virginia circuit court, a declaratory judgment that it had in fact acquired from Alliance the resource rights over the land. Alliance defended against this claim, and countersued for what Alliance called "slander of title" (an old English tort that had never once been recognized in the state of West Virginia's entire history). In brief, Alliance asserted that TXO was falsely diminishing public belief in Alliance's property rights. At bottom, this countersuit was an episode in a "hardball" contractual dispute about royalty rates.

That is, until the West Virginia courts got through with it. The trial judge rejected TXO's principal claim that any deal had been reached. The judge let a jury decide whether Alliance's title had been slandered. The jury accepted Alliance's slander of title suit and condemned TXO to pay $19,000 to Alliance (essentially the amount of Alliance's lawyer's costs in defending against the declaratory suit by TXO). Alliance had no other losses.[22]

So far, this sounds unexceptional—the case was a close call in a hardball dispute, TXO lost, and the damages are the equivalent of a loser-pays rule that folks like me have advocated for a long time. I have not yet mentioned that Alliance was a local company, while TXO was a fully owned subsidiary of U.S. Steel. That explains,

[21] TXO Production Corp. v. Alliance Resources Corp., 509 U.S. 443 (1993).

[22] See *id.* at 451.

perhaps, why the jury also condemned TXO to *ten million dollars* in punitive damages, i.e., 526 times the compensatory award.[23]

TXO had great confidence in its appeal. In *Haslip* the punitives were "only" 4 times punitives and the Supreme Court had said this was "close to the line."[24] Moreover, West Virginia's instructions to the jury on punitives were so totally devoid of standards as to make a mockery of the Supreme Court's demand in *Haslip* for at least minimum guidance. [Here was the standard as stated by the West Virginia Supreme Court, when it heard the appeal: We are compelled by the United States Supreme Court to set punitive damages standards if our decision is to pass constitutional scrutiny, so we hereby distinguish between "really mean" defendants and the "really stupid" defendants.[25] For the really *stupid* defendant, punitives can be 10 times compensatories. For the really *mean* defendant, punitives can be 500 times compensatories. Since this defendant "failed to conduct [itself] as a gentleman", it was "really mean", and 526 times punitives is close enough to 500, so we uphold the trial court's award.[26]]

The Supreme Court affirmed the West Virginia Supreme Court's ruling, 6-3, saying that its standard passed constitutional scrutiny. Justices White and Souter joined Justice O'Connor in dissent this time. On the one hand, O'Connor was no longer alone on the court in thinking that there were *some* punitive damage awards that could not pass constitutional muster. On the other hand, this case looked like the mother of all punitive awards, and if six justices found *it* constitutional, one wondered what could possibly offend due process.

This was the darkest hour. It was three years before dawn broke in Act IV.

D. BMW of North America, Inc. v. Gore *(Alabama, 1996)*[27]

Mr. Gore purchased a new BMW from an authorized Alabama dealer. He loved his car until he took it in for service one day, when

[23]This seemed "quite likely" to Justice O'Connor as well. *Id.* at 489 (O'Connor, J., dissenting).

[24]Pacific Mut. Life Ins. Co. v. Haslip, 499 U.S. 1, 23 (1991).

[25]TXO, 509 U.S. at 452 n.15.

[26]See *id.* at 473 (O'Connor, J., dissenting).

[27]BMW of North America, Inc. v. Gore, 517 U.S. 559 (1996).

he was casually informed by a mechanic that a wing of his car had been repainted. It turned out the car had been scratched during maritime transport from Germany. BMW had, it turns out, a nationwide policy of repairing pre-delivery paint chips and scratches to new cars so long as the cost of repair did not exceed 3 percent of the car's suggested retail price. (If repairs cost over 3 percent of the value of the car, it was not sent to the dealer, but was removed from new vehicle inventory and given to the sales team to use as a demonstrator, then sold at auction.) This particular paint repair cost *way* under the 3% limit, and it was also legal under Alabama's consumer protection law, as it had always been understood.[28] So BMW had shipped the car to its Alabama dealer, who had sold it as a new car to Mr. Gore.

Learning all this, Gore brought suit for compensatory and punitive damages against BMW, alleging that his car had a lower resale value because of the repainted part; he considered himself a victim of the tort of fraud. Again, we have a local plaintiff suing an out-of-state defendant. The jury returned a verdict finding BMW liable for compensatory damages of $4,000, the alleged difference in resale value between a "concours" car and one that had a repainted part. The jury also assessed $4 million in punitive damages, on the grounds that BMW of North America had likely repainted 1,000 cars (at $4,000) over the years.[29] Alabama appellate courts reduced the punitive award to $2 million, which they decided was not "grossly excessive" under the *TXO* standard because that amount constituted 500 times compensatories[30].

Finally, a majority of the Supreme Court had had enough. By a 5-4 margin (Justices Breyer, Kennedy, O'Connor, Souter and Stevens constituting the majority), the Court held that a combination of the lack of any real wrongdoing by BMW, the lack of notice that any punitive award was possible or even that its marketing was illegal in Alabama, the consideration of non-Alabaman touch-ups which were surely not violations of Alabama law, and the huge discrepancy between compensatories and punitives all combined to make this

[28] *Id.* at 562–64. Specifically, the $601.37 cost of repainting was about 1.5 percent of the car's suggested retail price. *Id.* at 564.

[29] *Id.* at 564–65.

[30] See *id.* at 567.

award unconstitutional. The Court didn't give any firm boundaries as to what *would* be a maximum limit, but said *this case* was beyond that limit in these circumstances.

Three dissenters, Justices Thomas, Ginsburg, and Rehnquist, essentially held that the federal Constitution could not place any limits on states in determining punitive damages. I have, above, indicated why I find this reasoning faulty—it abstracts from the private-public divide that is intrinsic to our constitutional structure. Justice Scalia, for his part denied that the Due Process Clause of the Constitution could ever affect damages in federal or state court.

There were some procedural decisions following *BMW v. Gore*, but substantively the Supremes did not revisit the issue of punitive damages until 2000, when they decided Act V, perhaps the most interesting case of them all.

E. State Farm Insurance v. Campbell *(Utah, 2003)*[31]

In 1981, Curtis Campbell was driving his wife down a two-lane highway in Cache County, Utah. He decided to pass, in one fell swoop, *six* vehicles traveling ahead of him. Campbell did not have enough space to pass all six. For his part, Todd Ospital was driving a small car approaching from the opposite direction, at a speed somewhat in excess of the speed limit. Campbell was headed right toward Ospital. To avoid a head-on collision, Ospital swerved onto the shoulder, where he lost control of his automobile, which came back onto the road and collided with a vehicle driven by Robert G. Slusher. Ospital was killed and Slusher was permanently disabled. The Campbells escaped unscathed, in fact they never collided with anyone—they got back in their lane safe and sound just in the nick of time thanks to Ospital's sacrificial decision to leave the road.

In the ensuing tort suits against Campbell by Ospital's estate and by Slusher, Campbell insisted he could not be at fault since he never collided with anyone (!), and since Ospital was speeding. Campbell's insurance company, State Farm, incredibly declined offers by Slusher and Ospital's estate to settle their respective claims for the modest policy coverage limit of $50,000 (i.e., $25,000 per plaintiff). In deciding to take the case to trial, State Farm ignored the advice of one of its own investigators, assuring the Campbells that "their assets were

[31] State Farm Mut. Auto. Ins. Co. v. Campbell, 538 U.S. 408 (2003).

safe, that they had no liability for the accident, that [State Farm] would represent their interests."[32] To the contrary, a jury determined that Campbell was 100 percent at fault, and a judgment against him was returned for $185,849, way more than the amount of State Farm's coverage.[33]

At first, the insurance company refused to cover the $135,849 in excess liability, since Campbell had purchased only $50,000 of coverage. State Farm's lawyer told the Campbells, "You may want to put 'for sale' signs on your property to get things moving."[34] Nor was State Farm willing to post the required *supersedeas* bond to allow Campbell to appeal the judgment against him. Campbell thus hired his own lawyer to appeal the verdict. While this appeal was pending, in late 1984, Slusher and Ospital's estate contacted him. The three parties reached an interesting agreement whereby Slusher and Ospital's estate agreed not to execute their judgments against the Campbells' house. In exchange, the Campbells agreed to pursue a bad-faith tort suit against State Farm, in which they would be represented by Slusher's and Ospital's estates' attorneys. The Campbells also agreed that Slusher and Ospital's estate would have a right to play a part in all major decisions concerning the bad-faith suit: no settlement between Campbell and State Farm could be concluded, in other words, without Slusher's and the estate's approval. Last but not least, Slusher and Ospital's estate would receive 90 percent of any verdict Campbell obtained against State Farm.[35]

In 1989, the Utah Supreme Court denied Campbell's appeal. State Farm then decided to pay the entire $185 thousand to Slusher and to Ospital's estate. This meant that the Campbells had suffered no damage (other than their lawyer's fees, which State Farm also agreed to cover) from the insurance company's incompetence (or worse). The Campbells nonetheless filed (as they had promised the Slushers and Ospital's estate they would) a new tort suit against State Farm,

[32] *Id.* at 413.

[33] *Id.*

[34] *Id.*

[35] *Id* at 413–14. By the way, I am not a Utah expert, but sale of a tort claim is illegal in most states. This was a sale of 90% of a tort suit—former adversaries, all Utah residents, were now in league against the out-of-state corporation. Keep that in mind.

alleging both fraud and "intentional infliction of emotional distress."[36] The trial court initially granted State Farm's motion to dismiss that suit for lack of damages (remember—no harm, no tort suit in private ordering), but that ruling was reversed on appeal. Now State Farm had to defend itself. In the first phase, the jury determined that State Farm's decision not to settle for $50,000 was unreasonable. The second phase of the trial would determine damages. Remember that there were *no* pecuniary damages (because State Farm had paid the excess award, though it was not contractually obliged to do so).[37] There *was* arguably emotional distress during the short period when the Campbells thought they were going to lose their home. Emotional distress, however, is not recoverable unless it was intentionally inflicted, and (as per my comment in a footnote above) no one can seriously claim that State Farm is a sadistic company bent on inflicting emotional distress on its clientele. State Farm argued during phase II of the trial that its decision to take the case to trial was an "honest mistake," and that it certainly did not warrant punitive damages. The Campbells introduced evidence that State Farm's decision to take the case to trial was a result of a national "scheme" to meet corporate fiscal goals by capping payouts on claims, not just in Campbell's case, but across the country.[38] (It is pretty clear that State Farm was being parsimonious, to say the least, though I might wonder out loud who wants to pay the insurance premiums that would be required to insurance companies that *over*pay claims?)

Just before the fraud and "intentional infliction" trial, the Supreme Court decided *BMW of North America, Inc. v. Gore*, summarized above. Based on that decision, State Farm moved for the exclusion of evidence of all out-of-state conduct. The trial court denied State Farm's motion. The jury then found $2.6 *million* in emotional distress for the Campbells, who (to repeat) had not lost one cent and were therefore not eligible for distress damages under classic tort doctrine.

[36] *Id.* at 414. The intentional infliction allegation was that in advising the Campbells to sell their home, State Farm was deliberately torturing them. The absurdity of this claim is hopefully self-evident—few corporations make money by torturing their customers, though admittedly some may make money through fraud. The fraud allegation was that the Campbells had been misled to believe State Farm was looking out for their interests.

[37] *Id.*

[38] *Id.* at 415.

How did the jury arrive at this amount? We will never know for sure, but likely the jury knew that 90 percent of this amount, or $2.34 million was going to the Slusher and Ospital families pursuant to the agreement. Likely the jury wanted to give $260,000 in emotional distress damages to the Campbells. This would be totally illegal if done explicitly, because the Slusher and Ospital families had settled their suit and had no cause of action against State Farm. In addition, however, the jury awarded Campbell (i.e., the Slusher and Ospital parties, to the tune of 90 percent) *$145 million* in punitives, to punish State Farm for aggressive defense practices throughout the country. The trial court reduced the $2.6 million in compensatories to $1 million, and the punitives from $145 million to "only" $25 million, under the *TXO* "really mean" standard. The Utah Supreme Court then reinstated the original award in its entirety. State Farm appealed that reinstatement to the United States Supreme Court.[39]

This time the decision was 6-3. Chief Justice Rehnquist abandoned his previous position and joined the majority, leaving Justices Scalia, Thomas, and Ginsburg alone in dissent.

The majority this time tried to provide an indication that certain trial court activity would no longer be tolerated:

- Don't *ever* again use legal out-of-state behavior to calculate punitive damages. Out-of-state behavior can be invoked to establish a pattern of bad faith or maliciousness, but in that case, it has to be the same behavior as the behavior being impugned.[40]
- Don't *ever* give more than 9 times compensatories as punitive damages, the Court said, unless there is a "particularly egregious act that has resulted in only a small amount of economic damages."[41]
- Moreover, in cases like this one, where the compensatory damages adjudged by the jury are extremely generous, do not exceed around one time punitives.[42]

[39] *Id.* at 416.

[40] See *id.* at 421–33. Interestingly, this part of the Campbell ruling undoes much of the Gore case—BMW's legal painting of cars in other states, which the Court had excluded, would possibly be probative now.

[41] *Id.* at 425 (citation omitted). "Single-digit multipliers are more likely to comport with due process . . . than awards with ratios in the range of 500 to 1, or, in this case, of 145 to 1." *Id.* (citation omitted).

[42] See *id.*

Joan Claybrook and Ralph Nader claimed that *Campbell* is a victory for them. Why? Part of this is spin, but I think Claybrook and Nader were happy that the Court has gone up from 4 times compensatories ("close to the line" in *Haslip*) to 9 times compensatories. They were also glad that the Court felt it could not touch the compensatories themselves. Surely, there is no way on earth that the Campbells, who cavalierly tried to pass six vehicles at once and drove off into the sunset leaving two devastated families in their wake, had $1 million in pain and suffering inflicted on them because *State Farm* aggressively came to their defense. What is to stop the next jury that wants to sock it to an out-of-state corporation from finding $*50 million* in so-called compensatory pain and suffering, and zero punitives? Money is fungible, after all.

F. Philip Morris v. Williams *(Oregon 2002)*[43]

The plaintiff in *Williams* was the widow of a long-time smoker. This widow alleged that Philip Morris deceived her husband into not quitting smoking. According to the wife, the late Mr. Williams said that "the tobacco companies don't even say they're cancer sticks, so I can smoke them."[44] Although his wife apparently helpfully pointed to the myriad warning labels on cigarette packages and herself corroborated the government's stern warning told that cigarettes would kill her husband, Mr. Williams allegedly responded: "This is what the Surgeon General says, it's not what [the] tobacco company says."[45] According to his wife, Williams gave no credence to the surgeon general's warnings because he believed that the tobacco companies would simply not sell a harmful product. His widow testified at trial that, "[H]e would say 'Well, honey, you see I told you . . . cigarettes are not going to kill you, because I just heard this so-and-so guy on TV, and he said that tobacco doesn't cause you [sic] cancer!'"[46]

Now, I cannot speak for you readers, but I know of no one on the planet Earth who talks like the decedent allegedly did, and I

[43] Philip Morris USA v. Williams, 127 S. Ct. 1057 (2007).

[44] Joint Appendix at 153a, Philip Morris USA v. Williams, 127 S. Ct. 1057 (2007) (No. 05-1256).

[45] Williams v. Philip Morris Inc., 48 P.3d 824, 835 n.15 (2002), vacated by 127 S. Ct 1057 (2007).

[46] Joint Appendix, *supra* note 44, at 138a.

know of no one who thinks that no seller could possibly fib about the dangers of the product he was selling. Of course, the jury can choose to believe whom it will, and to no one's surprise it chose to believe Ms. Williams, the local plaintiff. (Is the jury interested in buying a bridge in Brooklyn from me?) What possible motive could the plaintiff have to "embellish," after all?

That said, tobacco companies' behavior over the years has certainly been reprehensible on many different levels. *Thank You for Smoking* is a nice caricature of Big Tobacco's awful behavior. But awful behavior does not tort damages merit! Tort damages are awarded following proof of wrongdoing, causation, and damages as I have indicated above. Causation was established when the jury believed the astounding rendition by Ms. Williams. As to damages, well, punitive damages are essentially awarded in cases of intentional tort. Here, I guess, fraud is the intentional tort du jour. Mr. Williams managed to be defrauded despite his wife's and the government's best efforts to set him straight. This jury awarded $79.5 million in punitive damages against Philip Morris, which appealed to the Supremes on the ground that the award violated the rules set forth in *State Farm v. Campbell*.[47]

A bare majority of the Court (Justices Alito, Breyer, Kennedy, Roberts, and Souter) agreed with the tobacco giant. The Oregon court had allowed evidence on harm caused to smokers across the country in the damages phase of the trial—a tactic presumably allowed by *State Farm v. Campbell* for the narrow question of whether punitives at all should be granted. Ah, reasoned the majority, the court didn't take enough care to ensure that the jury then prevented itself from considering those self-same facts (the number of national victims) in order to fix the amount of punitive damages.[48] The Court did not address the amount of the punitive damages, which Philip Morris had argued were grossly excessive. Instead, the Court focused on whether the jury improperly took into consideration the alleged harm that Philip Morris' conduct caused to smokers who were not parties to the litigation in order to calculate said punitives.

How are judges to instruct juries following *Williams*? Courts will now have to craft jury instructions allowing global misfeasance to

[47] Williams, 127 S. Ct. at 1061.

[48] *Id.* at 1063.

entitle a plaintiff to punitives, but forcing it out of the jury's mind when calculating punitives. This is impossible to enforce except by saying (as the Court explicitly refused to state) that the punitive award for this plaintiff was just too high. We can look forward to years of litigation and circuit splits trying to sort out what the Court hath wrought.

And so we come to the end of a very rocky and unsettled road. The Supremes have no coherent view of punitive damages. Justice Stevens in *Williams* seemed to admit as much, when he harkened for the good ol' days of Excessive Fines (recall that Oregon takes 60 percent of Williams' booty), rashly rejected as an argument in *Kelco*. This is a mess, a royal mess, and we're in for much more to come.

IV. Conclusion

I end where I began—by recalling the purpose of tort law, i.e., full compensation for wrongfully inflicted private losses.

As long as judges allow local juries to punish out-of-state corporate defendants to enrich individual local plaintiffs, tort law will be defiled. As long as that happens, in my opinion, the Supreme Court must continue to intervene on constitutional grounds. Whether it be by striking down punitive damages or by rejecting the standardless "pain and suffering" awards made more attractive in *Campbell*, the Court will have to uphold the fact that private ordering is the domain of civil litigation, while public ordering requires a slew of constitutional protections. The 1989 *BFI* decision denying that punitives are fines is what, in my opinion, has prevented the Court from going down this logical and principled path.

Looking Ahead: October Term 2007

*Glenn Harlan Reynolds**

Last year's Supreme Court term was notable in at least one way: It lived up to the prediction, made in this space last year by Professor Peter Rutledge,[1] that Justice Anthony Kennedy would solidify his position as the "swing voter" on the court. Justice Kennedy found himself on the majority side in every single 5-4 decision last term.[2] Likewise, predictions that Chief Justice Roberts would move the Court were borne out to a substantial degree.[3]

Nonetheless, changes in the Court tend to occur gradually—Harry Blackmun, after all, initially voted with Warren Burger so often that they were called "the Minnesota Twins," but that was only at first. Cases selected for the coming term may shed more light on where the Court is likely to head in coming years, and provide some sense of the kind of issues that the Court, or at least some of its members, regard as particularly important. This all-too-brief Essay will look at some of the highlights from next year's docket. (Will predictions made here turn out as well as those made by Professor Rutledge? One can hope.) It will also discuss the Supreme Court's diminished caseload, the Court's relationship with the courts of appeal, and the implications of, and possible remedies for, this mismatch in output.

*Beauchamp Brogan Distinguished Professor of Law, The University of Tennessee College of Law. Thanks to Sybil Richards of the University of Tennessee Law Library for the caseload numbers for the Court of Appeals and Supreme Court.

[1]Peter B. Rutledge, Looking Ahead: October Term 2006, 2005–2006 Cato Sup. Ct. Rev. 361 (2006).

[2]Linda Greenhouse, In Steps Big and Small, Supreme Court Moved Right, New York Times, July 1, 2007, at A1, available at http://www.nytimes.com/2007/07/01/washington/01scotus.html.

[3]David G. Savage, High Court Has Entered a New Era, Los Angeles Times, July 1, 2007, at A1, available at http://www.latimes.com/news/nationworld/washigntondc/la-na-scotus1jul01,1,4832858.story? ("Working with a 5-4 majority, Roberts prevailed in nearly all the major cases.").

I. Free Speech and the Internet

Williams v. United States[4] deals with the constitutionality of 18 U.S.C. §2252A(a)(3)(B), which prohibits knowingly advertising, promoting, presenting, distributing, or soliciting any material that reflects the belief, or that is intended to cause another to believe, that the material is illegal child pornography. The question before the Supreme Court is whether this prohibition is unconstitutional on grounds of vagueness and overbreadth. A statute is "vague" if its language is so unclear that a person of reasonable intelligence cannot tell what it prohibits, opening the way to arbitrary and discriminatory enforcement. A statute is overbroad if it significantly prohibits conduct that is protected by the First Amendment as well as conduct that is not.

In an online chat room, defendant Williams had shared nonpornographic pictures of children—and adults digitally manipulated to look like children—with an undercover federal agent. Williams promised, but did not deliver, genuinely pornographic pictures of children, and was charged with "pandering" under § 2252A(a)(3)(B). Before the Eleventh Circuit, Williams argued that the statute was overbroad and vague. The Eleventh Circuit found that it was, and struck down the statute:

> First, that pandered child pornography need only be "purported" to fall under the prohibition of § 2252A(a)(3)(B) means that promotion or speech is criminalized even when the touted materials are clean or nonexistent . . . In a noncommercial context, any promoter . . . be they a braggart, exaggerator, or outright liar . . . who claims to have illegal child pornography materials is a criminal punishable by up to twenty years in prison, even if what he or she actually has is a video of "Our Gang," a dirty handkerchief, or an empty pocket.[5]

The government's justification was that shutting down a market in child pornography requires banning all promotional speech, regardless of whether it actually involves child pornography. The Eleventh Circuit disagreed, holding that "the government may not

[4] 444 F.3d 1286 (11th Cir. 2006).

[5] *Id.* at 1298.

suppress lawful speech as the means to suppress unlawful speech."[6] It added: "The Government must do its job to determine whether illegal material is behind the pander."[7] Since the statute bans "pandering" whether illegal material is present or not, the Eleventh Circuit found it overbroad and, hence, unconstitutional.

Williams' vagueness challenge also received a friendly reception from the court of appeals. The void-for-vagueness doctrine, the court observed, exists for three reasons:

> (1) to avoid punishing people for behavior that they could not have known was illegal; (2) to avoid subjective enforcement of the laws based on arbitrary or discriminatory interpretations by government officers; and (3) to avoid any chilling effect on the exercise of First Amendment freedoms. Thus, to pass constitutional muster statutes challenged as vague must give a person of ordinary intelligence a reasonable opportunity to know what is prohibited and provide explicit standards for those who apply it to avoid arbitrary and discriminatory enforcement.[8]

These concerns are heightened, it said, where a criminal statute is involved, and where First Amendment rights are implicated, given the greater danger of constitutional deprivations due to arbitrary or discriminatory enforcement.[9] And the court seemed to regard § 2252A(a)(3)(B) as rather obviously vague:

> This language is so vague and standardless as to what may not be said that the public is left with no objective measure to which behavior can be conformed. Moreover, the proscription requires a wholly subjective determination by law enforcement personnel of what promotional or solicitous speech "reflects the belief" or is "intended to cause another to believe" that the material is illegally pornographic. Individual officers are thus endowed with incredibly broad

[6] *Id.* at 1304 (quoting Ashcroft v. Free Speech Coalition, 535 U.S. 234, 255 (2002)).

[7] *Id.*

[8] *Id.* at 1305–06 (citing Grayned v. City of Rockford, 408 U.S. 104 (1972)).

[9] *Id.* at 1306.

> discretion to define whether a given utterance or writing contravenes the law's mandates.[10]

The appellate court imagined numerous examples of harmless speech that might contravene the statute: ''good pics of kids in bed,'' or ''little Janie in the bath—hubba, hubba!'' as sent, along with innocuous photos, by a grandmother. Such speech is not child pornography and is protected by the First Amendment. It thus found the pandering provision void for vagueness.

The *Williams* case reaches the Supreme Court at a time when there is increasing concern regarding illegal activities using the Internet, and a general move toward increasing regulation of Internet activities.[11] On the other hand, the most troubling cases involve real harm to real children, at the hands of stalkers and pedophiles, rather than the somewhat more rarefied harm addressed by the pandering provisions of § 2252A(a)(3)(B).[12] The Court's disposition of the case is likely to depend on whether a majority of justices regard Congress's effort to suppress the market for child pornography as sufficiently important to justify some infringement of speech, and whether those justices also regard the Eleventh Circuit's view of the statute's vagueness and overbreadth as compelling, or as exaggerated and subject to control via case-by-case analysis. Playing into this analysis may be the heightened power of law enforcement in the highly charged area of child pornography cases, where an accusation may be nearly as destructive as a conviction, as a reason for greater judicial strictness in statutory interpretation.

II. Dormant Commerce Clause

Despite calls from some academics, and even some members of the Court,[13] to lay the Dormant Commerce Clause to rest, it remains

[10] *Id.* An interesting question: Since, to avoid vagueness, a statute must be understandable by people of ordinary intelligence, is a determination by judges that the statute cannot be understood capable of being reversible error? Or is it inherently self-validating? Or, alternatively, might we conclude that there are statutes that judges cannot understand, but that are nonetheless clear to people of ordinary intelligence?

[11] Neil Munro, Regulating Fantasy, National Journal, June 30, 2007, at 34.

[12] Alexander Burns, Your Space, National Journal, June 30, 2007, at 32 (describing predators' use of the Internet to target underage victims).

[13] See, e.g., Camps Newfound/Owatonna, Inc. v. Town of Harrison, 520 U.S. 564, 611 (1997) (Thomas, J. dissenting).

alive. Existing doctrine forbids states from discriminating against interstate commerce, or from regulating commerce in a way that places an undue burden on interstate commerce. *Kentucky Department of Revenue v. Davis* may provide the next opportunity for the Court to abolish or to reinforce the doctrine.

Davis involves a claim that Kentucky's income tax system, by exempting income from bonds issued by the state of Kentucky or its political subdivisions from tax while taxing income from bonds from other states, discriminated impermissibly against interstate commerce. The Kentucky Court of Appeals held that it did,[14] and the Kentucky Supreme Court denied review.

Noting that "state laws discriminating against interstate commerce on their face are 'virtually *per se* invalid,'"[15] the Kentucky court held that the Kentucky statute was facially discriminatory and hence invalid.

Though the case is in some sense one of first impression—no case specifically addresses the exact same issue—the discriminatory nature of the law makes the outcome seem rather unexceptional.[16] That the Supreme Court granted certiorari, just one year after its decision in *DaimlerChrysler Corp. v. Cuno*,[17] however, suggests that at least some of the justices wish to address the question of state tax incentives on the merits, after dismissing *Cuno* on standing grounds.[18]

One potential issue not raised in the opinion below or in the petition for certiorari, but suggested in some prior Supreme Court dissents, is whether the Dormant Commerce Clause result might be reached via the Privileges and Immunities Clause, which prohibits some forms of discrimination against out-of-state citizens. Previous

[14] Davis v. Dep't of Revenue, 197 S.W.3d 557 (Ky. Ct. App. 2006).

[15] *Id.* at 562 (quoting Fultron Corp. v. Faulkner, 516 U.S. 325, 331 (1996)).

[16] See Camps Newfound/Owatonna, Inc. v. Town of Harrison, 520 U.S. 564 (1997) (finding preferential tax exemption for in-state charities violative of the Dormant Commerce Clause); New Energy Co. v. Limbach, 486 U.S. 269 (1988) (striking down ethanol sales credit limited to ethanol from Ohio or from states extending reciprocal tax treatment to Ohio-produced ethanol).

[17] 126 S. Ct. 1854 (2006).

[18] See Brannon P. Denning, DaimlerChrysler Corp. v. Cuno, State Investment Incentives, and the Future of the Dormant Commerce Clause Doctrine, 2005–2006 Cato Sup. Ct. Rev. 173 (2006) (discussing *Cuno* and Supreme Court Dormant Commerce Clause doctrine).

Supreme Court caselaw has found that the imposition of higher tax rates on nonresidents than on residents violates the Privileges and Immunities Clause,[19] which might well be extendable to the unequal availability of tax exemptions as well. This is certainly not a case in which the lower court can be said to be off the reservation, suggesting that the Supreme Court's willingness to grant certiorari involves a desire to tinker with doctrine, not merely to correct an erroneous interpretation below.

III. Presidential Powers

Can the president determine the steps necessary for states to take in complying with U.S. treaty obligations? And are states bound to honor treaty obligations of the federal government in implementing their own criminal justice systems?

Those are the questions raised in *Ex parte Medellin*,[20] in which a Texas court found in the negative. This case may well prove to be among the most important of the term, as it addresses core aspects of the foreign affairs power and of federalism.

Jose Ernesto Medellin was a Mexican national convicted and sentenced to death for the gang rape and murder of two teenage girls in Houston. After his appeals were completed, Medellin filed a petition for habeas corpus claiming a violation of his rights under Article 36 of the Vienna Convention on Consular Relations.[21]

Article 36 of the Vienna Convention provides that foreign nationals accused of a crime shall have free access to consular officials

[19] Austin v. New Hampshire, 420 U.S. 656 (1975); see also Gillian E. Metzger, Congress, Article IV and Interstate Relations, 120 Harv. L. Rev. 1468 (2007) ("Congress's dormant commerce clause authority is especially significant to congressional power under the Privileges and Immunities Clause, given the overlap between the activities to which both clauses apply. Although the Privileges and Immunities Clause prohibits only state discrimination that affects nonresidents' fundamental rights, much of nonresidents' economic activity falls into that category for Article IV purposes. Thus, invoking that clause the Court has struck down state laws that tax nonresidents at rates higher than residents, charge nonresidents higher license fees for engaging in commercial activities, and impose residency requirements as a prerequisite for certain forms of employment.") As Prof. Metzger notes, there is considerable overlap between the Privileges and Immunities Clause of Article IV and the Dormant Commerce Clause, and this case may well fall within that area of overlap.

[20] 223 S.W.3d 315, 332 n.105 (Tex. Crim. App. 2006).

[21] Vienna Convention on Consular Relations and Optional Protocol on Disputes, art. 36, Apr. 24, 1963, 21 U.S.T. 77, 100–01, 596 U.N.T.S. 261, 292–93.

from their home nation, that the accused shall be notified of these rights, and that upon request the imprisoning state shall notify the consular officials of the arrest or imprisonment.

After a somewhat complex procedural history, Medellin's case came before the Texas Court of Criminal Appeals. In the interim, however, the International Court of Justice had ruled in the *Avena* case that the Vienna Convention confers individual rights, and that the United States was in violation of the Convention.[22] President Bush responded by issuing a memorandum directing state courts to give effect to the *Avena* decision.

The Texas Court of Criminal Appeals was unmoved. Claims under Article 36, it held, are subject to procedural default to the same degree as other claims.[23] In addition—and more importantly—the presidential memorandum represented an unconstitutional usurpation of power on the part of the president:

> We hold that the President has exceeded his constitutional authority by intruding into the independent powers of the judiciary. By stating "that the United States will discharge its international obligations under the decision of the International Court of Justice in . . . [*Avena*], by having States courts give effect to the decision . . . [,] the President's determination is effectively analogous to that decision. In *Sanchez-Llamas,* the Supreme Court made clear that its judicial "power includes the duty to 'say what the law is.'" And that power, according to the Court, includes the authority to determine the meaning of a treaty "as a matter of federal law." The clear import of this is that the President cannot dictate to the judiciary what law to apply or how to interpret the applicable law.[24]

In a lengthy discussion, the Texas court distinguished other cases in which presidential foreign affairs power intruded into the realm of the judiciary, and concluded that Medellin's claims failed.

This case—and its tangled procedural history, which includes both state and federal *habeas corpus* petitions and a previous Supreme Court grant of certiorari that was dismissed as improvidently

[22] Case Concerning Avena and Other Mexican Nationals (Mex. v. U.S.), 2004 I.C.J. 12 (Mar. 31).

[23] Medellin, 223 S.W.3d at 332 n.105.

[24] *Id.* at 335 (quoting Sanchez-Llamas v. Johnson, 126 S. Ct. 2669, 2684 (2006)).

granted—illustrates the difficulty of integrating the national foreign affairs power with the domestic operations of the states. It also illustrates, as so many difficult cases in this realm do, the advantage of legislation: A federal statute, spelling out the duties of state courts in cases involving foreign nationals, would avoid the problems that produced this case.

The case combines some interesting crosscurrents in the *zeitgeist*, setting one theme in current international affairs and legal thinking—increased skepticism regarding executive powers—against another: increased solicitude for foreign criminal defendants and international law. With both federalism issues and questions about the judicial and executive roles involved, it seems likely to produce a plethora of opinions from various members of the Court regardless of outcome.

IV. Criminal Law

When is a gun not a gun? When it's the equivalent of money. That is, sort of, the argument made by the defendant in *United States v. Watson*.[25]

Watson was convicted of violating 18 U.S.C. § 924(c)(1)(A), which criminalizes the "use" of a firearm during and in relation to drug trafficking. The Supreme Court has previously held in *Bailey v. United States* that "use" of a firearm means "active employment."[26]

Watson purchased a firearm for drugs. The unloaded firearm was provided to him in exchange for OxyContin tablets. Unfortunately for Watson, the purchase was part of a government sting operation, and he was arrested. Watson entered a plea bargain, but reserved the question of whether receiving an unloaded gun as payment for drugs constitutes "use" of a gun in a drug transaction. The question is whether the firearm's role in this transaction is "active employment," or whether it was merely a passive form of payment. This is a subject on which the circuits are currently split.

The case itself is only moderately interesting, but the Court's handling of this question should shed some light on the interpretive style of the Roberts Court and its new members. The statute seems pretty clearly to have envisioned firearms "use" in a gun-slinging,

[25] 191 Fed. Appx. 326 (5th Cir. 2006).

[26] 516 U.S. 137 (1995).

Miami Vice sense. On the other hand, the firearm was certainly used here, but as payment. The "tough on crime" interpretation leaves Watson in jail; the narrow, "rule of lenity" approach probably lets him go free. The Court's choices may prove revealing.

V. Habeas Corpus

In the cases of *Al Odah v. United States*[27] and *Boumediene v. Bush*,[28] the District of Columbia Circuit held that the Military Commissions Act of 2006 barred habeas corpus actions by detainees. The Supreme Court denied certiorari in April despite what many commentators regarded as substantial tension with *Rasul v. Bush*.[29] In a highly unusual action, however, the Supreme Court reversed itself and granted certiorari in these cases on June 29.[30]

Congress had responded to the Supreme Court's decision in *Hamdan v. Rumsfeld*, which found the military commissions established to try suspected terrorists unconstitutional, by passing the Military Commissions Act of 2006, which was intended to bar habeas corpus claims by detainees.[31] The questions presented are extensive:

Questions presented by Boumediene:

1. Whether the Military Commissions Act of 2006, Pub. L. No. 109-366, 120 Stat. 2600, validly stripped federal court jurisdiction over habeas corpus petitions filed by foreign citizens imprisoned indefinitely at the United States Naval Station at Guantanamo Bay.
2. Whether Petitioners' habeas corpus petitions, which establish that the United States government has imprisoned Petitioners for over five years, demonstrate unlawful confinement requiring the grant of habeas relief or, at least, a hearing on the merits.[32]

[27] 321 F.3d 1134 (D.C. Cir. 2003).

[28] 476 F.3d 981 (D.C. Cir. 2007).

[29] 542 U.S. 466 (2004).

[30] According to Lyle Denniston, this may not have happened since *Hickman v. Taylor* 60 years ago. Lyle Denniston, Court Switches, Will Hear Detainee Cases, ScotusBlog, June 29, 2007, at http://www.scotusblog.com/movabletype/archives/2007/06/court 1.html.

[31] 126 S. Ct. 2749 (2006).

[32] Petition for Writ of Certiorari, Boumediene v. Bush, 127 S. Ct. 3078 (2007) (No. 06-1195), available at 2007 WL 680794.

Questions presented by Al Odah:

1. Did the D.C. Circuit err in relying again on *Johnson v. Eisentrager*, 339 U.S. 763 (1950), to dismiss these petitions and to hold that petitioners have no common law right to habeas protected by the Suspension Clause and no constitutional rights whatsoever, despite this Court's ruling in *Rasul v. Bush*, 542 U.S. 466 (2004), that these petitioners are in a fundamentally different position from those in *Eisentrager*, that their access to the writ is consistent with the historical reach of the writ at common law, and that they are confined within the territorial jurisdiction of the United States?

2. Given that the Court in *Rasul* concluded that the writ at common law would have extended to persons detained at Guantanamo, did the D.C. Circuit err in holding that petitioners' right to the writ was not protected by the Suspension Clause because they supposedly would not have been entitled to the writ at common law?

3. Are petitioners, who have been detained without charge or trial for more than five years in the exclusive custody of the United States at Guantanamo, a territory under the plenary and exclusive jurisdiction of the United States, entitled to the protection of the Fifth Amendment right not to be deprived of liberty without due process of law and of the Geneva Conventions?

4. Should section 7(b) of the Military Commissions Act of 2006, which does not explicitly mention habeas corpus, be construed to eliminate the courts' jurisdiction over petitioners' pending habeas cases, thereby creating serious constitutional issues?[33]

The central issue is whether habeas corpus jurisdiction extends to prisoners at Guantanamo, and whether Congress can strip away that jurisdiction. The United States has taken the (somewhat implausible) position that the base at Guantanamo Bay is not within the jurisdiction of the United States, and hence not within the territorial jurisdiction of U.S. courts. This position was upheld by the D.C.

[33]Petition for Writ of Certiorari, Al Odah v. United States of America, 127 S. Ct. 3067 (2007) (No. 06-1196), available at 2007 WL 671010.

Circuit in *Al Odah v. United States,*[34] and reversed by the Supreme Court in *Rasul v. Bush.*[35] Congress then passed the Detainee Treatment Act of 2005,[36] which barred habeas corpus jurisdiction by "any court, justice, or judge." The Supreme Court then held in *Hamdan v. Rumsfeld* [37] that the Detainee Treatment Act did not strip federal courts of habeas corpus jurisdiction in pending cases. Congress responded by passing the Military Commissions Act of 2006,[38] barring habeas corpus jurisdiction regarding aliens detained as enemy combatants. In *Boumediene,* the D.C. Circuit held that this statute barred habeas relief for Boumediene et al., and that it did not work an unconstitutional suspension of the writ.

Some experts seem to think that a Supreme Court reversal is likely in light of the Supreme Court's sudden shift on certiorari,[39] and that seems plausible. There seems no reason to infer a sudden desire to *uphold* the D.C. Circuit based on these actions. But while it seems quite likely that the Court will overturn the D.C. Circuit, what rule it will announce in doing so is unclear. While some commentators have in the past argued that the U.S. government faces substantial limitations under the Constitution even in its dealings with aliens outside of United States territory,[40] it seems unlikely that the Roberts Court will abandon the principle of *Verdugo-Urquidez*[41] to adopt such an expansive rule. On the other hand, it seems reasonably clear that Congress's legislative intent was to bar such habeas petitions, and the *pas de deux* engaged in by the Court and Congress thus far will require a certain amount of fancy footwork on the part of the justices if the result is not to look like a pure judicial power play—though

[34] 321 F.3d 1134 (D.C. Cir. 2003).

[35] 542 U.S. 466, 483–84 (2004).

[36] Pub. L. 109–148, 119 Stat. 2680 (2005).

[37] 126 S. Ct. 2749 (2006).

[38] Pub. L. 109–366, 120 Stat 2600 (2006).

[39] This is extremely unusual, and it is probably a pretty good sign that a reversal is likely. See, e.g., Orin Kerr, Supreme Court Agrees to Take Guantanamo Bay Cases, The Volokh Conspiracy, at http://volokh.com/posts/1183133554.shtml (June 29, 2007).

[40] See, e.g., John A. Ragosta, Aliens Abroad: Principles for the Application of Constitutional Limitations to Federal Action, 17 N.Y.U. J. Int'l L. & Pol. 287 (1985).

[41] U.S. v. Verdugo-Urquidez, 494 U.S. 259 (1990) (constitutional protections do not extend to aliens who have not formed a "voluntary attachment" to the United States).

this may be vitiated by the turnover in congressional control since that legislation's passage.

VI. Preemption

States are growing more enthusiastic about regulating tobacco, but this sometimes creates conflict with federal law. That's what *New Hampshire Motor Transport Association v. Rowe*[42] is about. Maine's Tobacco Delivery Law was designed to regulate direct-to-consumer sales of tobacco via the Internet, etc., and made it illegal to knowingly deliver tobacco products to a Maine consumer if those products were purchased from an unlicensed seller. The effect of this rule was to require carriers to treat tobacco products differently from other products, making timely deliveries more difficult. Carriers sued, arguing that these requirements were preempted by the Federal Aviation Administration Authorization Act of 1994 (FAAAA).[43] The FAAAA provides that a state

> may not enact or enforce a law . . . related to a price, route or service of any motor carrier . . . with respect to the transportation of property.[44]

Further, a state

> may not enact or enforce a law . . . related to a price, route or service of an air carrier or carrier affiliated with a direct air carrier through common controlling ownership when such carrier is transporting property by aircraft or by motor vehicle.[45]

Package delivery services like UPS are covered by these provisions, raising the question of whether the Maine provision "related to a price, route, or service." Both the district court[46] and the court of appeals for the First Circuit held that it did.[47]

[42] 448 F.3d 66 (1st Cir. 2006).

[43] Pub. L. 103–305, § 601, 108 Stat. 1569, 1605 (2006).

[44] 49 U.S.C. § 14501(c)(1) (2007).

[45] 49 U.S.C. § 41713(b)(4)(A) (2007).

[46] New Hampshire Motor Transport Ass'n v. Rowe, 377 F. Supp. 2d 197 (D. Me. 2005).

[47] 448 F.3d 66 (1st Cir. 2006).

The State of Maine argued before those courts that the FAAAA was intended to preempt only *economic* regulation, and not regulation based on the state's police powers. This argument has a certain force, but also offers the potential for a drastic narrowing of FAAAA preemption, since state police powers are virtually boundless. Maine's argument also stresses that caselaw on FAAAA preemption is based on cases involving preemption under the Employee Retirement Income Security Act (ERISA), and that the scope of ERISA preemption has since narrowed. The First Circuit found this argument unpersuasive, but perhaps the Supreme Court will feel differently. Its treatment of this issue, at any rate, is likely to shed light on the Roberts Court's general views on statutory construction and state-federal relations.

VII. Right to Keep and Bear Arms

This year's wild-card case is one that, as of this writing, is not even on the certiorari docket.[48] But it is a case that, in some ways, may actually be more influential if the Supreme Court doesn't get around to hearing it.

The case is *Parker v. District of Columbia*,[49] a D.C. Circuit case involving the District's draconian anti-gun laws. The result—an individual rights decision striking down those laws—was unusual. The Supreme Court has said little on the Second Amendment since its opinion in *United States v. Miller*,[50] which left things rather unsettled,[51] and court of appeals caselaw on the meaning of the Second Amendment was for many years rather shallow and conclusory.[52] More recently, there have been some signs[53] that

[48] Indeed, as I write this, the petition for certiorari has not been filed, but such a filing is expected. See Lyle Denniston, Second Amendment Case Headed to Court, ScotusBlog, July 16, 2007, at http://www.scotusblog.com/movabletype/archives/2007/07/second_amendmen.html.

[49] 478 F.3d 370 (2007).

[50] 307 U.S. 174 (1939).

[51] For more on the Miller opinion, see Brannon P. Denning & Glenn H. Reynolds, Telling Miller's Tale, 65 Law & Contemp. Probs. 113 (2002).

[52] Brannon P. Denning, Can the Simple Cite be Trusted? Lower Court Interpretations of United States v. Miller and the Second Amendment, 26 Cumb. L. Rev. 961 (1996).

[53] See, e.g., United States v. Emerson, 270 F.3d 203 (5th Cir. 2001) (finding an individual right to arms under the Second Amendment).

the circuit courts are taking notice of new scholarship[54] suggesting an individual right to arms under the Second Amendment, but not much action in terms of striking actual federal firearms laws.

In *Parker*, however, the D.C. Circuit faced something that other courts had not—a federal law, avoiding any questions of incorporation posed by state laws, and one that went well beyond any conception of mere "reasonable regulation," as the District's gun law effectively prohibited private ownership and use of firearms.

The District of Columbia's attorneys argued that the Second Amendment protected only a right to bear arms while actively serving in a state militia, a right that would leave no private conduct protected, leading the D.C. Circuit to observe: "In short, we take the District's position to be that the Second Amendment is a dead letter." After an extensive review, the D.C. Circuit concluded that the Second Amendment protects an individual right to arms, and that such a right includes a right to own handguns, and that the District of Columbia gun laws in question infringed that right.

For gun-rights advocates, *Parker* was a big win, as was the D.C. Circuit's denial of *en banc* review. As this is written, the Supreme Court has not yet docketed a petition for certiorari in this case, though it is likely that one will be filed: A loss for the District of Columbia in the Supreme Court would be a major defeat for backers of gun control, since it would mean that every gun control law would be subject to some degree of constitutional scrutiny. Though many gun control laws would undoubtedly withstand any degree of scrutiny likely to be imposed by the Court, merely having to acknowledge the constitutional issue would complicate matters considerably, and the more intrusive forms of gun control might well be found unconstitutional. Concern about these consequences is probably why the District of Columbia took so long to make a decision on filing for certiorari that it was forced to ask for an extension of time.[55]

[54] See, e.g., Glenn Harlan Reynolds, A Critical Guide to the Second Amendment, 62 Tenn. L. Rev. 461 (1995); William Van Alstyne, The Second Amendment and the Personal Right to Arms, 43 Duke L.J. 1236 (1994). See also David B. Kopel, What State Constitutions Teach about the Second Amendment, 29 N. Ky. L. Rev. 827 (2002).

[55] See Second Amendment Case Headed to Court, *supra* note 48. ("[The] petition would have been due Aug. 7, but city officials said Monday that they would ask Chief Justice John G. Roberts, Jr., for a 30-day extension of time to file the case.").

How likely is that? Experts as eminent as Laurence Tribe and Mark Tushnet disagree:

> Tushnet believes that if the Court grants certiorari, it will ultimately overturn the decision of the D.C. panel. "My gut feeling is that there are not five votes to say the individual-rights position is correct," he says. "[Justice Anthony] Kennedy comes from a segment of the Republican Party that is not rabidly pro-gun rights and indeed probably is sympathetic to hunters but not terribly sympathetic to handgun owners. Then the standard liberals will probably say 'collective rights.'"
>
> But Tribe is less confident of that prediction. Should the case reach the Supreme Court, he told *The New York Times*, "there's a really quite decent chance that it will be affirmed."[56]

Supreme Court vote counting is a perilous business, but I don't see five clear votes to sustain *Parker.* On the other hand, I was surprised by the outcome in the D.C. Circuit, and Laurence Tribe's skills at Supreme Court vote counting certainly exceed mine.

The legal commentariat seems to regard this as an important case, with Mike O'Shea suggesting that *Parker* might overshadow the rest of the Court's caseload in the coming term:

> It's not often that the Supreme Court takes up the core meaning of an entire Amendment of the Bill of Rights, in a context where it writes on a mostly clean slate from the standpoint of prior holdings. If the Court takes the case, then October Term 2007 becomes The Second Amendment Term. *Parker* would swiftly overshadow, for example, the Court's important recent cert grant in the Guantanamo cases.
>
> How many Americans would view *District of Columbia v. Parker* as the most important court case of the last thirty years? The answer must run into seven figures. The decision would have far-reaching effects, particularly in the event of a reversal . . . there is a way more straightforward comparison that a whole lot of average Americans would be making. That's a comparison between the Court's handling of the

[56] Elaine McArdle, Lawyers, Guns and Money, Harvard Law School Bulletin, Summer 2007, available at http://www.law.harvard.edu/alumni/bulletin/2007/summer/feature_3.php.

> enumerated rights claim at issue in *Parker*, and its demonstrated willingness to embrace even non-enumerated individual rights that are congenial to the political left, in cases like *Roe* and *Lawrence*. "So the Constitution says *Roe*, but it doesn't say I have the right to keep a gun to defend my home, huh?"[57]

O'Shea suggests that the pressure that this case might bring may encourage the Court to deny certiorari rather than face such a comparison. Of course, the calculus on these issues may vary among individual justices, and there are likely to be consequences to *not* granting certiorari as well.

Should the Supreme Court wind up hearing this case, it will be an interesting test of the power of academic legal thought. Second Amendment caselaw is sparse, and many of the opinions are unenlightening. On the other hand, there is a comparatively large body of legal scholarship on the Second Amendment, with most—though by no means all—of it tending toward supporting the reasoning and outcome in *Parker*. In the absence of precedent, it will be interesting—and, to some law professors, perhaps humbling—to discover how much impact this scholarship has on the Supreme Court's thinking.

VIII. Taking it Easy: The Supreme Court's Workload

One trend that has not shown any alteration since the appearance of the Roberts Court is the Supreme Court's reduced caseload. In the past term, the Supreme Court produced 68 decisions after argument, plus four summary opinions, for a total of 72 decisions on the merits.[58] This number of 68 decisions after argument is the lowest in the Court's recent history, with the previous year seeing 71. By contrast, October Term 1990 saw 106 decisions on the merits, a number that itself was lower than the Court's output in the 1970s: in the 1973 term, the Court produced 129.[59]

[57] Mike O'Shea, The Second Amendment Term?, Concurring Opinions, at http://www.concurringopinions.com/archives/2007/07/the_second_amen_1.html.

[58] ScotusBlog, figures at http://www.scotusblog.com/movabletype/archives/Workload.pdf.

[59] Glenn Harlan Reynolds, Marbury's Mixed Messages, 71 Tenn. L. Rev. 303 (2004). I make a similar point in this piece, but as Mike Graetz once told me, you have to say something three times in print before anyone pays attention. This is number two.

By contrast, the caseload of the federal courts of appeal, whose work is nominally supervised by the Supreme Court, has skyrocketed. In 2006, the federal courts of appeal produced 34,580 decisions on the merits.[60] In 1973, by contrast, the courts of appeal produced a mere 777 decisions on the merits.[61] A Court that decided 129 cases on the merits could plausibly oversee a system of inferior courts that decided 777. But can a Court that decides 68 cases on the merits plausibly oversee a system that decides 34,580? Perhaps it can, if the federal judicial system is running like a piece of perfectly functioning machinery, with a failure rate of a fraction of one percent. I will leave it to the reader whether that is a plausible account of the current situation. My own feeling, however, is that it is not, which is why I characterized the Supreme Court's supervision as nominal.

Indeed, although—as the habeas cases above demonstrate—the Supreme Court is capable of overseeing a court of appeals closely on occasion, it seems that the federal courts of appeal may in some cases exercise control in the other direction. The Supreme Court's Commerce Clause jurisprudence in *Lopez* and *Morrison,* for example, seems to have succumbed to foot-dragging by the courts of appeals,[62] leading ultimately to retrenchment and a "false dawn" of federalism.[63] Like a puma with a herd of buffalo, the Supreme Court may pick off the occasional outcast or straggler, and perhaps encourage the herd to stick more tightly together, but it is not in a position to choose the direction the herd will take tomorrow, or even to halt a stampede.

To be fair, the enormous expansion of the courts of appeals' caseload has probably contributed more to the Supreme Court's limited ability to exercise any real supervision than has the Supreme Court's own unwillingness to hear more cases. And the problem has gotten

[60] Administrative Office of the U.S. Courts, available at http://www.uscourts.gov/cgi-bin/cmsa2006.pl.

[61] See Reynolds, *supra* note 59.

[62] Glenn H. Reynolds & Brannon P. Denning, Lower Court Readings of Lopez, or What if the Supreme Court Held a Constitutional Revolution and Nobody Came?, 2000 Wis. L. Rev. 369; Brannon P. Denning & Glenn H. Reynolds, Rulings and Resistance: The New Commerce Clause Jurisprudence Encounters the Lower Courts, 55 Ark. L. Rev. 1253 (2003).

[63] Ilya Somin, A False Dawn for Federalism: Clear Statement Rules After Gonzales v. Raich, 2005–2006 Cato Sup. Ct. Rev. 113 (2006).

bad enough that the Judicial Conference of the United States has begun to take a hand in trying to resolve circuit splits over statutory interpretation.[64] There have also been proposals to create a National Court of Appeals that would sit between the circuits and the Supreme Court,[65] though this is a cure that would likely dilute the Supreme Court's powers further.

What remedy is appropriate is beyond the scope of this Essay, which has already run long enough. But the vast growth of the court of appeals' caseload relative to that of the Supreme Court leads to conclusions that may be uncongenial in the context of this Essay, and this journal: It may be that the Supreme Court doesn't matter as much as it once did. Statistically, the odds that any particular court of appeals decision will reach the Supreme Court are negligible. Nor, as the *Lopez-Morrison* example illustrates, do Supreme Court precedents necessarily trickle down to affect decisions in the circuits. For the vast, vast majority of litigants, the court of appeals *is* the Supreme Court, in effect.

The glamour attending the Supreme Court tends to obscure this. But while everyone focuses on the Supreme Court, the real and in almost all cases effectively unreviewable power is exercised by the courts of appeals. That power is less controversial because it is exercised less often in ways that make waves: like good bureaucrats, the courts of appeals tend to avoid controversy, and to make their output sufficiently boring that few will bother to read it in search of the controversial bits anyway.

One response to this—and one that I certainly endorse—is to start paying more attention to lower courts. Unfortunately, it is not clear who besides the legal academy will be willing to do so, and it is not at all clear that the legal academy has any great interest in doing so either. Court of appeals scholarship is not booming in tandem with the caseload.

Another response is to pay far more attention to the confirmation process where appeals court judges are concerned. The political system has done just that in recent years, of course, and although

[64] Jacob Scott, Article III En Banc: The Judicial Conference as an Advisory Intercircuit Court of Appeals, 116 Yale L.J. 1625 (2007).

[65] See Fed. Judicial Ctr., Structural and Other Alternatives for the Federal Courts of Appeals: Report to the United States Congress and the Judicial Conference of the United States 75–83 (1993).

this has sometimes been portrayed as the creeping politicization of a process that was once less politicized, it turns out to make a good deal of sense: As the decisions of the courts of appeals become less and less subject to a realistic possibility of review, the question of who is making those decisions assumes much greater importance.

Yet another response—one likely to be more effective than the others, if it can be implemented—is to remedy the caseload explosion at the circuit court level. That explosion since the early 1970s is no doubt the product of many causes, but the "regulatory explosion" that came with the expansion of federal power under the Commerce Clause and the creation of new federal regulatory agencies like OSHA and EPA, and the accompanying rise in interest groups intended to lobby and influence them, undoubtedly played a major role.[66] It is probably just not possible for the Supreme Court to police a judicial system that itself is big enough to police a government as big as the federal government has become in the past half century or so. Reducing the extent of federal responsibilities, and returning them to a scope that more closely resembles the Framers' intent,[67] would likely also reduce the caseload of the federal courts to something more manageable.

Such a change would be far more than a judicial reform, of course, and I see no great likelihood of its occurring any time soon. I hope, however, that I am wrong, as I doubt that the Supreme Court, in any plausible incarnation, can provide meaningful review over a judicial system as busy as the one we have now. That does not make the Supreme Court's docket less interesting, perhaps, but it does suggest that it is less important than is generally believed.

[66] Jonathan Rauch, Demosclerosis: The Silent Killer of American Government 50–57 (1994) (describing the rapid explosion of interest groups as a function of expanding government authority beyond traditional limits).

[67] For more on this topic, see Glenn H. Reynolds, Kids, Guns, and the Commerce Clause, Cato Policy Analysis No. 216 (Oct. 10, 1994).

Contributors

Hans Bader is Counsel for Special Projects at the Competitive Enterprise Institute (CEI), specializing in constitutional law. He is a 1994 graduate of Harvard Law School, where he served as an editor of the *Harvard Journal of Law & Public Policy*. Before coming to CEI, he worked at the Center for Individual Rights, where he litigated federalism, First Amendment, and civil rights cases, such as *United States v. Morrison* (2000) and *Gratz v. Bollinger* (2003). His clients included students, professors, and educational institutions. He has also worked at the U.S. Department of Education and the law firms of Skadden, Arps, Slate, Meagher & Flom LLP, and Nossaman Guthner Knox & Elliott LLP. After graduating from law school, he served as law clerk to the late federal district judge Larry Lydick.

Lillian R. BeVier is the David and Mary Harrison Distinguished Professor at the University of Virginia Law School. She has been teaching at Virginia since 1973. The courses she has taught have included Property, Intellectual Property (Copyright and Trademark), and Constitutional Law with an emphasis on the First Amendment. Professor BeVier earned her undergraduate degree from Smith College and received her J.D. from Stanford Law School in 1965. At Stanford, she was a Revising Editor on the Law Review and elected to the Order of the Coif. Professor BeVier has written extensively and been published widely on a variety of legal topics. Since 1985, with *Money and Politics: The First Amendment and Campaign Finance Reform* in the *California Law Review*, many of her publications have considered the First Amendment implications of campaign finance regulation. In the fall of 2003, Professor BeVier was a visiting scholar at the National Constitution Center in Philadelphia. She currently serves as vice-chair of the Legal Services Corporation and is chair of the Board of the Martha Jefferson Health Services Corporation. In addition, she serves on the national Board of Visitors of the Federalist Society.

Hon. Danny J. Boggs was born in Havana, Cuba, October 23, 1944. He grew up in Bowling Green, Kentucky, and then attended Harvard College. He received his A.B., *cum laude*, from Harvard in 1965, after twice winning the Coolidge Debate Prize. He attended the University of Chicago Law School on a Mechem Scholarship, was elected to law review, and won the Hinton Moot Court competition. After receiving his J.D. in 1968, and being elected to Order of the Coif, he taught at the law school for the 1968–69 academic year. He then returned to Kentucky, where he served as deputy commissioner of the Department of Economic Security (1969–70), legal counsel to the governor (1970–71), and legislative counsel to the minority in the State House of Representatives (1972). Subsequently, he served as assistant to the solicitor general of the United States (1973–75), assistant to the chairman of the Federal Power Commission (1975–77), and deputy minority counsel to the United States Senate Energy Committee (1977–79). He then left government and entered private practice. He returned to serve as assistant director of the White House Office of Policy Development and special assistant to the president of the United States (1981–83) and deputy secretary of the U.S. Department of Energy (1983–86). In 1986 he was appointed by the president to the United States Court of Appeals for the Sixth Circuit. Following his appointment to the bench, he led three missions under the auspices of the United States Department of State, teaching American jurisprudence at the judicial academy of the Soviet Union (May 1991), the Commonwealth of Independent States (October 1991), and Russia (June 1993). By appointment of the chief justice of the U.S. Supreme Court, he served on the Advisory Committee on Appellate Rules of the Judicial Conference of the United States from 1992 until 1994. From 1994 until 2000, he served on the Judicial Conference Committee on Automation, and chaired its Budget Subcommittee. He served as chair of the Appellate Judges Conference of the American Bar Association in 2001–02. On October 1, 2003, Judge Boggs became chief judge of the Sixth Circuit.

G. Marcus Cole is a professor of law, Helen L. Crocker Faculty Scholar, and Academic Associate Dean for Curriculum at Stanford Law School. His scholarship focuses on the law of bankruptcy, corporate reorganization, and venture capital. Professor Cole takes an empirical law and economics approach to research questions such as why corporate bankruptcies increasingly are adjudicated in Delaware, and what drives the financial structure of companies backed by venture capital. He has been a national fellow at the Hoover Institution, and has scholarly interests that range from classical liberal political theory to natural law and the history of commercial law. He serves on the board of directors for the Central Pacific Region of the Anti-Defamation League of B'nai B'rith, and on the editorial board of the *Cato Supreme Court Review*. Before joining the Stanford Law School faculty in 1997, Professor Cole was an associate in commercial litigation with the Chicago law firm of Mayer, Brown & Platt, and he clerked for Judge Morris Sheppard Arnold of the U.S. Court of Appeals for the Eighth Circuit.

Robert Corn-Revere is a partner in the Washington, D.C., office of Davis Wright Tremaine LLP, specializing in First Amendment, Internet, and communications law. He serves as counsel in a wide array of First Amendment litigation involving the Communications Decency Act, the Child Online Protection Act, Internet content filtering in public libraries, public broadcasting regulations, and export controls on encryption software. He successfully argued *United States v. Playboy Entertainment Group, Inc.*, in which the U.S. Supreme Court struck down Section 505 of the Telecommunications Act of 1996 as a violation of the First Amendment. He served as lead counsel in *Motion Picture Association v. FCC*, in which the U.S. Court of Appeals for the D.C. Circuit vacated video description rules imposed on networks by the Federal Communications Commission. He also successfully petitioned Governor George E. Pataki to grant the first posthumous pardon in New York history to the late comedian Lenny Bruce. In 1999 Corn-Revere was listed on a 30th Anniversary Roll of Honor by the American Library Association Office of Intellectual Freedom and the Freedom to Read Foundation for his role as lead counsel in *Mainstream Loudon v. Board of Trustees of the Loudoun County Library*. Prior to joining Davis Wright Tremaine LLP, Corn-Revere served as chief counsel to interim Chairman James H. Quello of the FCC. He is an adjunct scholar to the Cato Institute.

Brannon P. Denning is an associate professor of law at Samford University's Cumberland School of Law in Birmingham, Alabama. Prior to joining the Cumberland School of Law in 2003, Professor

Denning taught at the Southern Illinois University School of Law in Carbondale, Illinois for four years. At Cumberland, Professor Denning teaches Constitutional Law I & II, the First Amendment, and Professional Responsibility. Professor Denning has written extensively on the Commerce Clause, the dormant Commerce Clause doctrine, the constitutional amending process, the confirmation process, the Second Amendment, and on foreign affairs matters. His articles have appeared in the *American Journal of International Law, Constitutional Commentary, Foreign Affairs*, the *Minnesota Law Review*, the *William and Mary Law Review*, and the *Wisconsin Law Review*, among other journals and periodicals. He has also collaborated with Yale law professor Boris I. Bittker on a treatise on the Commerce Clause and is co-editor of a one-of-a-kind coursebook on gun control and gun rights. Professor Denning earned a B.A. in political science, *magna cum laude*, from the University of the South in Sewanee, Tennessee. He received a J.D., *magna cum laude*, from the University of Tennessee in 1995, and an LL.M. from Yale University in 1999.

Samuel Estreicher is of counsel to the labor and employment and issues and appeals practices of Jones Day. His practice focuses on a wide range of issues affecting the employment relationship, including designing ADR systems; training supervisors for performance-based management and employee involvement initiatives; advising clients in OFCCP, EEO, and labor relations compliance; and representing clients in individual, global HR management, and class EEO and wage and hour litigation. In addition, Sam is the Dwight D. Opperman Professor of Law at New York University School of Law and director of the Center for Labor and Employment Law and the Institute of Judicial Administration. He has published several books, including leading casebooks in labor law and employment discrimination and employment law; edited conference volumes on sexual harassment, employment ADR processes, and cross-global human resources; and authored more than 75 articles in professional and academic journals.

Erik S. Jaffe is a solo appellate attorney in Washington, D.C., whose practice emphasizes the First Amendment and other constitutional issues. He is a 1986 graduate of Dartmouth College and a 1990 graduate of Columbia Law School, where he was the articles editor of the *Columbia Law Review*. Following law school he clerked for Judge Douglas H. Ginsburg on the U.S. Court of Appeals for the D.C. Circuit, practiced for five years at Williams & Connolly in Washington, D.C., clerked for Justice Clarence Thomas on the U.S. Supreme Court during the October 1996 term, and then began his solo appellate practice in 1997. Since 1999 Jaffe has been involved in 24 cases at the merits stage before the U.S. Supreme Court. He represented one of the successful respondents in the First Amendment case of *Bartnicki v. Vopper* and authored Cato's amicus briefs in *Wisconsin Right to Life v. FEC*, *Randall v. Sorrell*, and *McConnell v. FEC*. Jaffe also has authored amicus briefs in cases such as *Republican Party of Minnesota v. Kelly* (judicial speech), *Zelman v. Simmons-Harris* (vouchers), *Watchtower Bible and Tract Society v. Village of Stratton* (anonymous speech), *Veneman v. Livestock Marketing Association* and *United States v. United Foods, Inc.* (compelled advertising), *Boy Scouts of America v. Dale* (freedom of expressive association), and *United States v. Morrison* (Commerce Clause). He is the chairman of the Federalist Society's Free Speech and Election Law Practice Group.

Michael I. Krauss is a professor of law at George Mason University School of Law. Professor Krauss earned his B.A. *cum laude* from Carleton University, his LL.B. *summa cum laude* from the Université de Sherbrooke, and his LL.M. from Yale Law School, where he was a Commonwealth Scholar. Before coming to George Mason in 1987, he was Columbia University's Law and Economics Fellow in 1981 and has taught at the law schools of Seattle University, University of Toronto, and the Université de Sherbrooke. Professor Krauss has also clerked for Canadian Supreme Court Justice Louis-Phillipe Pigeon, practiced law in Quebec City, and served on Quebec's Human Rights Commission. Today, Professor Krauss is a member of the Board of Governors of the National Association of Scholars, sits on the advisory boards of several think tanks, is an academic fellow of the Foundation for the Defense of Democracies, and is a Salvatori Fellow of the Heritage Foundation.

Thomas Lambert joined the faculty of the University of Missouri School of Law in the fall of 2003 from the Chicago law firm of Sidley Austin Brown & Wood, where he practiced antitrust litigation from

2000 to 2003. Prior to entering law school, Lambert was an environmental policy analyst at the Center for the Study of American Business at Washington University in St. Louis. He then attended the University of Chicago Law School, where he was a Bradley Fellow and served as comment editor of the law review. After graduating with honors in 1998, he clerked for Judge Jerry E. Smith of the U.S. Court of Appeals for the Fifth Circuit. He then spent a year as the John M. Olin Fellow at Northwestern University Law School. Professor Lambert's scholarship focuses on regulatory theory and business law. He is a regular contributor to "Truth on the Market," a weblog devoted to "academic commentary on law, business, economics, and more." Professor Lambert teaches Contracts, Business Organizations, Antitrust Law, and Environmental Law. He is a recipient of the Graduate Professional Council's Gold Chalk Award for Excellence in Teaching.

Mark K. Moller is a senior fellow at the Cato Institute and the editor in chief of the *Cato Supreme Court Review*. Moller earned his B.A., *magna cum laude*, from Duke University in 1994, a J.D. with honors at the University of Chicago Law School in 1999, and an LL.M in common law legal history and theory (first class honors) from the University of Cambridge in 2000. After graduation, he practiced law at Gibson, Dunn & Crutcher LLP for three years, with a focus on complex class litigation and appellate litigation. He is the author of "The Rule of Law Problem: Unconstitutional Class Actions and Options for Reform" (*Harvard Journal of Law and Public Policy*) and "Class Action Lawmaking: An Administrative Law Model" (*Texas Review of Law and Politics*). Moller's commentary has appeared in a variety of publications, including the *Washington Post*, *Slate*, and *Reason*. He frequently comments on the Supreme Court on television and radio. In the fall, he joins the DePaul University College of Law as an assistant professor of law.

Andrew P. Morriss is currently at Case Western Reserve University in Cleveland where he is the Galen J. Roush Professor of Business Law and Regulation. Morriss graduated *cum laude* from Princeton University in 1981 and earned a law degree with high honors and a master's of public affairs degree from the University of Texas at

Austin in 1984. Morriss clerked for U.S. District Judge Barefoot Sanders in Dallas and then worked for the Texas Rural Legal Aid. In 1994, he earned a Ph.D. in economics from the Massachusetts Institute of Technology. Morriss' ideas have been published in numerous scholarly journals including the *New York University Law Review*, *Texas Law Review*, and *William & Mary Bill of Rights Journal*. Morriss speaks frequently on issues of liberty and the role of the courts.

Roger Pilon is vice president for legal affairs at the Cato Institute. He holds Cato's B. Kenneth Simon Chair in Constitutional Studies and is the founder and director of Cato's Center for Constitutional Studies. Established in 1989 to encourage limited constitutional government at home and abroad, the center has become an important force in the national debate over constitutional interpretation and judicial philosophy. Pilon's work has appeared in the *New York Times, Washington Post, Wall Street Journal, Los Angeles Times, Legal Times, National Law Journal, Harvard Journal of Law and Public Policy, Notre Dame Law Review, Stanford Law and Policy Review, Texas Review of Law and Politics*, and elsewhere. He has appeared, among other places, on ABC's Nightline, CBS's 60 Minutes II, National Public Radio, Fox News Channel, CNN, MSNBC, and CNBC. He lectures and debates at universities and law schools across the country and testifies often before Congress. Before joining Cato, Pilon held five senior posts in the Reagan administration, including at State and Justice. He has taught philosophy and law and was a national fellow at Stanford's Hoover Institution. Pilon holds a B.A. from Columbia University, an M.A. and a Ph.D. from the University of Chicago, and a J.D. from the George Washington University School of Law. In 1989 the Bicentennial Commission presented him with the Benjamin Franklin Award for excellence in writing on the U.S. Constitution. In 2001 Columbia University's School of General Studies awarded him its Alumni Medal of Distinction.

Glenn Harlan Reynolds is the Beauchamp Brogan Distinguished Professor of Law at the University of Tennessee. After graduating from Yale Law School, he served as law clerk for Judge Gilbert S. Merritt of the United States Court of Appeals for the Sixth Circuit. He then practiced law in the Washington, D.C. office of Dewey Ballantine before joining the Tennessee faculty. Professor Reynolds teaches Constitutional Law, Advanced Constitutional Law, Administrative Law, and Internet Law. He is the author of *The Appearance of Propriety: How the Ethics Wars Have Undermined American Government, Business, and Society* (with Peter W. Morgan), and *An Army of Davids: How Markets and Technology Empower Ordinary People to Beat Big Media, Big Government, and Other Goliaths, as well as Outer Space: Problems of Law and Policy* (with Robert P. Merges). Reynolds has also published numerous articles in the *Columbia Law Review, University of Pennsylvania Law Review, Virginia Law Review, Wisconsin Law Review, Vanderbilt Law Review, Tennessee Law Review* and numerous specialty journals. He also founded the InstaPundit weblog.

Laurence H. Tribe is the Carl M. Loeb University Professor at Harvard University and a Professor of Constitutional Law at Harvard Law School, whose faculty he joined in 1968 at the age of 26. Born of Russian Jewish parents in Shanghai, Tribe entered Harvard College at 16, won the national intercollegiate debate championship at 19, and graduated *summa cum laude* in Mathematics and *magna cum laude* from Harvard Law School before spending a year clerking for Justice Mathew Tobriner of the California Supreme Court and then a year clerking for Justice Potter Stewart of the U.S. Supreme Court. While on the Harvard faculty for the past thirty-nine years, Professor Tribe has written 115 books and articles, including his treatise, *American Constitutional Law*, which has been cited more frequently by courts in the U.S. and abroad than any other legal text published since 1950. He has testified often at the invitation of committees of the House and Senate, is frequently called on to advise state and foreign governments and agencies, helped write the constitutions of South Africa, the Czech Republic, and the Marshall Islands, and is a much sought-after oral advocate, having prevailed in over three-fifths of the many appellate cases he has argued, including thirty-six arguments in the U.S. Supreme Court. More than half of Professor Tribe's legal work has been pro bono. Voted the best law professor at Harvard in 2001, Tribe has always been a popular but demanding teacher, counting among his many students Chief Justice John Roberts, Senator Barack Obama, former Stanford Dean Kathleen Sullivan, and a number of his current colleagues at Harvard and elsewhere. Elected to the American Academy of Arts and Sciences at the age of 38, Professor Tribe has won international recognition as an interdisciplinary intellectual. He was selected by the National Constitution Center in Philadelphia as one of its two Visiting Scholars for 2006–07 and has delivered influential public lectures for such groups as the Electronic Freedom Foundation and, most recently, the American Academy in Berlin in March 2007 and the Progress and Freedom Foundation in Aspen in August 2007.

ABOUT THE CATO INSTITUTE

The Cato Institute is a public policy research foundation dedicated to the principles of limited government, individual liberty, free markets, and private property. It takes its name from *Cato's Letters,* popular libertarian pamphlets that helped to lay the philosophical foundation for the American Revolution.

Despite the Founders' libertarian values, today virtually no aspect of life is free from government encroachment. A pervasive intolerance for individual rights is shown by government's arbitrary intrusions into private economic transactions and its disregard for civil liberties.

To counter that trend, the Cato Institute undertakes an extensive publications program that addresses the complete spectrum of policy issues. It holds major conferences throughout the year, from which papers are published thrice yearly in the *Cato Journal,* and also publishes the quarterly magazine *Regulation* and the annual *Cato Supreme Court Review.*

The Cato Institute accepts no government funding. It relies instead on contributions from foundations, corporations, and individuals and revenue generated from the sale of publications. The Institute is a nonprofit, tax-exempt educational foundation under Section 501(c)(3) of the Internal Revenue Code.

ABOUT THE CENTER FOR CONSTITUTIONAL STUDIES

Cato's Center for Constitutional Studies and its scholars take their inspiration from the struggle of America's founding generation to secure liberty through limited government and the rule of law. Under the direction of Roger Pilon, the center was established in 1989 to help revive the idea that the Constitution authorizes a government of delegated, enumerated, and thus limited powers, the exercise of which must be further restrained by our rights, both enumerated and unenumerated. Through books, monographs, conferences, forums, op-eds, speeches, congressional testimony, and TV and radio appearances, the center's scholars address a wide range of constitutional and legal issues—from judicial review to federalism, economic liberty, property rights, civil rights, criminal law and procedure, asset forfeiture, tort law, and term limits, to name just a few. The center is especially concerned to encourage the judiciary to be "the bulwark of our liberties," as James Madison put it, neither making nor ignoring the law but interpreting and applying it through the natural rights tradition we inherited from the founding generation.

Cato Institute
1000 Massachusetts Ave., N.W.
Washington, D.C. 20001